How to Do *Everything* with

Macromedia Flash

Bonnie Blake

Osborne/McGraw-Hill

New York   Chicago   San Francisco
Lisbon   London   Madrid   Mexico City
Milan   New Delhi   San Juan
Seoul   Singapore   Sydney   Toronto

Osborne/**McGraw-Hill**
2600 Tenth Street
Berkeley, California 94710
U.S.A.

To arrange bulk purchase discounts for sales promotions, premiums, or fund-raisers, please contact Osborne/**McGraw-Hill** at the above address. For information on translations or book distributors outside the U.S.A., please see the International Contact Information page immediately following the index of this book.

How to Do Everything with Macromedia Flash™ 5

234567890 CUS CUS 01987654321

ISBN 0-07-212714-7

Publisher:	Brandon A. Nordin
Vice President &	
Associate Publisher:	Scott Rogers
Acquisitions Editor:	Megg Bonar
Project Editor:	Pamela Woolf
Acquisitions Coordinator:	Alissa Larson
Technical Editor:	Mitch Thomas
Copy Editor:	Sossity Smith
Developmental Editor:	Steve Bain
Indexer:	Irv Hershman
Computer Designers:	Lucie Ericksen, Elizabeth Jang
Illustrators:	Michael Mueller, Lyssa Sieben-Wald
Series Design:	Mickey Galicia
Series Cover Design:	Dodie Shoemaker
Cover Illustration:	Tom Willis, Joseph Humphrey

This book was composed with Corel VENTURA™ Publisher.

Dedication

To Rose, who gave me some great celestial inspiration for this book.

For Stephen, too.

About the Author

Bonnie Blake, MFA, has been an adjunct assistant professor of computer graphics for the College of New Rochelle, and has taught at Parsons School of Design, both located in New York. She is currently an adjunct assistant professor of digital media at Ramapo College in Mahwah, New Jersey. In addition, she develops and teaches Web and multimedia course content for corporations and training organizations. She is also an award-winning creative director, specializing in Web design and multimedia. Bonnie is the author of the best-seller online course, Flash ActionScript 5.0 located at onehandson.com. She is currently co-writing a book that deals with the deconstruction of a Flash designer's movies.

Contents

Acknowledgments

I would like to thank the team at Osborne who I worked so closely with, including Megg Bonar, Pamela Woolf, and Alissa Larson. You were a pleasure to work with. Let's do it again sometime. Also, thank you Roger Stewart for your kind words of encouragement.

Thanks Doug Sahlin for doing such a wonderful job and saving the day. You too are a pleasure to work with. I'm glad we clicked so well on this book.

Thank you Mary Cicitta for your endless Flash research, editing, content expertise, input, and other forms of help with this project.

Special thanks to Dale Kroll, Matthew Luciano, and Kelly Kiernan for your creative input when I was at a loss for words.

Last but not least, the woman whose name always appears in so many acknowledgement sections of books, thank you Margot Maley Hutchinson.

Introduction

There seem to be two categories of Web authors: those who use Flash and those who have heard of it and are anxious to learn it. Nowadays, Flash has become such a common nomenclature; the designer or programmer who has never heard of it is a rare creature. In addition to the product itself being a known quantity, Flash movies are popping up everywhere in the media today. Many of the cartoons our kids watch on television are Flash driven. Gaming software is moving toward becoming more Flash-based, not to mention Flash presence on the Web, where nearly every award-winning site uses Flash technology. There is no doubt that Flash has arrived, and it's quickly escalating the world of multimedia to its most sophisticated level.

I believe you'll find *How to Do Everything with Macromedia Flash™ 5* a vibrant, not-to-be-without resource for the seasoned Flash user, offering easy to look-up references for questions of a more advanced nature. It is also perfect for the beginner who might be intimidated by the Flash interface, which can be kind of scary the first time you set out to make a Flash movie. Either way, this book addresses both ends of the learning spectrum.

Being a Web designer myself, I thought about what my wish list might be for a book about Flash if I were just beginning to learn the program. At the top of this wish list would be a book that cuts through the pedantic analysis and focuses on the point. Specifically, this book reviews what Flash does, how you would benefit from using Flash, and how you would go about using it the right way. I think you will agree that this book achieves the perfect balance; it simplistically hones in on the salient points of the software, while leaving you with a thorough understanding of all Flash topics.

The Structure of This Book

There are four parts to this book. The chapter subjects are arranged in order of complexity, starting with the more basic aspects of Flash and building up to the final chapters, which examine the programs' advanced features, specifically interactivity. The parts of this book are organized into the following categories:

Part I—Create Flash Movies

This section is designed to give you an overview of what Flash is all about, its vector capabilities, why it's so essential, and the process you use to actually build a movie in Flash. It sets the stage for the rest of the book and familiarizes you with basic Flash lingo and concepts. This part of the book also covers the basic drawing tools, the Flash interface, and how to use it.

Part II—Add Color, Style, and Design to Your Flash Movies

Part II introduces the very important concept of creating objects in Flash and manipulating the properties of these elements, such as scale, color, position, and so on. Also discussed are the transformation of objects and the many special techniques you can use to create exciting visual effects. Importing and exporting vector art, bitmaps, audio, and video from today's most popular programs is examined in detail as well. This part provides you with a solid overview of all facets of beginner to intermediate Flash and provides an excellent reference for even the most experienced Flash authors.

Part III—Flash Animation Techniques

Part III covers all facets of animation including frame by frame, shape, and motion tweening. The concept behind animation is also discussed in depth. Symbols are introduced in this section including buttons and movie clip creation. Step-by-step, tutorial-like examples are provided to accelerate your learning curve. Key figures are posted on the Web site for you to deconstruct and examine.

Part IV—Build Interactive Movies

In this part, ActionScript, the scripting language behind Flash interactivity, is introduced in a simple, easy-to-understand manner. This information is particularly useful for the non-programmer because scripting concepts are discussed in laymen's terms. This makes it fairly easy for you to jump right in and immediately start adding simple interactivity to your movies. For those of you who are ready to take ActionScript to the next level, Chapters 14 and 15 provide a more advanced study of the language, providing step-by-step instructions on how to create common interactive effects, with some complex tasks reviewed as well. Movie clips and their relation to interactivity are also examined in depth. Finally, this section ends with a complete synopsis on how to prepare your movie for publishing to the Web or other media.

Appendix A   This appendix has a complete list of all shortcut keys is provided in this appendix.

Appendix B   This appendix has a list of various resources you can call upon related to Flash technology. This includes a comprehensive list of Flash-based, award-winning Web sites—sites that range from the simple to complex and ActionScript-driven movies that will keep you up at night wondering how these authors made them. This appendix is equipped with a complete list of sites you can visit to download source code to see how others might have created that effect you're looking for. Also included are learning resources, technical references, tutorials, and sites that offer audio, sound loops, and video downloads for use in your Flash movies.

Web Site

Throughout the book there are examples of various techniques that can be created in Flash movies. All the major figures in the book are posted on Osborne's Web site at www.osborne.com. I believe you will find this particularly helpful, especially when more advanced techniques are covered in the second half of the book. I'm sure you'll find that having access to the source code of a Flash movie will truly augment your learning experience.

Conventions Used in This Book

Because Flash is for PC and Mac users alike, there are certain things to keep in mind when reading this book. The interface is nearly identical on both platforms, although the screen captures for this book were done in Windows. In a few isolated cases where the screen displays differently, Mac screen shots were also used.

When shortcut keys are listed next to menu commands, the Windows version is listed first and the Mac version second with a slash separating the two; for example, CTRL+ALT/OPT+CMND.

Notes are set apart from the body copy and include important issues you should be aware of regarding Flash. *Tips* are set apart as well and include helpful hints to streamline the creation of your Flash movies.

When you are presented with several menu options to select in sequence, they appear as so: Window | Panels | Character, with a "pipe" character dividing the menus' names.

Conclusion

My goal was to produce a book that provides a complete reference for every aspect of Flash that you could possibly want to use. This was not intended to be a book you would read once, put away, and never use again. Instead, my expectation was to write a desktop companion you would be able to keep at your fingertips and refer to time and time again, whenever you have a question or issue with the program. I believe I achieved this goal and I hope you enjoy reading this book as much as I did writing it.

—Bonnie Blake

Part I

Create Flash Movies

Chapter 1

Plan Your Flash Project

How to...

- ■ Understand Flash Concepts
- ■ Publish Flash Movies
- ■ Create or Import Artwork
- ■ Animate Your Artwork
- ■ Publish Your Movies on the Web
- ■ Use the Document Library
- ■ Edit Flash Preferences

The fact that you have this book in your hands means that you want to harness the power of Flash 5, the premier software for creating interactive movies and Web sites for the Internet. If you have never used Flash before, the interface, panels, and all the features the program has to offer might intimidate you. If you are a seasoned Flash veteran, you have probably already opened the hood so to speak and explored both the familiar and the new aspects of Flash. Throughout the course of this book, you will learn to use all the Flash features to create compelling, highly interactive movies for your Web designs that keep visitors returning time and again. In this chapter, you will learn some basic Flash concepts and receive an overview of workflow in a typical Flash project, which will aid you in planning future projects you create with Flash.

Understand Flash Concepts

Flash began life as a vector-based program that was capable of creating impressive animations for Web pages. Over the past few years, the programmers at Macromedia have revised the program, adding more elements, and giving Web designers a program with the power to create fully interactive Web sites at a fraction of the file size required by other media. Flash 5 is recognized as the leading Web authoring program for creating vector-based animations (known as Flash movies) for Web sites.

During the course of a typical Flash project, you create objects using the Flash drawing tools and animate them along the Timeline. You segregate the different assets used in your movies using layers. You add interactivity to and control the flow of your movie with ActionScript. While you are creating the movie, you edit everything within the main Flash workspace. You can preview your handiwork in the workspace, or test the movie with the Flash Player. When everything is performing as you planned, you publish the movie in Flash's native SWF (pronounced *swiff*), or one of the other available formats for use in a printed document or as part of a multimedia presentation.

Understand Flash Image Formats

Flash uses two types of graphics: vector-based and bitmapped (sometimes referred to as *raster*). The objects you create with Flash drawing tools are vector-based. Bitmap images on the other hand are comprised of pixels, tiny dots of colors that are assembled to create the final image. When you see an image displayed on a Web page, it is generally a bitmap image.

The biggest difference between bitmap images and vector-based graphics is the way they are displayed on a computer screen. Bitmap images are resolution dependent. The size resolution of a bitmap image is measured in pixels per inch. The standard resolution of bitmap images used on the Web is 72 pixels per inch. When you resize a bitmap image, pixels are redrawn and the host program adds data where there was none. Decrease the size of a bitmap image and the host program removes pixels; increase the size of a bitmap and the host program adds pixels. This inevitably leads to distortion.

Vector-based images, on the other hand, are drawn using mathematical formulas. When you resize a vector-based graphic, the image is redrawn by changing one or more parameters of the original formula. For example, if you increase the size of a vector-based circle, the radius of the circle is changed and the object is redrawn without distortion. Vector-based images scale very well, even when enlarged to many times their original size. The only time noticeable distortion might occur in a vector-based image is when you resize an object with a complex gradient fill.

Bitmap Images

Bitmaps are best suited for displaying real-world images, such as photographs of people or landscapes. Most of the images you view on Web sites are bitmapped. In fact, the two main image formats used on the Web, GIF and JPEG, are bitmap file formats. Some of the images you see displayed on Web pages, such as buttons, backgrounds, and user interfaces may start out as vector-based images that were created in programs such as FreeHand, Illustrator, or CorelDraw, but they ultimately end up as bitmapped JPEGs and GIFs when incorporated into images for Web pages. Figure 1-1 shows an example of a bitmap image that you might use on a Web page.

FIGURE 1-1   Example of a bitmapped image

Bitmap images, whether real-world images, such as photographs, or navigational images, such as buttons and icons, are generally created in programs such as Adobe Photoshop, Jasc's Paint Shop Pro, Corel's Photo-Paint, or Macromedia's Fireworks. The file size of a bitmap image is usually larger than similar graphics created with vector-based drawing tools. The notable exception is a vector-based image that relies heavily on complex gradients (blends of two or more colors).

There are a number of other important differences between bitmaps and vector images that are summarized in a table in the "Bitmaps Versus Vectors" section, later in this chapter.

Vector Graphics

Vector images, such as those created with Macromedia FreeHand, Adobe Illustrator, CorelDraw, and Flash are generally made up of lines (sometimes called strokes), shapes (or objects), and fills (both solid and gradient). Within most illustration programs, you can edit the lines and objects an infinite number of ways, including manipulating the individual points that make up the object's path.

When you create artwork in a paint or photo-editing program, you don't have the same flexibility when it comes to editing lines and shapes as you do with an illustration or a drawing program. The amount of editing you can achieve with a bitmap image depends on the power of your photo-editing software. Generally, you are limited to changing the color characteristics of the image or modifying the image using the filters or masks within your photo-editing program.

Figure 1-2 shows the control points in a curved line drawn in an illustration program.

Flash creates images using vectors, as you'll learn as you read through this book. Flash can also import and use bitmapped images, which gives you a great deal of flexibility when producing Flash content.

Bitmaps Versus Vectors

Both bitmaps and vector-based images have good and bad points. Table 1-1 summarizes some of the differences between the two file types.

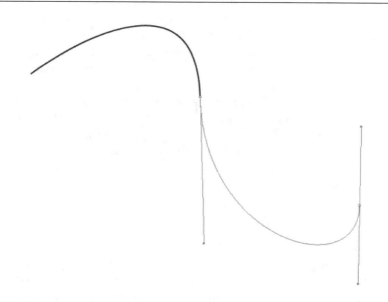

FIGURE 1-2   Example of a vector-based image

Bitmaps	Vector-based
Larger file sizes	Smaller file sizes
Good choice for real-world images	No real-world images
Not easy to edit in terms of lines and shapes	Easy to edit lines and shapes
Browsers recognize JPEGs and GIFs without the need for plug-ins	Plug-ins generally needed to view images with vector-based file formats
Not well-suited for animation	Perfect for creating animations
Easier to learn to create	Harder to learn to create
Don't scale very well	Scale easily without distortion

TABLE 1-1   Bitmaps Versus Vectors

Understand Flash Symbols and Instances

Symbols are reusable artwork in the form of images, animations, or buttons. When you convert an object created with one of the drawing tools into a symbol, it is stored in the document *Library*. Sounds also are added to the document Library. You can use a symbol from the document Library anywhere within a movie. An occurrence of a symbol is known as an *instance*. You can modify many parameters of an instance, such as its size, tint, and opacity. However, you cannot modify the symbol's basic shape; it remains constant with every instance.

You use symbols to reduce the file size of a movie. No matter how often you use a symbol in a movie, once the movie is published, the Flash player needs to download a symbol only once and then redraw it wherever an instance of it occurs along the Timeline. Symbols also reduce editing time. When you edit a symbol, Flash updates all instances of it to reflect the change.

Explore the Workspace

The Flash workspace shown in Figure 1-3 is composed of a large rectangular area called the *stage*. Directly above the stage is the Timeline. The Flash stage is your movie set with you as the director. You create the objects for your movie on the stage and then direct the action by animating objects along the Timeline.

To the left of the stage is a floating toolbox that you use to create objects, select objects, modify objects, and change the view of the stage.

Toolbox   Timeline   Panels

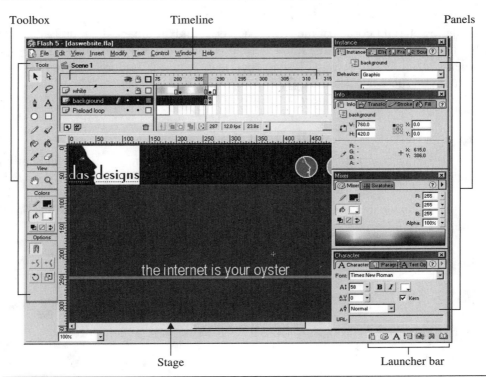

Stage   Launcher bar

FIGURE 1-3   The Flash workspace

Modify Your Movie with Panels

The Inspectors that you might have used in earlier versions of Flash have now been replaced with panels in Flash 5. You use panels to edit and modify certain parameters of the objects in your Flash movie, such as the font style and size of text objects, the colors of objects, and certain characteristics of the sounds in your movies. Panels also are used to align objects. Each panel group is broken into tabbed sections. Click one of the tabs to open a panel.

Panels can be opened, collapsed, or hidden. In Chapter 2 you will learn how to line up panels. Panels are used for many different functions in Flash. You will learn how to use individual panels in future chapters as the need arises. Figure 1-3 shows the default panels aligned to the right side of the workspace.

Explore the Flash Launcher Bar

In the lower-right corner of the workspace is a handy toolbar called the Launcher bar (refer to Figure 1-3). The Launcher bar consists of gaily colored icons that when clicked launch certain Flash applications. You can use the Launcher bar to start any of these applications: Info panel, Mixer panel, Character panel, Instance panel, Movie Explorer, Object Actions panel, or the document Library.

Save Time with Context Menus

Flash provides you with several context menus that contain commands and options relevant to the current selection. To access a context menu, right-click/CTRL-click a selected item in the Timeline, in the document Library, or on the stage. Figure 1-4 shows the context menu that appears when you right-click/CTRL-click a symbol on the stage.

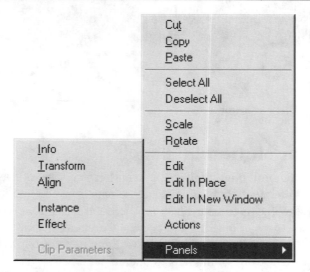

FIGURE 1-4   Context menus contain commands and options that are pertinent to a selected object

Organize Your Movie's Assets with the Document Library

Earlier in this chapter, you learned the significance of symbols and instances. All symbols that you create are stored in the document's Library. Objects you import, such as bitmap images, vector graphics created in other programs, and sounds, also are stored in the document Library. You use the Library to organize the assets used in your movie. An organized Library is invaluable when you are creating a large production. Figure 1-5 shows a typical document Library.

Library folders and items   Library preview window   Narrow State button

Wide State button

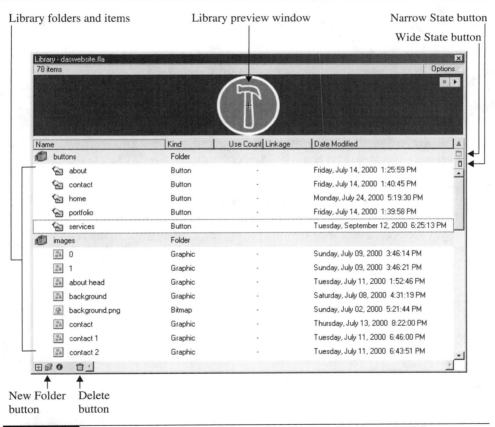

New Folder   Delete
button   button

FIGURE 1-5   All the symbols used in a movie are stored in the document Library

The Library in Figure 1-5 is displayed in Wide State so you can see all its features. Notice the Library window is split into two sections. The top section shows you a preview of what a selected item looks like; the bottom section is a catalog of Library folders and items. If the selected symbol is a movie clip, button, or sound, a Stop and a Play button appear to the right of the symbol in the preview window. Click the Play button to preview the item as it will appear in the movie.

To use a symbol from the Library, click the item in either section of the Library window, drag it onto the stage and Flash will add the item to the currently selected layer.

Change the Size of the Library Window

When you first open the document Library, it is displayed in its Narrow State mode. You can change the size of the Library window by doing one of the following:

- Click the Wide State button to expand the window.

- Click the Narrow State button to display only the Name column.

- Drag the lower-right corner of the window to resize it.

Use the Library Options Menu

You use the Library Options menu shown on the next page to perform various Library maintenance tasks such as adding and deleting folders and items. You also can edit selected items using commands from the Library Options menu. To open the Library Options menu shown in the figure, click the triangle to the right of the word Options.

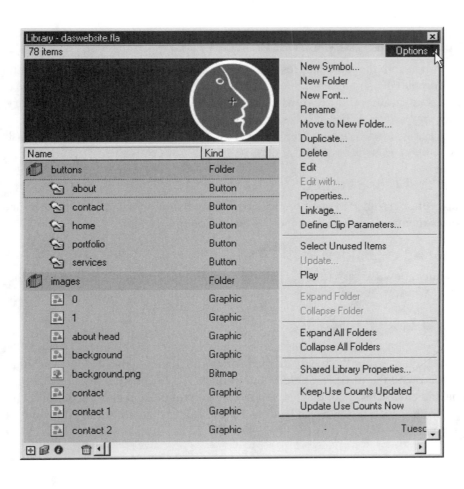

Organize Library Content in Folders

After you absorb the material presented in this book, you will find yourself creating more complex Flash movies, which inevitably means you will end up with some large document Libraries. Fortunately, you can organize the content of the Library by creating folders. When you create a new symbol, or import an item into your movie, Flash stores it in the currently selected folder. If no folder is selected, Flash adds the item to the root of the Library.

Open and Close Folders

Double-click a folder to open or close it. Alternatively, you can open the Library Options menu and choose Expand Folder or Collapse Folder.

Create a New Folder

To create a new Library folder, click the New Folder button at the bottom of the Library window or choose New Folder from the Library Options menu.

Name a Folder

When you give a folder a unique name, it helps you to quickly identify the folder's contents. Flash gives the newly created folder the default name of Untitled folder, appended with the next available folder number. To rename the folder, select its name and enter a new name. Choose a name that will make it easy to identify what's in the folder, such as the name Buttons for the folder that stores the buttons used in the movie.

Delete a Folder

To delete a folder that is no longer needed, select it, and then click the Delete button at the bottom of the Library window. Alternatively, open the Library Options menu and choose Delete. This button also is used to delete individual Library items.

 *When you delete a folder, you also delete all of the items in it. Deleting a folder cannot be undone.*

Move Items to Different Folders

After you organize your document's Library with folders, you can transfer an object from one folder to another by selecting the object and then dragging and dropping it into the desired folder.

Maintain Some Order in the Library

If you experiment with many different items in a movie, you can end up with items in the Library that are not used. This clutter makes navigating the Library more difficult and also bloats the file size of the published movie. When creating a complex project, keep the Library in good order by deleting unused items. To delete an unused item, open the Library Options menu, choose Select Unused Items, and Flash will select and highlight all items not used in the document. To delete the selected items, click the Delete button at the bottom of the Library window or choose Delete from the Library Options menu.

 Think twice before deleting any item from the Library. Deleting Library items cannot be undone.

Use Preset Items from the Common Libraries

Flash 5 has several Common Libraries with ready-to-use items for your movies, such as buttons, graphic symbols, and sounds. To use a Common Library item in one of your movies, choose Window | Common Libraries and then choose the desired library from the submenu. Select the desired item from the Common Library and drag it into the current document's Library. Alternately, you can drag the item from the Common Library directly on to the stage and Flash will add it to the current document's Library.

Create Your Own Custom Library

If you find yourself using many of the same buttons, symbols, or sounds in your work, you can store them in a custom Library for future use. To create a custom Library, create a new Flash document and then create or import the items you want to include in the custom Library. If you create the items from scratch, make sure to convert them to the proper symbol behavior. After creating the assets for the custom Library, name the file and save it in Flash's native FLA format. Store the file in the Libraries folder, which is located in the Flash application folder on your computer's hard drive. The next time you launch Flash, your custom Library will appear in the Custom Libraries submenu.

Plan Your Flash Movie

Before rushing headlong into creating objects for a Flash movie, a bit of pre-planning will save you hours of work later on. It is always a good idea to have a handle on the assets you will need to create your movie. For example, if you are incorporating sound in your production, will you use the presets that come with the Flash Sound Library, or will you need to import them? Another important consideration is the graphic objects you will use in your production. Will you create them with the Flash drawing tools, or import them from another source?

Many Flash authors prefer to create a storyboard of their movies. A *storyboard* is a series of sketches you create, generally on paper, to depict the major event changes that will occur in your movie. If the movie is to be used as a full-fledged Web site, it is a good idea to sketch out the interface. The storyboard sketches need not be elaborate. Your goal is to have a visual representation of what you are creating. The sketches will aid you when it comes time to choose a document size and set the other parameters for the movie.

Putting your project on paper also has the advantage of giving you some idea of the overall size of the project. For example, if while planning your project you find you will end up with a lengthy Timeline, you can plan on breaking the movie into scenes to manage the workflow better.

When creating movies there are a number of other questions you must ask yourself. For example, what size will the final movie be? Will you be publishing for the Web, a standalone movie, or designing a business presentation? You may even want to create the content with several formats in mind.

Asking yourself some of these questions and getting some honest answers before starting a Flash project will save you time in the long run. For example, when you open a new file in Flash, the stage area opens at a default size. Based on the information you learned while creating the storyboard, you might want your movie to be larger or smaller. For example, an ad banner that you create for a Web page is usually sized at 468 pixels by 60 pixels. To create an ad banner in Flash, you would need to resize the stage to the ad banner size.

Create a Flash Movie

Building a Flash movie, even one with only a few frames and objects, often requires you to use many of the tools that Flash contains. A typical Flash project may involve several stages, for example, creating the artwork, animating objects, and adding interactivity with ActionScript—the scripting language that is used in Flash.

As you create the movie, you use layers to organize the movie's assets, you use the Timeline to create action through time, and you use the document Library to manage the assets of your movie. In the next few sections, you will see a typical workflow for a Flash project that shows you how these different pieces come together.

Create the Document

The first step in creating a Flash movie is to create the document that you use while creating and animating the objects in your movie. If you are creating a complex movie, or are part of a team working on a Flash project, you will save the document between sessions to preserve any work you do in the individual sessions. When you save a Flash document in its native FLA format, all the assets used to create the file are stored with it. When you reopen the file, you can make changes and additions to the movie as needed.

If you have planned the movie out ahead of time, you will know exactly what the dimensions of your document need to be to flesh out your project. You also will know what background color to choose, and what frame rate to choose for your document. In Chapter 3 you will learn how to create a new document and set the other parameters for a new movie.

Create the Artwork

You can create all your artwork in Flash, or you can choose to import clipart or artwork that you have created in other digital imaging programs. Throughout the remainder of this book, you will learn different methods for creating and importing artwork from different sources.

Create Artwork in Flash 5

Flash 5 has a large selection of tools housed in the Toolbox that enable you to create original artwork. You can draw lines and edit them by changing their shape, and you can create objects and fill them with different colors and gradients. You can combine objects and lines to create sophisticated artwork. You can even use Flash 5 to create stunning navigational elements for Web pages. In Chapter 4 you will learn to use the Toolbox to create and edit objects for your movies.

There are a growing number of Web site designers that use only Flash to create entire Web sites. These sites are generally quite attractive, featuring animation and sound… a true multimedia, interactive experience that you can share with anyone using a modem and a modern Web browser with the Flash 5 Player plug-in.

Import Vector-Based Artwork

If you have an illustration program, such as FreeHand, Illustrator, or CorelDraw, you can use it to create vector-based artwork that can be imported into Flash for use in your movies. In fact, if your illustration program is fairly new, chances are that you can use it to create the frames for the movies. You can, for example, create a layered image in Adobe Illustrator and export the file such that the layers become separate frames in your final animation. If you use Macromedia's FreeHand to create your vector artwork, there is a special import dialog box that allows you to specify how Flash imports the FreeHand document's layers and pages into your movie. You will learn how to import images into Flash in Chapter 9.

Import Bitmap Images

Although bitmapped images add to the overall file size of your movies, it is possible to import bitmaps and use them to add another dimension to your Flash 5 movies. Used judiciously, the addition of bitmaps can have quite an impact on the final movies you create in Flash 5. Many times a bitmap image is the only way to present an image in Flash; for example, if your client is a photographer and you are displaying his or her portfolio. You will learn how to use bitmap images in your movies in Chapter 9. After reading this chapter, combine your imagination with some experimentation and you will find ways to make good use of imported bitmaps in your Flash movies.

Animate with Flash

Although Flash 5 can be used to create simple vector-based artwork, its true strength lies in the fact that it enables you to create high-impact, quick-loading, Web-based animations.

As you work through this book, you will learn all the techniques you need to create animations with Flash 5. You'll also learn how to use the various tools, such as the Timeline, keyframes, tweening, and more. These tools, all included in Flash 5, help you quickly and easily create animated content that you can publish to the Web.

You can create animated movies for the Web and for presentations. As well, you can create high-end, animated multimedia interfaces for your Web sites.

For example, by using the various tools in Flash 5, you can create animated ad banners that can be used to advertise a Web site.

NOTE   *The Flash plug-in has become so ubiquitous that many Internet advertisers want their publishers to accept Flash content. You can often get a premium if you will accept Flash content ad banners on your site as opposed to static material.*

Understand the Flash Timeline

The Timeline, shown in Figure 1-6, is the large window directly above the stage.
The Timeline window in this figure has been expanded so you can see all its
features. The Timeline is composed of *frames, layers*, and the *playhead*. You use
layers and frames to organize the contents of your movie. You create animation by
changing the attributes of objects along the Timeline. You create major changes in
keyframes. When you drag the playhead along the Timeline, you get a rough preview
of the action from keyframe to keyframe. You will learn how to use the Timeline
and animate objects in Part III of this book.

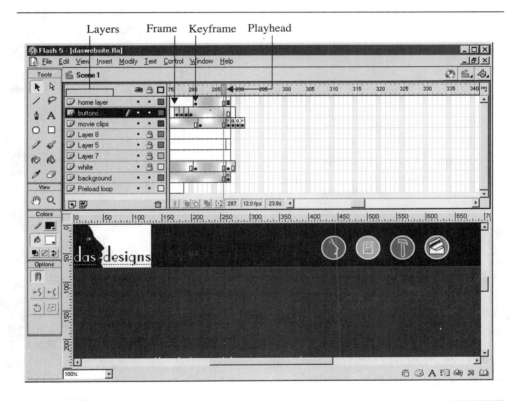

FIGURE 1-6   You create action over time by making changes along the Timeline

In Figure 1-6, notice that each layer has its own Timeline. Each layer's name is noted in a column on the left side of the Timeline window. At the top of the Timeline window is the Timeline Header that is broken down into individual frames. You can navigate along the Timeline by clicking the playhead and dragging it to the desired frame. At the bottom of the Timeline window is the Timeline Status Display, which indicates the current position of the playhead, the movie's frame rate, and the elapsed time to the current frame.

Preview Your Movie with the Controller

You can preview the movie within the workspace by clicking and dragging the playhead along the Timeline. You can generate a more accurate preview of your movie's action by using the Controller shown here. The Controller buttons (Stop, Rewind, Step Back, Play, Step Forward, and Go To End) function similarly to your VCR remote control device.

 *You also can preview your movie by pressing* ENTER *or* RETURN. *To step backward one frame at a time, press* <. *Press* > *to advance forward one frame at a time.*

Add Interactivity to Your Movie

You use Flash ActionScript to add interactivity to a movie. ActionScripts can be as simple as a one-line instruction that tells the Flash Player to halt a movie at a certain frame while awaiting input from a user, or they can be a complex series of actions that combine to create dazzling effects when a user's mouse rolls over a button. The uses for ActionScript are almost limitless. For example, you can also use ActionScript to create games, e-commerce catalogs, and online quizzes. Flash 5 has enough actions to warrant an entire book on the subject. In Chapter 14 you will learn to use the most popular Flash actions to add interactivity to your movies.

Publish and View Flash Movies

After you create a movie, it's time to share your Flash wizardry with the rest of the world. Flash comes with several features that make it easy for you to publish (or export) and view your Flash movies. Whether you want to create standalone content, create business presentations, or publish multimedia, interactive content to the Web, Flash makes a great choice.

View Flash Movies

When you install Flash the Standalone Player is installed by default. You can use the Standalone Player to view Flash movies you, and others, have created. To run the player, choose Start | Programs | Macromedia Flash 5 | Standalone Player (see Figure 1-7).

With the Player open, you browse to any SWF file to open and view that file in the Player.

You also can make your Flash movies run as standalone applications. In other words, you can create movies that can be played without the need for a Web browser or a standalone player. What this means is that you can create executable movies and distribute them to family, friends, and even to people over the Internet.

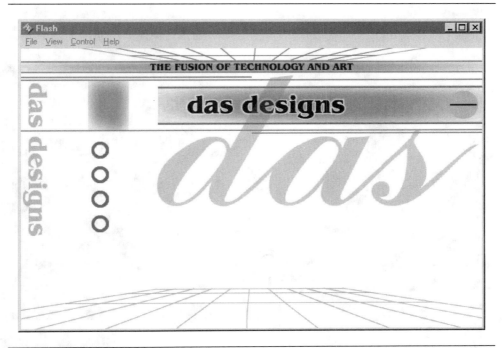

FIGURE 1-7   Running the Flash 5 standalone player

Publish Your Flash Movies

One of the biggest reasons why you want to create Flash movies is so that you can publish them on the World Wide Web. Flash 5 makes it easy to publish your movies. After you create a movie you publish it (as well as save it or export it). You will learn how to publish your movies in Flash's native SWF format as well as several other formats in Chapter 16. Figure 1-8 shows a published movie as it appears in the Internet Explorer Web browser.

Publish Your Movies on the Web

One of the biggest reasons to learn Flash 5 is so that you can create multimedia—interactive content for the Web. Flash content creators are in big demand on the Web. Knowing how to create and publish Flash content for the Web gives you

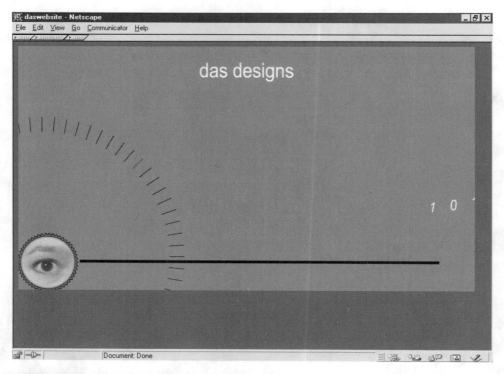

FIGURE 1-8 Movies published in Flash's SWF format can be viewed in Web browsers with the Flash Player plug-in

a tremendous marketing advantage over Web designers who only know how to create standard HTML Web pages. Even being able to create Flash ad banners can be a big plus in the world of the Web.

Flash 5 has all the tools you need to easily publish Flash movies to the Web. Of course there's more to it than that; you must first create a Flash movie.

Before you dive in and start creating content, you must become familiar with the Flash 5 interface. Even if you've used drawing or painting programs before, you may be surprised by some of the tools used in creating Flash animations. Not to worry, though, by the time you finish reading Chapter 2, you will use the Flash interface as though it were something you had been doing forever.

As you learn how to use the Flash interface and tools, you might find that some of the program's features don't suit your working style or run properly with your processor. Take a few moments to read the following section and you will know which items in Flash you can configure to suit your method of working.

Edit Flash Preferences

The designers of Flash set the program up to satisfy the working habits of most users. However, you can edit Flash preferences to suit your own working preference or to compensate for your processor. To open the Preferences dialog box, choose Edit | Preferences.

After you open the Preferences dialog box, you have three tabbed sections to choose from. Click the General tab (selected by default) to edit General preferences and modify the following options to suit your preferred work habits.

- In the **Undo Levels** section, enter a value between 0 and 200 to set the number of undo and redo levels. Choosing a high value uses more of your computer's memory.

- In the **Printing Options** section (Windows), choose Disable PostScript to disable PostScript while printing to a PostScript printer. This option is deselected by default. Use it only if you are experiencing problems while printing to a PostScript printer.

- In the **Select Options** section, Shift Select controls the manner in which you select multiple objects. When Shift Select is enabled (the default), holding down the SHIFT key while clicking additional objects adds them to the selection. If this option is disabled, you add additional objects to a selection by clicking them.

- In the **Select Options** section, enable the Show Tooltips option and Flash displays a tooltip when you move your cursor over a button or an icon.

- In the **Timeline Options** section, choose Disable Timeline Docking and Flash displays the Timeline as a free-floating window.

In the Timeline Options section, choose Use Flash 4 Selection Style to select frames as you did in Flash 4. Choosing this option gives you the ability to create additional frames by clicking and dragging the last frame on the Timeline.

In the Timeline Options section, choose Flash 4 Frame Drawing to display blank keyframes with unfilled circles.

- In the **Highlight Color** section, choose Use This Color, click the color swatch, and then choose a color from the palette. After you okay the new preferences, Flash displays selected items with the chosen color. To display selected items with the current layer's outline color, choose Use Layer Color.

- In the **Actions Panel** section, choose Normal mode or Expert mode. Choose Normal mode and Flash will automatically generate ActionScript when you select an action. Choose Expert mode and you can manually enter lines of ActionScript code directly into the Action Panel's text box.

The second tab in the Preferences dialog box is used to edit the way Flash handles the Pen tool and to modify drawing settings. The settings for the Pen tool are covered in Chapter 4. To modify the other drawing settings, click the Editing tab and in the Drawing Settings section, adjust the following parameters:

- **Connect Lines**—The option you choose in this section determines how close the end of one line must be to another before snapping to it. Choose from Must Be Close, Normal, or Can Be Distant. The setting also determines how close a line must be to true vertical or horizontal before Flash draws it that way.

- **Smooth Curves**—The option you choose in this section determines how much Flash smoothes a curve you create with the Pencil tool using the Smooth or Straighten mode. Normal works well for most users. If your mouse-drawn objects look a bit crude, choose the Smooth option.

- **Recognize Lines**—The option you choose for this parameter determines how close to straight a line must be before Flash draws it that way. If you are an accomplished computer artist, either Normal or Strict works well. Choose Tolerant for maximum assistance from Flash.

- **Recognize Shapes**—The option you choose for this parameter determines how precisely you must draw shapes such as rectangles, ovals, or triangles before Flash redraws them that way. The Normal or Tolerant settings work well for most users. Turn this option off for no assistance from Flash.

- **Click Accuracy**—The option you choose in this section determines how close your mouse must be to an item before Flash recognizes it. Choose Strict, Normal, or Tolerant.

- **Clipboard**—The settings in this section determine how Flash handles items copied to the clipboard from other programs. To modify clipboard preferences, click the Clipboard tab and adjust the following options to suit your working preference:

  - In the Bitmaps section (Windows) choose an option from the Color Depth menu. This setting determines the Color Depth Flash assigns to clipboard objects you copy from other programs and then paste into a movie.

  - In the Bitmaps section (Windows) choose an option from the Resolution menu. This setting determines the resolution Flash assigns to objects you paste into a movie from the clipboard. Stick with the default setting (Screen) unless you are creating high-resolution movies for multimedia presentations.

  - In the Bitmaps (Windows only) section, enter a value in the Size Limit field to determine how much of your computer's RAM is used when copying a bitmap image to the clipboard. Increase this value if you are working with large or high-resolution bitmap images. Enable the Smooth option to apply anti-aliasing to clipboard bitmaps.

  - In the Gradients section (Windows only), choose a menu option to determine the quality of gradient fills. Choosing a higher quality increases the time needed to copy graphics. This setting affects only the gradient quality when you paste copied objects to non-Flash applications. The gradient quality of clipboard items are unchanged when you paste them within Flash.

■ In the PICT Settings section (Macintosh), for Type, choose Objects to copy clipboard data as vector artwork. Alternatively, select one of the bitmap formats to convert clipboard data into a bitmap image. Enter a value for Resolutions. To include PostScript data with copied objects, select Include PostScript. Specify a Gradient setting to determine the quality of a gradient used in a PICT when pasted to an application outside of Flash. This setting does not alter Gradient quality when a PICT is pasted within Flash.

■ In the FreeHand Text section, choose Maintain Text as Blocks and you will be able to edit clipboard text copied from FreeHand and pasted into Flash.

Chapter 2

Learn to Use the Flash Interface

How to...

- Grasp the Stage Concept
- Navigate Through Time
- Layer Your Flash Objects
- Set Onion Skin Options

Often, when you try to tackle a new program like Flash, your computer screen can have some pretty intimidating features displayed on it, like foreign-looking windows, panels, and terms you're simply not familiar with. Before you get down to real production, it's best to familiarize yourself with the software interface. Because Flash is such a feature-packed program, starting with the basics ultimately speeds up your learning curve.

Grasp the Stage Concept

Your movie comes alive on the Flash stage, and this is the first element you'll see when you open a new file in Flash. All your images and animations are created on this stage. When you choose to create art in Flash (as opposed to importing it from another program) the stage is where you do all the drawing, painting, and editing of the lines and shapes that become the objects in your movie. You can see the main editing area within the stage in Figure 2-1.

The stage also contains a couple of other very useful areas that we'll get to know better in this chapter.

Directly above the main editing area you'll see the Layer section and the Timeline. You use layers to help keep your artwork in order. Layers act as transparent overlays and as such, help provide a stacking order for the elements on the stage. The Timeline works in conjunction with the layers and houses the frames of the movie. You can move back and forth through the Timeline and edit separate frames and groups of frames as you do so. Figure 2-2 shows the stage with a Flash file loaded.

You'll notice that there are several layers available in this file and that the topmost layer is active (it's showing a different color from the other layers, and it is called Steering Wheel).

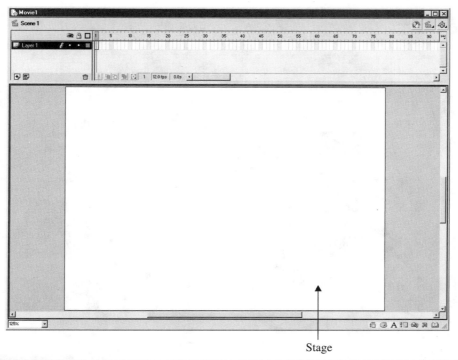

Stage

FIGURE 2-1   The Flash stage

You also should be able to see that the 10th frame is selected in the Timeline. This means that the elements in this frame comprise the tenth frame of this particular Flash movie.

We'll take a more detailed look at layers and the Timeline a little later in this chapter.

Learn the Editor Window

The Editor window is where you draw, paint, and manipulate lines, shapes, and text that will eventually become part of your Flash artwork or movies. To see how the Editor window works and to get used to drawing lines and shapes in the Editor window, try the following exercise:

1. Open Flash. Doing so will automatically start a new file, which you'll see as a blank white canvas on the stage.

Timeline

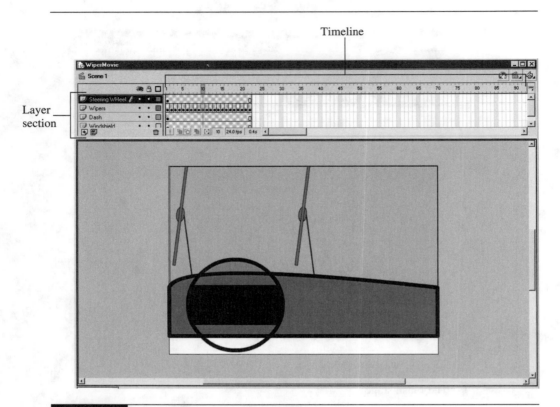

Layer section

FIGURE 2-2   The stage, layers, and Timeline

2. Using your mouse, click the Fill Color icon in the Toolbox. Doing so will bring up a small color palette from which you can choose the fill color that will be used as you create different shapes. Choose any color you want (see Figure 2-3).

3. You can repeat the process for the stroke color if you want. The color you choose here will be used for the color of the outline of the object you draw.

4. With the two colors selected, click the Oval tool in the Toolbox. It's the icon that has a small circle in it. You can see in Figure 2-3 that it has a small square around it indicating that it's currently selected.

5. Move your mouse into the Editing window. While holding down the left mouse button, drag the mouse to define an ellipse or oval shape. You'll

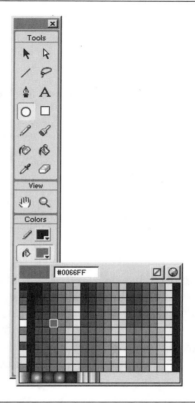

FIGURE 2-3   Setting the fill color

see the shapes being drawn as you move your mouse over the editing area. The shape will appear as a white oval with a thin black outline. Once you release the mouse button, the shape will be drawn in the fill and stroke colors you selected (see Figure 2-4).

Now that you have just drawn your first object in Flash and you're on your way to creating many amazing Flash graphics and animations.

You can edit the ellipse you've just drawn quite easily. For example, you can move it within the Editing window. To do so, select the Arrow tool (it's the small black arrow button in the upper-left corner of the Toolbox) and use it to draw an area around the ellipse you've drawn.

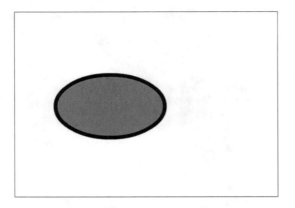

FIGURE 2-4 A filled and stroked ellipse drawn in Flash

You'll notice that the object changes and that it seems to be covered in a fine mesh. This mesh signifies that the ellipse is selected and that you can now edit it. With the ellipse selected, click and drag it to a new location in the Editing window (see Figure 2-5).

The Oval tool and Arrow tool are just two of the many Flash tools that you'll be using to create and edit different objects. We'll look at more of the drawing tools and their options later in this chapter.

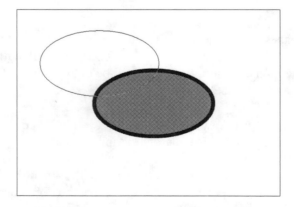

FIGURE 2-5 Moving the ellipse

Customize Toolbar Views

The tools you use most often can be displayed so that they're right at your fingertips. Flash makes it easy to customize the stage to suit your personal working style.

If you're new to Flash, the default setup will take a little getting used to. When you feel comfortable with the Flash environment, you can experiment with the interface and customize the stage to suit your personal preferences. Various panels that you see in the Flash interface are discussed in the following section.

Access Toolbars (Opening, Closing, Standard, Status, Controller)

There are quite a few toolbars and panels visible by default when you first launch Flash. As well, there are even more that remain hidden until you need them. All the various tools and panels windows can be toggled on and off via the View and Window menus.

View Menu   Under the View menu you have access to the Timeline and the Work Area (see Figure 2-6).

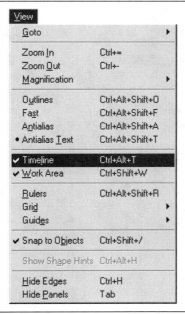

FIGURE 2-6   The View menu

You can toggle the Timeline on and off by choosing it under View | Timeline. Most often you'll want to leave it on because you'll be working with different layers or animations.

The appearance of the Work Area in the Flash window can be altered. Removing the check mark under View | Work Area moves the Editing window to the upper left of the stage and sets the zoom level to 100%.

Experiment with changing this setting to get the feel for how it works and how the view of the Flash window changes when you do so.

Window Menu   The Window menu offers a full selection of panels that make it easy to modify the properties of any elements in Flash (see Figure 2-7). For example, you can toggle on and off the Tools panel, for example, from within the Window menu.

You can access the various panels under Window | Panels, as seen in Figure 2-7. The panels that you can use are set into different areas. When a choice in an area contains a check mark, that means it is the panel you can currently see in the Flash window. For example, you can see a check mark next to the Info choice: This means that the Info panel should be visible in the Flash window. If an area has no choices

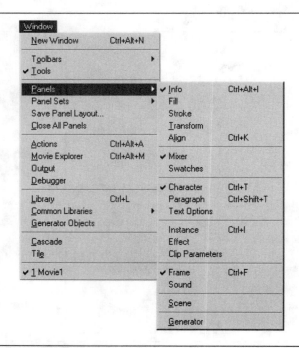

FIGURE 2-7   The Window menu

marked it means that the panel is not currently visible. For example, the Instance/Effect/Clip Parameters area in the menu has no choices selected. To open that particular panel, simply select one of the choices from the menu. Likewise, to close a panel, remove the check mark from the current choice for that particular panel.

You might notice as you open and close the various panels that some open as new panels and that some replace other panels.

You can open whichever panels you need based on the work that you're doing. Because it's so easy to open and close the various panels, you shouldn't worry too much about which ones are visible and which aren't at any given moment. In fact, if you're working on a computer with limited screen resolution, you might want to leave most of the panels turned off until they're needed to help you with a particular task.

Aside from the panels that are available under the Window menu, you can toggle the Toolbox on and off. Unless you want a wider viewing area on your stage, you will want to keep the Toggle Toolbox on. Otherwise, you might accidentally toggle off. Then when you go looking for the Toolbox, it has disappeared. Because having the Toolbox disappear can be frustrating, it's not a bad idea to familiarize yourself with how to get it back if it disappears. To turn on and off the display of the Toolbox, simply choose Window | Tools. Removing the check mark from the menu choice (choose Window | Tools) will remove the Toolbox, and clicking the same choice again will bring the check mark and the Toolbox back into view.

Below the Panels choice are a couple of options: You have the Save Panel Layout and Close All Panels options.

The Save Panel Layout enables you to save the way you've set up your stage. This can be handy if other people will be sharing the same computer where you're working on your Flash movies, or if you always use the same panel configuration. Using the Save Panel Layout, you can easily personalize the panels to your taste and work habits. You also could use this option to create several settings that you might use for different purposes. For example, you might save a certain setting to do your audio editing, another setting for creating animations, and so on.

Once you've saved your panel layout, it will be accessible under Window | Panel Sets. Any panel layouts that you've saved also will be available under this menu choice. As well, you can go back to the default Flash layout by choosing Window | Panel Sets | Default Layout.

The Close All Panels option is a quick way to close all the current panels. Note that this option is not a toggle, though. If you use this option to close all the panels, you can only get them back by opening each in turn from the Window | Panels menu.

You should experiment with different settings so that you can get used to opening and closing the different panels.

Dock and Undock Toolbars

The Toolbox has a special setting that you can use to "dock" it to the main window. To see how this works, click the title bar of the Toolbox. Doing so will dock the Toolbox to the left side of the main Flash window (see Figure 2-8).

This prevents the Toolbox from being moved around the screen. If you don't want to work this way, though, you can release, or undock, the Toolbox by double-clicking its title bar.

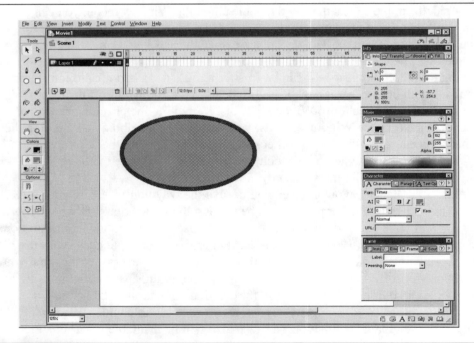

FIGURE 2-8   Docking the Toolbox

Line Up the Panels

Although you can't dock the various panels, you can line them up to each other quite easily. This helps keep your workplace organized. Customize the position of panels in any manner to suit your personal working style.

To line up your panels, move one into place by clicking and dragging it by its title bar. When you've got it positioned where you want the panels to line up, release the mouse button to drop it into place. Grab another panel by its title bar and move it towards the first panel. As you get close to the first panel, you'll notice that the panel you're dragging seems to jump towards the first panel. This jumping effect is known as "Snap To", and it's an effect that we'll later use to help line up lines, shapes, and text.

With the first and second panels joined together, move the remaining panels into place below them. Once you've got the panels lined up to your satisfaction, you might want to use the Save Panel Layout option under the Window menu to save your layout.

Now that you've got the Toolbox and the various panels laid out, it's time to start exploring the drawing tools and their options.

Access Drawing Tools and Options

Since Flash is a vector-based program, no doubt you'll be producing a lot of your movie directly on the Flash stage using the drawing tools. Flash drawing tools include many of the tools you're familiar with if you're used to working in drawing programs. All the drawing tools are available in the Toolbox (see Figure 2-9).

In Figure 2-9 you can see the Tools, View, Color, and Options areas. The Tools area contains the various tools you can use to create and edit lines, shapes, and text in Flash.

The View tools enable you to change the view of the Editing window. You can zoom in and move around the Editing window to make it easier to edit your objects.

The Color area enables you to set the colors for the various drawing tools.

Below the Color area is the Options area. This area is context sensitive, meaning that it changes depending on the current tool. This area will make available the options for the current tool you're working with. If you've seen an available option that you can't access, chances are that the option was only for use with another tool.

FIGURE 2-9   The Flash Toolbox

To select any tool, simply click its icon in the Tools area. Doing so will make that tool available to you. For example, earlier in this chapter, you selected the Oval tool and used it to draw an elliptical shape in the Editing window. You then used the Arrow tool to select the shape and to move it around the Editing window. We'll see, and use, the rest of the different tools throughout the remainder of this book as we create Flash images and movies.

Navigate Through Time Using the Flash Timeline

The Timeline is one of the most important concepts in Flash when you start animating your graphics. When you understand the concept of the Timeline, the making of moving objects will fall much more easily into place. The Timeline is where you coordinate the timing of your animations, and it's also where you control the layers that make up your animations.

Essentially, the Timeline enables you to control a movie's content over time. That is, you can have objects appear, disappear, move, and change over time.

Control Timeline View (View and Size the Window)

When you first open Flash, the Timeline appears at the top of the screen. However, as with the other controls in Flash, you can change how and where the Timeline appears in your work area. You can easily dock the Timeline to the bottom or sides of the main application window. As well, you can have the Timeline appear in its own window or be removed from the display altogether.

To move the Timeline, simply click and drag it by its title bar into the new position. In Figure 2-10, I've docked the Timeline to the bottom of the main window.

If you want to move the Timeline to a new location but don't want it to automatically dock itself to the top, bottom, or one of the sides of the main window, simply hold down the CTRL key (in both Mac and Windows) while dragging it to the new location.

You can hide the Timeline all together by choosing View | Timeline (see Figure 2-11).

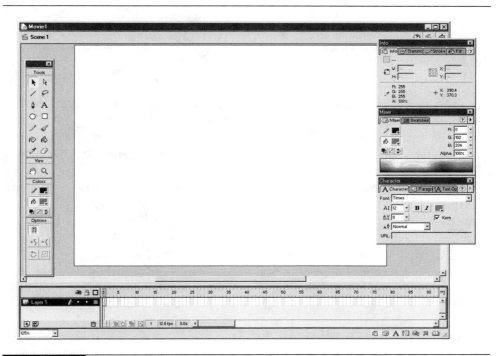

FIGURE 2-10   Docking the Timeline at the bottom of the stage

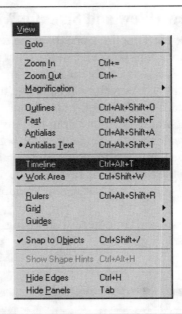

FIGURE 2-11 Hiding/showing the Timeline

The View | Timeline menu choice is a toggle. If the Timeline is visible, this menu choice will hide it, and if the Timeline is hidden, the menu choice will make it visible again. Hiding the Timeline is a great way to free up space when you're working. However, having it visible is a great asset when you're creating animations. Of course, it's a simple matter to toggle it off and on... the best of both worlds.

If you prefer to keep the Timeline visible as you work, you can always resize it to take up less screen real estate. To resize the Timeline, simply click and drag the bar between the Timeline and the application window if the Timeline is docked. If the Timeline is not docked, click and drag the lower-right corner as you would with any other GUI window. Figure 2-12 shows a docked Timeline window being shortened.

You also can change the length of the layer name fields. To do so, simply click and drag the vertical bar between the layer's section and the Timeline section in the Timeline window. This can be helpful if you use longer names for your layers.

Set the Timeline Options

To further customize the Timeline, you can adjust the size of the frames, tint them, and see a preview.

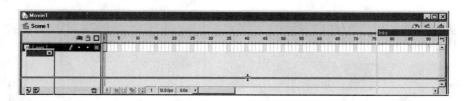

FIGURE 2-12   Resizing the Timeline

To adjust the size of the frames, click the Frame View button. You'll find it in the upper-right corner of the Timeline window. Clicking the button will display the Frame View pop-up menu (see Figure 2-13).

From the same menu, you can choose to set/unset the Tinted frames option. You also can choose whether to see a preview or a preview in context. Choosing Preview will display thumbnails of each frame scaled to fit the Timeline frames (see Figure 2-14).

Preview in context will show thumbnails of each frame's content, including any extra space included in the frame.

Layer Your Flash Objects

Layers are powerful tools in any digital graphics program, and Flash is no exception when it comes to the Layers tool. Layers enable you to control many aspects of your animation—you can change the order of layers, allow layers to be visible, or not, and more.

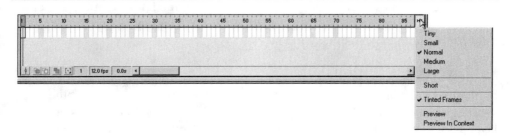

FIGURE 2-13   Resizing the Timeline's frames

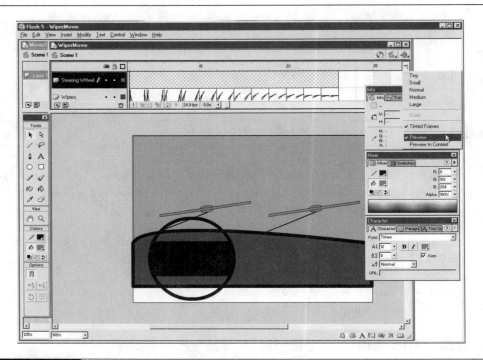

FIGURE 2-14 Previewing frames in the Timeline

Layers are like transparent sheets of acetate sitting over one another. When you create a new layer and add an object to it, the rest of the layer allows other, underlying objects and layers to show through except where the new object covers them.

Most layer options can be controlled directly from the left side of the Timeline. You can add and delete layers, toggle them on and off, and move and reorder them right from within the Timeline window.

Set Layer View Options

Sometimes in a complex multi-layer movie, it helps to be able to turn off the visibility of a particular layer for several reasons. There might be objects on one layer sitting underneath objects on a higher layer. The only way you can see the underlying objects is to make the other layer invisible. This is almost like temporarily removing your clear piece of acetate from the stack of layers to gain a better perspective of what lies underneath. The other issue is that sometimes it's impossible to select an object, especially if it's small or just a thin line, when it's overlapping

2

many other objects. Or you might just need to view a layer by itself on a clear background. Turning on and off the visibility of a selected layer can help you zero in on a particular object without the clutter of objects on surrounding layers.

You can toggle all layers on or off by clicking the Show/Hide All Layers icon. It resembles an eye, and you'll find it just above the topmost layer. You can use this icon to quickly hide all layers, for example, and then turn on only a select few.

You can toggle the visibility of separate layers by clicking the small dot icon below the Show/Hide All Layers icon in any of the layers (see Figure 2-15).

When the visibility of a layer is turned off, the layer is still visible when the movie is tested (Control | Test Movie) or published. Only guide layers become invisible when the movie is tested or published. Guide layers exist only for the purpose of providing guidelines that can be followed as a guide for placement of objects on a regular layer. The visibility of a layer guide can be turned on and off also. However, whether they're turned on or off on the stage, the layer guides are always invisible when the movie is published or played.

Add and Delete Layers

It's simple to add or delete layers. To add a layer you can click the Insert Layer icon. You'll find the icon in the lower-left corner of the layer section of the Timeline window. You also can add a layer by choosing Insert | Layer from the menu.

Another method that you can use to create a new layer is to right-click/CTRL-click a layer. Doing so will bring up the context menu, enabling you to choose Insert layer.

Any added layer will be placed above the currently active layer. To make a layer active, simply click in its title. Active layers are colored darker than inactive layers, and they contain a small icon that resembles a pencil, indicating that you can edit the objects in that layer.

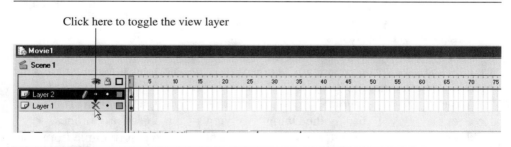

FIGURE 2-15   Toggling the view of a layer

Deleting a layer is as easy as creating one. You can click the Delete Layer icon in the lower-right corner of the layer section of the Timeline. The icon resembles a small trash can. You also can right-click/CTRL-click the layer you want to delete and choose Delete from the context menu.

Move and Reorder Layers

Part of the power of layers comes from the fact that you can easily reorder them, moving upper layers below others and vice versa.

To move a layer, click on its title in the layer section of the Timeline and drag it into place.

Create a Guides Layer (Snap-To, Rulers, Visible, Units, and so on)

There will be times when you might want some help lining up the various objects you've created. You can get some help in the form of a guide layer. To create a new guide layer, click the Add Guide Layer icon in the lower-left corner of the layer section of the Timeline.

Set Onion Skin Options

Onion skins help you visually track the path of an animation. If you've ever peeled an onion, you'll know that onion skins are partly translucent and that you can see several layers at a time. Because the skin is only partly translucent, though, the underlying layers are only partly visible. This is the case with onion skins in Flash. Using the Onion Skin option helps you in placing objects in frames on an animation, much as traditional animators flip between transparent cells to follow the direction of their animations. They also help keep your animations smooth. Without being able to see where an object has come from and where it's going, it's impossible to create an illusion of fluid movement.

To see the onion skin view of your animation, click the Onion Skin icon. The Onion Skin icon is the second button from the left in the lower-left corner of the Timeline (see Figure 2-16).

The icon acts as a toggle, meaning that if the view is off, clicking the icon will turn it on and vice versa. Having the Onion Skin view on can be a big help in placing objects in your animation.

To the right of the Onion Skin icon is the Onion Skins Outline icon. This is also a toggle that will display the Onion Skin view of the objects as outlines.

The next icon to the right is a toggle that enables you to edit multiple frames at once. This can be handy when you want to transform several objects/layers at the same time.

Click here to toggle the Onion Skin view

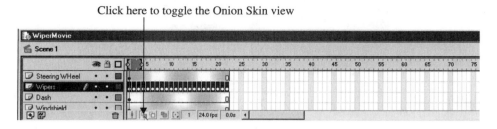

FIGURE 2-16   Toggling the Onion Skin view

The final Onion Skin icon enables you to choose how many skins, or frames, you'll see in relation to the current object/layer.

You can choose to see two frames on either side of the current frame, five frames on either side of the current frame, or all the frames in your animation (see Figure 2-17). Onion skins are discussed in detail in Chapter 10.

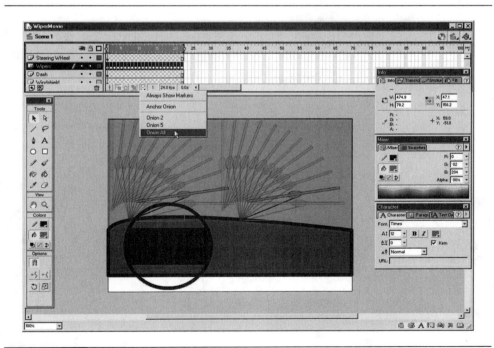

FIGURE 2-17   Viewing all frames in Onion Skin view

Chapter 3

Build a New Flash 5 Movie

How to...

■ Create a New Flash Document

■ Set Properties for Your New Movie

■ Save a Flash Document

■ Open an Existing Flash Document

■ Create Scenes for Your Movies

■ Navigate Your Movie

■ Manage Your Movies with the Movie Explorer

Flash 5 is a wonderfully diverse program that you use to create vector-based animations for the Internet, stand-alone presentations, and multimedia presentations. When you launch Flash to create a movie, the program presents you with a blank document set to default parameters. You adjust the parameters of the document to suit the media you're using to present your Flash movie. If you're creating a movie for streaming presentation in a Web browser, you adjust the different options to create the smallest possible file size. If, however, your movie will become part of a CD-ROM–based multimedia presentation, file size is not a factor and you can choose settings that create smooth action and high-quality images.

In this chapter, you will learn how to create and set up a new Flash movie. You also will learn how to use assets from previously saved Flash documents, as well as break a movie into scenes. You also will learn to navigate the Timeline and to manage your movie with the Movie Explorer.

Create a New Flash Document

When you launch Flash, the program creates a blank document set to the default parameters. There will be times when you need to create a new movie while editing another one, or create a new movie after saving a Flash document for another project. To create a new movie choose File | New. Flash creates a new document 550 pixels by 400 pixels with a frame rate of 12 fps (frames per second) on a white background. You can change these settings to suit the final destination of your movie. Figure 3-1 shows the default Flash document in the workspace.

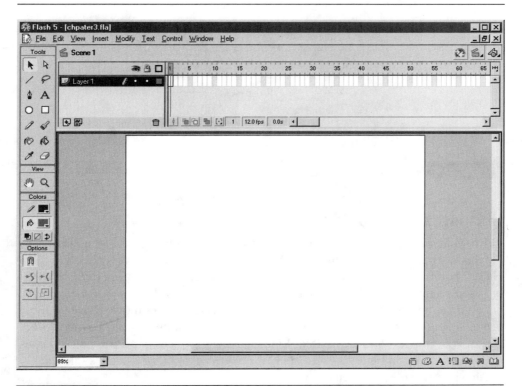

When you launch Flash the program creates a new document set to the default parameters

Set Properties for Your New Movie

The default document parameters might be perfectly suited for your Flash movie. However, if the default document's properties aren't suitable for your movie's intended destination, you can change them easily. You can modify the movie's properties at any time, but it's better to set the properties right after you create the document. Then you won't have to worry about resizing and realigning the graphics you use to create your movie. To set the properties for your movie, choose Modify | Modify Movie and Flash opens the Movie Properties dialog box shown in Figure 3-2.

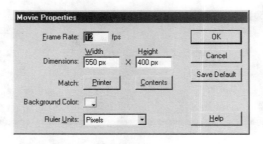

FIGURE 3-2   You modify a movie's properties in the Movie Properties dialog box

Choose Your Movie's Size

The default size of a Flash movie is 550 pixels by 400 pixels. The size of a Flash movie determines the size of the published SWF file. You can, however, modify the HTML publish settings so that the movie occupies a certain percentage of the Web browser, no matter what the size of the original document is. This however might distort the graphics, especially if you use bitmap images in your movie. It is best to decide upon the size of the movie prior to the beginning of the project. To modify the size of your movie, enter the desired Width and Height values in the Movie Properties dialog box shown in Figure 3-2. To apply the new size to the movie, click OK and Flash will resize the document.

Decide on a Frame Rate

The frame rate you choose for your movie determines how many frames Flash uses to display one second of action in your published Flash movie. The default frame rate for a movie is 12 fps, which is well suited for most interactive movies you create. If, however, you are packing a lot of action into a movie, you might need to increase the frame rate. Select a higher frame rate between 15–24 fps to create smoother action in your movies. The only penalty you pay for an increased frame rate is a larger file when the movie is published. To change your movie's frame rate, enter a new value in the Movie Properties dialog box's FPS field, previously shown in Figure 3-2, and click OK to apply the new frame rate.

After initially setting up the movie, you might find it necessary to change the frame rate. If the motion in your action sequences appears jerky, increase the frame rate. If you increase the frame rate, you will need to add frames between the start and finish of any sequence to maintain the timing of the movie. For more information on working with frames, see Chapter 10.

> **TIP** *To quickly access the Movie Properties dialog box, double-click the Frame Rate window below the Timeline.*

Choose Background Colors

The background color you choose for your Flash movie is displayed behind the artwork you create and animate on the stage. The default background color of a Flash movie is white. To change the default background color, click the Background Color swatch shown in Figure 3-2. Flash opens the color palette shown next and your cursor becomes an eyedropper. Click a color from the palette to select it. Flash displays the new color in the Background Color swatch. Click OK to apply the new background color to the document.

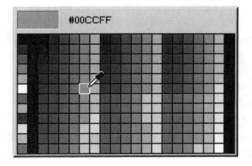

Choose Ruler Units

The default ruler unit for a Flash document is pixels, which means that Flash uses pixels as the unit of measure to record the position and size of objects in your movie. Most of your Flash work will end up being displayed on the Internet. Web pages and desktop sizes are all measured in pixels—a good reason for sticking with pixels as the ruler unit for the document. If however your movie will incorporate imported assets that use a different unit of measure, open the Movie Properties dialog box, previously shown in Figure 3-2, click the triangle to the right of the Ruler Units field, and choose a unit of measure from the drop-down menu. Your choices are Inches, Points, Centimeters, Millimeters, and Pixels (the default). Click OK to apply the change.

Save a Flash Document

During the course of a typical Flash project, you create objects, import graphic images, animate objects along the Timeline, and add interactivity to your movie by creating ActionScripts. Given the complexity of a typical Flash movie, you might find yourself creating the finished project over the course of several work sessions. When you save a Flash document in its native FLA format, you can open the file at a later date to edit it, or share the file with another Flash author working on the project.

To save a Flash document, choose File | Save and Flash will open the Save As dialog box. Navigate to the folder where you want the save the file, name it, and then click OK. Flash will save the file and all the assets used to create it to your hard drive for future use.

> **TIP** *Computer graphics programs such as Flash use up a lot of your system's resources. At times the program might use enough of your system's resources to lock up your computer, at which time you will lose any changes made in the current session. To avoid this, it is advisable to save your work early and often.*

Open Existing Flash Movies

After you save a Flash file, you can edit it at any time by opening the file. To edit an existing Flash project, you open the document as saved in Flash's native FLA format. Upon opening an FLA file, you can edit any asset used to create the file, or add additional elements to the file. To open an existing Flash file, choose File | Open and Flash displays the Open dialog box. Navigate to the folder where the file is stored, select it, and then click OK to open the file.

You also can preview a published Flash movie in the authoring environment by opening it. When you open a movie published in Flash's native SWF format, the Flash Player plays it in a preview window within the authoring environment. To open a published Flash movie, choose File | Open and Flash displays the Open dialog box. Navigate to the folder where the published movie is stored, select it, and then click OK to open and play the file.

Use Assets from Other Movies

When you create symbols, import bitmaps, or add sound to a movie, they are stored in the document Library. The document Library's assets can be used as needed within the movie, which saves you the effort of creating or importing similar objects throughout the course of a project. When a Flash document is saved, the document's Library is saved with the FLA file.

When you create a new Flash movie, you can use assets from another document's Library by choosing File | Open As Library. Flash opens the Open as

Library dialog box. Navigate to the folder the Flash file is stored in, select the file, and then click OK. Flash opens the saved file's document Library. To use an asset from the other document's Library, select the asset by clicking its name and dragging it onto the stage or directly into the current document's Library, as shown here. The asset now becomes part of the current document's Library. After you add the needed assets from the other document's Library, close it.

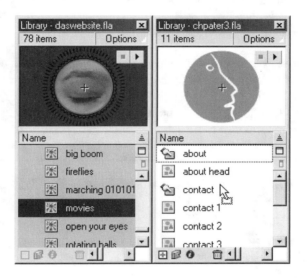

Control View Options

When you create a complex Flash movie, the various components of the movie are stored in your processor's memory. As your Flash projects increase in complexity, the demands on your processor increase, sometimes to the point where Flash slows down the redraw of an object, or slows down an animation as you test the movie in the authoring mode. When this happens, you can speed things up again by changing the way Flash draws objects on the stage. You have four commands from the View menu that will speed up a movie's display in the authoring mode:

- Choose View | Outlines and Flash displays all objects as outlines.

- Choose View | Fast and Flash displays the shapes and colors of objects without antialiasing.

- Choose View | Antialias and Flash applies antialiasing to all shapes and bitmaps in your movie. This display option gives you the best idea of what your finished Flash production will look like, but might slow down the display speed when previewing animation. Use this mode if you have a fast processor and a video card capable of displaying 24-bit color.

■ Choose View | Antialias Text and Flash applies antialiasing to all text objects in your movie. As a rule, you want to choose this option (which is enabled by default) to accurately display text used in your movies.

Use Grids

Although it is not visible when you create a new document, Flash always provides you with a grid, which you can use to align objects to each other and the grid. You can choose to display the grid, change the grid's spacing and color, and choose whether objects snap to grid points. Choose View | Grid | Show Grid and Flash will display the grid shown in Figure 3-3.

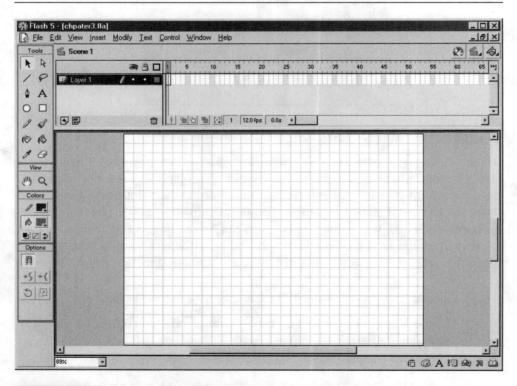

FIGURE 3-3   You use the grid to precisely align objects to themselves and specific points on the stage

3

Use Grid Snapping

You can use the Flash grid in two ways: first as a visual reference when you manually align objects to grid intersections, and second as a virtual reference where Flash snaps objects to intersecting grid points. Choose View | Grid | Grid Snapping and Flash will snap an object to grid points as you move it across the stage.

When you employ Flash to align objects to grid points, the point where an object aligns to the grid is dependent on where you select the object. Every object you create has a bounding box with a handle in its center, and one for each extremity of the bounding box. As you drag an object, the handle (an unfilled dot) you are dragging the object by becomes larger and darker when it nears a grid intersection point.

Edit the Grid

The default grid will display a light gray line every 18 pixels along the document's width and length. You can modify the grid spacing and color to suit the document you are editing. Choose View | Grid | Edit Grid and Flash displays the Grid dialog box shown here.

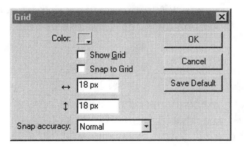

Change Grid Color

To modify the color of the grid lines, open the Grid dialog box as previously outlined, click the Color swatch, and select a color from the palette. Select a color that contrasts well with the background color of your document. Click OK and Flash changes the grid to the color you specified.

Change Grid Spacing

To change the grid spacing, open the Grid dialog box as outlined previously and enter the desired values in the width (the horizontal double-headed arrow) and height (the vertical double-headed arrow) fields. Click OK and Flash redraws the grid lines using the spacing you specified.

Change Grid Snapping Accuracy

You can change how close an object must be to a grid intersection before Flash snaps the object to the grid. To change grid snapping accuracy open the Grid dialog box as outlined previously. Click the arrow to the right of the Snapping Accuracy field and choose an option from the drop-down menu. The effect of the different options will vary depending on the size of your document and the spacing of the grid. Normal works best in most instances. Choose Must Be Close or Always Snap if you have specified wide grid spacing.

Use Rulers

Flash has another hidden tool that you use to align objects in your movies: rulers. When you choose View | Rulers, Flash displays a vertical and horizontal ruler as shown in Figure 3-4. The rulers use the unit of measure you specified with the Modify Movie command. If you did not modify the Ruler Units option when you set up the movie, the rulers use pixels, the Flash default, as their unit of measure.

When you select an object on the stage and move it, Flash displays two small lines on each ruler, which correspond to the object's width and height. As you move an object across the stage, these reference points follow, giving you a preview of the object's current position. You can use these reference points to accurately position an object on the stage. You also use rulers to create guides for your document.

Use Guides

Another option you can use to align and position objects in your movies is guides. Guides are visual references that you create and position where needed. You can create horizontal and vertical guides. You can create as many guides as you need. Guides will not be visible when the movie is published. An example of using guides would be aligning a series of navigation buttons to a vertical guide. To create guides for your document, you must first make the rulers visible by choosing View | Rulers.

To create a vertical guide, click the vertical ruler and drag to the right. As you drag, a small vertical line appears on the horizontal ruler, giving you a preview of the vertical guide's position. When the guide is in the desired position, release the mouse button and Flash creates a lime green colored horizontal guide.

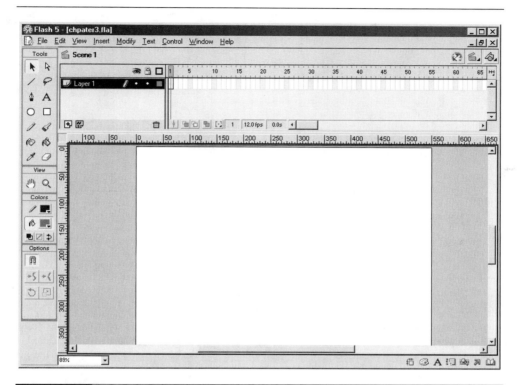

FIGURE 3-4   You use rulers to precisely align items to a specific position on the stage

To create a horizontal guide, click the horizontal ruler and drag down. As you drag, a small horizontal line appears on the vertical ruler indicating the current position of the guide. When the guide is in the desired position, release the mouse button. The following illustration shows a vertical and horizontal guide added to a document.

To toggle the visibility of guides, choose View | Guides | Show Guides. When you choose this command Flash hides all visible guides from view. Select the command again and Flash reveals the hidden guides.

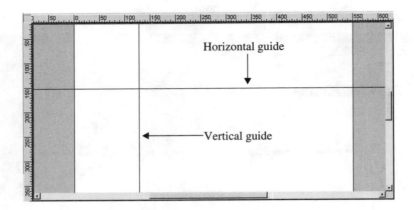

Use the Snap to Guides Feature

After you create a series of guides, you can have Flash snap objects to the guides by choosing View | Guides | Snap to Guides. After you choose this option, Flash will snap objects to guides as you drag the objects across the stage. The snapping takes place at the handle you chose when you selected the object. For example, if you select the object by its center, snapping will occur when the center of the object approaches a guide. If you select the object by one of its corners, snapping will occur when the corner approaches a guide. The object's handle (an unfilled dot) becomes darker and slightly larger when it approaches a guide that it can snap to.

 When you use the Snap to Guides feature, it's a good idea to disable snapping to the grid. If you have both options enabled at the same time, Flash has so many targets to snap to, it will be difficult to ascertain when Flash is snapping an object to the grid or to a guide.

Move Guides

After you create a guide, you can easily move it. As you near a vertical guide, a small arrow appears to the right of the cursor. Click the guide to select it and then drag it to the desired position. As you near a horizontal guide, a small downward pointing arrow appears to the right of the cursor. Click the guide to select it and drag it to the desired position.

Lock Guides

When you have a series of guides positioned just the way you want them, lock them to prevent inadvertently selecting and moving a guide when you meant to select an object. To have Flash lock all guides used in your document, choose View | Guides | Lock Guides.

Edit Guides

You can edit guides after you create them. You can change the color of guides and modify the snapping accuracy Flash employs when you align objects to the guides. Choose View | Guides | Edit Guides and Flash opens the Guides dialog box shown here:

3

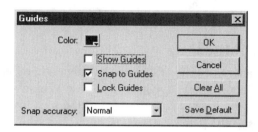

Change Guide Color

To change the color of guides in your document, open the Guides dialog box as outlined previously, click the Color swatch, and select a color from the palette. Select a color that contrasts well with the background color of your document. Click OK and Flash applies the selected color to all guides in your document.

Change Guide Snapping Accuracy

You can specify the amount of accuracy Flash uses when snapping an object to a guide. Snapping accuracy determines how close an object must be to a guide before Flash snaps the object to the guide. To modify guide-snapping accuracy, open the Guides dialog box as outlined previously. Click the triangle to the right of the Snap Accuracy field and choose an option from the drop-down menu. Click OK and Flash applies the new setting.

The default snapping accuracy of Normal works well in most instances. Choose Must be Close and the object must be close to a guide before Flash will snap the object to it. Choose Can be Distant and an object can be farther away from a guide before Flash will snap the object to the guide.

Break a Movie into Scenes

When you create a complex movie with lots of action, you end up with a Timeline of equal complexity. To prevent scrolling past an endless procession of frames and framesets to find a particular action sequence, you can break your movie into scenes. A movie with scenes is like a three-act play; after the finale of one scene, another starts.

When you create a new Flash document, it has one scene by default. If you know your production is going to involve a lot of frames and interaction, you can break it down into scenes right after you create the document. You also can create a new scene when your production reaches a point where it becomes obvious that editing the movie as a single scene would be a logistical nightmare. If your movie has a discernable beginning, middle, and end, you can break it down into three scenes, which will make editing your movie easier.

Use the Scene Panel

You use the Scene panel to create, delete, and arrange the order of scenes in your movie. To open the Scene panel shown here, choose Window | Panels | Scene. The Scene panel is essentially a window with a list of the scenes in your movie. The buttons at the bottom of the panel are used to duplicate, add, and delete scenes from your movie.

Create a Scene

You can create all your scenes after you create the document, or create a scene on the fly when it becomes obvious that the magnitude of your movie requires an additional scene. After you create a scene, you can cut and paste frames and layers from another scene into the new scene. To create a new scene, open the Scene panel as outlined previously, click the Add Scene button (the + icon at the bottom of the panel) and Flash will add a new scene to your movie.

Name the New Scene

You can name the scenes in your Flash movies. Naming scenes is a good habit to get into. The proper naming of scenes will make it easier for you to identify the scene's contents by its name. In addition, Flash will add the scene name to drop-down menus that are associated with certain actions you use when creating ActionScript. When you name a scene, choose a name that has meaning, one that will make the scene's contents identifiable by the name alone.

When you create a new scene, Flash gives it the default name of Scene followed by the next available scene number. To name a scene, click its current name and Flash will highlight it. Type a new name for the scene and then press ENTER or RETURN. Flash will now identify the scene by its new name.

Delete a Scene

You can delete a scene when it is no longer needed. To delete a scene, open the Scene panel, click the Delete Scene button that looks like a trash can, and Flash removes the scene from your movie.

CAUTION *Deleting a scene cannot be undone.*

Duplicate a Scene

You can duplicate an existing scene and use the entire scene or parts of it to create a new scene. When you duplicate a scene, Flash creates an exact copy, preserving the original scene's layer names, frame names, and action. To duplicate a scene, open the Scene panel as outlined previously, click the Duplicate Scene button that looks like an arrow pointing from one document to another and Flash creates a new scene duplicating all the elements in the original scene. Flash names the new scene by appending the original scene's name with copy. Rename the duplicated scene and delete any unwanted frames or layers.

Change the Order in Which Scenes Play

The scenes you create in Flash play in the order in which they were created. When you open the Scene panel and view the list of scenes in your movie, the last scene created appears at the bottom of the list. To rearrange the order in which scenes play, click the scene's name and drag it to a new position in the Scene panel.

Navigate Your Movie

As you create your movie, you will need to move freely to different parts of the movie to edit elements and add new elements to your production. You can manually navigate between frames, layers, and scenes, or use Flash 5's new Movie Explorer to quickly locate items in your movies.

Navigate the Timeline

When you add action to your movies, you navigate from one point on the Timeline to the next to select specific frames or framesets. A *frameset* is a set of frames between two keyframes. To select a specific frame on the Timeline, click it. To select a specific frame within a frameset, CTRL-click/CMND-click the frame.

You also can manually advance from frame to frame by clicking the playhead and dragging it across the Timeline. This also is known as scrubbing the frames. When you navigate in this manner, the objects within your movie will move, giving you a rough preview of the action. The following illustration shows a typical Timeline from a Flash movie.

Playhead

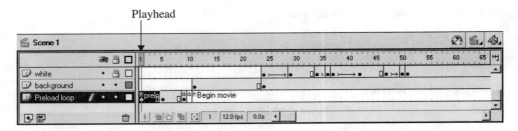

TIP   *An alternative method for navigating the Timeline is to use your computer's keyboard. To advance forward one frame at a time along the Timeline, press the > key. To navigate backward, press the < key.*

Navigate Between Scenes

After you create a movie with multiple scenes, you need to navigate from scene to scene to edit and fine-tune the content of your movie. You have three different options for viewing a scene in your movie. To view a particular scene, do one of the following:

- Choose View | Go to and select the name of the scene you want to view from the menu.

- Choose Window | Panels | Scene and select the name of the scene you need to edit in the Scene panel.

- Click the Edit Scene button and select a scene from the menu.

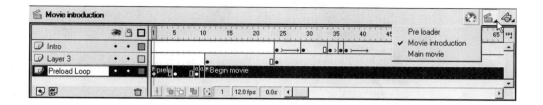

Navigate Between Layers

When you use layers to segregate items within your movie, you go from one layer to another to edit various elements. To navigate to a layer do one of the following:

- Click a layer's name.

- Click any frame in a layer's Timeline.

- Select an item on the stage that you know is on the layer that you want to select.

Manage a Movie with the Movie Explorer

New to Flash 5 is the Movie Explorer, a tool that enables you to view the components of your movie as a visual outline. You can use the Movie Explorer to select and edit specific assets in your movie. The Movie Explorer is customizable; you choose which elements of your movie are displayed. The Movie Explorer also can be used to navigate within your movie. To open the Movie Explorer, as shown in Figure 3-5, choose Window | Movie Explorer. An alternative method for opening the Movie Explorer is clicking the Movie Explorer button on the Launcher bar.

In default mode, the Movie Explorer displays all text objects, buttons, movie clips, artwork, and ActionScripts. To display or hide a particular group of elements, click one of the buttons shown in Figure 3-5.

In addition to displaying a particular group of items, you also can customize which objects within a group the Movie Explorer displays. For example, you can configure the Movie Explorer to display only buttons. To customize the items the Movie Explorer displays, click the Customize Which Items to Show button and Flash opens the Movie Explorer Settings dialog box shown next. Select the items you want the Movie Explorer to display and click OK.

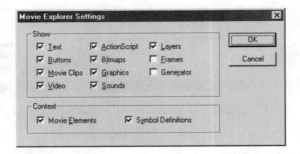

The Movie Explorer also enables you to find all instances of an item used in your movie. To find a labeled item, enter its name in the Find field and then press ENTER or RETURN. The Movie Explorer displays all instances of the item as shown here.

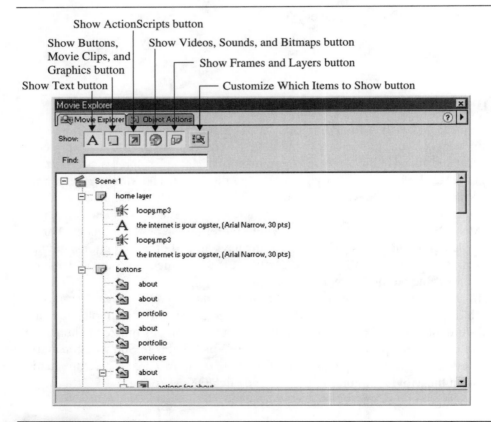

FIGURE 3-5   You use the Movie Explorer to view the elements of your production as a visual outline

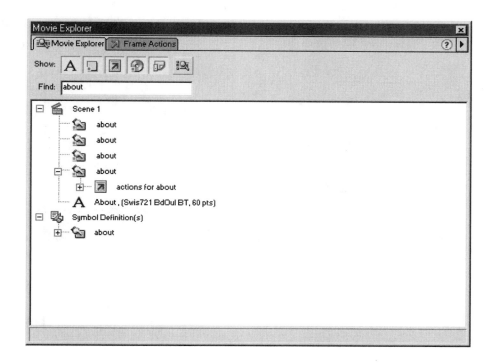

You also can use the Movie Explorer to edit symbols used in your movie. To edit a symbol, double-click its name in the Movie Explorer and Flash opens the symbol in Symbol-Editing mode. For more information on editing symbols and navigating the Movie Explorer, see Chapter 8.

The Movie Explorer has an Options menu that you can use to perform a variety of tasks on a selected item. To display the Movie Explorer's Options menu shown here, click the triangle near the upper-right corner of the Movie Explorer window.

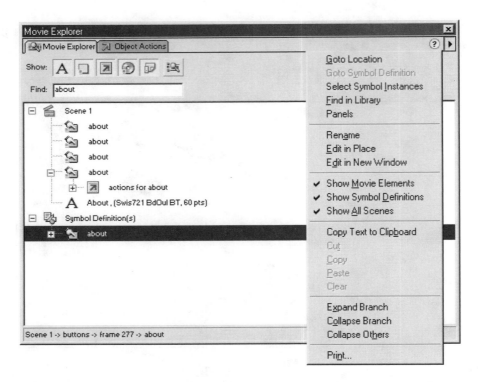

As you can see, you can use the Options menu in several ways: to navigate to a symbol instance's or a frame's location; to rename or edit a selected object; to cut, copy, or paste a selected object; or to expand or collapse a branch in the Movie Explorer. You also can expand a Movie Explorer branch by clicking the + icon to the branch's left or collapse it by clicking the − icon to the branch's left. Expandable branches are noted with a + icon to the left of the branch; collapsible branches by a − icon to the branch's left.

Chapter 4

Create Graphic Objects for Your Flash Movies

How to...

- Use the Toolbox
- Use the Stroke Panel
- Draw Lines and Curves
- Create Basic Shapes
- Combine Shapes to Create New Objects
- Change Your Viewpoint

To create a compelling Flash movie, you create colorful objects that you later animate along the Timeline. The graphic objects you create can either be imported into your movie or created within Flash itself. You use the Flash drawing tools to create vector-based artwork. If you are new to Flash, but an experienced veteran of vector drawing programs, you will notice that Flash has a decidedly different way of handling overlapping shapes and intersecting lines. In this chapter, you will learn to create objects with the drawing tools. You also will learn how to select and modify the shapes you create.

Locate the Right Tool in the Toolbox

The Toolbox is home to all of the tools you use to create and modify objects for your movies. The Toolbox, as shown in Figure 4-1, is comprised of four sections. The Tools section of the Toolbox houses the tools you use to create objects, select them, and modify them. The View section has two tools that you use to zoom in or out on objects, and pan your view of the stage. The Colors section has two color wells, one that modifies the object's stroke (outline) color, and one that changes the object's fill color. The Options section of the Toolbox contains the modifiers for a selected tool. Many of the tools have multiple modifiers; some have none. To select a tool from the Toolbox, click it. After you select a tool, Flash updates the Options section to display the tool's modifiers.

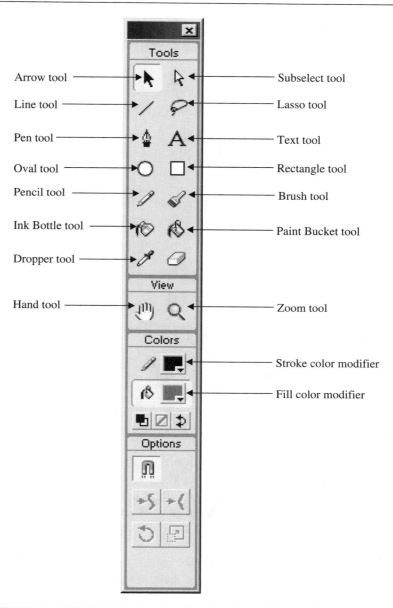

Arrow tool

Line tool

Pen tool

Oval tool

Pencil tool

Ink Bottle tool

Dropper tool

Hand tool

Subselect tool

Lasso tool

Text tool

Rectangle tool

Brush tool

Paint Bucket tool

Zoom tool

Stroke color modifier

Fill color modifier

4

FIGURE 4-1   You use tools from the Toolbox to create and modify objects

Create Objects for Your Movies

To create an object using one of the Toolbox's drawing tools, you click the tool to select it. After you select a tool, specify the stroke and fill colors for the object you are creating. After you select the stroke and fill colors, you adjust the tool's modifiers to control the performance of the tool and modify the type of shape it creates. To draw the object, drag the tool on the stage.

Select Fill and Stroke Color

After you select a drawing tool, you use the Colors section of the Toolbox to select the object's stroke (outline) and fill colors. You use the Stroke Color well to select the color for a line or a shape's outline. You use the Fill Color well to select a color or gradient fill for a shape. The Color section of the Toolbox and its controls are shown here.

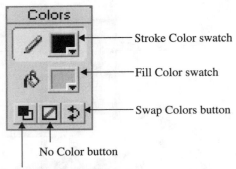

To select a Stroke color for an object you are creating with a drawing tool, click the color swatch to the right of the pencil icon. After you click the swatch, the cursor becomes an eyedropper and Flash opens a color palette. Click a color in the palette to select it. If you do not want a stroke color for the object you are creating, click the No Color button and when you create the shape, Flash applies the selected fill color, but no stroke color.

To select a fill color, click the color swatch to the right of the Paint Bucket icon. After clicking the swatch, Flash opens the color palette shown on the next page and your cursor becomes an eyedropper. This is the same color palette that you use to create a stroke color with the addition of seven gradient fills. A *gradient fill* is a blend of two or more colors. Click a color or gradient to select it. Flash applies the selected fill to the shape you create.

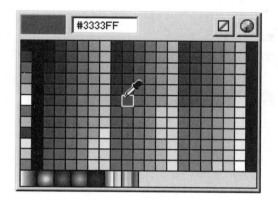

TIP   *To copy a solid color from an existing object, click the Stroke Color or Fill Color swatch, and then drag the Eyedropper on the stage. Move the Eyedropper over the object whose color you want to sample and release the mouse button. Flash displays the sampled color in the swatch's window and will apply it to the shape you create with the tool.*

At the bottom of the Colors section are three buttons that you use to modify the stroke and fill colors. Click the first button to restore the swatches to Flash's default black stroke color and white fill color. Click the No Color button after clicking the Stroke Color button and Flash will apply no stroke color to the object you create with the selected tool. Click the No Color button after clicking the Fill Color button and Flash will create a transparent fill for the object you create with the selected tool. Click the Swap Colors button and Flash will swap the fill color with the stroke color and vice versa.

Select the Line Style

When you use a drawing tool to create a line or an object with an outline, the default style is a solid one-pixel thick line (or stroke, as it is referred to in Flash).

You use the Stroke panel, shown below, to change a line's style, height, and color. You also can use the panel to create a custom line style.

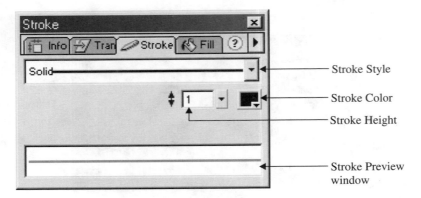

To create a line style other than the default, choose Window | Panels | Stroke. Click the triangle to the right of the Stroke Style field and select a style from the drop-down menu. To modify the height of the line, click the triangle to the right of the Stroke Height field and drag the slider up or down. Alternatively, enter a value between .10 and 10. To select a Stroke color, click the swatch and select a color from the palette. As you modify the line style, Flash updates the image in the Stroke preview window, giving you a preview of the modified line style.

Create a Custom Line Style

You also can use the Stroke panel to create a custom line style for the shape you create. To create a custom line style, open the Stroke panel as outlined earlier, click the triangle near the panel's upper-right corner and then click the Custom button. Flash opens the Line Style dialog box shown here.

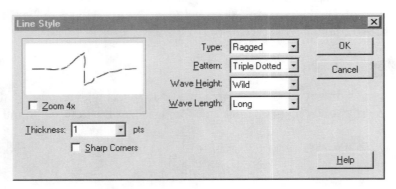

4

To begin creating a custom line style, click the triangle to the right of the Type field, and select an option from the drop-down menu. Each style has a different set of parameters. Next select the desired option from each of the style's parameter menus. To specify the line's thickness, click the triangle to the right of the Thickness field and drag the slider. Alternatively, enter a value between .10 and 10. Enable the Sharp Corners option and Flash will render abrupt transitions in the lines you create as sharp corners. As you create the custom line style, Flash creates a preview in the window on the left side of the dialog box. To finish creating the custom line style, click OK. Flash will display the line style in the Stroke Style window and apply it to all the shapes you create until you once again modify the line style.

Draw Lines and Curves

Flash provides you with one tool for drawing lines and three tools for drawing lines and curves. The Line tool enables you to create the simplest geometric shape, the straight line. You use the Pencil tool to create lines or geometric shapes. The tool has extensive modifiers that give you the freedom to create anything from a freeform line, to a recognizable geometric shape, such as a circle, rectangle, or triangle. You use the Brush tool to add calligraphic splashes of color to your movies. To create a line, path, or shape with point-to-point control, you use Flash 5's long-awaited addition to the Toolbox, the Pen tool.

With the Line Tool

To create a straight line, select the Line tool and then adjust the line style and select a stroke color as outlined previously. Click and drag on the stage to create the line. Hold down the SHIFT key while dragging to constrain the line to 45-degree increments.

With the Pencil Tool

You use the Pencil tool when you want to create a smudge-free virtual line that rivals your trusty 2B graphite pencil. You can use the tool to create freeform lines, or create outlines that you color with the Ink Bottle tool. If the outline you create is closed (the beginning and ending points meet), you can fill it with the Paint Bucket tool. You have three different pencil modes that give you varying degrees of assistance while creating the line.

To create a line with the Pencil tool, select the tool from the Toolbox and then select a line style, thickness, and stroke color as outlined earlier. In the Options section, click the Pencil Mode button and choose Straighten, Smooth, or Ink. Pencil modes are discussed in the next section. To create the line, click on the stage and drag. To constrain the line to 45-degree increments, hold down the SHIFT key while dragging.

What Are Pencil Modes? When you select the Pencil tool, the Pencil Mode button appears in the Options section of the Toolbox. You have three different modes that modify the performance of the Pencil tool. Figure 4-2 shows lines created with the Pencil tool in each mode.

To select a mode, click the Pencil Mode button, and Flash expands the button as shown on the next page. To select the desired mode, click the appropriate button. You have three Pencil modes to choose from:

- **Straighten**—Choose this mode to create a line comprised of straight line segments and interconnecting curves.

- **Smooth**—Choose this mode when you want to draw smooth flowing curved lines.

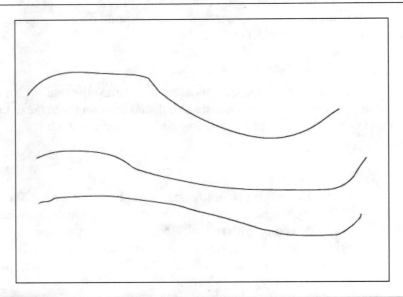

FIGURE 4-2 The type of line you create with the Pencil tool depends on which Pencil mode you choose

■ **Ink**—Choose this mode when you need to create a freeform line with no assistance from Flash. You might prefer this mode if you are an accomplished artist working with a digital tablet or if your movie calls for an irregular line.

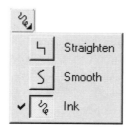

 *To quickly create a geometric shape with the Pencil tool, select the tool and then select the Straighten mode. Draw a shape resembling an oval, a rectangle, or a triangle, and Flash will transform your creation into its proper geometric shape.*

With the Brush Tool

You use the Brush tool when you need to add artistic splashes of color to your movie. The tool has modifiers that let you vary the shape of the brush tip, as well as the width of the brush. There's even a modifier you can use to vary the width of the brush stroke when drawing with most pressure-sensitive tablets. The modifiers for the Brush tool are shown here.

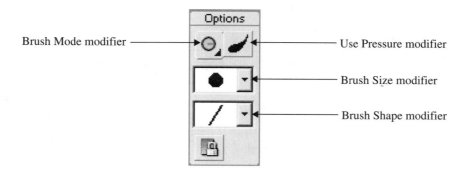

To create a brush stroke, select the Brush tool and select a fill color as outlined previously. Click the Brush Mode modifier button and choose an option. Brush modes will be discussed in the next section. To create a brush stroke that varies in width with your computer's pressure-sensitive tablet, click the Pressure Sensitive button. Click the triangle to the right of the Brush Size window and choose a brush size from the drop-down menu. To select a brush tip style, click the triangle to the right of the Brush Shape window and choose an option from the drop-down menu. To create the brush stroke, click anywhere on the stage and drag the tool.

What Are Brush Modes?   The Brush tool has four different modes that you use to control where color is applied with the tool. To select a Brush mode, select the Brush tool, click the Brush Mode button in the Toolbox's Options panel, and choose one of the following options:

- Choose **Paint Normal** to apply paint over existing lines and fills on the selected layer.

- Choose **Paint Fills** when you want to apply paint to all filled shapes and blank areas on the stage while leaving lines unaffected.

- Choose **Paint Behind** to apply paint behind existing lines and fills and apply color to blank areas of the stage.

- Choose **Paint Selection** when you need to apply paint within a selected filled shape while leaving lines and blank areas of the stage unaffected.

- Choose **Paint Inside** to apply paint within the filled shape where you begin the brush stroke without affecting surrounding lines, surrounding fills, and blank areas of the stage. If you like painting within the lines, choose this mode. Figure 4-3 shows how you can modify where brush stokes are applied with the different Brush modes.

With the Pen Tool

The Pen tool is a welcome addition to Flash 5. You can use it to create lines, outlines, or paths that you can use for animation motion paths. The Pen tool gives you point-to-point control over the shapes you create. With this tool, you can create straight line segments, curved line segments, or combine both for a truly unique line. When you create a line with the Pen tool, click to define the beginning and ending points for the line segment.

To create a straight line with the Pen tool, select the tool, and select a line style, thickness, stroke, and fill color as outlined earlier. Click the spot on the stage where you want the line segment to begin, and Flash creates a single corner point. Click the spot where you want the segment to end, and Flash adds another corner point, connecting the points with a straight-line segment as shown next.

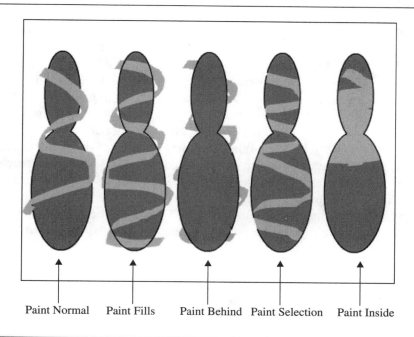

Paint Normal   Paint Fills   Paint Behind   Paint Selection   Paint Inside

FIGURE 4-3   The Brush mode modifier lets you choose how paint is applied with
the Brush tool

To add an additional segment to the line, click another spot on the stage. To
constrain a line segment to 45-degree increments, hold down the SHIFT key.

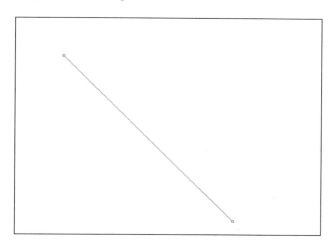

To complete drawing an open path with the Pen tool, double-click the last point. Alternatively you can CTRL-click/CMND-click anywhere on the stage. To create a closed path, click the first point you created and Flash closes the outline and applies the currently selected fill color.

To create a curved path with the Pen tool involves the same technique with a slight variation. Wherever you need to add a curve point to the path, you click and drag. As you drag, Flash creates a pair of tangential handles that define the shape of the curve. The direction and the distance you drag after clicking determines the length and slope of the handles. When the curve segment is the shape you desire, release the mouse button. You can now add additional curve points or corner points to create a path. If the shape of the path is not satisfactory, you can modify each point along the path with the Subselect tool, or you can add additional points to the path or delete unneeded points with the Pen tool. When you draw with the Pen tool, you can combine curve points and corner points, as shown here.

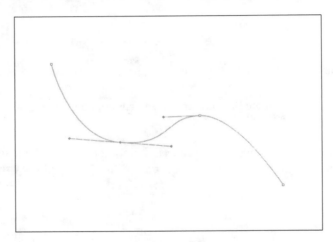

Modify Paths   Once you create a path with the Pen tool, you can easily modify it by manipulating the points that make up the path. You can add points or delete points, convert corner points to curve points and vice versa, or move points to modify a path. By default, Flash displays selected corner points as hollow squares and selected curve points as hollow circles.

To move a point along a path, select the Subselect tool, click the point you want to move, and drag it to a new position. When you release the mouse button, Flash readjusts the shape of the path to reflect the point's new position.

To nudge a point, select it with the Subselect tool and then use your keyboard's arrow keys to nudge the point in the desired direction. To nudge more than one point, select the first point with the Subselect tool, and add additional points to the selection by clicking them while holding down the SHIFT key. Alternatively, you can drag a marquee around the points you want to select with the Subselect tool. Use the arrow keys to nudge the selection of points to a new location.

To add a point to a path, select the Pen tool. As you approach the path, the cursor's icon changes to a plus (+) sign. Click to add a point to the path. Flash creates a new point along the path that you can modify with the Subselect tool.

To delete a corner point from a path, select the Pen tool and move toward the corner point you want to delete. As you approach the point, the cursor becomes a minus (−) sign. Click the point to delete it.

To delete a curve point from a path, select the Pen tool and move toward the curve point you want to delete. As you approach the point, the cursor becomes an angled (<) sign. Double-click the point (the first click converts the point to a corner point; the second click deletes it) to delete it. Alternatively, you can delete any point from a path by first selecting it with the Subselect tool and then pressing DELETE.

To convert a corner point to a curve point, select the point you want to convert with the Subselect tool, and while holding down the ALT/OPTION key, drag. As you drag, Flash creates a pair of tangential handles that define the shape of the curve point. When you release the mouse button, Flash redraws the path.

To convert a curve point to a corner point, click the point with the Pen tool. Flash collapses the point's handles as it converts it and redraws the path.

Adjust Pen Tool Preferences   You can edit the Pen tool to change the appearance of the Pen tool cursor, display line segments as you draw, or change the appearance of selected points to suit your working style. You modify the Pen tool's performance by choosing Edit | Preferences and then clicking the Edit tab. In the Pen tool section, you can adjust the following options:

- **Show Pen Preview**—Select this option and Flash creates a preview of each line segment as you move the cursor across the stage, before you create the end point of the segment.

- **Show Solid Points**—Select this option and Flash displays selected points as hollow points and unselected points as solid points.

- **Show Precise Cursors**—Select this option and Flash displays the Pen tool as a crosshair. Use this option when you need to align path points to precise locations along the grid.

Use the Text Tool to Quickly Create a Text Object

When you want to add the written word to a movie, you use the Text tool. Text in Flash can be animated, become a dynamic interactive element of your movie, or used to display a static message or word. The usage of text in Flash movies is covered in detail in Chapter 5. The section gives you a quick overview on how to create a block of text.

To create a text object for your movie, choose Window | Panels | Character and Flash opens the Character panel shown next. Click the triangle to the right of the Font style window and select a font from the drop-down menu. Click the triangle to the right of the Font size window and drag the slider to set the font size. The font size slider stops at 96 points. However, you can select a larger font size by entering a value into the field. If you want the text bold faced or italicized, click the appropriate button. To select a color for the text block, click the Text color swatch and click a color from the palette to select it.

After you have selected the options that determine how the text will look, select the Text tool. Click anywhere on the stage and begin typing. Flash will create the text block using the font style, size, and color you specified with the Character panel.

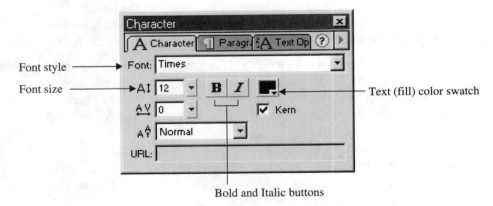

Create Basic Shapes

Flash gives you two basic shapes to work with: a rectangle and an oval. Although these are certainly rather humble shapes, they can be combined to become a whole greater than the sum of its parts. After you create a basic shape, you can modify it, move it, rotate it, skew it, or combine it with other shapes to create a new shape.

Basic Flash shapes are vector-based objects. If you are a veteran user of vector drawing software such as Macromedia's FreeHand, Adobe's Illustrator, or CorelDraw, you will quickly realize that Flash has a decidedly unique way of handling overlapping shapes and intersecting lines. After you become familiar with the way Flash treats vector objects, you will learn to use this unique behavior to your advantage.

With the Oval Tool

You use the Oval tool to create circles and ellipses for your Flash movies. The shapes you create with this tool can either be outlines, solid shapes with outlines, or simply a filled shape. You can use the oval tool to create shapes for your buttons, or use the tool to create artwork such as a cartoon character's eyes.

To create a shape with the Oval tool, select the tool and in the Options section of the Toolbox, select stroke and fill colors. To create an outline different from the single pixel Flash default, choose Window | Panels | Stroke. Modify the line style for the shape's outline as discussed previously in this chapter. To create the ellipse, click and drag the tool on the stage. As you drag the tool, Flash creates a bounding box that gives you a preview of the shape's size and position. To finish creating the rectangle, release the mouse button. To constrain the tool to drawing a circle, hold down the SHIFT key while dragging. Remember to release the SHIFT key before releasing the mouse button; otherwise, the tool will revert to its unconstrained ellipse mode.

With the Rectangle Tool

To add rectangular shapes to your movies, use the Rectangle tool. Rectangles make excellent borders for text objects and also work well for other vector-based artwork such as buildings. The Rectangle tool has one modifier that lets you create a rectangle with rounded edges.

To create a rectangle, select the Rectangle tool and in the Options section of the Toolbox, select a stroke and fill color for the rectangle. If you're creating a rectangle with a border, you can modify the border's line style by using the Stroke panel as outlined previously in this chapter. To create the rectangle, click anywhere on the stage and drag. As you drag the tool, Flash creates a rectangular bounding box, giving you a preview of the rectangle's size and position. When the rectangle is the size you want, release the mouse button. To constrain the tool to drawing a square, hold down the SHIFT key while dragging the tool. Remember to release the SHIFT key before releasing the mouse button.

To create a rounded rectangle, select the Rectangle tool and then select a stroke and fill color. Click the rounded rectangle button in the Toolbox's Options section to open the Rectangle Settings dialog box shown below. In the Corner Radius field, enter a value between 0 and 999. A value of 0 will create a rectangle with 90-degree corners. A value of 999 creates a rectangle with a gently curved corner. If you constrain the Rectangle tool to a square shape and enter a Corner Radius value of 999, you create a circle. After selecting a corner radius, click on the stage and drag to create the rounded rectangle. As you drag the tool, Flash creates a bounding box, giving you a preview of the rounded rectangle's shape and size. Release the mouse button to complete creating the shape.

TIP *To create the popular pill shape that's all the rage for Web page buttons, use the Rectangle tool, enable the Round Rectangle modifier, and specify a corner radius of 100. Drag the tool on the stage to create a rectangle that's long but not too tall and you've got an instant pill shape.*

Select and Edit Graphics with the Arrow Tool

The Arrow tool has a revered position in the upper-left corner of the Toolbox for good reason. It is one of the most versatile tools you have at your disposal. You use the Arrow tool to select objects, move objects, scale objects, rotate objects, and modify the shape of editable objects.

Select an Object Fill

When you create an object with both an outline (or stroke as it is referred to in Flash) and a fill, you are actually creating two separate objects that can be selected and edited independently. To select an object's fill, select the Arrow tool, position your cursor over the filled section of the object and click. Flash selects the fill as shown here. You can now edit the fill independent of the object's outline.

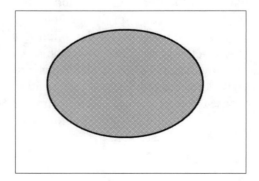

Select an Outline

You also can select only an outline with the Arrow tool. After the outline is selected, you can modify it with menu commands or other tools. To select an object's outline, select the Arrow tool and move your cursor over the object's outline. Click the outline to select it as shown here.

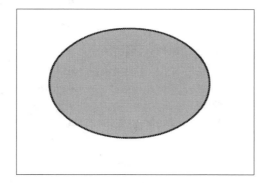

Select an Entire Object

You also use the Arrow tool to select an entire object. To select a filled object and its outline, select the Arrow tool and position your cursor in the middle of the object's fill. Double-click to select both the object and its fill, as shown here.

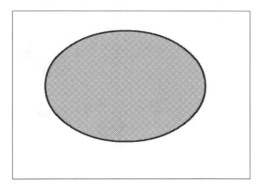

Select a Line

When you create a line with the Line tool, it is a single segment. However, when you create a line with the Pencil tool, it is a series of connected line segments. You can use the Arrow tool to select either a single line segment or the entire group of segments that make up the line.

To select a single line segment, select the Arrow tool, position your cursor over a line segment, click it, and Flash selects the single line segment. To select a single line segment and attached line segments, position your cursor over any line segment, double-click it and Flash will select the entire line.

Move an Object

After you select an object with the Arrow tool, your cursor becomes an angled arrow with a four-headed arrow just below it. Once this cursor appears, you can move the object anywhere on the stage.

Use the Arrow Tool's Modifiers

When you select the Arrow tool, Flash reveals the tool's five modifiers in the Options section of the Toolbox as shown next. By selecting the proper modifier you can align one selected object to another, smooth a line segment, straighten a line segment, scale an object, rotate an object, or skew an object. After you select an object with the Arrow tool, you activate the desired modifier by clicking its button.

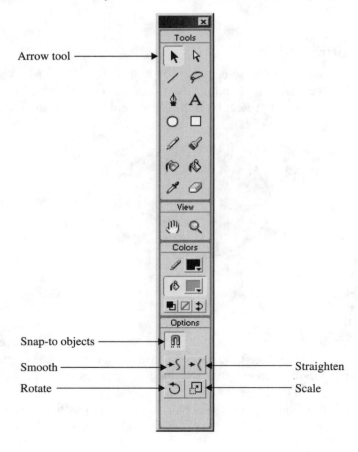

Snap-to Objects

When you enable the Arrow tool's Snap-to Objects modifier, you can precisely align one object to another. When you move one object toward another with this option enabled, Flash will snap the selected object to the other object. The actual point of alignment will depend upon where you select the object. If you select the object by its registration point (the object's center by default), the object's center will align to other objects. If you select the object by one of its corners, snapping occurs at the selected corner. If you select the object by top center, bottom center, right center, or left center, snapping occurs at the center selected.

Flash creates an unfilled dot to designate the point at which you selected the object. When you move close to an object that the selected object can snap to, the unfilled dot becomes larger and its outline becomes thicker. Release the mouse button and Flash will snap the objects together.

Smooth a Line

You can use the Arrow tool to take the kinks out of a line drawn with the Pencil tool. To smooth a line with the Arrow tool, select the line you want to smooth. If you're smoothing a line that is a series of connected segments, remember to double-click the line to select all attached segments. After selecting the line, click the Smooth modifier and Flash smooths the line. When you smooth a line, in addition to creating a smoother line, you are optimizing it, reducing the number of points that are used to make up the line. Click the modifier as many times as you need to produce the desired smoothing.

Straighten a Line

You also can use the Arrow tool to straighten a line. This Arrow tool modifier optimizes a line by converting curved segments to straight line segments. To straighten a line with the Arrow tool, select the line and its associated segments, click the Straighten modifier, and Flash will straighten the line. Click the modifier as many times as needed to produce the desired level of straightening.

Rotate an Object

You can rotate a selected object freely by enabling the Arrow tool's Rotate modifier. To rotate an object, select it with the Arrow tool, and then click the Rotate modifier. After you click the modifier, Flash creates eight unfilled dots around the object's perimeter as shown in the following. As you move your cursor toward one of the dots, it becomes four curved arrows. To rotate the object, click one

of the corner dots and then drag clockwise or counterclockwise. Release the mouse
button when the object is in the desired position.

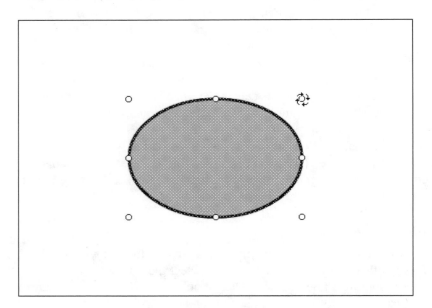

Skew an Object

You also use the Arrow tool's Rotate modifier to skew (slant) an object vertically
or horizontally. To skew an object, select it with the Arrow tool and then click the
Rotate modifier. Flash creates eight round handles around the object as shown in
the previous illustration. As you approach a point you can use to skew the object
horizontally, your cursor becomes a horizontal two-headed arrow; approaching a
point you can use to skew the object vertically changes the cursor to a double-headed
vertical arrow. To skew the object horizontally, click the round handle at top center
or bottom center and then drag left or right. To skew the object vertically, click the
round handle at the center of the left or right side and then drag up or down.

Scale an Object

You can use the Arrow tool to quickly resize an object by enabling the tool's scale
modifier. You can use this modifier to resize the selected object proportionately

or change its width or height. To resize an object with the Arrow tool, select it and then click the tool's Scale modifier.

After you enable the modifier, Flash creates eight square handles around the object as shown below. When you approach a point that can be used to resize the object proportionately, your cursor becomes a diagonal two-headed arrow. Click one of the corner handles and drag diagonally toward the center of the object to proportionately reduce the size of the object; diagonally away from the object's center to proportionately increase the size of the object. Release the mouse button when the object is the desired size.

To change the object's height, click either the top center or bottom center handle. When you approach a handle you can use to change the object's height, your cursor becomes a vertical dual-headed arrow. Drag toward the object's center to reduce its height; away from the object's center to increase its height. Release the mouse button when the object is the desired height.

To change an object's width, click either the handle on center of the object's left side, or the center of its right side. As you approach a handle that can be used to change the object's width, the cursor becomes a horizontal double-headed arrow. Drag toward the object's center to decrease its width; drag away from the center to increase it. Release the mouse button when the desired width is attained.

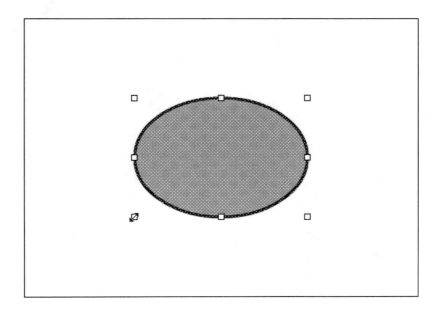

Reshape Objects with the Arrow Tool

You can use the Arrow tool to reshape any editable object you create with the drawing tools. When you select the Arrow tool and move it towards an editable object, the cursor changes, alerting you to the type of change you can apply. When you approach a curved line segment, or a curved segment that is part of a filled shape, a small curve appears below the cursor. An angled line appears when you approach a corner point.

You can modify an editable object with the arrow tool by altering the shape of curved segments, or adding corner points and then moving them. To alter a curved segment, select the Arrow tool and move your cursor toward the object you want to modify. When a curved line icon appears below the cursor, click and then drag the segment to modify it. If the curved segment is part of a filled shape, the entire object is modified, as shown here.

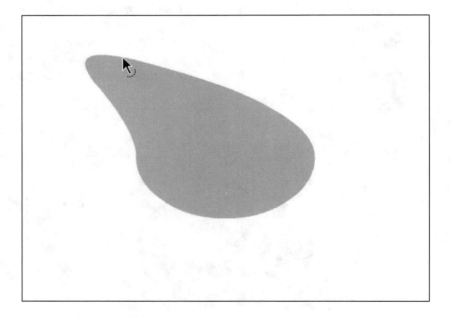

You can use the Arrow tool to add corner points to a curved segment. Add a corner point when you need to create an abrupt transition in the middle of a curved segment. To add a corner point to a curved segment, select the Arrow tool, hold down the CTRL/OPT key, and then click and drag the point on the curved segment where you want to add the corner point, as shown here.

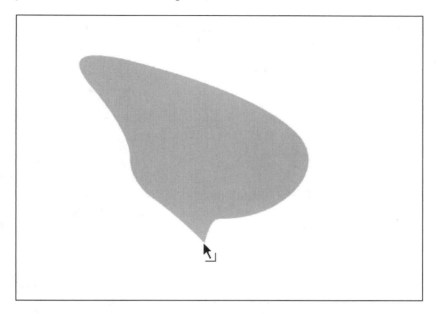

Create a Selection of Objects

You create a selection of objects when you need to edit several objects in one action, move a selection of objects, or create an object group. When you need to create a selection of objects, you can use the multi-functional Arrow tool or Lasso tool.

With the Arrow Tool

When you use the Arrow tool to create a selection of objects, there are two ways you can go about it. The default method of selecting several objects with the Arrow tool is to click one object, and then while holding down the SHIFT key, click other objects you want to add to the selection. If you prefer to add additional objects to a selection by just clicking them, you can change the default selection method by choosing Edit | Preferences to open the Preferences dialog and then, in the Selection Options section, disable the SHIFT Select selection option.

The other way you use the Arrow tool to select objects is by creating a marquee selection. To create a marquee selection, select the Arrow tool and then click and drag the tool down and across the stage, creating a rectangle around the objects you want to select. As you drag the tool, Flash creates a rectangular bounding box that gives you a preview of the marquee selection's area. Release the mouse button and Flash creates the selection. Selected objects will be highlighted for visual reference.

With the Lasso Tool

The Lasso tool looks like a cowboy's lariat. You use the Lasso tool in its default mode to create a free-form selection of objects, or in Polygon mode to create a point-to-point selection of objects.

In Free-Form Mode   To create a free-form selection, select the Lasso tool, click anywhere on the stage and drag around the objects you want to select. As you drag the tool, Flash creates a line that gives you a preview of the selection area, as shown here. When you have surrounded (lassoed) the objects you want to select, release the mouse button.

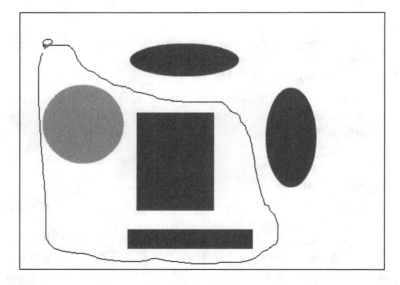

In Polygon Mode   When you use the Lasso tool in Polygon mode, you create the selection area by creating a point-to-point bounding box to define the boundary of the selection area. To create a point-to-point selection, select the Lasso tool and in the Options section of the Toolbox, click the Polygon Mode modifier, as shown below. Click anywhere on the stage to define the first point of the selection; click to create the second point, and Flash creates a straight line between the two points. Continue adding points until you have defined a selection area that encompasses all the items you want to select. Double-click to complete the selection and Flash highlights the items you have selected.

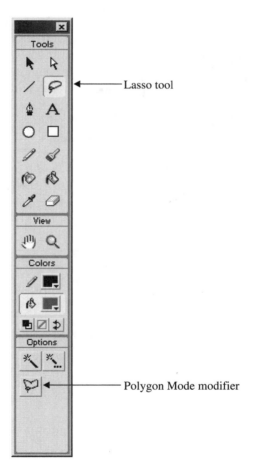

Lasso tool

Polygon Mode modifier

Work with Intersecting Lines

Every line you create with the Line tool is a single line segment. However, when you create one line, and then place another line over the top of it, the top line neatly cuts the bottom line into two sections, which you can select and treat as individual line segments. If you select the top line first, it is the one that loses its identity and is severed into two segments. Figure 4-4 shows two identical sets of intersecting lines. The set at the right has been separated with the Arrow tool.

Combine Shapes to Create New Objects

In most vector-based drawing programs, when you create one shape and then create another shape on top of the first shape, both shapes retain their identities. This, however, is not the case in Flash. When two shapes overlap, they either combine to create a new shape, or one shape will cut away from the other. At first, veteran users of vector-based drawing programs might be frustrated by the way Flash handles overlapping shapes, but you will soon learn to use this characteristic to create interesting shapes that would otherwise be extremely difficult to create. If you convert a shape to a symbol, it will retain its identity. Refer to Chapter 8 for more information on creating symbols.

> **TIP**　*You can group a single shape and it also will retain its identity. To group a single object, select it and then choose Modify | Group. For more information on creating object groups, refer to Chapter 6.*

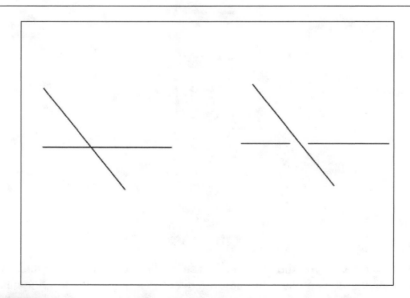

FIGURE 4-4　When you intersect lines in Flash, they lose their identities

Expand a Shape

When you overlap two objects of the same color, Flash combines them and they become a single entity that you can select and modify. You can use any of the Flash drawing tools to create the overlapping shapes you are going to combine. When creating shapes for the specific purpose of combining them, remember to create a shape with no stroke. If you overlap shapes with a stroke outline, the outline will thwart your intended purpose and cut out of the shape you select first. To expand a shape, create a second shape with the same color as the one you want to expand. Use the Arrow tool to select the second shape and then overlap it with the first. Click anywhere on the stage to deselect the shapes and then use the Arrow tool to select the new shape. Figure 4-5 shows two ovals that have been combined to create a new shape.

Subtract from a Shape

When you overlap two shapes of differing colors, one shape will cut a piece out of the other. For example, if you place a small green oval inside a large red oval, deselect the green oval, and then reselect and move the green oval beyond the red oval's boundary, there will be a hole inside the red oval, the same size as the green

FIGURE 4-5   Overlap two shapes with the same color and Flash combines them as one

oval you removed. You also can overlap shapes of differing colors. When you select one of the shapes and remove it, the shape you remove will take a cut out of the remaining shape. The area of the cut is equal to the area where the two shapes overlapped each other. You can use this Flash characteristic to create eyes for cartoon characters in your movies, or to create windows for buildings. In Figure 4-6 you see two circles with different colors on the left. On the right is the resulting shape after the smaller circle was removed.

Sample and Apply Colors to Your Objects

Color is a very important component of any Flash movie. Color attracts attention to key elements in your presentation and draws the viewer in. The combination of color and animation is a particularly potent duo.

Flash movies usually end up as part of Web pages, or as an entire Web site. In spite of the fact that Flash movies are compressed to small sizes when published, you still have to be judicious in the choice of colors that you use. Instead of

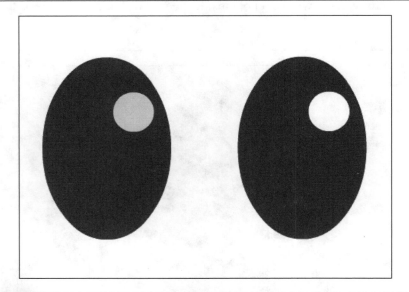

FIGURE 4-6   Overlap two shapes of different colors and Flash will cut one from the other

randomly picking colors out of the Flash palette, stick with a limited palette and then use the Ink Bottle tool, the Dropper tool, and the Paint Bucket tool to apply colors to the objects in your movie.

Use Ink Bottle Tool

You use the Ink Bottle to apply colors to lines and outlines in your movie, or as they are referred to in Flash, strokes. The Ink Bottle tool is a handy way to quickly apply a stroke color to several objects in your movie. The Ink Bottle tool is similar to the old-fashioned ink bottles used to fill fountain pens. The Flash Ink Bottle gives you a bit more latitude. In addition to specifying the stroke color, you also can apply a line style and line weight with the tool.

To fill the Ink Bottle, select the tool and then, in the Colors section of the Toolbox, click the color swatch to the right of the Pencil icon. Select a color from the palette as outlined previously in the "Select Fill and Stroke Color" section of this chapter. Choose Window | Panels | Stroke and then select the desired line style and weight as outlined earlier in the "Select the Line Style" section of this chapter.

To apply the stroke, click an object on the stage. Click a line segment to apply the stroke to it, or click the center of a filled object to apply the stroke to the object's outline.

Use the Paint Bucket Tool (Including Gap Size)

You use the Paint Bucket tool to apply solid colors, or color blends known as *gradients* to objects in your scene. You can use the tool to fill an existing outline you create with one of the drawing tools, or change an object's fill. The tool has modifiers that enable you to fill an outline with gaps.

To apply a fill with the Paint Bucket tool, select it and, in the Colors section of the Toolbox, select a solid fill color or gradient from the palette. You also can create a custom fill using the Fill and Mixer panels. You will learn to use the Fill and Mixer panels in Chapter 7. If the object you are filling was created with one of the drawing tools and has gaps, click the Gap Modifier button shown on the following page and choose one of the following options:

- **Don't Close Gaps** is the default setting. Flash will only apply the fill to objects with no gaps.

- **Close Small Gaps** tells Flash to apply the fill to an outline with small gaps.

■ **Close Medium Gaps** tells Flash to apply the fill to an outline that has medium gaps.

■ **Close Large Gaps** informs Flash that you want the fill applied to an outline with large gaps.

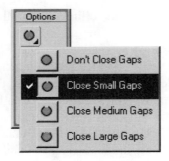

Click an object on the stage to apply the fill.

Use the Dropper Tool

You use the Dropper tool to sample fill and stroke colors and apply them to other objects in your movie. You can also use the tool to sample a bitmap fill, a technique that is covered in Chapter 9. To sample an object's stroke or fill, select the Dropper tool. As you move the tool toward an object, the cursor will change to signify what you can sample with the tool. If a Pencil icon appears under the Dropper tool, it is over a stroke; a Paintbrush icon signifies you can sample a fill. Click the stroke or fill to sample it. When you sample a fill, the Dropper tool becomes the Paint Bucket tool; sample a stroke and the Dropper tool becomes the Ink Bottle tool. To apply a sampled stroke, click a line or an outline. To apply a sampled fill, click an enclosed outline or filled object.

Use the Eraser Tool

When the rare occasion pops up and you do make a mistake, use the Eraser tool to right your wrong. The Eraser tool has modifiers that you use to control exactly what is erased. Use the tool to erase only lines, fills, or a combination thereof. When you select the Eraser tool, you have three modifiers, as shown here, which let you control which areas are erased, a modifier to soak up all an object's fill, and a modifier that lets you change the shape of the eraser.

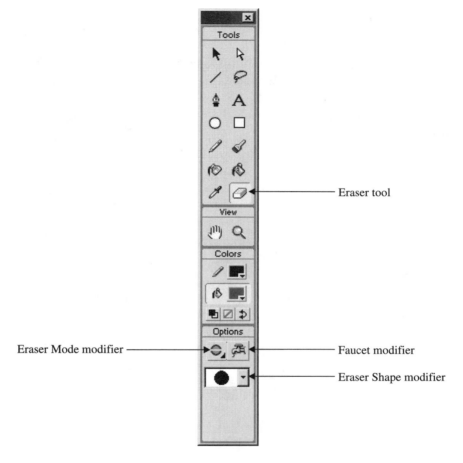

Eraser tool

Eraser Mode modifier

Faucet modifier

Eraser Shape modifier

Erase Shapes To erase an object with the Eraser tool, select the tool. In the Options section of the Toolbox, click the Eraser Mode button and then select one of the following options:

- **Erase Normal** causes strokes and fills on a layer to be erased as you drag the tool across them.

- **Erase Fills** causes only filled shapes to be erased; strokes and outlines are not affected.

- **Erase Lines** causes only strokes to be erased; filled objects are not affected.

- **Erase Selected Fills** causes a fill from a selected shape to be erased without altering its stroke.

- **Erase Inside** causes an object's fill to be erased from the point where you begin the eraser stroke without altering surrounding fills or strokes.

Click the Eraser Shape modifier and choose a shape from the menu shown here.

Drag the tool on the stage to erase objects.

 To quickly erase everything on the stage, double-click the Eraser tool.

Erase Fills The Eraser tool's Faucet modifier makes it easy for you to soak up all an object's fill or stroke. To completely erase a stroke or fill, select the Eraser tool, and then click the Faucet modifier as shown previously. Click an object's outline to erase a stroke; click its center to remove a fill.

Change the Views of Your Objects

When you create a complex movie, you often have many items on the stage. When this happens, you can change your view of the stage, by using the Hand tool, and/or use the Zoom tool to get a better view of individual objects in your movie.

With the Hand Tool

You use the Hand tool to pan (move) the viewpoint of the stage. The Hand tool is especially helpful when you've increased the magnification of the stage to a point where you can no longer see everything. To change your viewpoint of the stage, select the Hand tool, move it over the stage, and then drag left or right or up or down.

 To quickly select the Hand tool while using another tool, press and hold down the SPACEBAR *on your computer's keyboard. With the* SPACEBAR *still depressed, drag on the stage to change your viewpoint. When you release the* SPACEBAR, *the previously selected tool becomes active again.*

With the Zoom Tool

You use the Zoom tool to zoom in or out on objects in your movie. The Zoom tool's modifiers, as shown here, are used to increase or decrease magnification.

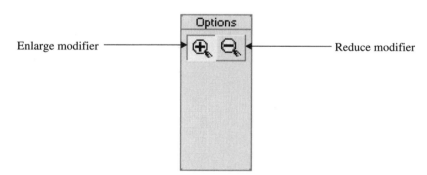

Enlarge modifier ———————————— Reduce modifier

To zoom in (increase magnification) on an object, select the Zoom tool and then click the Enlarge modifier. Click anywhere on the stage to zoom to the next level of magnification. Click again to zoom in tighter. Alternatively, drag a marquee around the objects you want to select.

To zoom out (decrease magnification), select the Zoom tool and then click anywhere on the stage to decrease magnification to the next lowest level. Click again to zoom out further.

> TIP   *To momentarily switch between zoom modes, press the ALT/OPT key. The tool's icon changes to reflect the new mode. Click on the stage to change magnification. Release the ALT/OPT key and Flash returns the tool to its previous mode.*

Alternatively, you can choose a preset level of magnification by clicking the triangle to the right of the Zoom Control window at the lower-left corner of the workspace. Choose a preset magnification from the drop-down menu, or enter a value from 8%–2,000%.

Part II

Add Multimedia to Your Flash Movies

Chapter 5

Create Exciting Text Effects

How to...

- Input and Edit Text
- Change the Look of Your Text
- Transform Your Text into an Object
- Create Text Fields with Form-like Behavior

The power of text should not be underestimated. It is a language, a communication form. Text brings together major forces in print and Web design. Its reach is long and wide as it often provides a subliminal message.

When using Flash, you can use text as both a design element and a message relayer. It will enhance your work and can make a dramatic, comedic, or thought-provoking statement to your audience.

There are many ways to design with text in Flash. There are also many things to consider: displaying fonts correctly, embedding fonts in movies, working with device fonts, and transforming your text into an object. Working with text in Flash will greatly enhance your Web site designs as you will see in this chapter.

Create and Edit Text Objects

Creating basic text in Flash is fairly easy and the program provides many ways to jazz up the look of your text. You can modify the size, color, scale, rotation, and skew, as well as change paragraph formatting. This chapter shows you how to modify the look of your text and, to build on these modifications, you'll learn how to apply many additional animation effects to your text in the section on multimedia in Part IV.

Flash text works with the Postscript or TrueType fonts installed on your system. When you use text in your movie, Flash embeds font information in the Flash Player file (the SWF file that's seen on the Web) so that, when the movie is played, the fonts display as you originally planned. Fonts, however, are far from being an exact science. There is little guarantee that your fonts will display correctly once the movie leaves your desktop. If the display of a font is important to you, there are a couple things you can do to control the fonts your audience will see.

One alternative is to use device fonts. There are three device fonts that come with Flash: sans, serif, and typewriter, as shown in Figure 5-1. If you use device fonts in your movie, the sans font will default to a font similar in appearance to

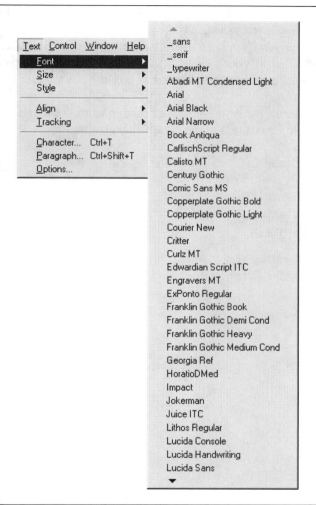

FIGURE 5-1   Use the Font list from the font menu to select a typeface

Helvetica, Arial, or Verdana. A serif font will default to a font that looks like Times Roman. A typewriter font will default to a font that looks like Courier. Ultimately, testing your movie on many different computers, platforms, and browsers is the best way to detect potential problems with fonts. But using the device fonts that come with Flash will give you a reasonable idea of what you can expect the viewer to see on their computer.

Device fonts are not embedded in the Flash Player files. Embedded fonts make the size of the movie larger because there is additional font information that accompanies the movie. This is another element to take into consideration when making font decisions. If your Flash file is ultimately being put up on the Web, you want the size of the file to be as small as possible, as smaller files mean faster download time for users.

The second alternative is to break your text apart so the text becomes a bitmap. We discuss breaking apart text at the end of this chapter.

 *To view Postscript fonts, you must have Adobe Type Manager (ATM) installed in your system. Windows 2000 does not require the use of ATM to display Postscript fonts.*

Create Basic Text

It's simple to create basic text in Flash. Go to the toolbar and select the Text tool, as shown in Figure 5-2. Drag the tool onto the stage where you want the text

Text tool

FIGURE 5-2   Access the Text tool from the toolbar

positioned. Notice the cursor transforms into a text-input icon (a crosshair with the letter "A" in the bottom right, as shown in Figure 5-3). Start typing, and you'll see that the Text Input icon now becomes an I-beam and a text box now surrounds the text.

As you type, the text box expands in width to accommodate the text you're typing. To move a text box to a different location, select the Arrow tool in the Tool palette and click, drag, and drop the box in its new position.

To modify text, select the Text tool from the toolbar and highlight the text you want to modify. With the text area highlighted, start typing over the old text. The new text will automatically appear where the old text was located.

Manipulate the Extended Text Box

Flash allows you to easily modify the shape of your text box. The simplest way to create text is to select the Text tool in the toolbar, choose a location on the stage, click, and start typing. This encloses your text in something called an *extended text box*. An extended text box displays the boundaries of the text you're inputting. If you were to modify the text (for example, by scaling or rotating), the text box would serve as a reference point for aligning the text. The text box enables you to view the text as a whole object instead of as separate characters.

Notice the round handle in the upper-right corner of the text block you just created, as Figure 5-4 shows. This indicates a text box handle. A *round* handle indicates a text box that will expand and contract in length indefinitely (unless you

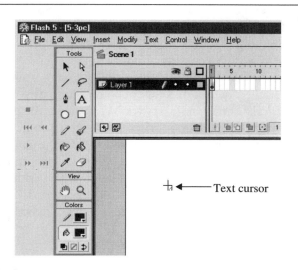

Text cursor

FIGURE 5-3   The text cursor turns into a Text Input icon when the Text tool is selected

| extended-width text box | ──Extended text box handle |

FIGURE 5-4   An extended text box is identified by the round handle in the upper-right corner

press ENTER to start a new line). The extended text box is primarily used for small lines of text. To enter more than one line of text with an extended text box, simply press ENTER, and continue typing. Otherwise, the text will continue on one line indefinitely.

Manipulate a Fixed-Width Text Box

A fixed-width text box has a width that is predetermined. Fixed-width text boxes are similar to extended text boxes in that they indicate the boundaries of the text they're enclosing. A fixed-width text box is a better choice when you're typing in a substantial amount of text such as a paragraph. Unlike an extended text box, a fixed-width text box will constrain to the width of the box you created. You can use the fixed-width text box for a small line of text, too. In fact, some designers who are accustomed to this method prefer to create their text with a fixed-width text box. The selection of an extended text box versus a fixed-width text box is a matter of designer preference.

To make a text box with a fixed width, click the Text tool in the toolbar, drag the icon to the stage, and click and drag the text box to the desired width. When you type text in a fixed-width text box, the type constrains to the parameters of the text box. The constraining function of the fixed-width text box is similar to the left and right margins in a word processing program. It creates its own soft return that conforms to the width of the box. Both the extended text box and the fixed-width box have no depth limit. You can make them both as long as you want. A square handle in the upper-right corner indicates you've created a fixed-width text box.

To modify the width of a text box, select the Text tool from the toolbar and click the text box to be modified. Drag your mouse over the square or round icon in the upper-right corner. The icon transforms into a double-headed arrow. Click and drag the square or round icon to reduce or enlarge the width, as shown in Figure 5-5. Modifying the width of both kinds of text boxes does not distort the actual text within the box. It just rewraps the text within the box, like changing margins in a word processing program.

fixed-width text box   Fixed-width
text box handle

FIGURE 5-5   Change the size of the fixed-width text box by dragging on its square handle

Convert a Text Box

To convert an extended text box into a fixed-width text box, select the Text tool
from the toolbar and click the text box to be modified. Drag your mouse over the
round icon in the upper-right corner. The icon transforms into a double-headed
arrow. Click and drag the icon to reduce or enlarge the width, as Figure 5-6 shows.
When you deselect the icon, it will transform into a square.

To convert a fixed-width text box into an extended text box, select the Text
tool from the toolbox and click the text box to be modified. Double-click the
square icon. The square icon transforms into a circle and snaps back to the last
character in the text box, indicating that the text box can now be extended.

Control the Look of Your Text

All objects in Flash, including type, have properties that can be set and changed.
There are many different ways to control the look of your text. To set or change
the font, size, and paragraph attributes of new or existing text, select Windows |
Panels | Character panel, as shown in Figure 5-7.

This will display the Character, Paragraph, and Text Options panels in a panel
grouping. These are known as Text panels. Display individual panel options by
clicking the appropriate tab at the top of the panel grouping (see Figure 5-8). The
selected tab will display the available options for that particular panel.

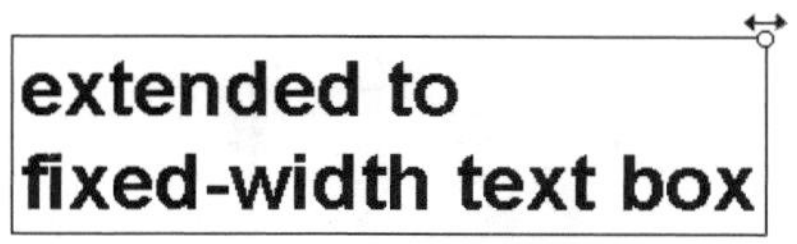

**extended to
fixed-width text box**

FIGURE 5-6   Change an extended text box into a fixed-width box by extending the
round handle

5

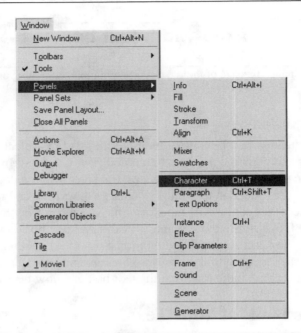

Use the Windows | Panels | Character panel to display font selections, type size, and more

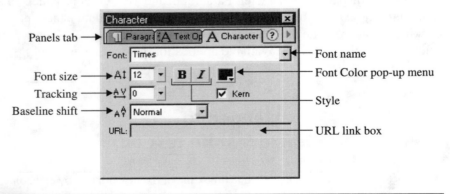

The Text Panel tabs selected, with the Character panel displayed

If you have a small monitor, the panel-grouping feature is great for economizing on space. Just like other windows, these panels are floating and can be docked anywhere on the stage.

The default display for the Character, Paragraph, and Text Options panels is as a grouped panel. You can tear off (or ungroup) individual tabs by clicking a tab and dragging it outside the panel group. Regroup tabs by dragging them onto another panel, as Figure 5-9 shows. Again, it's a space saver to eliminate unnecessary panels and tabs when you're not using them.

You also can close the panels you don't need by clicking the close button in that panel's window.

5

> **TIP**   *To close a window on the PC, click on the "X" in the upper-right corner of the window. To close a window on the Mac, click on the square in the upper-left corner of the window.*

You can add a tab back onto a panel by clicking and dragging the tab into the desired panel. When you release the mouse, the tab will be grouped into the new panel.

> **TIP**   *Panels are small windows and as such, move, close, and collapse just like any other window.*

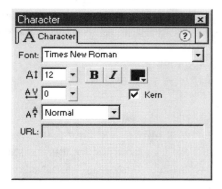

FIGURE 5-9   The Character tab separated from other tabs in the panel

Font properties also can be changed in the menu. The Text menu offers font, size, style, and tracking selections. These properties either can be set before you input text or the text can be highlighted and modified after it's created. To select a font, size, style, and tracking amount from this menu, go to Text | Font, Text | Size, Text | Style, or Text | Tracking. Each entry has a pop-up selection menu. Choose your options, and then click the Text Input tool on the toolbar. Click the stage and start typing. The text will display according to your menu selections. To modify already existing text with the options from the Text menu, highlight the text with the Text Input tool from the toolbar. Go to the Text menu and select your new options. The text will now reflect your new choices.

Set Font, Color, Size, Style, and Tracking for Your Text in the Text Panels

To change the appearance and size of the text in your Flash movie, one of your options is to use the Text panels. There are three text panels in total and they include the Character, Paragraph, and Text Options. Together, all three text panels default to a single group referred to as a *panel group*. Access a single text panel by clicking the Character, Paragraph or Text Options tab at the top of the panel group. The Text panels are a wonderful feature in Flash. You can position these panels anywhere you want on the stage and make instant changes to your text properties without having to search through a series of pop-up menus to do so. Use these panels to change the look of your text. There are many selections to choose from in these panels, which are reviewed in this section.

To set the appearance of text *before* you input the text, display the Text panels by selecting Window | Panels | Character. Select a font, color, size, style, and track amount. Then select the Text tool on the toolbar, click the stage, and begin typing.

NOTE   *Choosing any of the three panel group selections from the Windows menu (Character, Paragraph, or Text Options) will display the entire text grouping.*

To change the appearance of already existing text using the Text panels, highlight the text with the Text tool from the toolbar, as shown in Figure 5-10. Select Windows | Panels | Character to access the Character panel. In the Character panel, change the font, color, size, style, and tracking.

With text highlighted, select a font. This is the first option and is a pop-up menu listing all fonts available in your system as Figure 5-11 shows. Underneath font is the font size option; a sliding arrow bar that goes up and down gives you a variety of point sizes to choose from.

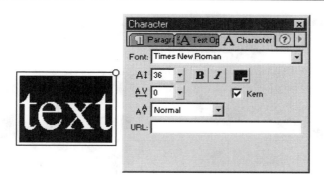

FIGURE 5-10   Text selected with the Character panel displayed next to it

To the right of the leading option are two font styles selections: Bold and Italic.
To the right of the styles is a pop-up color menu. Choose a color swatch from the
color palette to change the color of your text, as shown in Figure 5-12.

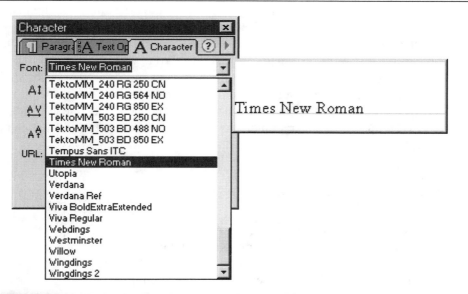

FIGURE 5-11   Selecting a font in the Font pop-up menu

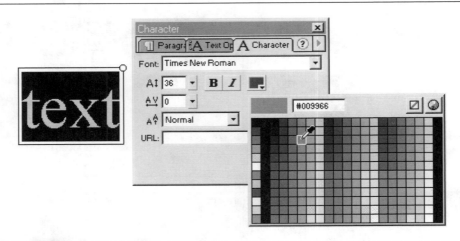

Selecting a color swatch in the Color pop-up menu

Underneath the Size setting in the Character panel is the text tracking option where you can customize the letter spacing of selected text. If you check the Kern box, Flash will automatically kern the text for you. The Text Tracking option also has a pop-up menu with a sliding arrow to select the tracking amount in points.

You can manually input leading (the space between your lines of text) and tracking (the space between letters) in the Character panel by highlighting the box that contains the text. With the Character panel displayed, you can type in a fixed number. You also can track between a highlighted block of text or in between two characters by selecting the text and holding down CTRL+ALT on the PC or OPTION+COMMAND on a Macintosh and simultaneously clicking on the left and right arrow keys. To track in even larger increments, hold down SHIFT+CTRL+ALT on a PC or SHIFT+OPTION+COMMAND on the Mac.

TIP *If you forget this key combination, go to View | Keyboard Shortcuts where you will find a complete listing of all shortcuts.*

Underneath the Tracking setting in the Character panel, you can specify a baseline for your text. This is useful for special text effects, scientific equations, or any design where you need the text to have an irregular baseline. The baseline of the text is the bottom of the text block. The default setting is "normal." Superscript puts the text above this normal baseline and displays the text in a smaller font. Subscript displays the text underneath the normal baseline and displays the text in a smaller font.

> **TIP**   *In addition to using the sliding arrow options to set the font, size, and tracking in the Character panel, you also can manually input this information in the box next to font, size, and tracking, where your choice of these items is displayed.*

You also can specify a link to a URL in this panel. If you're planning on putting this movie up on the Web, linking to a URL means when your Web viewer clicks on text you selected for linking, it will lead them to the location you indicated as your URL. URL stands for *uniform resource locater*, which in plain English is a Web address. The address can be an HTML file or a Flash Player file (SWF). The URL address will determine where the file is located. To link to another page (URL), select the text you want to link and type in the address of the URL.

Set Alignment, Margins, and Indents with the Paragraph Panel

Once you've created your text and set the appearance of this text, you may need to finish it off by setting Paragraph attributes. If your text is in a paragraph format, you need to make additional design decisions, such as alignment, indents, and line spacing. These settings are located in the Paragraph panel; as mentioned previously, the Paragraph panel is part of the Text Panel grouping. To activate the Paragraph panel in the Text Panel grouping, click the Paragraph tab.

As with the settings in the Character panel, you can assign the Paragraph panel settings before you input type, or you can modify pre-existing type by highlighting the text and selecting the settings. To modify text before you input, display the Character panel and choose the desired settings. In this section, each selection in the Paragraph panel is discussed.

To modify text after you've created it, select the Text tool from the toolbar, click and drag the cursor on the stage, and create a fixed-width text box. Type in a paragraph of text. Select Windows | Panels | Character. Click the Paragraph tab to access the Paragraph panel.

With the paragraph highlighted, play with the different settings in the Paragraph panel, as shown in Figure 5-13. The top section offers alignment features. You can align a paragraph left, center, right, or justified.

You can set left and right margins for your text using the icons in the bottom half of the Character panel. Underneath the margins are the first line indent option and the line spacing option, all of which are selectable by manually typing in the increments or by selecting a number using the sliding arrow. The icons again reflect the type of margin you're selecting. Play with different settings to familiarize yourself with the way it works.

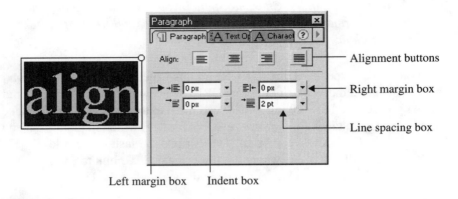

Use the Paragraph panel to set text alignment, margins, and indents

The Character, Paragraph, and Text Options panels also can be displayed by going to the Text menu and selecting Character, Paragraph, or Options. You also can modify the alignment of a paragraph by selecting Text | Align from the text menu. Text | Align will enable you to select text alignment from a pop-up menu.

Create Input Text and Dynamic Text

The third text panel in the Text panel grouping is the Text Options panel. This can be accessed by selecting Text Options in the Windows | Panel menu (see Figure 5-14). Use the Text Options panel to select text options for static text, such as we have been creating (text that isn't interactive), Input text, and for text that can be dynamically updated. Dynamic text is text that can be updated easily and quickly in a Flash movie without having to edit the actual Flash movie. The update instantly appears in your Flash movie when a text file is revised. Dynamic text is explained in more detail in the section "Create a Dynamic Text Field," later in this chapter.

To use the Text Option panel, select Windows | Panels | Character. Click the Text Options tab to access the Text Options panel. Note that Static Text, which is just plain text, is the default in the pop-up menu as Figure 5-15 shows. You are offered two checkbox options with this selection:

- **Use Device Fonts**—Fonts will *not* be embedded in the Player file with this option selected.

- **Selectable**—The viewer will be capable of selecting text in the movie but not manipulating it in any way.

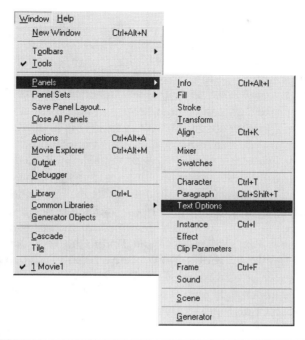

FIGURE 5-14   Text Options Panel is used for Static, Input, and Dynamic Text fields

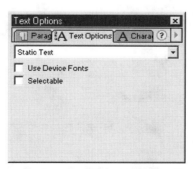

FIGURE 5-15   Static Text selected in the Text Options panel

Set Variables in a Text Field with Input Text

Input Text is the second selection in the Text Options pop-up menu. Input Text fields can possess powerful interactive capabilities. Although the capabilities of a Input Text field can be very complex, the basic premise behind the workings of it are simple. Input Text fields, like Dynamic Text fields, work with a script action called a variable. A *variable* is a name that's assigned to the text field. Variables are called such because they can change or vary at the designer's discretion. Variables can be assigned to objects as well as text. This in itself has amazing implications. It means you can transform an object into another object by changing a variable in a script. Variables need to be defined, so they are assigned a value. Your value can be either text or numeric. If you prompted your viewers to fill out a form where you wanted them to indicate their age, the *variable* may be a text box named "age," but the *value* of the variable is whatever number the user types in the text field. Variables are discussed in Chapter 15.

To create an Input Text field, select Input Text in the Text Options panel pop-up menu, as Figure 5-16 shows. Now create a fixed-width text box. Notice that when Input Text is selected in the Text Options panel, the rectangle handle that's located in the upper-right corner is now located in the bottom-right corner. This is how you identify an Input or Dynamic Text field. Your viewer can input text in this kind of text field. Use this option for forms, games, any concept where

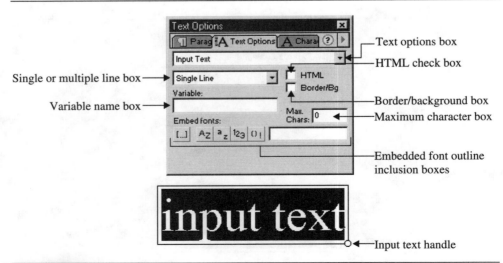

FIGURE 5-16   Input Text selected in the Text Options panel

you want the viewer to interact with the movie by typing in text, and dynamic updating of text as discussed previously.

When Input Text or Dynamic Text is selected, the third line in the Text Options panel prompts you for the variable we spoke of previously. This line requires you to input a name for your variable. You can name your variable anything you like.

Create a Simple Input Text Field with a Variable

This simple exercise will help you understand the concept of text fields and variables. You will create an Input Text field and duplicate the text field. The duplicate will have the same variable name as the original, so the value that the viewer types in will always match the text field with the same variable. This concept is often used on the Web where a site prompts you for your name. Then, throughout the site, your name is remembered, so the site appears personalized. The following series of steps shows you how to accomplish this technique:

1. Select the Text tool and display the Text Options panels (Windows | Panels | Character).

2. With the Character Panel tab selected, create a line of static Text. Make the text 24-point size and any font you want. In the Paragraph panel, select an alignment of flush right. Click the middle of the stage and type **Name**. This will be an extended text box.

3. Duplicate the word "Name" by clicking the word with the Arrow tool. Hold down the SHIFT+ALT/SHIFT+OPTION key, and drag downward a couple of inches. This duplicates the selected text and constrains its vertical alignment. In the *new* text box, highlight the text and replace it with the word "Hello."

4. Display the Text Options Panel tab. You will now create an Input Text box to the right of "Name." Select Input Text from the pop-up menu. Check Border/BG. When Border/BG is checked, the text field box will have a border around it in the movie. If you need the viewer to see where they should input type, check this box. Click and drag to make a text box to the right of the word "Name," that's large enough to accommodate a viewer's first name. Under Input Text, select Single Line. For Variable, type in the word **Name**. To speed up the process, duplicate this text field the way you did in step 3, and place the new text field to the right of the word "Hello." Now, both text fields are identical, with the same variable name.

5. We are finished with our simple page. Let's do one more thing before we test the movie. Let's make sure the baseline of the text field that the viewer will input will be aligned correctly with the baseline of the words "Name," and "Hello." Let's also check the color and the font the viewer will see when he or she inputs the text.

6. With the Text tool selected in the toolbar, click the top blank text field. Display the Text panels (Windows | Panels | Character). With the Character tab selected, choose the font, color, and style of the text the viewer will see when he or she types. Our sample illustration has the same properties as the Static Text block that says "Name."

7. Click the Paragraph tab. Align the blank text field left. Test the Input Text field out by typing a couple of characters in the blank text field box. You want the baseline of the Static text, "Name," to be aligned with the baseline of the text the viewer will input. Use your sample text to align the baselines of both text boxes. In the sample illustration, a guideline was placed on the baseline of the Static Text and the sample Input Text was used for alignment purposes. When you're finished aligning, *delete* the sample text in the text box. Repeat this alignment process for the Text Input box next to "Hello."

NOTE
If you don't delete the sample text, it will show up on the actual movie. Because you're just using it for alignment purposes, you don't want it to appear.

8. Test the Movie by selecting Control | Test Movie. Next to "Name," type in your name. Your name will appear simultaneously next to the "Hello" Text Input box because both text fields have the same variable as shown in Figure 5-17.

Variables can be assigned to text fields and movie clip instances. In our simple exercise, when the viewer inputs his or her name, that becomes the *value* of the text field, "name," and that variable and value remain consistent throughout this movie.

TIP
Text fields with variables can be used in conjunction with very complex scripts. Chapters 14 and 15 discuss ActionScript (the native scripting language of Flash) in more detail.

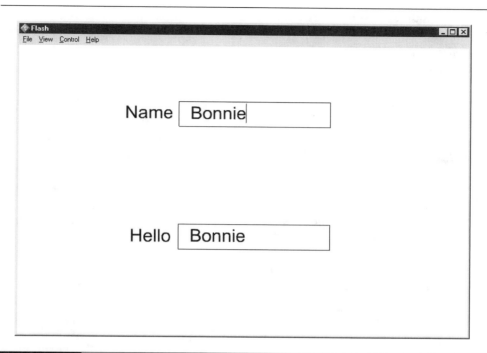

FIGURE 5-17   The finished exercise that utilizes Input Text fields

Other Options Made Available When the Input Text Option Is Selected

When selecting Input Text in the Text Options panel, there are other selections you can make to fine-tune your text field. These selections determine the style of the final Input Text field.

In the second pop-up menu that becomes accessible when you select, Input Text enables you to select from Single Line, Multiline, or Password. Single Line allows you to only type in one line of text. The Multiline selection enables the viewer to type in more than one line of text. When Password is selected, the viewer can type in a secret password that appears as asterisks, so someone looking over the viewer's shoulder won't know what he or she typed in.

Underneath Variable, there are six Embed Font options. The default is "Include entire font outline" (the first icon) and "Include outlines for punctuation" (the fifth icon). The middle icons represent, from the left, "Include outlines for uppercase,"

"Include outlines for lowercase," "Include outlines for number." The sixth box is a manual input box that enables you to specify font outlines for special characters. You also can specify the maximum number of characters the viewer can input by typing a number in the "Max Chars" text input box.

Create a Dynamic Text Field

A Dynamic Text field is called "dynamic" because Flash files can be updated quickly and easily while residing on a remote server. For a Dynamic Text field to work, it needs to know exactly what variable is being updated and where the update text is located. To do this, you create a simple text file that gives values to the Dynamic Text field variable in the targeted movie. The text file can be uploaded quickly to the server without ever having to revise the actual Flash Movie. This technique is used on sites that require quick and continuous updating, like weather, stocks, and news.

Create a Dynamic Text field by selecting Dynamic Text in the Text Options panel pop-up menu, as shown in Figure 5-18. The options in the Dynamic Text panel are the same as for Input Text. This is because Dynamic Text and Input Text are similar, because they both are changeable while a viewer is online. Input Text can be changed by the viewer, and Dynamic Text can be changed by the author on demand. To make a Dynamic Text field work, you need to assign a load Variable action to a frame in your movie. The load Variable action instructs the URL of a text file to load into a Dynamic Text field every time a viewer plays the movie.

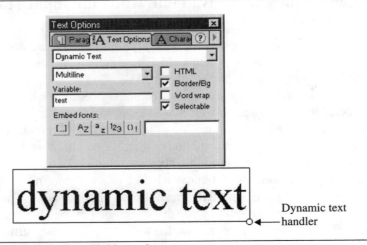

FIGURE 5-18   The Dynamic Text Field panel

The variables are defined as values in the text file. They load into the text fields in your movie because they have the same variable names.

The values of the variables are in the text file, so each time the text file is updated and uploaded to the site, the information in the Dynamic Text field reflects these changes. Because the text field can be revised instantly, this procedure is referred to as *dynamic text updating.*

The values from the text file that will load into the Dynamic Text field in the movie needs to be created in a URL-encoded format. The technical name for the URL-encoded format is "x-www-urlformencoded." It's a simple ASCII format that requires words to be strung together with no spaces (see Figure 5-19). Words are separated with a plus sign (+). An equal sign (=) is placed after a variable and before the value is declared. An ampersand is used to separate multiple variables in the same Flash movie, so if you have created more than one Dynamic Text field in your movie that needs updating, the same text file would address all variables.

Dynamic Text fields are simple to make yet can be a very powerful design element. Only text field variables can be updated dynamically using this technique. For more sophisticated forms and dynamic behavior that requires more than just simple text, you need to write a custom script or use a a program like Macromedia Generator.

Break Apart Your Text

As mentioned earlier, text is not always predictable when it displays on your viewer's system because you have no control over the way your movie will look. One way to ensure the font you've selected will display the way you want it to is to break text apart so it becomes an editable bitmap. This technique is great for a special font or a complex animation that uses text as a design element.

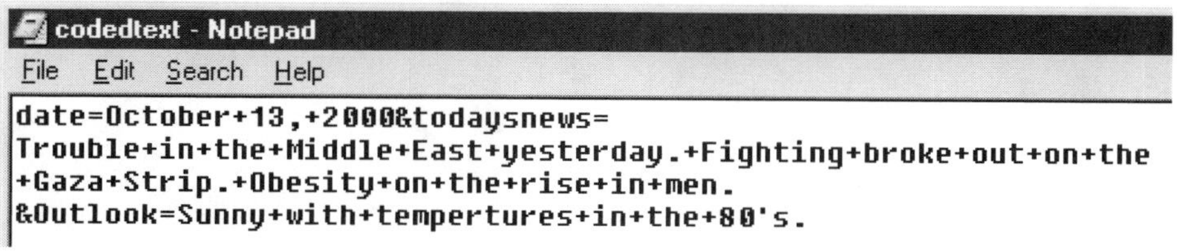

```
codedtext - Notepad
File   Edit   Search   Help
date=October+13,+2000&todaysnews=
Trouble+in+the+Middle+East+yesterday.+Fighting+broke+out+on+the
+Gaza+Strip.+Obesity+on+the+rise+in+men.
&Outlook=Sunny+with+tempertures+in+the+80's.
```

FIGURE 5-19   Sample of a simple text file with URL encoding

Breaking apart text is generally used for display text rather than lengthy paragraphs, because once you break the text apart, it's no longer editable as text. The text is treated as a graphical object rather than a font. In fact, it no longer is a font once you break it apart.

To use the Break Apart feature, create some text and from the Text panels (Character | Paragraph | Text Options) assign properties to the text such as font, color, size, and so on. Select the text with the Arrow tool. Go to Modify | Break Apart. The text is now an editable object. Each character is now a separate object, as Figure 5-20 shows. To group the letters together so they're not floating around as separate objects, go to Modify | Group. You can now manipulate the letters individually, too, if your design calls for it.

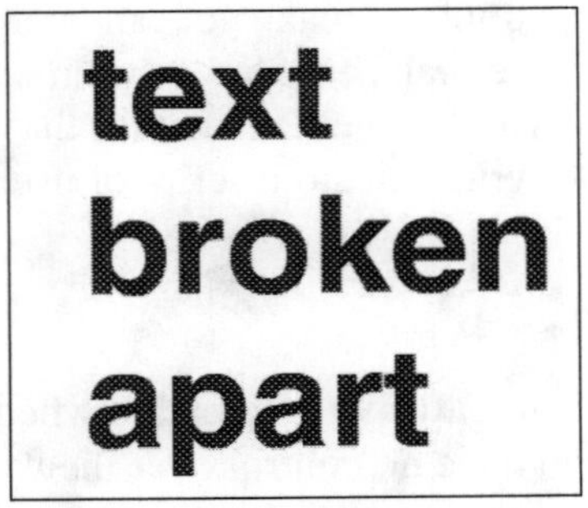

text broken apart

FIGURE 5-20   Text that has been broken apart in Flash

Chapter 6

Apply Transformations to Text and Graphics

How to...

- Change the Properties of an Object
- Use the Transformation Panel
- Control the Stacking Order of Objects
- Arrange Objects on the Stage
- Group and Ungroup Objects
- Get Details About Objects and Movies

Flash comes with a comprehensive suite of tools to modify the properties of objects and text. Although you can import both raster and vector graphics into Flash, the Drawing and Transformation tools are so complete, you can often compose your entire movie without ever leaving Flash.

The Transformation tools can be accessed from three different areas of the stage: the toolbar, the menu, and the Transformation panel. The way you access transformations is a matter of personal preference that ultimately hinges on which method simplifies your creation of Flash movies

Change the Look of Text and Graphics

You can use many of the tools in Flash to change the look of your text and graphics. Transformation tools are used to change the appearance of these objects. You can scale and rotate objects to change the size and angle of them. You also can skew an object if you want to distort its perspective. Text can be transformed as well.

Let's examine the Transformation options made available on the bottom of the toolbar as shown in Figure 6-1. There are two icons available that transform three properties of your objects.

Scale an Object

You can make a selected object smaller or larger by applying the scaling features. Before modifying the scale of an object, select the object first and then perform the scale. This is true of all of the Transformation tools. The tools must know what it is they're transforming before they work.

Scale an object visually by clicking the object and selecting the Scale icon in the Option portion of the toolbar. Eight square handles surround the boundaries of the object. When you mouse over these handles, the mouse turns into a

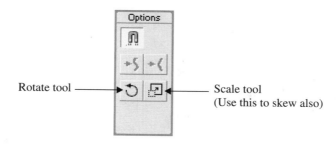

Rotate tool ————   —— Scale tool
                                          (Use this to skew also)

FIGURE 6-1   The Options portion of the toolbar where Transformation icons
are accessed

double-headed arrow. To scale the object, click and drag any of the eight squares
(see Figure 6-2).

You can enlarge or reduce the object to any size you want and extend the
object into the pasteboard area off the stage. If the object extends past the stage
when the movie plays, the only part of the object that will show is the part within
the movie dimensions. To constrain the scale of the object, hold down the SHIFT
key while dragging on one of the squares in the corners. This scales the object in
exact proportion to its original size.

You also can use the Scale command in the Modify | Transform menu to scale
an object. Scale an object in this manner by clicking the object and selecting
Modify | Transform | Scale, as shown in Figure 6-3. This works the same way as
the Scale icon on the Options portion of the toolbar. Scale by clicking and dragging
one of the eight scaling handles located on the boundaries of the object.

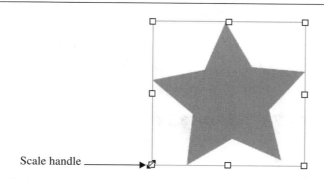

Scale handle ————

FIGURE 6-2   When you scale an object in Flash, square handles appear around
the boundaries

FIGURE 6-3   Picture of the Modify | Transform menu options

There are other ways to scale an object. Another method that's used frequently (when an object requires a specific size) is to scale an object with a numeric percentage. This is done by clicking on the object and selecting Modify | Transform | Scale and Rotate from the menu or CRTL+ALT+S/OPT+CMD+S. This displays the Scale and Rotate dialog box, as shown in Figure 6-4. In the Scale setting, type a percentage number and click OK. This method will always constrain objects to the proportion you're entering. For example, if you wanted to scale a rectangle 50 percent, the width and the height of the rectangle at 50 percent would be in perfect proportion to the original at 100 percent.

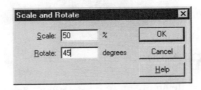

FIGURE 6-4   In the Scale and Rotate dialog box, you can enter in numeric proportions and degrees of a rotation

Undo a scale by clicking the object and choosing Modify | Transform | Remove Transform or CTRL+SHIFT+Z/CMD+SHIFT+Z. This removes any of the Transformations applied and returns the object to its original state.

Edit | Undo or CTRL+Z/CMD+Z will return the object to its previous state before you applied the transformation. In Edit | Preferences | General, you can specify the number of undo levels that can be applied up to 200 times. The default number of undos in the Preferences | General dialog box is 100. This means you can apply Edit | Undo to an object to return back to a previous state up to 100 times. Flash keeps track of the progression of your movie so elements can be undone to a certain point.

6

TIP   *Setting the Undo Levels to 200 times requires more system memory. If you're running Flash on an older system, increasing the Undo Levels could slow down your system's performance considerably.*

Rotate an Object

When you rotate an object, the angle of its direction is changed. Many interesting visual effects can be achieved by applying simple rotations to objects. Rotate an object visually by clicking the object and selecting the Rotate icon in the Option portion of the toolbar, as shown in Figure 6-5. Eight ring handles surround the boundaries of the object. When you mouse over these ring handles in the four corners of the object (the other four handles perform another function, which we discuss in the "Skew" section, later in this chapter), the mouse turns into a rotation icon, resembling the Rotate icon in the Options portion of the toolbar. To rotate the object, click and drag one of the four corner rings. To constrain the rotation, hold down the Shift key while dragging on one of the four corner squares. This will constrain the object in 45-degree increments. The other four ring handles are reserved for creating a skew effect.

As an alternative, you can use the Rotate command in the Modify | Transform menu. To do so, select the object and go to Modify | Transform | Rotate. This works the same way as the Rotate icon on the Options portion of the toolbar.

Rotate an object to a predetermined numeric degree by clicking the object and selecting Modify | Transform | Scale and Rotate or CRTL+ALT+S/OPT+CMD+S. In the Rotate setting, type a specific angle degree and click OK.

To further your choices, the Modify | Transform menu offers you two more rotation-related options: Rotate 90 degree CW, which rotates the object 90 degrees clockwise, and Rotate 90 degree CCW, which rotates the object 90 degrees counterclockwise (see Figure 6-6). Use these Transformation tools by clicking the object to be rotated and selecting the desired transformation from the menu. Click OK and the transformation will be completed.

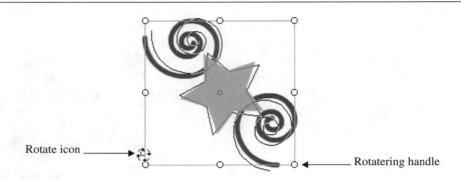

Rotate icon ⟶ Rotatering handle

FIGURE 6-5 The objects in this movie are rotated; note the Rotate icon appears when the Rotate ring handle in one of the four corners is moused over and clicked

A rotation can be undone by clicking the object and choosing Modify | Transform | Remove Transform (CTRL+SHIFT+Z/CMD+SHIFT+Z). This command completely removes the transformation. The Edit | Undo (CTRL+Z/CMD+Z) command returns the objects to their previous state, right before you applied the transformation.

Skew and Flip an Object

When you skew an object, you distort the object by applying a slant effect along an axis. This gives the object a quasi-3D effect on a two-dimensional plane, as is shown in Figure 6-7.

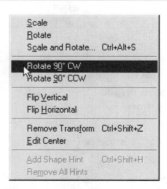

FIGURE 6-6 You can select from several rotation options in the menu

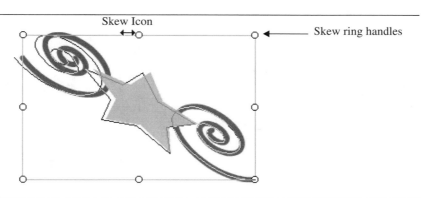

Skew Icon

Skew ring handles

FIGURE 6-7   The objects in this movie are skewed; the Skew icon appears when the Skew ring handle on one of the middle ring handles is moused over or clicked

The Rotate icon in the Options toolbar provides a quick way to apply a skew technique. Click an object and select the Rotate icon. Click and drag any of the four ring handles in the middle of the object boundaries. The cursor turns into a double-headed arrow when you are in skew mode.

You also can flip an object horizontally or vertically to create a mirror effect. The flip transformation options can be found in the menu under Modify | Transform | Flip Horizontal or Vertical.

Use the Transform Panel

The Transform panel gives you an organized summary of the transformations that have taken place or are about to take place on an object as shown in Figure 6-8. This panel can be used in place of, or in conjunction with, the Transform options on the toolbar, and/or the Transform menu. With this panel displayed, you can type and monitor the exact percentage or degree of the transformations (Scale, Rotate, and Skew) on a selected object. It also can be used to track the transformation properties of an object or for a comparison of one object versus another. To display the Transform Panel, go to Window | Panels | Transform.

To use the scale function, click on an object, and in the Transform panel, type a specified scale percentage. Click the Constrain box to scale the object in proportion. For Rotate and Skew, select the check button next to the entry fields, and type a rotate degree or a skew degree.

In the bottom-right corner of the Transform panel there are two icons. The first icon is the Copy and Transform icon. This applies the selected transformation to a copy of the original object and leaves the original object intact.

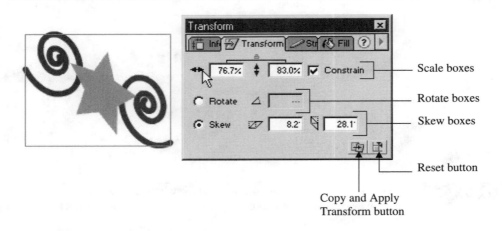

Scale boxes

Rotate boxes

Skew boxes

Reset button

Copy and Apply
Transform button

FIGURE 6-8   The Transform panel makes it easy to modify an object

The second icon is a Reset button, which returns the object to its original state if you decide you don't like the effect the transformations have on your object. If you're a beginner, it's easy to get carried away with these functions, especially the skew function, and end up with an undesirable effect. This function brings you back to where you started, so you can experiment freely, without fear of losing the shape of your original object.

Use the Snap-To Function

In the Options portion of the toolbar, the icon that looks like a magnet is a snap-to objects feature. Use this when you want to align two or more objects on your stage. To activate the snap-to feature, select an object and click on the Magnet icon. When it's active, the magnet highlights in white, and when you select an object, a snapping ring appears.

The snapping ring is a little round icon that appears when the object is selected on certain areas of the object. When the snap-to magnet on the toolbar is turned on, the snap-to rings act like magnets when one object is dragged near another object.

If the object is a circle or a rectangle, when you select it, the snap-to rings appear on either the bottom center, top center, left center, right center, dead center, or corners of the object (if the object is rectangular or the sum of its parts are rectangular in nature). These snap-to rings act as reference points when you align objects to one another. For example, if you wanted to align the top center of a rectangle to the left center of another rectangle, with the snap-to magnet turned on, you would select the top center snap-to ring of one object and drag it to the left center of the other object. The result would be the top center of one object being in perfect alignment to the left center of the other object, butted together (see Figure 6-9).

In a text block, the snap-to rings are active on the center of the text.

You also will note that if you grab an object by its snap-to ring and drag it around the stage, the size of the ring continuously changes from small to large in certain points on the stage. When the object nears a gridline, whether the grid is turned on or off in the View menu, the small ring will become larger when it nears a snap-to point on this grid.

To align an object with another, select the object and drag the snapping ring near another object. The selected object will snap to the other object.

6

Align Objects with a Snap-To Grid

You can use the grid function to align objects; it is available in the View menu under View | Show Grid or CTRL+'/CMD+'. Some designers like to use a grid to help them position objects. If you want to snap an object to a certain point on this grid, select View | Snap To Objects or CTRL+SHIFT+/ or CMD+SHIFT+/. This grid is only visible in Flash (it doesn't display when the movie plays), and it serves as a guide for alignment on the stage. Some designers find the grid annoying and prefer to use other alignment methods. You can customize the grid size and color by selecting View | Edit Grid or CTRL+ALT+G/CMD+OPT+G. In the Edit Grid dialog box, the color, space between the horizontal and vertical grid lines, and snap accuracy level (normal to always snap) can be adjusted.

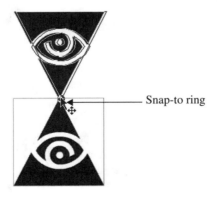

Snap-to ring

FIGURE 6-9   Illustration of the snap-to ring on an object, aligning with
             another object

Change the Stacking Order of Objects

All objects on the same layer have a stacking order. The stacking order is determined by the last object created on the stage. The first object created is behind subsequent objects. If you were to create a rectangle as an object on the stage, create another object on the stage, and position the second object on top of the first, the first object would be hidden by the second object. This is the natural stacking order of objects in Flash (see Figure 6-10).

The layer order in multilayer movies creates a type of stacking order. Each layer created is behind subsequent layers. So the first layer in the layer list is always on top of the layers underneath. Layer order can be reshuffled simply by clicking a layer and dragging it up or down in the layer list to reposition it.

Objects on a single layer can be stacked so that one object previously under another can now reside on top of that object. You can only change the stacking order of a grouped object or a symbol. When editable objects are stacked on top of one another, they exhibit bitmap-like qualities. Objects that are bitmapped inherently don't have a stacking order because all elements are on the same level. An editable object will cancel out another editable object when you deselect it, select it, and try to move it again. In some cases, the two objects may join together. Either way, the results can be disastrous if alterations are required at a later date. So if you're working on a complex one-layered drawing, it's a good idea to either group objects or make them into symbols to modify the objects at a later date.

To change the stacking order of an object in relation to another object, select one of the objects. In the menu, select Modify | Arrange | Send to Back or CTRL+SHIFT+↓ /SHIFT+OPTION+↓. This puts the object all the way back in stacking order. Modify | Arrange | Send to Front or CTRL+SHIFT+↑ / SHIFT+OPTION+↑ brings

FIGURE 6-10   A single-layer drawing with grouped objects stacked on one another

the object all the way forward in the stacking order (see Figure 6-11). If you had ten objects overlapping one another, and you clicked on the first object you created and selected Modify | Arrange | Send to Front, it would reshuffle the object to the top stacking position.

To move the stacking position of your object up one level or down one level instead of all the way back or all the way to the front, select Modify | Arrange | Send Forward (CTRL+↑/CMD+↑) or select Modify | Arrange | Send Backward (CTRL+↓/CMD+↓). This works well if your single-layer design requires multiple stacking, as is most often the case when working on a design of medium to difficult complexity.

NOTE *When an experienced Flash artist tackles a complex drawing, most often, he or she will create all the ancillary parts of the drawing as symbols. Symbols, like groups, stack easily and are simple to edit. Chapters 8 and 13 cover symbols in more detail.*

Lock and Unlock the Position of an Object

On a single-layer drawing with many components and multiple stacking orders, you may want to lock an object into place so you don't accidentally move or

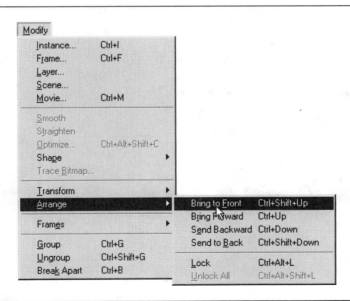

FIGURE 6-11   The stacking order functions in the Modify menu

change it while modifying other objects around it. This can be done with any objects that are grouped or symbols. To lock an object, click on the object with the Arrow tool. In the menu, select Modify | Arrange | Lock or CTRL+ALT+L / CMD+OPTION+L. The object will be visible, but you will be unable to manipulate it. To unlock the object, select Modify | Arrange | Unlock All or CTRL+ALT+SHIFT+L / CMD+OPTION+SHIFT+L. This unlocks all the elements on your stage that were previously locked.

Arrange Objects on the Stage

When you're creating a Flash movie with many objects on the stage, arranging the objects on this stage becomes an important issue. If your stage layout demands balance and it's cluttered with many objects, Flash offers a lot of options to help make your layout appear symmetrical.

You can align and distribute objects in relation to one another using the Align panel, as is shown in Figure 6-12. The Align panel is a floating panel that can be docked anywhere on the stage. This panel is packed with convenient features. In addition to the align and transform features in the panel, the size, height, and width

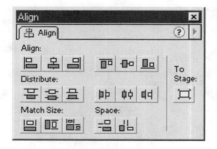

FIGURE 6-12   Align options from the Align panel set on selected objects

of two or more objects can be matched. You also can space objects evenly on a horizontal plane and/or a vertical plane. Aligned and distributed objects can be aligned and distributed to the actual stage if you click on the Stage button. Within this panel every possible scenario for alignment of two or more objects exists. The alignment options in the panel are represented as icons that are easy to interpret.

The Alignment options sit at the top of the panel. There are six options in this category: Left Edge, Horizontal Center, Right Edge, Top Edge, Vertical Center, and Top Edge.

Under the Align options are six Distribute options that display in the following order: Top Edge, Vertical Center, Bottom Edge, Left Edge, Horizontal Center, and Right Edge. The Distribute options distribute two or more selected objects (grouped object or symbol). The Alignment options align two or more objects (grouped object or symbol) according to the alignment icon you selected.

Under Distribute, there are three Match Size options: Match Width, Match Height, Match Width and Height. The Match size options match the dimensions of two or more selected objects (grouped object or symbol).

To the right of the Match Size options are two Space options: Space Evenly Vertically and Space Evenly Horizontally. The Space options space evenly either horizontally or evenly vertically two or more selected objects (grouped object or symbol).

The To Stage icon enables you to use the alignment features in conjunction with the stage as a whole. When this icon is selected, objects can be aligned in relation to the stage as well as to one another.

If you forget the purpose of any of the icons in this panel, when you mouse over each icon in the panel, an icon definition pops up. This feature is active on all panels in Flash and is particularly convenient in panels such as the Align panel that have options too numerous to remember if you don't use them frequently.

To use the options in the Alignment panel, first select the objects you want modified, and then click the appropriate icon(s) in the panel.

Figure 6-12 illustrates five individually grouped objects with different alignment features applied. In the Align options, Align Vertical Center was selected. For Distribute, Distribute Horizontal Center was selected, and all selected objects have been aligned to the stage.

In Figure 6-13, the same selected objects have now had the Match Size option, Match Height, applied to them. Note the heights of all selected objects are now identical.

The Alignment panel is a wonderful time-saving feature if you're creating movies that require balance and consistency in the layout.

FIGURE 6-13 Match Size option from the Align panel set on selected objects

Group and Ungroup Objects

In Flash, when you draw an object (with the exception of a text object), unless the object itself is grouped or a symbol, it behaves like a bitmap graphic. These kinds of objects are known as "editable objects" in Flash. If you select and move a rectangle with a stroke that has not been grouped unto itself, the fill will separate from the stroke. If you were to select and move the same rectangle with a partial marquee (creating an invisible rectangle around the entire object to select it), only the area selected with the partial marquee would move. Selecting an object that is not grouped will display bitmap behavior to this extent.

If you're used to drawing in classic drawing programs like Freehand or Illustrator, this behavior may seem foreign at first. But it's nice to have both vector (drawing) and raster (paint program, bitmap) features combined in the one software program. Also, in Chapter 12, you'll discover the expanded capabilities of editable objects.

If you want to manipulate an object more like a vector-based drawing package would (with the exception of a text object), you need to group an individual object once you create it. Group an object unto itself by first creating it. With the entire object selected, go to Modify | Group or CTRL+G/CMD+G (see Figure 6-14). Now when the object is selected, the boundaries of the object will display as a rectangle around the object.

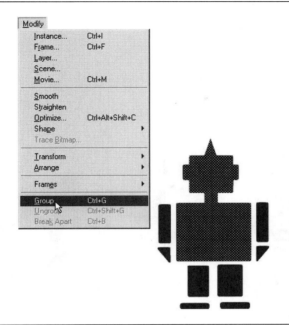

FIGURE 6-14   The Group command in the Modify menu

If you need to group an individual object that has not yet been selected, you must select the entire object with a marquee selection. Otherwise, the part that's not selected will not be included in the grouping (see Figure 6-15).

To ungroup an object from itself, click the grouped object and go to the menu. Select Modify | Ungroup or CTRL+SHIFT+G/CMD+SHIFT+G.

Group and Ungroup Groups of Objects

Not only can you group individual objects unto themselves, you can group several objects together to form one big group. This can be done with grouped objects, ungrouped objects, or symbols. In using this technique, you're essentially creating groups within groups. Groups of objects can contain or "nest" other groups within groups. The levels of these groupings can go on and on. There is no limit to the number of objects that can be grouped together.

NOTE   *Symbols possess group-like qualities too and also can contain groups within groups. In Chapter 8 graphic symbols are discussed, and in Chapter 13 buttons and movie clip symbols are covered.*

FIGURE 6-15 Selecting an ungrouped object with a selection marquee

You group objects together to help organize your layout and to economize on repetitive tasks like moving a set of objects to a new position on the stage. To group several ungrouped objects together, select the objects by clicking and dragging the Arrow tool to create a marquee selection. Drag the mouse from the top left (outside the area you're selecting) to the bottom right (outside the area you're selecting) of the window objects. This selects the area you want grouped. Then, select Go to Modify | Group. The objects will now be grouped together. You also can select objects by SHIFT+clicking on each object. When the SHIFT key is pressed while clicking on objects, each object clicked on becomes part of the selection.

To ungroup objects, click on the group and select Modify | Ungroup. This turns grouped object into an editable object. The color of a grouped object cannot be modified. It must be an editable object before color can be modified.

The color of a grouped object can be changed by entering the Group Editing mode. You can enter the Group Editing mode in one of two ways: double-click the object you want to edit or click the object and select Edit | Edit Selected. This brings you into the Group Editing mode (see Figure 6-16), which is indicated in the upper-left corner of the stage with a graphic icon and the name "Group." Additional modifications can be applied while in the editing mode. You can exit this mode in one of two ways: Click the Scene name in the upper-left corner of the stage or select Edit | Edit All from the menu. This returns the object to its grouped state.

Create a single grouping of grouped objects by selecting the objects you want to group and going to Modify | Group in the menu or CTRL+G/CMD+G. The grouped objects are now on a higher-level group (see Figure 6-17). To ungroup these objects, click on the group and select Modify | Ungroup or CRTL+SHIFT+G/CMD+SHIFT+G. This returns the grouped objects to their original state.

6

Group editing mode buttons

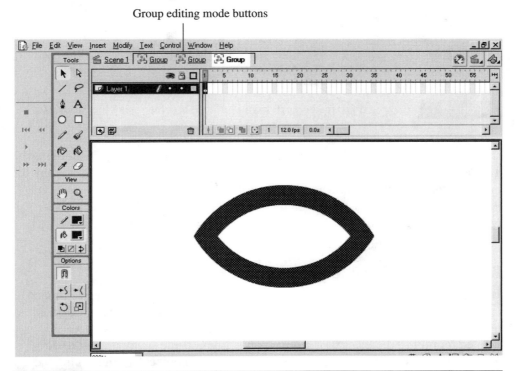

FIGURE 6-16   In Group Editing mode, the mode is labeled in the upper-left corner of the stage

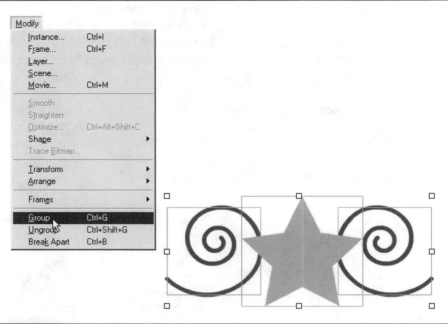

FIGURE 6-17   Selected grouped objects being grouped together using the Modify |
Group command from the menu

You can create a grouping hierarchy by grouping groups of groups, indefinitely.
The last group created becomes the highest-level group. Ungroup this hierarchy by
applying the Ungroup command to each group in the hierarchy. When you edit a
group, the hierarchy is displayed on the top left of the stage. Each time a level
within the group is accessed, another group icon appears next to the previous one
(refer to Figure 6-16).

Break Your Objects Apart

Breaking apart text was examined in the last chapter. The Break Apart command
can be applied to objects, symbols, and imported bitmaps as well as text. Break
objects apart to separate these elements into editable objects. For example, if you
wanted to modify the color of a grouped object, you could break it apart to do so.
You could also modify the color of this same grouped object by ungrouping the
object. To this extent, ungrouping and breaking apart an object is similar. Once
you break apart an object, it is not grouped and becomes a bitmap. Generally,
breaking apart is used for text and imported bitmaps.

The main difference between the Ungroup command and the Break Apart
command is that the Break Apart command is not reversible in some cases. Break

apart objects by clicking the object and selecting Modify | Break Apart or
CTRL+B/CMD+B.

You can break apart a Symbol instance, but the Break Apart command discards
what may be important information about that instance, such as frames and layers,
as well as breaking the link between the instance and the master symbol. When the
master symbol is updated, it no longer carries through to the instance that has been
broken apart. For more information about symbols, see Chapters 8 and 13.

Imported bitmap pictures can be broken apart too. Flash provides some fun tools
to manipulate a broken-apart bitmap. This is covered in Chapter 9, where importing
bitmaps are discussed in detail.

Get Details About Objects

Flash comes equipped with a helpful tool called the Info panel. The Info panel is
an essential utility because it gives you all the details you need to know about a
selected object, symbol, sound, or bitmap. Use the Explorer window to provide
you with a synopsis of the entire movie. The Explorer window is also a helpful tool
when you need to get details about objects. The Explorer window gives you a
detailed history of everything that was used to make a movie and what each element
was named, including the inner workings of symbols and scripts. The Info panel is
more for individual objects, whereas the Explorer window gives you the blueprints
of the bigger picture.

Use the Info Panel

Use the Info panel by clicking on an object and selecting Window | Panels | Info or
CTRL+ALT+I/CMD+OPT+I as shown in Figure 6-18. The default is a grouped panel,
including the Info, Transform, Stroke, and Fill tabs. If the other tabs make the panel
appear too cluttered for your taste, tear the Info panel away from the grouping to
display it separately.

The Info panel displays the name, width, height, and X, Y coordinates of the
object. The X, Y coordinate position indicated in this panel is determined by the
reference point of a selected object. To the left of the X,Y selections is a rectangle
icon with eight handles surrounding its boundaries, plus a center handle. The
highlighted handle represents the reference point of the current X, Y position. You
can change this reference point for alignment purposes by selecting one of the
other handles.

NOTE   *The handles that are dimmed indicate they are not available as an option.*

Selected
object(s)

Reference
point icon

X and Y position boxes

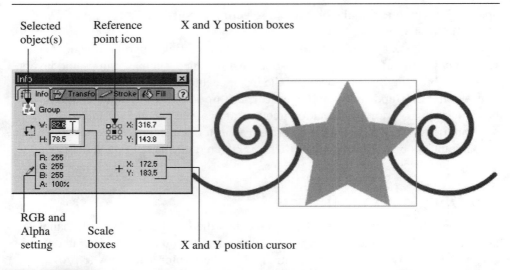

RGB and
Alpha
setting

Scale
boxes

X and Y position cursor

FIGURE 6-18   Use the Info panel to get information about a selected object

For example, if you needed to know the X, Y position of the top left of a circular object, you could click on the handle in the upper left of the rectangle icon on the Info panel to get the exact position.

Coordinates can be manually entered in the Info panel, too. If you need an object to be positioned at a particular spot on the stage, or require a specific width and height, type it manually. This is a very convenient feature because it enables you to modify an object with pinpoint accuracy.

In the bottom half of the Transform panel, the RGB setting of the object is indicated, as is the Alpha property (A). The RGB setting indicates the color of the selected object. The alpha indicates the level of transparency that's applied to the object. 100 percent alpha is an opaque color, and 0 percent is the absence of color (transparent). Get information about RGB values by mousing over the object you want to know about. The current X, Y position of the cursor is also indicated. As you move the cursor, the X, Y position is reflected in this portion of the panel.

Get Information from the Movie Explorer

The Movie Explorer Panel gives you a complete description of every component of an entire movie in detail, including the inner workings of objects, symbols, layers, frames, actions, sounds, and more (see Figure 6-19).

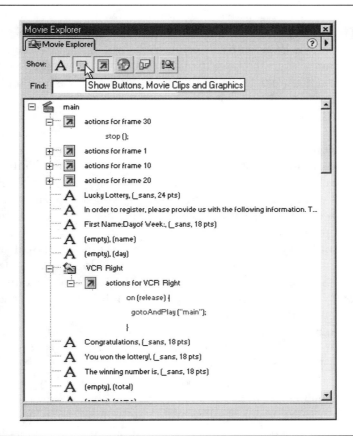

FIGURE 6-19   Use the Movie Explorer to track the history of a project

This panel is a very important addition to Flash 5 for the advanced user. When your movies become complex, with multiple layers, frames, movie clips, scenes, and complex actions, the Movie Explorer helps track the progress and review the history of the movie as you create it. It also can help you find and modify elements in the movie. This is particularly important when working with a production team. On a large Flash project, teams of people often work on different components of the same movie at different stages. One person can easily track the work of another with the Movie Explorer. It's even difficult to dissect components of your own movie when it becomes very involved. For example, let's say you completed a very complex Flash movie for a client and archived it. Six months later, the client requests extensive revisions on the movie. Chances are you won't remember exactly how it was constructed. The Movie Explorer, having kept track of all the internal work, could help bring the project back into focus for you.

Display the Movie Explorer by Selecting Window | Movie Explorer. The Movie Explorer also can be accessed from the Launcher icons in the bottom right of the stage, as shown in Figure 6-19. The Launched icon is a toggle button that shows and hides the Movie Explorer upon mouse click.

The Movie Explorer window is a collapsable hierarchy of all elements and events that have taken place in the current movie. Each time you change the movie, the Explorer window is updated to include new additions. Elements are arranged in a folder-like hierarchy with scenes, layers, symbol definitions, as well as other titles, acting as a container to organize elements in the movie. Plus and minus signs reside next to each container, enabling you to expand and collapse its contents. A plus sign indicates the presence of contents, whereas a minus sign indicates an empty container.

On the top of the Movie Explorer, you can extract the display of specified elements in the movie. The icons display in the following order: Text; Action Scripts; Video, Sounds and Bitmaps; Frames and Layers; and Customize Which Items to Show. The last selection, Customize Which Items to Show, enables you to customize your display selection.

Find text, ActionScript, video, sounds, bitmaps, frames, and layers by entering the name of item in the Find field. The Movie Explorer will go to that item in the Movie Explorer list.

Elements of the movie also can be edited from the Movie Explorer. Edit text by double-clicking the text in the Movie Explorer you want to change. Text can be edited directly in the Movie Explorer Window, and the change is immediately reflected on the stage. You also can access the editing mode for symbols by double-clicking the appropriate icon. This is a convenient feature when your movies contain a great deal of nested or invisible elements that are difficult to spot on the stage.

Once you get the feel for the many tools available in Flash, it's easy to transform the properties of objects in your movies. Because Flash movies are rich with multimedia elements, color is also an important property in your Flash movies. Chapter 7 covers all the fundamentals of using color in Flash to help move you to another plateau with your Flash learning experience.

Chapter 7

Apply Color and Line Styles to Text and Graphics

How to...

- Use Color in Flash
- Apply Colors to Graphics and Text
- Modify Fills
- Set Colors with Color Panels
- Apply Gradient Color
- Modify Gradients
- Apply a Style and Weight to Lines

One of the remarkable features of Flash is the richness and intensity of color display in a Flash Player file (SWF). On the Web, Flash color jumps out at you, helping to entertain your Web audience, giving you all the more reason to choose Flash for your Web design needs.

In Flash, you can assign color objects, text, symbols, as well as the background of the movie. Because Flash most often is used as a multimedia application for developing graphics on the Web, its color functions are slanted toward a multimedia-authoring environment.

How Does Flash Color Work?

The default color in Flash is the Web safe palette. The Web safe palette (sometimes known as the Web 216) consists of 216 colors identified by a hexadecimal code. It is made up of a combination of six digits and numbers. The hexadecimal code is used in HTML code as well as some other scripting languages. It represents a set of 216 RGB colors that can be seen on both PC and Mac monitors. RGB color is a mix of red, green, and blue pixels that create color on your monitor. Different intensity levels of red, green, and blue are mixed to create different colors. The number of colors that you can see on your monitor depends upon the range of intensity levels the monitor is capable of displaying. If a monitor is capable of displaying 256 colors in total, it's considered an 8-bit monitor. Color values are measured in bits. Red, green, and blue are color channels. Computers that display 8-bit (256 colors), 16-bit (approximately 16,000 colors), and 24-bit (approximately 16,000,000 colors) colors are based upon a mathematical calculation relating to the number of bits per channel that are needed to display each intensity value. For example, a 24-bit monitor is capable of displaying approximately 16 million colors and each color channel (RGB) can display up to 256 intensity values. 256(R)x256(G)x256(B) equals approximately 16 million colors. Monitors with different bit depths are calculated in a similar manner but with a different number of intensity values.

Use a Web Safe Palette

The concept behind a Web safe palette is simple. Color on the Mac and PC platforms displays differently. Examine the same Web page on a Mac and PC and the color difference is immediately apparent. As mentioned in the last section, a monitor set for 8-bit color is capable of displaying 256 colors. When creating art for the Web, you're delivering to an audience with a multitude of computers and multiplatforms. Because of this, 8-bit color is generally your target audience. Although many newer systems are capable of displaying 24-bit color (approximately 16 million colors for continuous tone display), it's safer to target a general audience and assume 8-bit as the standard.

Both Macs and PCs come with a default system palette of 256 colors. Out of those colors, 40 colors differ on each platform. This is where the Web safe palette comes in. The 216 colors it's made up of are identical on both platforms. This is not to say a specific color on one platform will look identical to the color on another. It means that if you assign a Web safe color to two or more objects on your Web page, the color on that Web page will match. If you assigned an RGB color in two or more places on a page that are not from the Web safe palette, on certain monitors, the colors may appear different. This can be a problem if you have an object sitting on a color background and the object is supposed to blend into the background. Certain viewers would see a border around the top object. This is one example where it may be essential to use a Web safe palette.

If you use regular RGB colors instead of the Web safe palette, certain monitors won't be capable of viewing these colors. In this case, the user's monitor will dither the colors it can't read. Dithering simulates color by juxtaposing colors similar to what was intended to create the visual illusion of the intended color. Dithering is not necessarily a bad thing and can work quite well in many cases. If you create multimedia for the Web, dithering is a fact of life. This is one reason why it's so important to test your Web pages and Flash movies on as many platforms and browsers as possible.

A Web safe palette is the default palette in Flash. Use a Web safe color by selecting the Fill color and Stroke color pop-up menus. These are available in the toolbar as well as in the panels for Swatch, Fill, Stroke, and Mixer (see Figure 7-1).

7

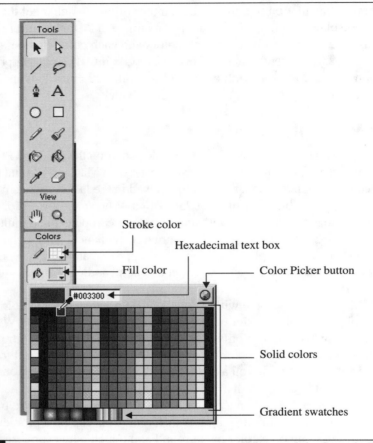

Stroke color

Hexadecimal text box

Fill color

Color Picker button

Solid colors

Gradient swatches

#003300

FIGURE 7-1   Apply a Web safe color swatch from the toolbar and the Swatch, Fill, Stroke, and Mixer panel

When you select a Web safe color in the toolbar and the Mixer panel, the hexadecimal number for the color appears in the top left of the pop-up menu as is displayed in Figure 7-2. As you click and drag on the swatches, the cursor turns into an eyedropper and the hexadecimal colors change as you mouse over each swatch.

When you select a Web safe color in the Swatch panel, the hexadecimals aren't displayed. Rather, the chosen swatch becomes the current color in the toolbar, and in the panels of the Fill, Stroke, and Mixer, where the hexadecimal equivalent is displayed by clicking on the Fill or Stroke colors.

FIGURE 7-2 Select a Web safe color from the Swatch panel

Apply Colors to Graphics and Text

It's simple to apply color to objects in Flash. Color can be applied before the object is created or used to modify an existing object.

To apply a fill or stroke color to an object or text before the object is created, select a fill and stroke color from the toolbar, Mixer, Fill, Stroke, or Swatch panels. When you select a fill color and a stroke color, these colors become the current color in all of the Fill Color and Stroke Color pop-up menus. After you select a color, create the object or text. The item will display in the currently selected Fill and Stroke color.

To modify the fill or stroke color of an editable object, select the object and then select the color from the toolbar, Mixer, Fill, Stroke, or Swatch panels. The object will display the chosen color. To modify the stroke of an editable object, click on the stroke until the entire stroke is selected; then modify the color in the Stroke panel.

This brings you to the Group Editing mode, where the object becomes editable. Change the color as you would on an editable object. To modify the color of a grouped object, double-click the object to enter the editing mode, or click once and select Edit | Edit Selected from the menu. The color of the other objects on the stage becomes dimmed indicating which object is being targeted. Select the new color. Exit the Editing mode by either clicking the Group icon in the upper left, double-clicking somewhere a blank part of the stage, or selecting Edit | Edit Selected from the menu (see Figure 7-3).

If objects are grouped within other groups, repeat the process of editing and exiting the editing mode as many times as it takes to get to the level of the object you want to edit. If you're using Edit | Edit Selected from the menu, once you enter the top-level editing mode, you can zero in on the object you want to edit by

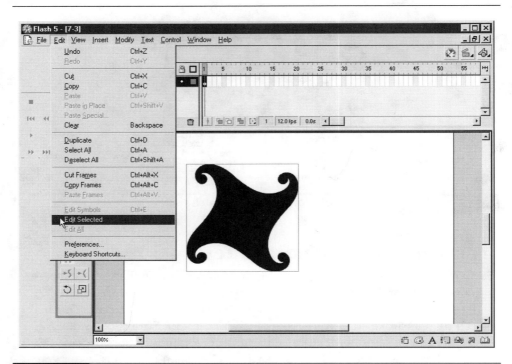

FIGURE 7-3   Edit the color of an object by entering the editing mode

clicking the object and selecting Edit | Edit Selected again. Because a group within a group creates a hierarchy, to get to the object you want to modify, you have to get beneath the first grouping. This subgroup is reflected in the icon hierarchy in the upper-left corner of the editing moe as is demonstrated in Figure 7-4. If text is within a group, the group must either be ungrouped before editing the text or the same methods for editing an object within a group can be used on text.

To modify the color of existing text, highlight the text with the Text tool from the toolbar and select a Fill color from the toolbar, Mixer, Fill, Stroke, or Swatch panels. The text will reflect the chosen color. A stroke cannot be added to text.

Modify Fills with the Shape Menu

Flash comes equipped with some creative ways to manipulate fills. These can be found in the Modify | Shape menu. The selections in this menu can only be applied to editable objects. You can change a line into a fill and make the fill of an object grow larger or smaller thereby changing the size of the object (see Figure 7-5).

Group Editing mode

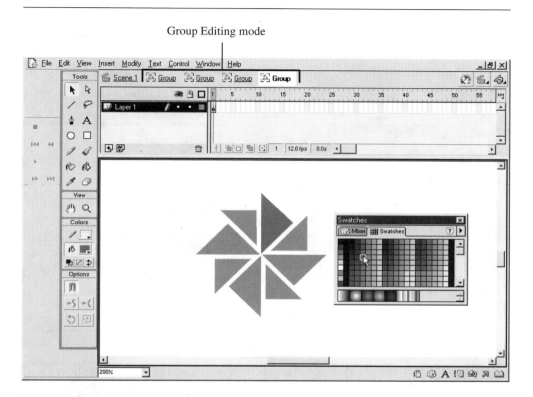

FIGURE 7-4   A group within a group is identified in the editing mode by the icons in the top left of the stage

You also can soften the fill edges of an object in the Soften Edges dialog box to make it appear soft and blurry. This is done by creating a gradient around the object, which fades into a transparent color. The Soften Edges option is wonderful for creating an effect usually associated with bitmap graphics as shown in Figure 7-6.

Convert a line to a fill by clicking a line and selecting Modify | Shape | Convert Lines to Fills as shown in Figure 7-7. Use this to convert what was previously a line into an object made from a fill. Expand or contract the size of a fill by selecting Modify | Shape | Expand Fill. The Expand Fill dialog box will appear as shown in Figure 7-8. Indicate the amount you want to enlarge or reduce the fill in the Distance box. Click Expand to make the fill larger or Inset to reduce the size of the fill. If you display the Info panel, the new size of the object will be reflected in the width and height boxes.

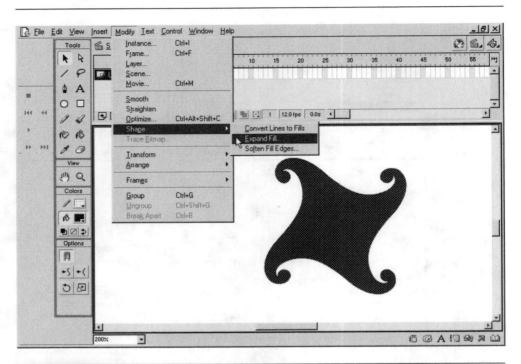

FIGURE 7-5   Modify the shape of an object by selecting one of the Shape options in the Modify menu

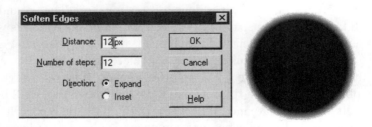

FIGURE 7-6   Blur the edges of an object with the Shape | Soften Fill Edges selection in the menu

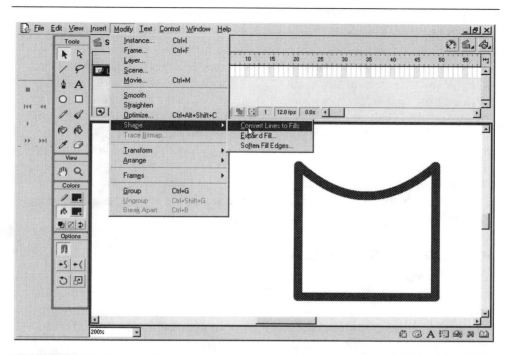

FIGURE 7-7 Convert lines to fills with the Modify | Shape | Convert Lines to Fills command

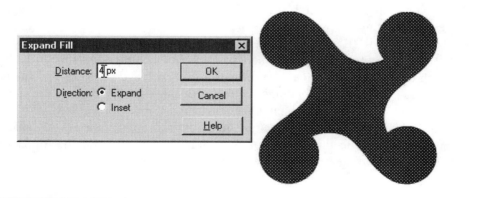

FIGURE 7-8 Expand or reduce the size of a fill in the Expand Fill dialog box

Blur the edges of a fill by selecting Modify | Shape | Soften Fill Edges. In the dialog box, indicate the distance amount you want the fill to expand or reduce. The default distance is four pixels. Select the number of steps the object will soften to. A large number of steps will create a softer edge, but the file will be larger. A small number of steps will create either a harder fill or more banding, depending on the distance you entered. A smaller number of steps creates a smaller file size. Caution should be used when entering a large number of steps. It can take forever to display on your monitor and on the Web. Applying soft edges with a limited number of steps is generally a safer choice. The default number of steps is four pixels.

Set the direction of the soft edge by clicking on Expand to make it larger or Inset to make the blur effect go inward. You can achieve some spectacular effects by experimenting with the Soften Edges settings.

Set Colors with the Flash Color Panels

In addition to setting Web safe colors, you can select or mix custom RGB colors. This is done with the Mixer Panel or the Color Picker dialog box in the Fill and Stroke Color pop-up menus. Once the RGB color is created, you can store the color in the bottom of the Swatch panel. Custom mixed colors are saved with the current Flash movie, not with the default application palette.

Use the Mixer Panel to Set Color

The Mixer panel offers a multitude of ways to set colors. Display the Mixer panel by selecting Window | Panels | Mixer. The Mixer Panel gives you the option of either selecting a Web safe color from the Fill and Stroke color boxes, mixing an RGB color, changing the Alpha of a color, or selecting colors from the Color Picker. (See Figure 7-9.)

To create an RGB color using the Mixer, select the Fill or Stroke icon. A pencil icon represents the Stroke, and a paint bucket icon represents the Fill. Click and drag on the Mixer. The cursor becomes a crosshair, and the RGB equivalent of the selection you're currently dragging over is displayed to the right of the panel. You also can set the Alpha, which is the transparency index of a color. An Alpha level of 100 percent is the default setting, representing a solid color. An Alpha level of 0 percent represents the absence of that color. Type a number in the Alpha value field or use the sliding arrow to select an alpha percentage.

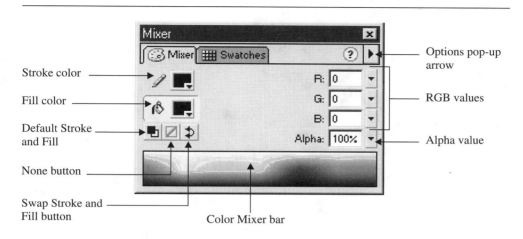

Stroke color

Fill color

Default Stroke and Fill

None button

Swap Stroke and Fill button

Options pop-up arrow

RGB values

Alpha value

Color Mixer bar

FIGURE 7-9   Mix or select a color from many different sources in the Mixer panel

Change the Mixer to reflect different color modes by clicking the pop-up menu on the top right of the panel as shown in Figure 7-10. The following options are available in this menu:

■ **RGB**   Select RGB mode if you want to create an RGB color.

■ **HSB**   Select HSB to make a color using the hue value, saturation, and brightness.

■ **Hex**   When the Hex mode is selected, the RGB color values are displayed in numbers and characters. Hex snaps the mixer to hexadecimal colors.

■ **Add Swatch**   Select this to add a color to the Swatch panel. You also can add a swatch to which an Alpha value was applied. This means you can create colors that are partially transparent.

NOTE   *If you're in Hex mode, a swatch won't be added because hexadecimal colors are represented in the default palette already. New RGB and Hex colors display on the bottom of the Swatch panel.*

7

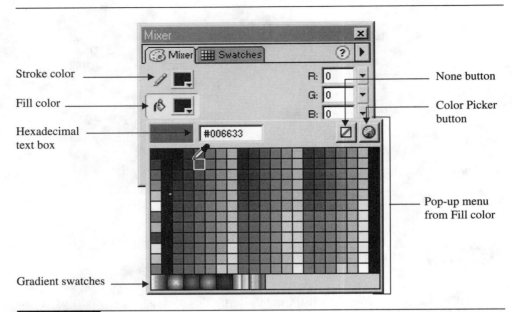

Stroke color

Fill color

Hexadecimal
text box

Gradient swatches

R: 0
G: 0
B: 0

#006633

None button

Color Picker
button

Pop-up menu
from Fill color

FIGURE 7-10 Select a color swatch from the pop-up menu in the Mixer panel

In the Mixer panel, there is a Default Fill and Stroke button under the Paint
Bucket. Click this to return the Stroke to white and the Fill to Black. Next to the
Default Fill and Stroke button is the None button. Select the None button if you
want a Fill without a Stroke or vice versa. Next to the None button is the Swap
Colors button. Swap the Fill color with the Stroke color and vice versa by clicking
this button.

NOTE *Transparent strokes can only be applied to new objects. To eliminate
a stroke from an existing object, select it (it must be ungrouped) and
manually delete the stroke.*

TIP *If the None button is not selectable in the toolbar, Mixer, or Stroke Panel,
click on the Stroke color in the Mixer, give it an Alpha of 0 percent. The
Stroke will appear clear. Now when you click the tool to create a new
object, the None button will become active.*

Use the Color Picker The Color Picker gives you even more color options to
choose from. Display the Color Picker dialog box by clicking on the Fill or Stroke

Color pop-up menus and selecting the Color Picker icon in the top right of the window as shown in Figure 7-11.

The Color Picker dialog box on the PC reflects the same selections available in the Mixer and Swatch panels with the exception of being able to mix a color with a Hue, Saturation, and Luminosity. On the Mac platform, the Color Picker has a different interface from on the PC. With the Mac version of the Color Picker (Figure 7-12), you can select a color from many different color modes. The color modes are listed to the left of the dialog box. When you select from a color mode,

7

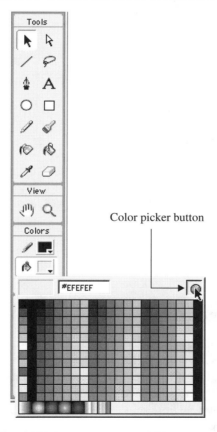

Color picker button

FIGURE 7-11   Display the Color Picker dialog box by clicking the pie icon in the upper right of the Fill and Stroke swatch panels

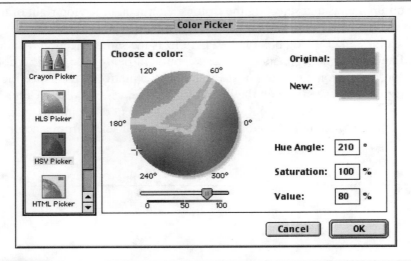

FIGURE 7-12 The Color Picker on the Mac differs from the Color Picker on the PC

choices related to that color mode are displayed in the right side of the dialog box. The following are the color mode options offered:

- **CMYK Picker** Use this to mix a CMYK color. Slide the pointers for each color bar to the left and right to assign CMYK color. The color percentages are displayed to the right of the color bar. The original color and a color preview appear in the upper right of the dialog box. Use this mode for movies that are going to print instead of the Web.

- **Crayon Picker** Use the Crayon Picker to select custom mixed colors that resemble crayons. Click on one of the crayons to select a color. The original color and a color preview appear in the upper right of the dialog box. These are RGB colors.

- **HLS Picker** Use the HLS Picker to choose the hue angle, saturation, and lightness of an RGB color. Click and drag on the color wheel to mix the hue angle and saturation of a color. The numerical equivalent of the hue angle, saturation, and lightness is listed to the right of the color wheel. Adjust the lightness of a color by dragging the pointer on the Value color bar. The original color and a color preview appear in the upper right of the dialog box.

- **HSV Picker** Use the HSV Picker to set the hue angle, saturation, and value of a color. The numerical equivalent of the hue angle, saturation, and value is listed to the right of the color wheel. Adjust the value of a color by dragging the pointer on the Value color bar. The original color and a color preview appear in the upper right of the dialog box.

- **HTML Picker** Set a Web safe color by clicking on Snap to Web color. Slide the pointers on the RGB bars to select a Web safe color. The hexadecimal equivalent of the chosen color is listed in the HTML box on the bottom right of the Color Picker dialog box. Turn off Snap to Web color to identify the hexadecimal equivalent of a non-Web safe color. The original color and a color preview appear in the upper right of the dialog box.

- **RGB Picker** Set an RGB color by sliding the pointers on the RGB bars. The numerical percentage values appear to the right of the dialog box. The original color and a color preview appear in the upper right of the dialog box.

Use the Swatch Panel to Select Color

Flash makes it easy to color objects. There are many different panels you can use to pick just the right colors for your movie. In the Swatch panel, you can select swatches to color objects or store colors you mixed from the Mixer panel. Access the Swatch panel by selecting Windows | Panels | Swatches. The Swatch panel lists the Web safe colors in the top portion of the panel. The bottom of the Web safe color is reserved for custom RGB colors you create as well as gradients. Flash comes with several default gradients; see Figure 7-13. New gradients that you create also are stored in this panel.

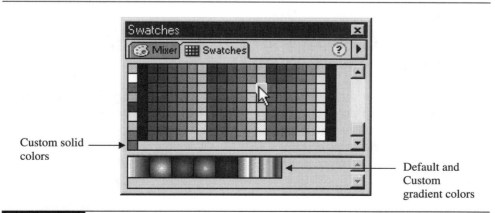

Custom solid colors

Default and Custom gradient colors

FIGURE 7-13   Use the Swatch panel to choose swatches or to store mixed colors

The pop-up menu in the upper right of the panel enables you to further customize the Swatch panel settings (see Figure 7-14).

The options in the pop-up menu are as follows:

- **Duplicate and Delete**   To duplicate or delete a swatch, click on a swatch you want to modify, and select Duplicate or Delete in the pop-up menu. If you duplicate a swatch, it will appear in the bottom of the swatch window. Deleting a swatch removes it from the swatch color table of this file.

- **Add or Replace**   Add or Replace color palettes by selecting these in the pop-up menu. The Import Color Swatch dialog box appears. You can add or replace color sets from other Flash files, color tables created in other programs (such as PhotoShop, Fireworks, and Director), and colors from GIF files.

- **Save Colors**   Colors can be saved in the Flash Color Set format or as a Color Table. Save colors by selecting Save Colors. A Save dialog box will appear. Target a place where you want the color palette saved. Color Table files are saved with an .act extension. Files with this extension can be imported into other programs, such as PhotoShop or Fireworks. Flash Color Set files are saved with a .clr extension. These color sets can be imported and exported into Flash movies.

- **Save as Default**   This makes the selected color palette the new default for that movie which replaces the Web safe default color set.

- **Clear Colors**   This deletes all colors from the current selection, leaving only black-and-white swatches.

- **Web 216**   Use this option if you want to return to the default palette.

- **Sort by Color**   Select Sort by Color to sort current colors by hues ranging from light to dark.

NOTE   *The difference between Add Color and Replace Color is that Add Color loads the new color set and retains the old set. Replace Color loads the new color and deletes the old color set. When you mix custom RGB colors and gradients, they are saved with the Flash movie. They are not saved in the program's preference file.*

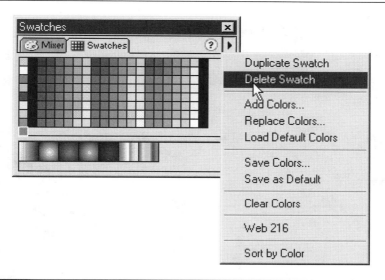

FIGURE 7-14   Use the pop-up menu on the Swatch panel to alter or customize the Swatch panel

Use the Fill and Stroke Panels to Set Color

The Fill and Stroke panels offer another way to apply color to an object. The color boxes are similar to the Fill and Stroke color box options in the toolbar.

Display the Fill panel by selecting Window | Panels | Fill. The default type of fill is Solid. From the pop-up menu, you also can select None, Linear Gradient, Radial Gradient, or Bitmap. A selection of None gives you a stroke with no fill. Linear and Radial Gradient give you a gradation of colors, which is discussed in the next section. Select Bitmap for adding color to imported bitmaps. Click the color box to display color swatches (see Figure 7-15). Notice the pop-up menu is the same menu as is in the Fill and Stroke color in the toolbar.

Display the Stroke panel by selecting Window | Panels | Stroke. Click the color box to display color swatches. A preview of the line with the settings you chose displays in the bottom of the panel (see Figure 7-16).

NOTE

Stroke color cannot be applied to a text object. To apply a stroke to text, it must be broken apart and made into an editable object. To break the text apart, click the text with the arrow tool and select Modify | Break Apart or CTRL+B *or* CMD+B.

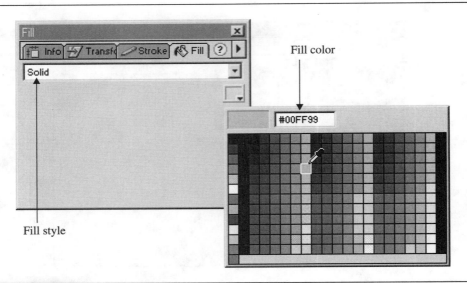

FIGURE 7-15   The Fill panel offers another way that you can apply fill color to an object

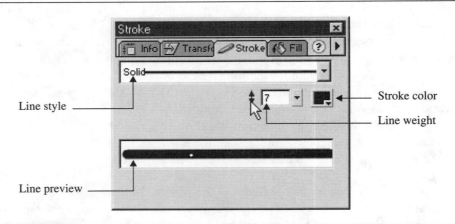

FIGURE 7-16   Select the Stroke panel to apply a stroke color value, style, and width

Apply a Gradient Color

Gradient color changes from one hue, saturation, alpha, color, or tint to another. There are many different effects you can create using gradient color. You can start with a solid color and fade out to no color; or you could have several colors in a gradient that gradually transform into one another. The possibilities are endless. In Flash you can control the color, as well as the way that colors blend into one another.

Generally, Flash produces pretty impressive gradients. Although colors are restricted on the Web, a Flash movie with gradients generally displays clearly with minimal banding on most systems. Banding is a sometimes undesirable result of gradients created in vector programs. Gradients in drawing programs are created from a series of bands of color that give the illusion of color gradually changing. If your computer doesn't make enough bands to give the illusion of a smooth transition of color, the bands become visible. Banding becomes even more of an issue if your beginning and end colors in the gradient are similar in hue and intensity. In this case, because the colors are similar, there are less color steps for the computer to interpret. Gradients in a Flash movie are far better quality than a gradient in a GIF file. Still, there's little guarantee that your gradient will look smooth on every viewer's platform, because there's such a wide variety of different configurations in cyberspace.

Create gradients with the Fill panel. Select Window | Panels | Fill. Under the Fill Type pop-up menu, there are two types of gradients you can select: Linear and Radial. A Linear fill gradates color in a straight horizontal or vertical direction. Use Linear fills for rectangular shapes or objects where you want the fill to appear in a straight line. A Radial fill gradates color in a circle. Use Radial fills for ellipses or any object where you want the gradation to appear radiating.

Gradients can be used on the currently selected object(s) or added to the movie's Swatch palette, where the color is stored permanently in the movie.

In the Fill panel, once you choose Linear or Radial as your gradient, a Gradient Definition bar appears at the bottom of the panel as is shown in Figure 7-17, with two pointers underneath the bar. To create a gradient, click on a pointer. A pointer will appear to the right of the color bar. Click the pointer color to display a pop-up menu and select a color. Now go to the next pointer and repeat the process. The swatch on the left is a gradient preview. To add more pointers to your gradient, click directly underneath the gradient definition bar, and a duplicate pointer will appear. Click that pointer and repeat the previous process. Sliding the pointers left or right adjusts and customizes the gradient. To delete pointers from the Gradient Definition bar, click and drag them off the bar.

7

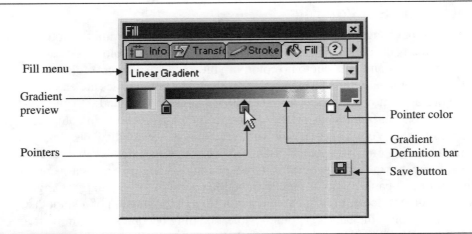

Fill menu

Gradient preview

Pointers

Pointer color

Gradient Definition bar

Save button

FIGURE 7-17 Use the Linear or Radial Gradient option from the Fill panel to create gradations

To save the gradient to the Swatch panel, go to the pop-up arrow to the right and click. Select Add Gradient. You can also save the gradient by clicking the Save button in the bottom right of the Fill dialog box. Display the Windows | Panels | Swatches panel. The gradient you just created appears in the bottom of the Swatch panel.

To apply a gradient to an object, click the object. From the Swatch panel, select a gradient. The object will change to the color you selected.

To create a Radial fill, display the Fill panel. Select the Radial option from the Fill menu. Repeat the same process as for a Linear fill. Notice the Radial fill radiates from the center. You can customize the way Linear and Radial gradients display, which we discuss in the next section.

NOTE *Gradients cannot be applied to the stroke of an object.*

Modify Gradients with Transform Fill and Lock Fill

Once you've assigned a gradient color to an object, there are ways to adjust the angle of the gradient, different stages of the gradient, and the way the gradient appears assigned to several objects on the stage. Use the Transform Fill option and the Lock Fill option to achieve some interesting gradient effects (see Figure 7-18).

Transform Fill The Transform Fill icon becomes available when you select the Paint Bucket in the toolbar window in the bottom right. This is a fun tool to use because you can create some dramatic effects by manipulating the size and the

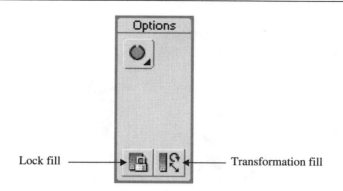

Lock fill ——————————→ ←—————— Transformation fill

FIGURE 7-18   Use the Transform Fill button and the Lock Fill button to create special
gradation effects

7

angle of the gradation. To use this tool, click the Paint Bucket tool in the toolbar.
In the Options portion of the toolbar, click the Transform Fill icon, located in the
bottom right. Then click an object with a gradient you want to change. If you
chose an object with a linear fill, two vertical lines will appear on either side of the
object. A ring handle appears in the center of the object and on the top of the line
to the right. On the right centerline, a square adjustment handle will appear, as
shown in Figure 7-19. These handles enable you to adjust, size, and rotate the
gradation on the selected object. To reduce or enlarge the gradient, click and drag
on the square adjustment handle. This can dramatically change the look of the
gradient. By shortening or elongating its length, you can give the gradation a
completely different look. Rotate the angle of the gradation by clicking the top
right ring handle and dragging to change the angle of the color. Change the center
point of the gradation by clicking and dragging on the ring handle in the center of
the object. This makes the center point of the gradation start at the new point
you've chosen.

Transforming a fill on a radial gradient is slightly different from transforming
a Linear fill. Because the color radiates in a circle, it requires a different kind of
adjustment. Select the Paint Bucket from the toolbar. Click the Transform Fill icon
on the bottom of the toolbar options. Click an object with a Radial fill. An ellipse
appears around the circumference of the object. There is a ring handle in the middle,
two ring handles, and a square handle on the right edge of the ellipse. Adjust these
handles by clicking and dragging. The ring handles rotate the direction of the
gradation, and the square handle reduces and enlarges the gradation. The ring handle

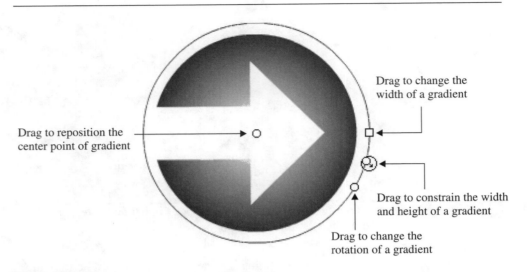

Drag to change the
width of a gradient

Drag to reposition the
center point of gradient

Drag to constrain the width
and height of a gradient

Drag to change the
rotation of a gradient

FIGURE 7-19   Use the adjustment handles to transform a gradient fill on an object

in the center of the object changes the center point of the object (refer to Figure 7-19) much like the center ring handle on a linear gradation.

Lock Fill   Use the Lock Fill option to adjust your color in a continuous gradation across several objects. Figure 7-20 demonstrates how a Lock fill can be used. In this figure, the text is broken apart and a gradation with a Lock fill has been applied separately to each character in the word. Instead of the gradation treating each character as a separate object with a separate gradation for each character, the characters are treated as one object with one gradation applied. This technique displays a kind of masking effect on a group of objects. It creates the illusion of a gradient in the background being masked by the objects you've created.

To create a Lock fill, let's review the steps that were used to create Figure 7-20. First, create a linear gradation using the steps from the previous paragraph on applying gradients. Then create some text on the stage. If you're using text for your Lock fill, it's a good idea to select a heavy weight font, so the locked gradation will stand out more. 100-point Arial Black was used for this figure. Click the text and break it apart using Modify | Break Apart or CTRL+B/CMD+B. Now you're ready to apply the gradient you created and lock it in place on all the text objects.

Select all the characters. For Fill color, select the gradient you just created. For Stroke color, click the None button. Each character will now have a separate gradient unto itself. However, you want the gradient to start at the first character

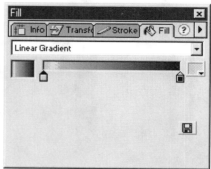

FIGURE 7-20   Apply a Lock fill to objects to create a continuous gradation on several objects

and extend through the last character as if it were one object. With the characters and Paint Bucket still selected, click on the Lock Fill button at the bottom of the toolbar. When activated, the Lock Fill icon becomes highlighted. Drag the mouse to the stage. The arrow turns into a paint bucket with a lock on the bottom right. Click any one of the objects to apply the Lock fill to the selected characters. Now go back to the Lock Fill icon and click it to deactivate. Click again on any one of the objects. The fill will now expand across all characters as a single fill.

TIP   *After applying a Lock Fill to a series of objects, you also can apply a Transform fill to change the size and direction of the gradient across the span of objects. To do this, select all Lock Fill objects and follow the procedure in the section on Transform fills.*

A technique similar to a Lock fill can be applied to a series of objects using the Paint Bucket. Select a series of objects with the Arrow tool. Select a gradient color from the Swatch panel. The color of the objects will now be the color of the swatch you chose. Select the Paint Bucket from the toolbar and click and drag the Paint Bucket over the selected objects, starting with the first object. The gradient will follow through from the first object to the last, in a similar manner to the Lock Fill tool (see Figure 7-21). Change the angle of the gradient by clicking and dragging across the selected objects on a diagonal. Change the center point by clicking on any object and dragging in any direction. This technique is more freestyle and unpredictable than the Lock Fill and Transform Fill, but in some cases, this quick technique might lend itself to the project you're working on.

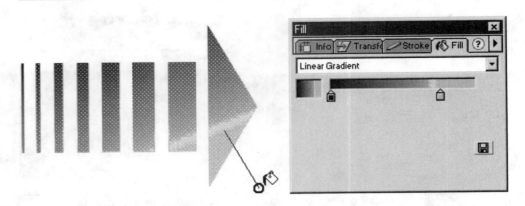

Dragging the Paint Bucket over several selected objects with gradient fills

Apply a Line Style and Width to a Stroke

In addition to setting the color of a stroke, you can set or change the style.
Flash offers an interesting array of line styles.

From the Style pop-up menu in the Stroke panel, you can select solid, hairline, dashed, dotted, and three custom line styles, as shown in the Figure 7-22.

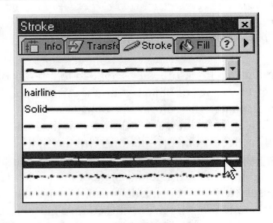

Change the style of a line by clicking on the Line Style pop-up menu in the Stroke panel

The width of a line can be between .25 and 10. There are two ways to indicate the weight in the Line Weight box:

- ■ Type the line weight manually.

- ■ Click the double-headed arrow. The line weight will be reflected in the Line Weight box.

A preview of the line displays on the bottom of the panel so you can see what the finished line will look like.

7

Chapter 8

Use Graphic Symbols, Instances, and Libraries

How to...

- Create Graphic Symbols
- Convert Objects to Symbols
- Edit Symbols
- Nest Symbols
- Place Instances
- Edit Instances
- Set Color with the Effects Panel
- Modify Instances with the Instance Panel
- Navigate the Movie Explorer
- Use the Common Library
- Use the Library Window

Symbols are an important feature of Flash. They are powerful because they lay the groundwork for animation and interactivity in Flash. When you learn how and when to make symbols, you'll be on your way to understanding advanced Flash.

In Parts I and II, the basics of Flash are covered, including creating objects and modifying their properties. To this extent, Flash mimics a typical drawing program. In Part III, symbols and instances are introduced, and Flash begins to depart from a basic drawing program and assumes the direction of a multimedia application.

Graphic symbols are the simplest type of symbols to create in Flash. In this chapter we will concentrate on the basics of symbols and how they work. Understanding graphic symbols paves the way for the creation of more complex symbols. Buttons and movie clips are additional kinds of symbols you can create in Flash. They can contain interactivity and animation capabilities and will be discussed in Chapter 13.

Symbols are objects you create with drawing tools, text tools, imported bitmaps, or vector art, and save in the Library window. A major difference between a graphic symbol and a regular object is that a symbol is stored in the Library and can be reused. Symbols dramatically reduce the file size of a movie because they're only saved within the movie once. Multiple uses of this symbol don't increase a file size. Every time you use a symbol from the Library, it's referred to as an *instance*. You can change the properties of an instance in many different ways. If you revise a symbol, the changes occur globally on all instances. This can minimize production time on large projects where an instance might be used numerous times. Symbols are a great help when organizing a Flash movie.

Symbols, like grouped objects, can be nested inside other symbols. When you revise a nested symbol, the main, or root symbol, automatically updates. Flash is a program that demands planning and organization, and symbols make it simple to organize your movie.

Some people create entire movies using only symbols instead of regular graphics. This is not to say everyone should work this way. Every Flash author has a unique working style, and you will ultimately be the best judge of how to make a successful movie.

Create Graphic Symbols

There are two ways to create a graphic symbol in Flash. You can make one from an existing graphic, or you can enter a special mode where your graphic symbol can be created. The first method is Convert Object to Symbol. The second method is Create New Symbol. These are both accessed from the Insert menu.

Convert an Object into a Symbol

Converting an existing object into a graphic symbol is easy. Use this technique if you have an existing object on the stage and, as an afterthought, want to convert it into a symbol. It also might be easier for some people to create the graphic symbol on the main Timeline if they're accustomed to working this way. Creating a new graphic symbol launches a special editing mode, and the objects in the main Timeline are not visible.

Convert an object to a symbol by selecting an object on the stage. Click the object. If the object contains more than one element, hold down the SHIFT key and click each element, or drag a selection marquee around the objects you want to convert. Just like on the main Timeline, the object can exist on a single layer or multiple layers.

With the entire area selected, go to Insert | Convert to Symbol as shown in Figure 8-1. The Symbol Properties dialog box appears (see Figure 8-2). Name the symbol in the Name box and click a Behavior type. Select Graphic for behavior. Notice Graphic is one of three selections. Movie Clip and Button are the other two. Click OK. Your object is now a graphic symbol. Display the Library

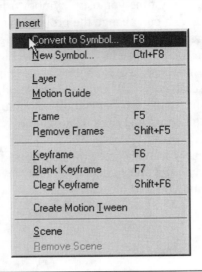

FIGURE 8-1 Convert an object to a graphic symbol with the Insert | Convert to Symbol menu selection

window by selecting Window | Library. The symbol you created appears in the Library. The icon to the left of the symbol name is the icon for the graphic. Symbol types are represented in the Library as Graphic, Button, and Movie icons.

Create a New Graphic Symbol

Creating a graphic symbol from scratch is just as easy as converting a graphic to a symbol. Create a new symbol by entering the Symbol Editing mode. The Symbol Editing mode has its own stage and Timeline separate from the main stage and Timeline. Most everything you can do to an object in the main stage can be done in the Symbol Editing mode too. In this sense, creating a graphic symbol is much like making a regular object. You can have multiple layers, groups of objects, import bitmaps, and vector art; add other symbols; and even create animations. The only restriction is adding sounds and actions, neither of which will work in a graphic symbol.

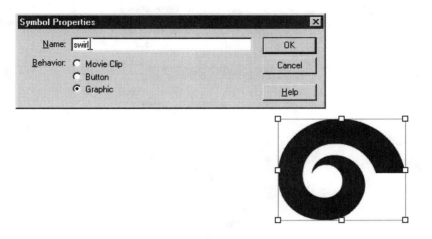

FIGURE 8-2   Name and choose the behavior of a symbol in the Symbol Properties
dialog box

NOTE

*Sounds and actions do work on movie clip symbols, and sound works with
button symbols. You also can change the behavior of a graphic symbol to
that of a movie clip or button by dragging the instance on the stage and
displaying the Instance panel. In the Type pop-up menu, the behavior can
be changed. This is discussed further in Chapter 13.*

Create a new symbol by selecting Modify | New Symbol. The Symbol Properties
dialog box appears (refer to Figure 8-2). Give the symbol a name. Click Graphic
for the Behavior and click OK. You're now in the Symbol Editing mode where
symbols are created and modified. The Symbol Editing mode looks just like the
main Timeline, only with a crosshair in the center of the stage. The crosshair is
used to target the center of the symbol you're about to create. When you're in
Symbol Editing mode, an icon and the name of the symbol being edited appear
in the upper-left corner of the stage, indicating you're in the Editing mode.

Create your graphic in the Editing mode, as shown in Figure 8-3. When you're
done, exit the Editing mode in one of two ways: Click the Symbol icon and Symbol
Name icon in the upper-left corner, or select Edit | Edit Movie. This brings you
back to the main Timeline and stage.

The Symbol Editing mode is similar to the Group Editing mode. A graphic
symbol makes an object or group of objects into one element. An object(s) that is
grouped becomes a single element too. They can be taken apart, modified, and put

FIGURE 8-3 Create a new graphic in the Symbol Editing mode

back together again in their original state. Both symbols and groups have separate editing stages, and both indicate you're in the Editing mode in the upper-left corner. You exit both modes the same way. They also are different from one another. Symbols can be used more than once and not affect the size of the movie. Certain symbol properties such as color and alpha can be modified, whereas this is not possible with grouped objects, unless you enter the Group Editing mode. As a whole, symbols offer more diversity, organization, and economy when dealing with larger projects.

Edit a Symbol

Edit an existing symbol by re-entering the Symbol Editing mode discussed in the previous section. There are a few ways to access this mode, and personal preference dictates which mode you use. First, you can double-click on an instance that's on the stage. This brings you into the editing mode that is indicated in the top left of the stage. You also can click on a symbol instance either on the stage or in the Library and select Edit | Edit Selected from the menu. The third method is to double-click the symbol in the Library. All three of these methods yield the same results, that is, accessing the Symbol Editing mode. Exit the Symbol Editing mode by either clicking on the Scene name in the upper-left corner of the stage, or select Edit | Edit Movie from the menu. The Symbol Editing mode enables you to modify the properties of a symbol as if it were a regular graphic object.

NOTE

When you modify an instance from the stage, other elements on the stage that are not related to that symbol will become dimmed. When you modify a symbol from the Library, the stage only contains the object being modified. Both methods will change all instances of this particular symbol.

Nest a Symbol Within a Symbol

8

Symbols offer a lot of diversity in the way you can build them. You can place groups of objects in a symbol, and you can edit a group that's within a symbol. When this is done, the Group Editing Mode icon will appear in the upper-left corner of the editing stage, to the right of the Symbol icon and name. You also can place symbols within symbols, which is referred to as *nesting* or *embedding*. Graphic symbols are often nested in complex graphics, buttons, or movie clip symbols. For example, let's suppose you were designing an animated cartoon of a person's face. An efficient way to plan this cartoon would be to create the different components of the face as graphic symbols: the eyes, nose, mouth, face, and eyebrows as shown in Figure 8-4.

The graphic symbols of the face would then be nested in movie clip symbols and animated on their own Timeline. The final face movie clip might then be nested in another movie clip symbol on another Timeline. Although the final symbol is a complex movie clip, it's easy to go back to each nested symbol and edit them in the Symbol Editing mode for each symbol. Graphic symbols are often the first building block for creating more complex symbols.

The graphic symbols we have been discussing are static symbols. You also can create an animated graphic symbol and place it on the main Timeline and stage as seen in Figure 8-5. The animation is created on the Timeline in the Graphic Symbol Editing mode. Notice when you place an animated graphic on the main Timeline, in order to see the animation, you have to add frames to the main Timeline. Otherwise, when you play the movie back, it still appears static.

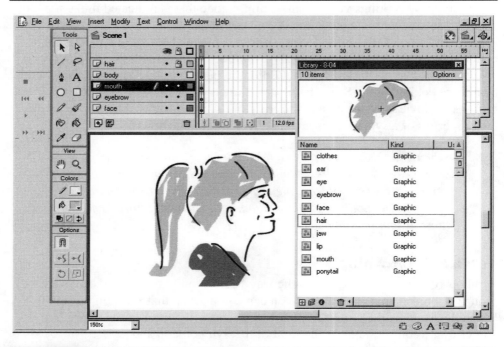

FIGURE 8-4   Create a graphic symbol of a cartoon face using existing symbols for the components of the cartoon face

Generally, movie clips are used more often to create animated effects. Unlike animated graphic symbols, movie clips run independently on their own Timeline, and they are probably one of the most significant and exciting features in Flash. Movie clips are discussed in more detail in Chapter 13.

Learn to Use Graphic Symbols

Symbols are much more versatile than a regular graphic. Symbols are stored in the Library, and every time you use one, an instance of that symbol is created. An instance is easy to position, edit, manipulate, and change back into a regular graphic object. You can edit a symbol from the Library easily by re-entering the Symbol Editing mode, where you created the original symbol. All these techniques make it easy for you to control symbols in your movie.

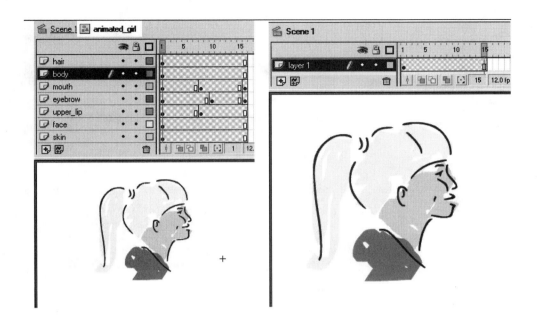

The animation in Symbol Editing mode   The graphic symbol on the main Timeline

FIGURE 8-5   A graphic symbol must span several frames on the main Timeline to view the animation in a movie

Placing an Instance

Create an instance by dragging a symbol from the Library to the stage. Symbols are stored in the Library until you need to use them. To view the symbols in your movie, select Window | Library. Any symbols, sounds, video, fonts, imported bitmaps, or graphics associated with your movie will appear in this Library. The Library serves as a container for these components (see Figure 8-6).

Select a graphic symbol from the Library. Symbols are depicted as three different icons: graphic, button, and movie clips (see Figure 8-7). This is how you distinguish between symbol types. The type of symbol, whether it is a graphic, button, or movie, defines the way the symbol will behave. For example, if an instance is a button, it might elicit interactive behavior.

If you click a graphic symbol in the Library, a preview of the symbol displays in the top of the Library. Drag it onto the stage. As soon as a symbol is on the stage, it becomes an instance.

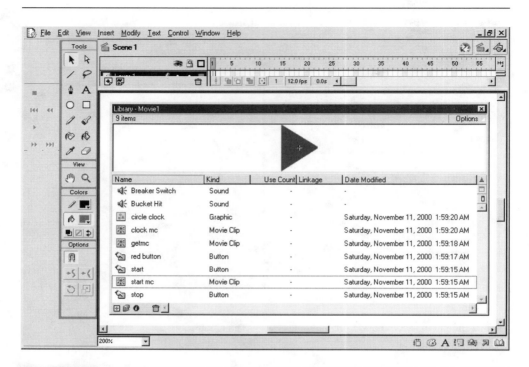

FIGURE 8-6 A library with symbols, sound, and imported bitmaps

Click on the instance, and you'll see the crosshair that indicates the center of the instance. This crosshair also is visible in the Symbol Editing mode and is used to target the position of your symbol. The crosshair is used as a reference point to align the instance on the stage. The default reference is the center of the object, but you can change the position of this crosshair if you want to reference the object from another point. Change the reference point by clicking on the instance and selecting Modify | Transform | Edit Center (see Figure 8-8). When you do this, the crosshair fill turns white and a rectangular bounding box surrounds the instance. Click and drag the crosshair to a new position on the bounding box (it creates a snap-to ring handle), or to the center of the instance. After the new position is set, click somewhere off of the object. Now when you select the instance, the crosshair appears in its new position. This is an important feature because it gives you more control over where a symbol is located in relation to others. The Edit Center command can be used with all types of symbols.

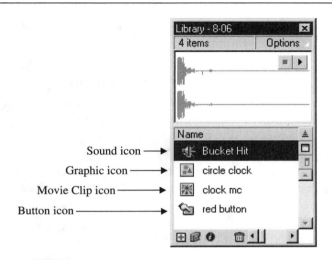

Sound icon

Graphic icon

Movie Clip icon

Button icon

FIGURE 8-7   A depiction of the Graphic, Button, and Movie Clip symbol icons
representing the kind of behavior a symbol elicits

Click and drag the crosshair to a new position on the bounding box (it creates
a snap-to ring handle), or to the center of the instance. After the new position is
set, click somewhere off the object. Now when you select the instance, the crosshair

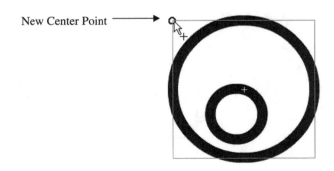

New Center Point

FIGURE 8-8   Edit the center of an instance using the Modify | Transform | Edit
Center command

appears in its new position. This is an important feature because it gives you more control over where a symbol is located in relation to others. The Edit Center command can be used with all types of symbols.

Edit an Instance with the Transformation Tools

An instance is much like any other object. Just like any other object, you can apply the transformation tools from the toolbox, Transform panel and the Modify | Transform menu. Figure 8-9 shows an instance being skewed from the Transform panel and as you can see, it's treated just like any other object except there's a crosshair in it that identifies it as a symbol. The main difference is, you can reuse and transform this and other instances as many times as you like and the size of the movie will remain the same.

Convert Instance Back Into a Graphic

Let's say you created a symbol and then needed one of the instances to return to an editable object state. You can break a link from an instance to a symbol. When a

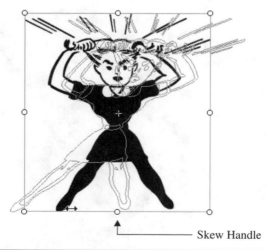

Skew Handle

FIGURE 8-9   Use any of the transformation tools on an instance

symbol is revised, all instances update too. An instance that has been broken apart no longer has any association with the symbol. It becomes an independent graphic.

You can break apart all types of symbols. When you break apart symbols with layers, animation, sound, and interactivity, you lose everything but the static object. Objects grouped and nested within the symbol remain intact when the symbol is broken apart.

Break apart a symbol by clicking a symbol and selecting Modify | Break Apart (see Figure 8-10). This breaks apart the symbol the same way it does for text and graphic objects. You could use this technique for several purposes. For example, let's say you created a symbol with a very complex illustration, and you wanted to

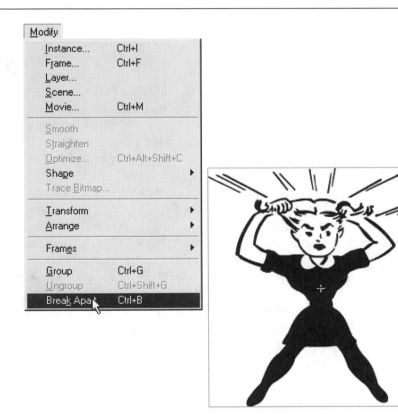

FIGURE 8-10   Break apart a symbol by selecting Modify | Break Apart from the menu

8

use a part of the illustration to create another illustration. You could break the object apart, extract the part you needed, and create a new symbol from the new illustration without affecting any other elements of the movie.

Set and Modify Instance Properties

In addition to the transformation tools, you can set or modify properties using the Effect panel. The Effect panel enables you to change the color properties and alpha settings of an instance. You also can modify properties of a symbol by modifying an instance in the Instance panel. Both of these panels are frequently used in conjunction with movies that contain symbols.

Use the Effect Panel

The Effect panel enables you to apply color to an instance. The manner in which you modify color on an instance is different from the way you modify color on a regular object. Color is applied to an instance in the Effect panel, as shown in Figure 8-11. If you edit color in the Symbol Editing mode as opposed to using the Effect panel, color is updated on the symbol and subsequent instances. You can achieve some very powerful effects by changing the properties of an instance, especially in an animated movie, where you can change the opacity or color of an object over time.

Click on an instance and display the Effect panel by selecting Windows | Panels | Effect. (If the Effect panel is displayed without selecting an instance, the bottom part of the menu will be dimmed.) The Effect panel is docked in a group with the Instance, Frame, and Sound panels. The default pop-up menu says "None" to indicate that no effect has been added to the selected object. Click the pop-up menu to display options. The selections are as follows:

- **Brightness**—Select Brightness to make the instance lighter or darker in increments that range from 100% for pure white to -100% for black.

- **Tint**—Set the Tint amount and the RGB percentages of a selected instance with the sliders next to each box. Click and drag on the slider or type a number in manually in the boxes. You also can select a Tint color from the Flash color pop-up menu or use the color bar at the bottom of the panel. Use the color bar just like the color bar in the Mixer panel.

■ **Alpa**—Set an Alpha to modify the opacity of an instance. Use the sliding bar or type in a percentage in the box. A 0% setting on an instance makes the object transparent, and a 100% setting is total opacity.

■ **Advanced**—The Advanced setting enables you to apply tint and color effects to the selected instance. Adjust RGB color and Alpha with the sliders associated with that particular color. In addition, you can increase your palette selections by using the RGB and Alpha settings within the container. You can alter the intensity of an RGB multiplied by the current color. The added value appears in the boxes to the right. The numbers in the right boxes can be set with sliders or typed in (see Figure 8-12). Experiment with the sliding bars to create custom color effects.

The Effect panel becomes particularly powerful when you start to use symbols for animating. The color of a symbol can be interpolated gradually from one color to another, or an instance can fade in and out of the stage by changing the Alpha settings. The Effect panel will be used for this purpose in Chapter 13.

8

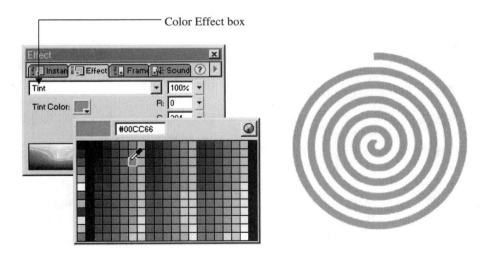

FIGURE 8-11   Change the color of an instance by applying color from the Effect panel

FIGURE 8-12   Play with different RGB color and the Alpha of an instance with the
Advanced menu in the Effect panel

Use the Instance Panel

The Instance panel gives you information about a selected instance. You also can
modify and edit a symbol from which the instance came from and adjust a script
from within this panel. If you're working on a movie that has a lot of symbols,
the Instance panel provides a quick and easy way to make modifications. Click
an instance and display the Instance panel by selecting Windows | Panels | Instance
(see Figure 8-13). If the Instance panel is displayed without selecting an instance,
the pop-up part of the menu won't display. The Instance panel is docked in a group
with the Effect, Frame, and Sound panels. The current behavior of the instance is
indicated in the pop-up menu. The behavior indicates the type of instance and how
that instance behaves. The three selections are Graphic, Movie Clip, and Button.
The name and symbol type of the instance is indicated in the upper-left corner. The
name and icon refer to the symbol in the Library window. You also can change

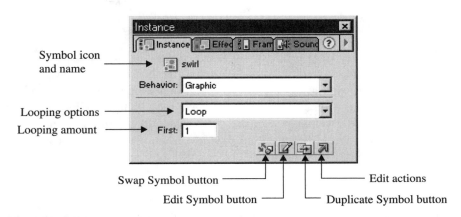

Symbol icon and name

Looping options

Looping amount

Swap Symbol button

Edit Symbol button

Edit actions

Duplicate Symbol button

FIGURE 8-13   Change additional instance properties with the Instance panel

8

the behavior of an instance. For example, if you wanted an instance of a graphic symbol to behave like a button, you could change it here. Change an animated graphic symbol into a movie clip so it could play on its own Timeline. When you change the behavior of an instance, it doesn't affect the symbol in the Library.

Depending on what type of instance you're selecting, the bottom half of the panel changes to display the following options:

■ **Behavior: Graphic**—If you select Graphic as your behavior type for your symbol, loop options become available. Looping is an action applied to animations and refers to the number of times an animation plays within a movie. The pop-up menu in the second half of the panel gives you three looping options: Loop, which plays as long as the movie is playing; Play Once, which plays once and stops; and Single Frame, which displays only one frame of the animation sequence. When Single Frame is selected, enter the frame number you want displayed on this instance (see Figure 8-14). Loop and Play Once enable you to indicate a frame number you wanted to play from. In order for the looping options to work properly, you need to use a Stop action on the main Timeline to stop the frames in the main Timeline from controlling the looping.

- **Behavior: Button**—If you select Button as the behavior type for your symbol, from the options portion of the panel, you can select Track as Button or Track as Menu Item. Use Track as Button for a single button and Track as Menu Item for pop-up menus (see Figure 8-15).

- **Behavior: Movie Clip**—When you select Movie Clip as the behavior type on a symbol, the movie clip can be named in the Name box. Name movie clips when you want to refer to a movie clip in a script. For example, if you wanted a button, when clicked, to duplicate a movie clip, the button would target the movie clip instance by the name assigned. On the bottom of the Instance panel, there are four icons that add additional functionality to this panel (see Figure 8-13). From the bottom left, they are as follows:

- **Swap Symbol**—Select Swap Symbol to replace an instance. This feature replaces an instance with another, but retains all the settings from the original instance, including actions and effects. Click the Swap Symbol icon to display the Swap Symbol dialog box. Click the symbol in the dialog box you want to swap with. You also can make a copy of the selected symbol

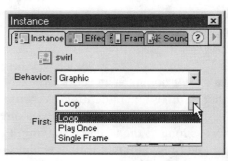

FIGURE 8-14   If you've created an animated graphic symbol, you can change the looping options on an instance in the Instance panel

by clicking on the Duplicate Symbol icon in the bottom-left of the dialog box. Duplicate a selected symbol if you need multiple copies of that symbol that differ slightly from one another. The new copy appears in the Library. This method of duplication is a great time saver as opposed to creating different symbols from scratch.

■ **Edit Symbol**—Selecting Edit Symbol brings you to the Symbol Editing mode as discussed in the previous section on editing symbols.

■ **Duplicate Symbol**—The Duplicate Symbol icon works the same as the Duplicate Symbol icon in the Swap Symbol dialog box, making a copy of the selected symbol. You also can duplicate a symbol from the options pop-up menu in the Library window.

■ **Edit Actions**—Click the Edit Actions icon to display the Object Actions window. Add actions to a selected symbol with Edit Actions. You can activate the Actions window from two other places on the stage: the Window | Actions menu and from the Show Actions icon on the Launcher bar.

Get Information on Symbols and Instances

You often need quick information about an instance. The Instance panel indicates the kind of behavior a symbol elicits. The Info panel gives you the name, type, location, and size of a selected instance. In addition to the Instance and Info panels, you also can gather important information about instances using the Movie Explorer window. The Movie Explorer tracks every element of the movie, including use of symbols. Instances can sometimes be hard to keep track of and to this extent, the Movie Explorer is a big help.

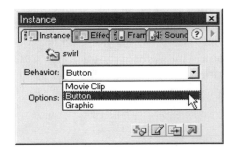

| FIGURE 8-15 | When you select a button instance, the Instance panel enables you to change the options on that instance |

Use the Movie Explorer

When movies become more complex, with multiple layers, movie clips, and nested symbols with actions on instances and frames, it becomes harder to track different elements and their history. It's particularly hard to track instances because they can take on so many different personas. Multiple instances from one symbol can have different actions attached to them, be swapped, be duplicated, or be changed into a different type. Figure 8-16 shows the Movie Explorer from a movie of moderate complexity. This panel is packed with useful features to help you zone in on any element in the movie. Display the Movie Explorer in the Launcher bar by clicking the fifth bar from the left. You also can display this panel by selecting Window | Movie Explorer. The Movie Explorer window's default display is docked in a group with the Object/Frame Actions panel. The Movie Explorer also is discussed in Chapter 3.

The Movie Explorer has six Show icons at the top of the window that enables you to customize your display. From the left, you can display one of the following types:

- ■ Text

- ■ Buttons, Movie Clips, and Graphics

- ■ ActionScripts

- ■ Video, Sounds, and Bitmaps

- ■ Frames on Layers

- ■ Customize Which Items to Show. Click this mode to display the Movie Explorer Settings dialog box (see Figure 8-17) where you can custom select the items you want displayed.

Under the Show icons, there's a Find feature. Type in the name of anything in the movie (instance, frame, symbol, imported video, sound, and so on) and the Explorer will take you to its position in the Movie Explorer Hierarchy.

A pop-up menu can be accessed by either clicking the triangle in the upper-right corner of the Explorer window or right-clicking/CTRL-clicking as shown in Figure 8-18. Different options become available depending on what type of object, layer, frame, or action you select.

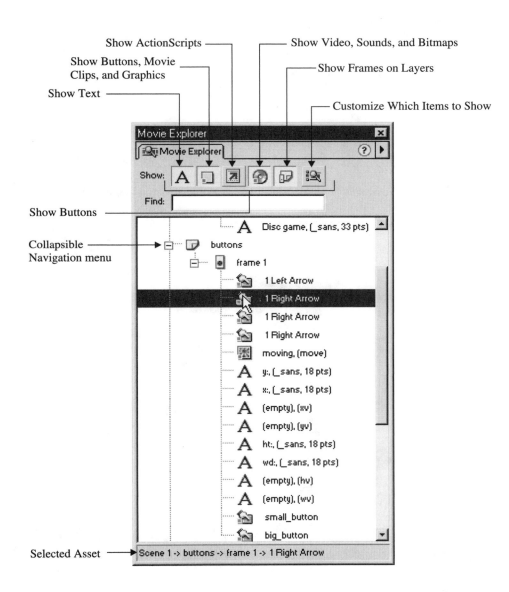

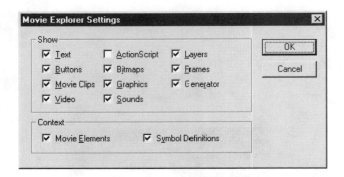

FIGURE 8-17 The Movie Explorer Settings dialog box can be accessed from the Customize icon

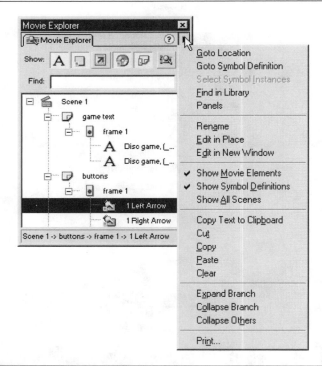

FIGURE 8-18 Display the pop-up menu in the Movie Explorer window to fine-tune your viewing options

When you click an element in the Explorer window, you can select from the following options in the pop-up menu:

- **Goto Location**—Select Goto Location to jump quickly to a selected element in the Explorer.

- **Goto Symbol Definition**—Select this option to jump directly to a symbol definition. Symbol definitions list all the elements used to create the symbol in a collapsible branch folder. In order for this to be selectable, Show Symbol must be selected.

- **Select Symbol Instances**—This option jumps directly to an instance listed under the Symbols Definitions in the Movie Explorer. For this to be selectable, Show Movie Elements must be selected.

- **Find in Library**—Select this option to jump directly to an item in the Library window.

- **Panels**—This option displays panels relevant to the element selected. Hold down the ALT/OPT key and double-click any element to display panels too.

- **Rename**—Select Rename to give the element a new name.

- **Edit in Place**—This enables you to edit an object you've selected in the Movie Explorer right on the stage.

- **Edit in New Window**—Choose Edit in New Window if you want to edit a selected element in a new window.

- **Show Movie Elements**—This option shows elements neatly organized in scenes.

- **Show Symbol Definition**—This displays all information associated with a selected symbol.

- **Copy Text to Clipboard**—Select this option to copy selected text to the Clipboard for use in another part of the movie or a text editor.

- **Cut, Copy, Paste, Clear**—Use these old standbys to reshuffle, duplicate, and eliminate items from the Movie Explorer.

8

- **Expand and Collapse Branch and Collapse Others**—Click any of the triangles associated with a branch of the navigation tree to expand and collapse a branch on a selected item. This navigation technique helps clean up the appearance of the windows in complex movies.

- **Print**—To print the Movie Explorer, select this option.

The Movie Explorer is packed with features to make it easy for you to navigate even the most complicated movie.

Use the Common Library

The Common Library is separate from the Library you store symbols in. It is filled with ready-made graphic symbols, buttons, sounds, movie clips, and Smart Clip extensions that make it easy for the beginner to add interactivity to their movie (see Figure 8-19). This Library is saved within the application.

Use the Common Library to grab quick symbols and sounds. This can be a time-saving device for creating simple elements. You also can add symbols, sounds, and Smart Clips to the permanent Library. Add your own objects to the Common Library by creating a movie containing the Library elements you want included in the permanent Library. Save the file to the Flash Application Library folder on your computer. The new Library elements will display by name the next time you open the Common Library. Delete Library items by removing them from the Library folder in the Flash application.

Display the Common Library by selecting Window | Common Libraries. A pull-down arrow lists six different types of Libraries you can display:

- **Buttons**—This Library contains a large list of interactive buttons including LED styles, VCR styles, arrows, circles, and bars.

- **Graphics**—Graphics offers a meager selection of graphics as of this writing. The only reason to take a peek at this Library is it provides a good demonstration on how to build a graphic symbol from other symbols.

- **Learning Interactions**—This selection is new to Flash 5 and is a noteworthy addition for beginners. It contains prefab interactive movie clips along with instructions that you can customize for instant programmable behavior. It serves as a tutorial-like example of Smart Clips. Create drag-and-drop functions, text field elements, multiple choice, and hot spots, albeit with the restrictions of a prefab script (see Figure 8-20).

■ **Movie Clips**—This Library also offers a limited selection of movie clips that you can browse through.

■ **Smart Clips**—Smart Clips include click box, menu, and radio button movie clips. These are little movie clips with standard interactivity attached to them (see Figure 8-21). After you position them, they can be easily customized using the Clip Parameters panel in the Window | Panels | Clip Parameters. More Smart Clips can be obtained from the Macromedia site (www.macromedia.com). They are listed under Extensions on the site. Additional resources for Smart Clips and Extensions can be found in Appendix B.

■ **Sounds**—This library contains a broad selection of small sounds that are perfect for attaching to buttons, frames, or events.

NOTE   *If you've added Extensions to Flash, some will appear in the Common Library window.*

8

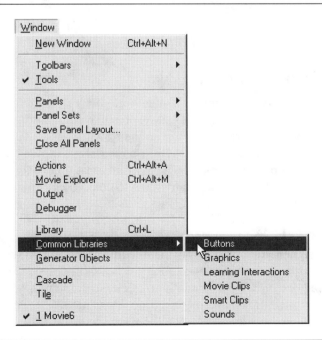

FIGURE 8-19   The Common Library offers ready-made symbols as well as templates to add simple interactivity to a movie

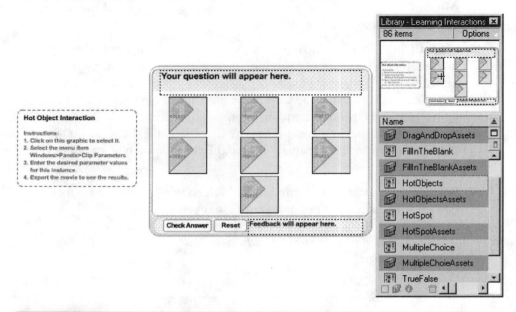

FIGURE 8-20   Display Learning Interactions from the Common Libraries to use a ready-made interactive template

Navigate the Library Window

As you become a more experienced Flash author, you realize the importance of organization in your movie. A complex movie can have hundreds of elements including several movie clips all running on their own separate Timelines. Most often, you'll be creating and gathering all the assets of the movie before you begin. A well-organized Library will help you easily find what you're looking for when you build your movie. Flash offers many tools to help you customize and organize your Library just the way you want it.

The Library window is a container for symbols, imported sound, bitmaps, vector drawings, and videos. Display the Library by selecting Window | Library from the menu. When you click on a name, the image associated with it appears in a preview window at the top of the Library. The scroll down Library window lists in a horizontal array the name and kind of element, the number of times an instance has been used, links, and the last time it was modified. Customize the window to expand and contract horizontally using the Wide State and Narrow State buttons in the upper-right of the window. Reverse the viewing order of elements by clicking on the Sort button in the upper-right corner of the window, as shown in Figure 8-22.

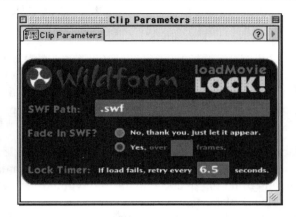

FIGURE 8-21   Sample of the Load Movie Lock Smart Clip in the Parameters panel that was downloaded from the Macromedia site

8

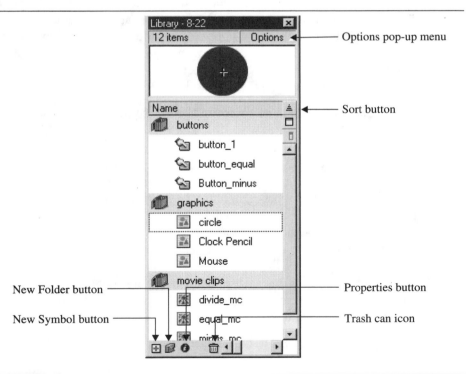

FIGURE 8-22   The Library window

When you click on an element, four buttons on the bottom right become active. From the left, the four buttons perform the following functions:

- **New Symbol button**—Click the first button to create a new symbol. The Symbol Properties dialog box appears. This is where you select the behavior of the symbol before moving on to Symbol Editing mode. Use this as an optional way of creating a new symbol, as opposed to using the menu selection Insert | New Symbol.

- **New Folder button**—The second button is the New Folder button. Click this button to create a folder within the Library. Name the folder by clicking and dragging over the name and typing over it. The Library window navigates like a standard window on the Mac and PC. You can create folders to further subdivide your assets. Click the folder to expand and contract the contents of a folder.

- **Item Properties button**—Click a symbol and select the Properties button to modify the properties of a symbol. This displays the Symbol Properties dialog box. This is the same dialog box that appears when you double-click on a symbol in the Library window, or double-click an instance on the stage, but with the addition of an edit button. Click on another behavior type to change the behavior of the selected symbol. Click on the Edit button to enter the Symbol Editing mode.

- **Trash Can icon**—Click an object and select the trash can to delete it from the Library.

To use a symbol in your movie, click on the layer you want the asset to appear, select the symbol in the Library, and drag it to the stage to create an instance.

The Options menu in the upper-right of the Library window offers even more options to help organize and manage your Library assets. Access the options in the pop-up menu by clicking on the triangle in the upper-right corner.

The pop-up options in the Library Options menu are as follows:

- **New Symbol**—Select this to display the Symbol Properties dialog box. This dialog box also can be accessed from the New Symbol button on the bottom left of the window.

- **New Folder**—Select this to create a new folder in the library. A new folder also can be created by clicking on the New Folder button on the bottom left of the window.

- **New Font**—This displays the Font Symbol Properties dialog box. Use this dialog box for font symbols. Font symbols are created for shared Library items for fonts to be shared across multiple sites.

- **Rename**—Select this option to rename a symbol.

- **Move to New Folder**—This displays the New Folder dialog box where you can create and name a new folder. This dialog box also can be accessed from the New Folder button on the bottom left of the window.

- **Duplicate**—This option displays the Symbol Properties dialog box and enables you to duplicate and rename an element.

- **Delete**—This deletes an element from the Library. The delete function also can be accessed from the Trash Can button on the bottom left of the window.

- **Edit**—Edit brings you to the Symbol Editing mode of a selected symbol.

- **Edit With**—This selection displays an Open dialog box that enables you to edit a bitmap in the program it was created in.

- **Properties**—Properties displays the Properties window associated with a selected object in the library.

  - If a symbol is selected in the Library, the Symbol Properties dialog box will display.

  - If a bitmap is selected in the Library, a Bitmap Properties dialog box appears. The Bitmap Properties dialog box allows you to update a revised bitmap from this location, import another bitmap into the symbol, and choose a compression type. Compression can be GIF, PNG, or JPEG. Check smoothing for antialiasing of the bitmap.

  - If a sound is selected in the Library, a Sound Properties dialog box appears. In this box you can import another sound, update the current sound, test the sound to hear it, change the Export settings, and set the Compression Rate. Compression options include Default, ADPCM, MP3, and Raw, all of which are discussed in Chapter 9.

  - If a font is selected in the Library, the same Font Properties box is displayed as in the New Font selection.

8

■ If a video clip is selected, the Video Properties dialog box appears. A movie imports in a QuickTime Movie (MOV) format. You can change the name of the video and indicate the path of the video (where the movie resides).

■ **Linkage**—This displays the Symbol Linkage Properties dialog box (see Figure 8-23). Use this dialog box to assign linkage properties to a selected element. You can set up symbols so they can be linked to other movies. Use the Symbol Linkage Properties dialog box by giving the element an Identifier Name. Check one of the three buttons:

■ **No Linkage**—This is the default setting for all movies.

■ **Export This Symbol**—Click Export This Symbol to define a Shared Library element. The movie must be saved before the Library can be shared with another movie. Once you choose Export in the Linkage Properties dialog box, the linkage information on the element in the Library changes to "Export." To link the defined element as a shared Library, go to another movie file or create a new one. Select File | Open As Shared Library. From the dialog box, open the shared Library file, select it, and click OK. The shared Library appears. Drag these items into the new movie's Library. Notice the linkage information on the element in the Library changes to "Import."

■ **Import This Symbol From URL**—Use this selection if you want to put a shared Library in another location other than the movie you're currently working on. You must specify the different URL in the input box. Shared Libraries are automatically saved with the SWF file of the movie, but you can change the location of the shared Library by using this option.

■ **Define Clip Parameters**—This feature displays the Define Clip Parameters dialog box. Use this for setting the parameter values on a Smart Clip. Smart Clips are ready-made interactive elements that you can customize by defining the parameters in a template format.

■ **Select Unused Items**—This highlights and identifies elements not yet used in your movie.

■ **Update**—Use this feature to update any imported graphics that have been revised in an outside program.

- **Play**—This selection plays any interactive or animated element in Flash such as sound, buttons, and movie clips. Use this to test an interactive or animated element. You also can test an interactive or animated element by clicking the Play triangle in the upper-right corner of the Preview window in the Library.

- **Expand and Collapse Folders**—This opens and closes selected Library folders. You also can double-click on the folder in the Library to expand or collapse the folder.

- **Expand and Collapse all Folders**—This feature opens or closes all folders in the Library.

- **Shared Library Properties**—This displays the Shared Library Properties dialog box where you can indicate a URL you want to share a library with.

- **Keep Use Counts Updates and Update Use Counts Now**—These selections update the number of times an instance from the Library has been used in the movie. The total is indicated in the Use Count in the Library window.

The Library window is used frequently when creating multimedia movies. Because it contains a multitude of ways to display, manage, and customize your Library, it's a big help when it comes to organizing your project.

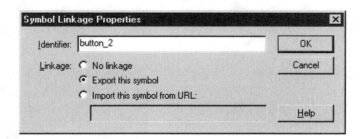

Choosing Linkage from the Library Options menu enables you to define and link shared Library items

Chapter 9

Add Pictures and Sound to Your Flash Movies

How to...

- Understand Graphics Created in Other Programs
- Import Graphics into Your Flash Movie
- Import File Sequences
- Use Vector Graphics
- Use Bitmapped Images
- Import and Assign Sounds
- Access Sound from the Sound Library
- Link a Sound

Flash is packed with an impressive array of drawing tools. Some authors never leave the Flash environment to create a movie. Still, others are addicted to their favorite drawing programs. Some programs offer features you just can't replicate in Flash. Most Flash authors find a happy medium by combining Flash drawing features with those from other programs. Either way, Flash offers great flexibility to accommodate both methods, enabling you to customize your movie just the way you like.

Understand Graphics Created in Other Programs

You can import both vector and raster images into a Flash movie. Remember, vector drawings are associated with drawing programs while raster graphics are associated with paint programs.

To take full advantage of the import features and be able to further manipulate those images, it's important to understand the difference between vector- and raster-based graphics.

Understand Vector Graphics

Vector graphics are defined with mathematical precision. An object created in a vector-based program is described with a series of lines and curves that move from point to point to create a shape. Vector objects have properties that can be modified. You can group, move, scale, rotate, duplicate, change the color, and much more with vector art. You also can assign a stacking order to objects and change this order at will. Unlike bitmaps, vector graphics maintain their quality at any scale, as shown in Figure 9-1. They are resolution-dependent, giving them consistent quality in print or in multimedia. The drawing features of Flash are vector-based, as are programs like Macromedia FreeHand and Adobe Illustrator. Use vector graphics for logos, technical drawings, or any art where precision is important.

Understand Raster Graphics

Raster graphics are *bitmaps*. Bitmaps are created from pixels arranged on a grid. Each pixel is assigned an RGB color value and the juxtaposition of pixels creates the illusion of an object. Zoom up on a bitmapped image in its native program, or even in Flash, to see how the pixels are arranged in a grid-like order. The larger you zoom the image, the more the pixels appear as a group of squares. Zoom in enough and the image no longer resembles the original art; it will look more like an abstract painting. Zooming in on a bitmap provides a good idea of how a bitmap is made. Programs such as Adobe PhotoShop are raster-based applications.

Bitmaps (also known as raster graphics) are very different from vector art. When you modify a bitmap, you change the properties of each pixel within the selected area. If you reduce or enlarge a selected bitmap, the pixels reduce or enlarge within the scheme of the pixel grid. Enlargement of a bitmap can cause a "pixelated" effect (see Figure 9-2) and seriously downgrades the quality of the original image. Bitmaps have resolution issues too. *Resolution* is a mathematical

9

FIGURE 9-1   An illustration created in a vector maintains quality when it's scaled to 300% of its original size

FIGURE 9-2   When the illustration from Figure 9-1 is transformed into a bitmap and scaled up, the pixels become visible

calculation relating to the way images display their final output, which could be various forms of print or multimedia (Web, video, and slides). The higher the resolution of the image, the clearer the image will display or output.

At higher resolutions, pixels become more densely populated and as a result, display a better quality picture. The image size increases too. This might not be a problem if the final output is for print. If the bitmap is being put up on the Web, bigger files mean longer download times, and on some systems, crashes. The standard resolution for a bitmapped image being prepared for the Web is 72 dpi (dots per inch). When creating bitmaps in a paint program, plan to make the art either the same size or larger than the final output. This helps eliminate pixelated or jagged edges.

Paint programs enable you to smooth out the edges of pixels. This is a technique known as *antialiasing*. Antialiasing creates extra pixels around an object that provide a more gradual transition of color from the object to the background. Antialiasing can create problems if the background in the paint program is not the same color as the background in your Flash movie. For example, if you save antialiased art as a transparent GIF, a halo of the remains of the background color can appear around the edges of the image. Fortunately, the newer paint programs provide ways to eliminate halos around antialiased objects.

Creating, manipulating, and saving bitmaps in an appropriate format is a whole book unto itself. If you plan on using bitmaps in Flash, you need to familiarize yourself with the file-saving methods for Web media in your program to ensure a smooth transition into Flash.

Import Graphics into Your Flash Movie

When you create graphics in other programs for use in Flash, they must be saved in a file format that Flash recognizes. Flash imports many different file formats from paint programs, drawing programs, animation programs, as well as many more. Systems with QuickTime 4 and later installed give you additional file format capabilities and cross-platform compatibility on Macintosh and Windows-based systems. Although it's easy to import art into Flash, there are some rules and issues you should familiarize yourself with to help you decide what program and file format might best suit your needs.

Import from Fireworks and FreeHand

FreeHand and Fireworks are Macromedia's drawing and image manipulation software programs. Flash is very forgiving when importing from Fireworks and FreeHand, and many different import options are available.

When exporting art from Fireworks to be placed in a Flash file, you can use any of the following formats:

■ **PNG**—This is Fireworks native format.

■ **SWF**—SWF is Flash's native format and also imports flawlessly into Flash.

■ **Illustrator 6**—When saved in this format, the file assumes an extension of .ai, the Adobe Illustrator file format. Certain elements, such as gradients in vector drawings, will be lost in this conversion.

■ **GIF**—GIF is an indexed color (256) file format. Although you can import a GIF format into Flash from Fireworks, the SWF format is so comprehensive, there would be little reason to do so.

The preferred import format for Fireworks to Flash would be either the PNG or SWF formats. When you import a PNG format into Flash, the Fireworks PNG Import Setup dialog box appears, as shown in Figure 9-3. Use this dialog box to further refine the import. There are two options:

■ **Import Editable Objects**—Check this option if you want the object to behave as a vector, preserving groups and layers. Importing Editable Objects provides a clean import that's editable in Flash. There are three

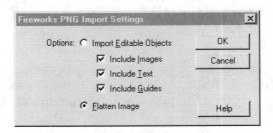

FIGURE 9-3   When a PNG file from Fireworks is imported into Flash, the PNG Import
Setup dialog box offers the import options

sub-selections in this category. Select Include Images to include bitmapped
images that are part of your Fireworks file. Check Include Text to bring
along font, style, size, and make Fireworks text editable in Flash. Check
Add Guides to include guides from Fireworks.

- **Flatten Image**—Check Flatten Image if you want art imported as a bitmap.
  This option eliminates layers and frames, as well as transparent backgrounds.

You also can copy and paste a graphic from Fireworks into Flash by clicking
the object and selecting Edit | Copy from the Fireworks Menu (CTRL+C/CMND+C).
Select Edit | Paste (CTRL+V/CMND+V) from the Flash menu to paste the graphic
on the Flash stage. This copies the object into Flash as a bitmap with an opaque
background.

NOTE   *When you import an object into Flash, it always appears on a new layer.*

FreeHand files (7.0 or later) import seamlessly into Flash. In fact, Macromedia
offers both FreeHand and Flash in a packaged suite to encourage using them together.
Although FreeHand files can be imported in many different formats into Flash,
most often, you'll import files from FreeHand in a *FH* format. FH is the native
file format for FreeHand. This format offers more options than other methods for
retaining the integrity of FreeHand art in Flash. When you select an FH format for
import, the FreeHand Import dialog box displays (see Figure 9-4). You can custom
select several settings from the dialog box:

- Mapping refers to the way FreeHand pages translate onto the Flash stage.
  You can map a FreeHand page to a scene or a keyframe in Flash. Mapping

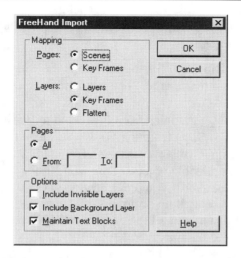

FIGURE 9-4   FreeHand files being imported into Flash in an FH format can be customized in the FreeHand Import dialog box

to Scenes places all pages in the FreeHand document in a separate scene. Mapping to Keyframes places every page in the FreeHand document in separate keyframes.

■ FreeHand layers can be mapped to Flash layers too by checking the Layers option. Check Keyframes if you want your FreeHand layers to be mapped into individual keyframes in Flash. You also can check Flatten as an option if you want the FreeHand document to be one frame, one layer. The other convenient feature in this dialog box is the ability to specify a particular page or pages for import from FreeHand to Flash (in FreeHand, you can create multiple pages).

Additional options at the bottom of the dialog box areas include

■ **Include Invisible Layers**—This option imports invisible layers along with your layers containing objects. Use this feature for files that have certain layers made invisible in FreeHand that you need to view in Flash to complete a picture.

■ **Include Background Layer**—If your FreeHand file contains an intricate or hard to replicate background layer, you might choose to bring it with you.

Or perhaps there is some guide on the background layer that you need as a guide in Flash. In either case, it might be essential for you to retain the background layer.

■ **Maintain Text Blocks**—This option keeps the width of text blocks intact from one program to the other. The text is then editable in Flash.

You can copy and paste graphics from FreeHand to Flash by selecting the object and choosing Edit | Copy from the Fireworks menu (CTRL+C/CMND+C), and then selecting Edit | Paste (CTRL+V/CMND+V), from the Flash menu. This copies the objects into Flash as editable objects. This works quite well for quick simple things and can be a time-saver if you don't need to save your FreeHand art or retain layers. You can display both programs, create art in FreeHand, copy it and paste it into Flash, albeit without all the customized options. Objects on multiple layers will appear stacked on one layer.

There are other issues to keep in mind when importing from FreeHand to Flash. If you select Layers from Options, each object will appear on separate layers in Flash. If you copy and paste objects on multiple layers from FreeHand to Flash, they will appear on the same layer and in the stacking order they were created in.

Gradient objects can carry up to eight colors from FreeHand to Flash. If you're going to import a gradient from FreeHand to Flash, it's best to try and stick with eight colors. Otherwise Flash has to create clipping paths to simulate the gradation. Clipping paths could mean trouble because the file size can increase dramatically. Blends from FreeHand to Flash also are interpreted as separate paths, which also increases the file size. When imported in an SWF format, FreeHand 8 and over gradients are converted to Flash gradients.

If for some reason you opt to import a FreeHand file into Flash as an EPS (or perhaps you receive one from another source and you have to make use of it), you need to click Convert Editable EPS in the FreeHand Export dialog box. Otherwise it won't appear on your Flash stage.

Import from Other Programs

Although Flash is most friendly to programs in the Macromedia family, there are other popular programs and formats you can import from. Adobe Illustrator is a vector program like FreeHand. Flash does a nice job of importing and exporting Illustrator files 6 and earlier. The preferred Illustrator format for importing into Flash is the AI format. However in Illustrator 9, you can now import to the SWF format. The same features that apply to FreeHand when imported in the SWF format, apply to Illustrator 9. Gradients aren't supported in versions of Illustrator before version 5. Bitmaps are supported in version 6. You also can copy and paste between Illustrator and Flash.

> **NOTE** *Although you can import Illustrator files from version 7 and earlier, Macromedia suggests saving as an Illustrator 6 or below file as a guideline.*

When art is imported from Illustrator, the elements used to make the objects are grouped together and the stacking order is maintained in Flash. Layers created in Illustrator are also recognized in Flash (see Figure 9-5).

Files generated from Adobe Photoshop, ImageReady, and other popular programs can be imported into Flash using any of the appropriate extensions listed in Table 9-1. See Table 9-2 for a listing of file extensions you can use with Flash 5 and QuickTime 4.

FIGURE 9-5   Art saved in Illustrator in an AI format (version 6) and imported into Flash maintains layers and stacking order

9

File type	Extension	Windows	Macintosh
Adobe Illustrator (version 6.0 or earlier)	.eps/.ai	Yes	Yes
AutoCAD DXF	.dxf	Yes	Yes
Bitmap	.bmp	Yes	No
Enhanced Windows Metafile	.emf	Yes	No
FreeHand	.fh7/ .ft7/ .fh8, .ft8/ .fh9/ .ft9	Yes	Yes
FutureSplash Player (Older version of Flash)	.spl	Yes	Yes
GIF	.gif	Yes	Yes
JPEG	.jpg	Yes	Yes
PICT	.pct/.pic	No	Yes
PNG	.png	Yes	Yes
Flash Player (Flash native format)	.swf	Yes	Yes
Windows Metafile	.wmf	Yes	No
WAV Audio	.wav	Yes	No
AIFF Audio	.aif	No	Yes

TABLE 9-1   File Formats that Can Be Imported into Flash

File type	Extension	Windows	Macintosh
MacPaint	.pntg	Yes	Yes
Photoshop	.psd	Yes	Yes
WAV Audio	.wav	Yes	Yes
AIFF Audio	.aif	Yes	Yes
Silicon Graphics	.sai	Yes	Yes
TGA	.tgf	Yes	Yes
PICT	.pct/.pic (as bitmap)	Yes	Yes
QuickTime Image	.qtif	Yes	Yes
QuickTime Movie	.mov	Yes	Yes

TABLE 9-2   Import File Formats in Flash 5 if User is Running QuickTime 4 and Higher

Import File Sequences

You also can import file sequences generated from 3D programs (such as Infinity 3D, Adobe Dimensions, MetaCreations Poser, and Logomotion), CAD programs (such as AutoCAD), or any program that can automatically generate sequential files. A file sequence is a series of files that, if viewed together, would give the illusion of a flipbook or a frame-by-frame animation. Flash recognizes a group of files as sequential if the files have the same names but end in sequential numbers.

To import sequential files, go to File | Import. Navigate to the folder containing the files you want to import. Click the first file in the numerical file sequence. On a PC, click the Open button. On a Mac, click the Add button and Import buttons. An alert displays: "This file appears to be part of a sequence of images. Do you want to import all the images in the sequence?" Click Yes. The sequence will import into Flash. The files appear on a single layer and sequentially occupy the frames on that layer. The total number of frames equates to the number of sequential files you imported.

When you import a sequence, you create a frame-by-frame animation in Flash. You can create some of your 3D effects using sequences from programs such as Adobe Dimensions, as shown in Figure 9-6. Using sequential files to create a frame-by-frame animation (especially sequential files from 3D programs) can add some exciting effects to your Flash movie that would otherwise not be attainable. A word of caution about file size. Files from 3D programs, depending on how they're rendered, can be big. Careful attention should be paid to keeping the file sizes low. Even the most spectacular Flash Movie is anticlimactic when you have to wait too long for it to play.

With a multi-frame movie in Flash, you also can export a file sequence to another program. Do this by selecting File | Export Movie from the menu. The Movie Export dialog box appears. In Windows, type in a filename and select a Save As Type in the pop-up menu (see Figure 9-7). The Export options are as follows:

- QuickTime Sequence (.mov)
- Animated GIF (.gif)
- Wave Audio (.wav)
- EMF or WMF Sequence (.emf or .wmf)
- EPS 3.0 Sequence (.eps)
- Adobe Illustrator Sequence (.ai)

9

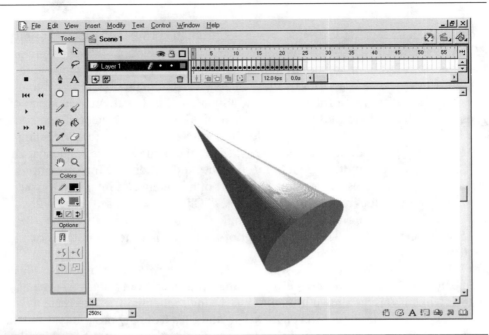

FIGURE 9-6 Import a sequence of files into Flash from a program such as Adobe Dimensions to create a 3D frame-by-frame-animation sequence

- ■ DXF Sequence (.dxf)
- ■ Bitmap Sequence (.bmp)
- ■ JPEG Sequence (.jpg)

Your export selection depends on what program you're exporting to. Consult the program's user manual to determine which file format is best to use.

The Movie Export dialog box on a Mac is slightly different from the dialog box in Windows (see Figure 9-8). Type in the name for the first file of the sequence in the Save As box. The pop-up menu for Format is identical to the Save As Type pop-up menu in Windows with a couple of exceptions. PICT sequence is available on the Mac and WAVE Audio (.wav); EMF sequence (.emf); and WMF (.wmf) sequence are not available. (If QuickTime 4 or higher is installed on a system, the WAV format becomes available on the Mac.)

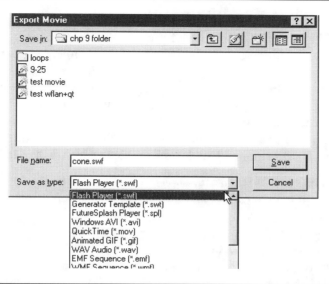

FIGURE 9-7 The Export dialog box in Windows displaying the Save As Types available for exporting a sequential file series

9

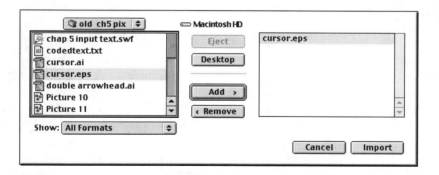

FIGURE 9-8 The Export Movie dialog box on the Mac platform differs from the Export Movie dialog box in Windows

Import QuickTime Movie Files

Movies saved in the QuickTime movie format (.mov) can be imported into Flash. Movies from video-editing programs such as Adobe Premiere and AfterEffects or 3D animation programs can be brought into your Flash movie. To import a QuickTime movie in Flash 5 and have all elements work correctly, your system must be running QuickTime 4 or later. A Flash Track has been added to QuickTime 4. The QuickTime Flash Track is a track just for Flash so when it's published (exported) as a QuickTime movie, it retains many of the features of the original Flash movie. Imported QuickTime movies reside on the Flash track too.

> **TIP**   *If your PC or Mac is running a version of QuickTime older than 4, you can download the QuickTime Player from www.apple.com/quicktime.*

To import a QuickTime movie into Flash, select File | Import. Select the QuickTime movie you want to import and click Open (PC) or Import (Mac). A static picture of the movie appears on the stage of the current layer. When you import a QuickTime movie, it appears on only one keyframe of a layer. To see the full animation of the movie, you have to add frames to that layer. Add frames by clicking the keyframe where the QuickTime movie resides in. Press the F5 key repeatedly to add frames. Or, add frames by clicking on a blank frame and pressing the F5 key. This will fill in the all frames up to the keyframe.

> **NOTE**   *Some older versions of video-editing programs might not be compatible with QuickTime 4. Check to make certain your program is compatible with QT 4 before you load it.*

Because the Frame rate in Flash might not match the frame rate of your QuickTime movie, you might need to adjust the frame rate in the imported QuickTime movie before you export it to encourage smooth playback of the movie in Flash. Consult your software's user manual for frame rate setting information.

An Imported QuickTime movie must always be linked to your Flash file. It exists apart from the Flash file and its path must be identified for it to work properly. To set the path of the movie, display the Library window and select the QuickTime movie in the Library, as shown in Figure 9-9. Go to the Options pop-up menu in the Library and click Properties. The Video Properties dialog box displays. Click the Set Path button and locate the source of the QuickTime movie. With the movie selected, click Open. The correct path of the movie is now set.

If you try to test the QuickTime movie using Control | Test Movie, it doesn't work, which can be rather disconcerting. Nor can you view it in any of the

FIGURE 9-9 Set the path of a QuickTime movie in the Library with the Video Properties dialog box

File | Publish Preview settings. You can preview the movie on the Timeline by selecting Control | Play (see Figure 9-10). The reason you can't see it in Preview mode is because SWF file types can't display QuickTime video.

FIGURE 9-10 Test your imported QuickTime movie by scrubbing over the frames with the playhead

A Flash movie with an imported QuickTime movie must be exported as a QuickTime movie. In File | Publish Settings, the basic setting should be as follows:

- **Formats tab**—For Type, select, Flash (.swf), HTML (.htm), and QuickTime Movie (.mov).

- **Flash tab**—For Version select Flash 3 from the pop-up menu. This will convert your Flash Player file into 3.0.

When your Flash file is exported to a QuickTime format, there are some limitations in what can display. Animations on the main Timeline work and basic actions will work. Only the first frames of movie clips appear. Because you can't see movie clips, movie clip actions don't work either. See Chapter 15 for a detailed description on how to publish a QuickTime movie.

When importing QuickTime movies, another issue to be considered is size. QuickTime movies are large, so tricks have to be pulled out of your hat to get the file size down. One technique you can use to pare down the size of your Flash file is to first make your movie as small as possible by eliminating unnecessary frames and lowering the frame rate. Then save your movie in a sequential file format (PCT or BMP); the files will have the same name, ending with sequential numbers

Most video editing, 3D, and 3D animation programs enable you to save in a sequential format. If the sequential files are from a program such as Premiere, you can bring your files into a photo-editing program such as PhotoShop, and then further manipulate and resave them. Then import the sequence into Flash, as shown in Figure 9-6. If your sequence is from a video-editing program or a bitmapped 3D program, you can further reduce the size of the sequence images by using the Trace bitmap technique. This is discussed in the section "Use Bitmapped Images," later in this chapter

In addition, you can eliminate any unnecessary frames in the sequence to save on file size. Sometimes a choppy look that has an interesting frame-by-frame rhythm can work well as a design technique. You could also make symbols out of the sequential files and reuse them to further save on space.

Use Vector Graphics in Your Flash Movies

As mentioned in the previous section, vector graphics are made in drawing programs such as FreeHand and Adobe Illustrator. Although Flash is a vector-based program, some artists like to take advantage of features in other drawing programs. FreeHand has a perspective grid to help shape an object into a 3D shape. It also contains all sorts of interesting fill textures. Illustrator is packed with filters that enable you to distort paths. Some people are so accustomed to drawing in one package, they don't care to learn a new one. Fortunately, Flash makes it easy to import vector drawings.

Drawing programs were originally intended for print, although the latest releases of FreeHand and Illustrator address the increasing need for Web features in vector programs. RGB color should always be used when making art for Flash because CMYK color doesn't translate well into RGB. If you can import in an SWF format, your color and art will always translate well when brought into Flash

Although vector art in general tends to be smaller than bitmaps, using many complex paths can increase file size. When creating vector art for import into Flash, make certain you use the program's utilities for minimizing points on a path, or plan in advance to eliminate unnecessary paths.

The standard Import dialog box on Mac and Windows is different. When you import on a Mac, the dialog box is split into two sides. The left side is where you navigate the computer to find the file. The Show pop-up menu on the bottom of the dialog box enables you to specify the format you're searching for (see Figure 9-11). Click the file to be imported and select the Add button. You can add more than one file to the list on the left. When you've selected the file(s) you want, click the Import button.

In Windows, the Import dialog box is a single box that enables you to navigate the hard drive. Select a single file in the middle of the dialog box. Select Files of Type on the bottom to narrow down your file search (see Figure 9-12). When you've selected the desired file, select Open.

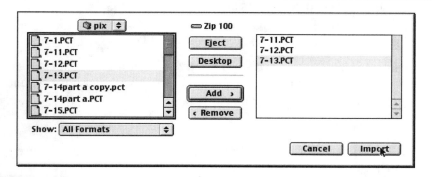

FIGURE 9-11   The Import dialog box on the Mac platform

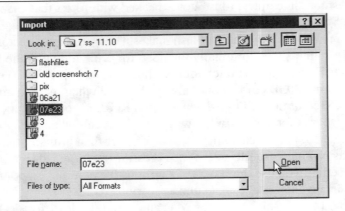

FIGURE 9-12   The Import dialog box in Windows

Export Vector Graphics to Other Programs

In addition to being able to import vector graphics into Flash, you can export vector graphics from Flash into other programs. You might like a drawing feature in Flash that's not available in another program. I love the way Flash handles painting of fills and strokes, so I often import drawings I make in Flash to Illustrator. Still other artists might create a logo in Flash and need to use it for a print application. There could be many reasons to export a graphic from Flash.

To export an image, select File | Export Image from the menu. In the File Export dialog box in Windows, name the file and indicate as Save as Type from the pop-up menu. The export formats are as follows:

- **Flash Player (.swf)**—The native format for Flash.

- **Generator Template (.swt)**—The native format for Macromedia Generator, a program often used in conjunction with Flash for advanced interactivity and Web e-commerce sites.

- **FutureSplash Player (.spl)**—An older player version.

- **Enhanced Metafile (.emf) and Windows Metafile (.wmf)**—These formats are exclusive to Windows.

- **EPS 3.0 (.eps)**—Encapsulated Postscript. Flash can only be exported to older EPS formats.

- **Adobe Illustrator (.ai)**—Native file format for Adobe Illustrator.

- **AutoCAD DXF (.dxf)**—This is a format used in AutoCAD 2D and 3D.

- **Bitmap (.bmp)**—Bitmaps are used for Windows applications and are similar to PICT files on the Mac.

- **JPEG Image (.jpg)**—Joint Photographic Experts Group. Creates 24-bit continuous tone art, if system is capable of viewing 24-bit color. This format doesn't support Alpha channels. JPEG is lossy compression (which creates image deterioration).

- **GIF Image (.gif)**—Graphics Interchange File. This supports indexed color (256 color palette) and produces medium to low quality export.

- **PNG Image (.png)**—Portable Network Graphic Format. This is the native file format for Fireworks and supports 8-bit, 24-bit color, and Alpha channels.

SWF and AI file formats will export as editable vectors. Export to an SWF format if you're using FreeHand 8 or Illustrator 9. This gives you a clean export with color, path, and layer support. The other formats will export as bitmaps. AI file formats 5 and earlier do not support gradient fills, and 6 and older do not support the export of bitmaps. There is a plug-in that comes with Flash 5 called Flashwriter. This plug-in offers enhanced export capability to Illustrator 8 and earlier files.

In the Mac Export dialog box, type a name in the Save As box and select a Format from the pop-up menu. The format types on the Mac are the same as for Windows with the following exceptions: Mac exports to a PICT (.pict, .pct) format instead of a Bitmap (.bmp). Enhanced Metafile and Windows Metafile formats are only available on the PC.

Use Bitmapped Images

Bitmapped images are usually generated from paint programs or photo-editing programs. Some artists turn vector art from illustration programs such as FreeHand and Illustrator into bitmaps to take advantage of filters and techniques that can be applied to raster images.

The ability to import bitmapped graphics is an exciting feature of Flash, although caution must be used when doing so. Even bitmaps saved in low resolution can have file sizes that push the limit on the Web. When you think of the old guideline for graphics on the Web (one second per kilobyte for a system with a 28.8 modem), a bitmap that's 100k in size is way too big to use in a movie that is being designed for Web use. Flash does compress files when it creates SWF files, but if you load a movie with several bitmaps, your audience could have a long waiting time while it loads. This is precisely why some Web designers avoid bitmaps altogether.

There are tricks you can use to pear down the movie file size even with bitmaps. You can import 8-bit images into Flash, which will display 256 colors or less, or 24-bit images that can display up to 16.7 million colors. 24-bit images display beautifully on monitors capable of viewing 24-bit color, but dither on an 8-bit display. In either case the safest bet once you've chosen an image format, is to test the movie on many different platforms and on many different browsers so you can anticipate what your audience is seeing.

Import a bitmap into Flash the same way you import a vector image. Go to File | Import in the menu. The Import dialog box is slightly different on the Mac platform versus Windows, as shown in Figures 9-11 and 9-12. On the Mac, select the file on the left side, click the Add button, and the file you select appears on the right. When you've selected the file(s) you want, click the Import button. In Windows, select the file in the Import dialog box. Select Files of Type on the bottom of the dialog box. Your bitmap will appear on the current layer. The bitmap formats you can import from are listed in Table 9-1.

Make a Symbol from a Bitmap

If you plan on using a bitmap more than once, save on file size by making it into a symbol. It can be any symbol type: graphic, button, or movie clip. This also affords access to the Effect panel, where you can change the color and Alpha of a symbol. Some interesting effects can be created with this technique. Figure 9-13 shows a bitmap graphic symbol in an animation that has a motion tween applied to it. In the first frame, the symbol has an Alpha of 20% applied to it. The last frame has an Alpha of 100%. In between the Alpha is interpolated. Because the bitmap is a symbol, the file size doesn't change. There are many other animation techniques you can employ using a bitmapped symbol.

FIGURE 9-13   A bitmapped graphic symbol with a motion tween applied to it to interpolate an Alpha effect

Set or Modify the Properties of a Bitmap

When you import a bitmap into Flash, it appears in the Library. The Library assigns a bitmap icon to the image and gives it a Type of Bitmap. The Options pop-up menu in the Library enables you to set and modify properties of a bitmap.

There are several ways to access the Bitmap Properties dialog box. You can select Properties from the Options menu, or right-click/OPT-click to display the options available to that selection. Double-clicking the image displays the Bitmap Properties dialog box too. You can choose from several options, as shown in Figure 9-14. The top of the box provides you with file information: when it was created and the size. The following options are also available:

■ Check Allow Smoothing for an antialias effect. This will smooth any rough edges.

■ Choose a Compression format. You can select from Photo (JPEG) or Lossless (PNG/GIF). If color and image detail are important, JPEG is the best choice. Use Document Default Quality enables you to either keep the previous setting or re-enter a new value of quality between 1 and 100 in the Quality box. You cannot change the image quality of a JPEG image in the Publish settings dialog box. If you need to modify the quality setting, it must be done in the native program or in the Bitmap Properties dialog box.

9

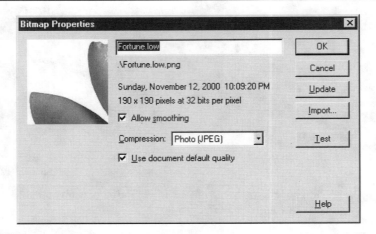

FIGURE 9-14 The Bitmap Properties dialog box enables you to change settings on an imported bitmap

■ The Update, Import, and Test buttons enable you to update the file throughout the movie, import it to another format, and test the quality of your new settings. The new settings ratio appears on the bottom of the dialog box when you test the settings.

Edit a Bitmap

If you need to modify a bitmap in its native program, you can launch the program in Flash. To do this, select the bitmap in the Library. From the Options menu, click Edit With (or right-click/OPT-click to display the options available for this image). This displays the External Editor dialog box. Navigate your hard drive to find the application the bitmap was created in. When you select the application, it will appear in the File name box. Under Types of File, Executable Files (.exe) is the default selection. Once you locate the program, click OK. The file opens in the program it was created in. Make your changes and re-save the document. When you return to Flash, the edited version will now be in the Library. If you have an instance of this bitmap on the stage, the change will be reflected in that also.

On the Mac platform, Flash recognizes the native program of your bitmap and lists the Program in the Options Menu. For example, if you selected a file in the Library that was created in Adobe PhotoShop, and you displayed the Options menu, the selection above Edit With would be Edit in Adobe PhotoShop. It must recognize the program the bitmap was saved in for this feature to work. This is a nice feature because it eliminates having to search for the native program on your hard drive.

Trace a Bitmap

Being able to trace a bitmap serves many purposes. If the correct settings are chosen, you can substantially reduce your movie file size. If it's not done the right way, it can increase the size of the file beyond belief. You also can create some cool effects using this technique. When you trace a bitmap, Flash paints over it and renders it as vector art—your bitmap is gone. Sometimes it adds a great effect; sometimes it can make your bitmap look like an unrecognizable blob. Because the results can be unpredictable, you need to experiment with the settings to get just the right effect.

To use this technique, select a bitmap on the stage. Choose Modify | Trace Bitmap. The Trace Bitmap dialog box appears as shown in Figure 9-15. You can customize tracing options in this box to achieve a variety of results. From the options are as follows:

- **Color Threshold**—The default is 100. Choose between 1 and 500. Increasing the threshold decreases the number of colors used to trace the image.

- **Minimum Area**—The default setting is 8 pixels. You can enter a value between 1 and 1,000 pixels. This sets the number of neighboring pixels surrounding a dominant color. A low number gives you more areas of color because there's less pixels surrounding a color.

9

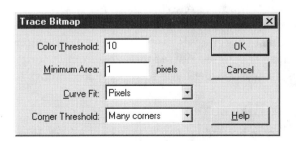

FIGURE 9-15   The Trace Bitmap dialog box enables you to select from several settings to refine your tracing

- **Curve Fit**—From the pop-up menu, select from the following:

  - **Normal**—This is the default setting.

  - **Pixels, Very Tight, Tight, Smooth, Very Smooth**—These options determine the smoothness of an outline. Pixels have many points for detail and Very Smooth has less points between curves.

- **Corner Threshold**—From the pop-up menu, select from the following options to determine the way edges will look:

  - **Normal** is the default setting.

  - **Many Corners** gives the resulting trace more detail.

  - **Few Corners** gives the resulting trace less detail.

 In some cases, these settings might cause the file size to become too large. Check the resulting file size before settling on the image.

Flash recommends the following settings for a decent looking trace:

- Color Threshold of 10

- Minimum Area of 1 pixel

- Curve Fit with Pixels

- Corner Threshold of Many Corners

A trace can only look as good as the original. If the quality of the bitmap is substandard, the trace will be too. Also certain bitmaps with a lot of detail or dark colors don't lend themselves to being traced. I've had much success tracing clip art objects with transparent backgrounds from stock photo collections. They come out looking very clean and almost not recognizable from the original bitmap (see Figure 9-16). This tracing uses the Flash recommended settings for tracing a bitmap.

Break Apart a Bitmap

Breaking apart a bitmap is another way to jazz up your art. When you break apart a bitmap, the selected picture becomes broken up into an editable object. These objects can be modified by filling them with color and applying transformations like scale, rotate, and skew. You also can make the bitmap the current color in the Color Options pop-up menu or in the Color Panel. With this option, you can actually fill any object using the broken apart bitmap as the color fill.

FIGURE 9-16   A bitmap from the PhotoDisc Object Series Collection looks impressive
when traced

To be able to paint with the broken apart bitmap, select the bitmap and choose
Modify | Break Apart. With the bitmap selected, the fill color option now reflects
the chosen bitmap. You can now fill objects with it. If you deselect the object and
want to use it as a fill again, select the Eyedropper in the Toobox. The Fill Color
option will change back to the selected bitmap that's been broken apart. Use this
technique to create mask-like effects with the Paintbrush, as shown in Figure 9-17,
or to fill objects with bitmap background effects such as clouds or a landscape.

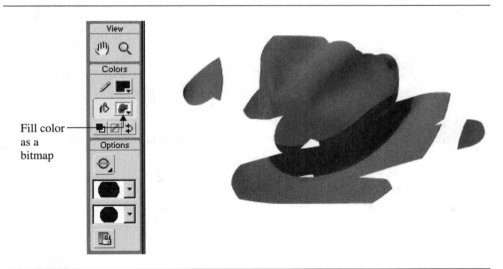

FIGURE 9-17   A paint brush with a broken apart image substituting for a color creates
a mask-like effect

To break apart a bitmap and modify the fill colors, select a bitmap on stage and choose Modify | Break Apart. In the Toolbox, select the Lasso tool. The Options portion of the Toolbox now displays the Magic Wand tool, Magic Wand properties, and the Polygon tool. The Magic Wand tool enables you to select an area within the image to modify its properties.

To customize the selected area, you can set the properties of the Magic Wand tool by clicking the Magic Wand Properties icon. This displays the Magic Wand Settings dialog box (see Figure 9-18). In this dialog you can set the Threshold and Smoothing.

- The Threshold can be set between 1 and 200 pixels. The Threshold number determines how close the colors have to be in hue to be included in the selection. A low setting indicates a more exact selection, picking only colors similar to the few pixels you have selected. A higher number gives you a broader and more diverse selection of pixels.

- The Smoothing options are Pixels, Rough, Normal, and Smooth. Pixels gives you a pretty rough edge selection. Smooth evens out the pixels on the edge of your selection. The middle selections of Rough and Normal fall somewhere in the middle in edge smoothness.

NOTE *Pictures with contrasting colors or broad areas of color are easier to select from.*

To use the Magic Wand, set the properties if needed. Then, click the Magic Wand icon and click the broken apart bitmap. Your selection is now editable with the Paint Bucket or the Transformation tools. To color the selected object, with the object selected, click the Paint Bucket. You can apply a fill or gradient as you would to any editable object in Flash.

To transform the object, click the part of the object you want to transform using the Magic Wand tool, then select it with the Arrow tool. The Transformation tools now become available in the Options portion of the Toolbox (see Figure 9-19). Move, scale, rotate, or skew the selection as you would any object in Flash.

You also can use the Transformation options by choosing Modify | Transform. This selection offers additional transformations such as flipping horizontally or vertically. Your third option is selecting the Transformation tools from the Transformation panel. Display the Transformation panel by choosing Window | Panels | Transform.

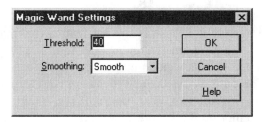

FIGURE 9-18   Click the Magic Wand Properties icon to display the Magic Wand
Settings dialog box

The Polygon icon enables you to custom an area by clicking from point-to-point until the first point meets the last. After your selection is complete, you can change the color or use the Transformation tools as with the Magic Wand selection.

9

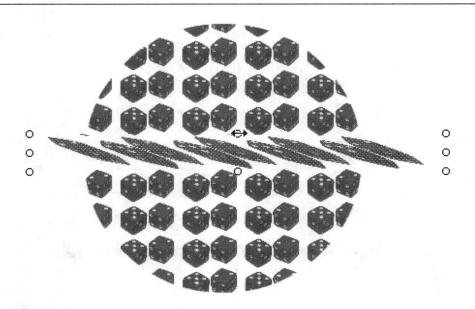

FIGURE 9-19   You can scale, rotate, or skew a broken apart bitmap with the
Transformation tools

Import and Assign Sounds

The ability to import sound into Flash is another feature that makes Flash a well-rounded-multimedia program. To understand sound in Flash, it's important to understand how sound works on a computer.

Sound on your computer is digital, and it exists in the form of a file that you can open and modify, just like any other program. The sound you hear from other sources, is analog. To modify the sound, you need a sound-editing program. Sound is depicted in the form of sound waves (see Figure 9-20). You can modify the properties of a sound wave in many ways: You can change the tempo, insert and delete tracks, delete part of the sound, re-mix it, and make many other changes.

Sound can be digitized from a number of sources including CDs, recordings, cassettes, or live audio. Many audio-editing programs are available on Windows and Mac platforms to enable you to make modifications to this digitized sound. On the Windows platform, there are programs such as Cool Edit 2001, Sonic Foundry, Cakewalk, and Goldwave to name a few. On the Mac there are Beatnik, Cakewalk, Cubase, mEdit, PEAK, and many more. Web sites such as askjeeves.com and zdnet.com offer a plethora of information on Windows and Mac audio-editing programs, including features, reviews, demo versions, and freeware editing programs.

Understand How Digital Sound Works

Digital sound is known as sampled sound. It's recorded by taking samples of a sound every fraction of a second and storing the sound in bits and bytes. The

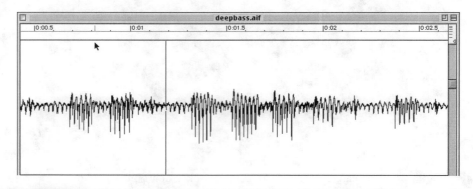

FIGURE 9-20   Sample of a sound wave from a digital sound

sample rate indicates the number of times the samples are stored, and the sample size is information stored on the sound. A high sample rate and sample size equates to better sound resolution. Sample frequencies are measured in hertz (Hz) or kilohertz (kHz).

The most common frequency settings are

- **44.1 kHz**—This produces the cleanest sample and is the standard CD quality.

- **22.05 kHz**—Usually a good choice for music for the Web. Produces acceptable quality.

- **11.025 kHz**—This is voice quality or AM radio quality.

The bit resolution is the number of bits used to describe a sound sample. An 8-bit sample size uses 256 units of data to describe the current sound level. A 16-bit sample size uses approximately 65,000 units of data to describe the current sound. The higher the bit rate, the clearer the sound and the larger the file. Stereo sound makes for file sizes twice the size of the original.

The formula for determining the final bite size of a stereo recording is

```
rate sample x recording x (bit resolution ÷ 8) x 2 = sample size
```

The formula for determining the final bite size of a mono recording is identical to that of stereo, only it is multiplied by 1 because it has a single audio track.

Because this formula might seem a little obscure, the following are some sample rates that will give you a better idea of how frequency, resolution, and length of recording work in conjunction with one another and what kind of results they yield:

- A 60-second sound with a 44.1 kHz sample rate that's 16-bit stereo is 10.5 MB in size. This produces superior quality sound. The same file in mono and in 8-bit is approximately half the size.

- A 60-second sound with a 22.1 kHz sample rate that's 16-bit stereo is 5.25 MB in size. This produces average quality sound, but the size is large. The same file in mono is approximately half the size.

9

■ A 60-second sound with a 22.1 kHz sample rate that's 8-bit mono is 1.3 MB in size. This is probably the best bet for the Web in terms of balancing quality with file size.

■ A 60 second sound with a 11 kHz sample rate that's 8-bit stereo will be 1.3 MB in size, so low, stereo is barely recognizable. Good for voice recordings on Web, the mono version of this equation is approximately half the size.

The trick to keeping the file size down while not sacrificing too much quality is to sample the sound as a loop. *Looping* a sound means you extract a tiny piece of a sound and visually match the beginning of the sound wave to the end of the sound wave so when it plays back it sounds like one continuous sound. You can program the looping of a sound in Flash too. In fact, looping is an action in Flash that's automatic. You have to tell Flash how, when, the number of times, or on what event you want the sound to loop, or if you want it to loop at all. Assigning sound to buttons and movie clips is discussed in Chapter 13, and controlling sounds with ActionScript is discussed in Chapter 14.

Import a Sound File

When sound is imported into Flash, just like a picture file, it must be compressed and saved in a format that's recognizable to Flash. The following sound file formats can be imported into Flash:

■ **AIFF (.aif)**—This format is the standard Mac sound format. Windows with QuickTime 4 can read AIFF files.

■ **WAV (.wav)**—This format is the standard sound format for Windows. Macs with QuickTime 4 can read WAV files.

■ **MP3 (.mp3)**—MP3 format is becoming an increasingly popular file format because of its impressive compression capabilities. It can reduce the size of an audio file considerably and still retain good sound quality. It is both Mac and Windows compatible.

The following file formats can be imported into Flash with QuickTime 4 or higher installed on your system:

■ Sound Designer II (Mac)

■ Sound Only QuickTime Movies (Windows and Mac)

■ Sun AU (Mac)

■ System 7 Sounds (Mac)

■ WAV (Windows and Mac)

Importing a sound into a Flash file is as easy as importing a graphic. From the main menu choose File | Import to display the Import dialog box. Navigate to the sound file and click it. Click Open in Windows or click Import on the Mac. Nothing appears on your stage because you're importing a sound. Although digital sound is represented graphically as sound waves, Flash does not depict the sound this way on the stage. Rather, it is displayed as a sound wave in the Timeline and in the Library.

Imported sound is stored in the Library. To see the sound you import, choose Window | Library. Sound is depicted with a loudspeaker icon. When you click on a sound in the Library, the graphical representation of the sound wave is shown in the top of the Library, as shown in Figure 9-21. Sample the sound by clicking the control arrow in the top right of the sound wave. Stop the sound by clicking the square stop button.

9

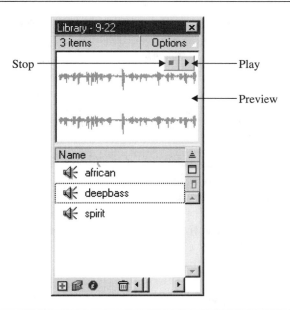

FIGURE 9-21   Imported sound is stored in the Library in Flash; sample the sound by clicking the arrow button in the upper right corner of the sound wave

Export a Sound File

To edit the properties of a sound, you need to access the Sound Properties dialog box. Do this in one of several ways: Double-click the Sound icon in the Library, or right-click/OPT-click to access the options selectable for this object. Select Properties to display the Sound Properties dialog box. This box enables you to compress or re-compress your sound in another format. For example, if you've imported a WAV file and want to re-compress it in an MP3 format to get the size down, this is the dialog box where you make it happen. You also can change a sound and test the quality results of several different compression ratios.

Figure 9-22 shows the Sound Properties dialog box displayed on a sound residing in the Library named "african". This box is used to specify the sound's export settings. The name of the sound file appears on the top of the dialog box. Under the name, the file path, date, and specs on the sound file in its current state are displayed. In this case, the file named "african" has a sample rate of 22 kHz, stereo, a bit depth of 16, and its duration in seconds is 2.3 seconds. The size of this audio file is 203.8 kb, which is pretty sizable for 2 seconds of an audio clip. In the Compression box, you can experiment with different compression formats and ratios. Test the results by clicking the Test button.

> **TIP**   *You also can set export settings for sound in the Publish Settings dialog box, which is discussed in Chapter 16. If you didn't select export settings in the Sound Properties dialog box, you can assign export settings to sounds in the Publish dialog box. You also can ignore the export settings in the Sound Properties dialog box. Do this by selecting Override. Use Override if you want to retain two sets of files to be used for different purposes, with different audio export settings.*

The Compression pop-up menu offers the following compression formats: MP3, ADPCM, and Raw. When you select from one of these three compression formats, additional menu selections become available relating to the format you selected. If you select MP3 as your compression, you can also set the Bit Rate and Quality of the sound file from pop-up menus to the right of the selection. The Bit Rates range from 8 kbps (kilobytes per second) on the low end of the sound spectrum to 160 kbps on the high end. From Quality, you can select Fast, Medium or Best. Fast Quality is smaller in size than Best Quality. When you select different bit rates, the resulting file information appears underneath the Quality setting. Experiment with different settings by clicking the Test button in this dialog box. Notice the difference in sound quality between a file with a bit rate of 8 versus a file with a bit rate of 48 kbps.

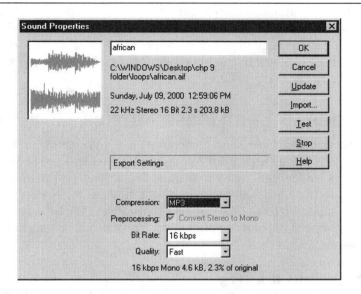

FIGURE 9-22   In the Sound Properties dialog box, you can set the sound compression ratio, test the sound, update it, and change it all together

If you select Adaptive Differential Pulse-Code Modulation (ADPCM) as your compression, you can Select a Sample Rate from the pop-up menu that gives you a range from 5 kHz–44 kHz. You also can select ADPCM Bits in a pop-up menu from the 2–4. Mono or stereo settings can be checked also. It is commonly used in voice technologies and digital phone networks. It compresses well (although not as well as MP3) and as such is a viable choice for keeping file sizes on the low side. This compression format was the default setting on older versions of Flash and is useful for short sounds you might use on button events.

Raw enables you to export uncompressed sound. With Raw compression selected, you can change the sample rate from 5 kHz–44 kHz as well as choose mono or stereo setting. Raw audio offers big file sizes and lossless compression. This wouldn't be an option you would choose for movies being put up on the Web. There might be some special circumstance where you might need to use this format. As a general rule for beginners and intermediate Flash users, just ignore it.

NOTE *MP3 sound requires the Flash Player version 4 and above to be heard.*

Use the Import button to assign another sound to the currently selected one. The currently selected sound will become the newly selected sound. This is a useful technique if you need to globally update instances of sound. Select Update if a sound has been changed in another program. Click Update, and the sound will automatically update.

Assign Sounds to Your Flash Movies

You've probably noticed that Flash technology on the Web is chock full of sounds these days. With the new MP3 compression standard and streaming capabilities, it's made sound easier to use and to hear on the Web than ever before. Getting sound from its original source into your movie is pretty easy to do.

Once you import your sounds, they become stored in the Library. To make the sound work, you need to put it in your movie. You can add sounds to layers, buttons, and movie clips.

Add a Sound to a Layer

Assigning a sound to a layer is simple. Sounds can be added to more than one layer too. You can use layers as if they were separate sound channels. To add sound to a layer, select a keyframe or frames on this layer. Click a sound in the Library and drag the sound to the stage. The sound wave appears in the frames on the layer. If you test the movie at this point, the sound loops once. You can modify the properties of the selected sound and sync the sound to the frames in the movie using the Sound panel. Going back to the stage, select the sound wave on the layer and display the Sound panel by choosing Modify | Panels | Sound, as shown in Figure 9-23. The Sound panel enables you to do minimal editing on the selected

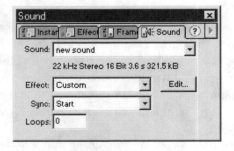

FIGURE 9-23   Use the Sound panel to loop, sync, and edit a selected sound to your movie

sound. It's convenient to be able to do this, especially if you don't have access to an audio-editing program.

At the top of the Sound panel is the name of the selected sound. Under the name, details about the sound are listed: the sample and bit rate, length of the sound in seconds, and the size of the file. The additional settings are available in the Sound panel:

- **Effect**—Use Effects apply different sound effects to your sound. From the pop-up menu you can choose effects from the following:

    - **None**—This is the default for no application of effects. It also removes previously applied effects.

    - **Left Channel and Right Channel**—Use one of these options to play in one of the selected channels.

    - **Fade Left to Right or Fade Right to Left**—Use one of these options to fade a sound from one channel to another.

    - **Fade In or Fade Out**—Select one of these options to gradually fade in or out the loudness of a sound.

    - **Custom**—The Custom selection displays the Edit Envelope dialog box as shown in Figure 9-24. You can customize your effect with this box.

- **Sync**—The Sync option synchronizes sound to the movie. The options are as follows:

    - **Event**—When you sync on an event, the sound will synchronize to an event that elicits an action. For example, a sound might play on a layer when a button is clicked or moused over.

    - **Start**—A sound with a start and stop sync starts playing when the movie loads.

    - **Stop**—Select Stop if you don't want the sound not to play when the movie loads. Use this if you want the sound to play on an event.

    - **Stream**—This option makes sound keep up with the animation in the movie, so the sound doesn't fall out of sync with the animation. The number of frames determines the length of a streaming sound. MP3 sounds synchronized for streaming must be recompressed in the Sound Properties dialog box.

9

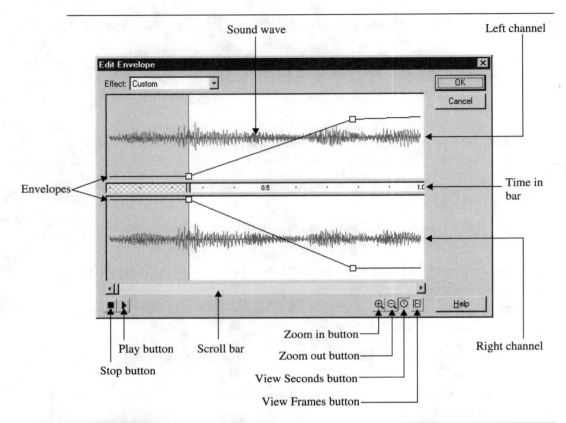

Sound wave

Left channel

Envelopes

Time in bar

Play button

Scroll bar

Stop button

Zoom in button

Zoom out button

Right channel

View Seconds button

View Frames button

FIGURE 9-24 The Edit Envelope dialog box displays automatically when Custom is selected as an effect; click the Edit button to access it on other effects

- **Loops**—Loops indicate how many times a sound will repeat a play action. If you want the sound to play throughout an animation, enter a number larger than the duration time of the animation. Looping doesn't work well with streaming sounds. When a sound is streamed, frames are added to the movie to keep up with the animation. Looping can conflict with streaming because each time the sound loops, the file size increases unnecessarily. Type in a number for the number of times you want the sound to loop.

Use the Edit Envelope Dialog Box

The Edit Envelope dialog box becomes available when you select Custom from the Effect selection in the Sound panel (refer to Figure 9-24). This dialog box enables you to further customize the predefined effects. In fact, if you select an effect like Stop; Start; Fade Right to Left; or Left to Right, and then click the Edit button, the Edit Envelope will graphically display the results of that effect. If you alter the sound envelope on a predefined effect, when you click OK, the effect returns to Custom because you've now created a new effect.

The Edit Envelope dialog box displays the selected effect in the top left of the box. This is your starting ground for modifying the sound. The sound waves are displayed one on top of another, the top representing the Left Channel and the bottom representing the Right Channel. The Envelope Handles are the little squares attached to the Envelope lines. Click and drag these square handles to change the way a sound comes in and goes out. Add handles to the envelope by clicking anywhere on the envelope line. Notice when you add a handle, a mirror handle appears in the other channel. When you drag up and down on a handle, this action is not mirrored in the other channel. However, horizontal dragging of the handle is reflected on both channels.

In between the left and right channels are the Time In and Time Out controls. This enables you to control where sound starts and stops. If you want to loop the sound and need to tweek In and Out points, you can do it with these tools. To use the Time In and Out Controls, click and drag them to the new points where you want the sound to begin and end. Toggle between Frames and Seconds in the bottom-right corner of the window to help select your In and Out points.

In the bottom right of the box, you can select the Zoom In and Out icons to magnify the sound waves for pinpoint precision when setting the options in this box. The bottom of the box offers a scroll bar so if the magnified sound wave exceeds the size of the box, you can scroll left and right. The bottom left of the box offers sound controls to test the state of the current sound. Use this to experiment with envelope settings and test them.

Access a Sound from the Sound Library and Link a Sound

Flash comes with a large selection of sounds located in the Common Library. The sounds in this Library are small, short, and are perfect for attaching to buttons on mouse events. To display these sounds, choose Window | Common Libraries | Sounds. The Sound panel displays. These sounds are stored permanently in the Flash application folder. Common Library sounds have the same properties as the sounds you import. You can change the properties of these sounds in the Sound Properties dialog box and in the Sound panel.

9

You also can link sounds in the Library to another movie. Do this by assigning linkage properties. Select the sound you want to link from the Library. From the Options pop-up menu, select Linkage. The Symbol Linkage dialog box appears. Type in an Identifier name and click Export This Symbol. Now this sound can be used in a Shared Library or on a Sound Action. Select File | Open as Shared Library to share sounds from one Library to another. Share a Library on the Web from one movie to another by posting the Library on the Web. When a sound is linked, the sound resides outside the file. A movie calls the Shared Library posted on the Web to find the sound. The Identifier names the linked sound. Identifiers also are used to identify a sound when adding Sound actions.

Add Sound to Button and Movie Clip Symbols

Sounds can not only be added to layers, they also can be added to buttons and movie clips in Symbol Editing mode. When you add a sound to a button, you add it in the Button Editing mode (see Figure 9-25). Buttons are created on their own custom Timeline. Sound for buttons are placed on a separate layer from the button layer.

Button sounds are usually short because they often serve as button events. For example, when you click a mouse, which would signify an event, you might have a short sound happen. You also can add a sound to a button on mouse over. When a user drags his mouse over a button, it could make a sound. Sounds from the Common Library are often used on button states. Attaching sounds to buttons is discussed in detail in Chapter 13.

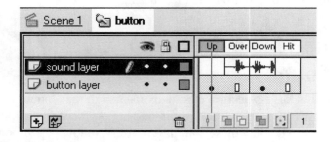

FIGURE 9-25   Add sound to button states on a separate layer

Movie clip symbols run independently on their own Timeline (see Figure 9-26). Sounds can be added to movie clips on their own layer in the movie clip Editing mode the same way they're added to the main Timeline. Sounds are added to movie clip layers the same way they are added to a layer in the main Timeline.

Sounds on movie clips can be controlled with actions. For example, you could have a button that when pressed, stop a movie clip with a sound attached to it. Another button could start the sound in the movie clip when pressed. Flash is so versatile when it comes to movie clips, there is no end to what you can do with sounds in movie clips. Using sounds in movie clips is discussed further in Chapter 13.

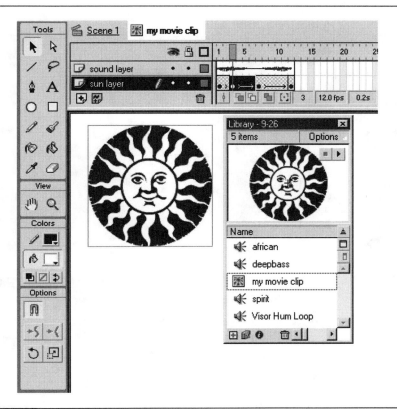

9

FIGURE 9-26   Sound is added to a layer in the Movie Clip Editing mode the same way it's added in the main Timeline

Part III

Flash Animation Techniques

Chapter 10

Learn the Basics of Flash Animation

How to...

- Think Like an Animator
- Plan Your Movie
- Animate on Different Time Sequences
- Animate on Different Layers
- Make Keyframes
- Create Frame-by-Frame Animations
- Test Your Animation
- Set Onion Skins

Animation is a major feature of the Flash authoring environment, and Flash animation is a feast for the eyes. It engages the audience in a way that static graphics just can't do. Years ago, animation was created on stand-alone systems with proprietary software. The kind of animation you can now make in Flash was an enigma back then, only seen on TV and in movies. Animators were highly skilled technicians who had both the technical expertise and artistic know-how to conceptualize linear animation. The last decade brought professional animation and video editing capabilities to the desktop, an achievement we never thought possible ten years ago. With computers getting bigger and better every day, animation is no longer the mystery it used to be. Animation is accessible to you on your desktop, and it's relatively easy to create in Flash.

Think Like an Animator

Animation in its most simplistic terms is graphics in motion. To understand the way an animator thinks, let's consider animation in its most primitive state.

First, let's consider flip books. You've probably seen a flip book, where each page in the book represents a slight movement or change, so that when the book is flipped quickly, the elements on the page appear in motion. Then remember the old animated Disney movies. Armies of artists were recruited to create hand-drawn, individually rendered frames. Artists would create keyframes where major shifts in movement occurred within the animation and then sculpt the rest of the secondary frames around them. The in-between frames were the interpolation of movement between one keyframe to another. This is where the term "tween" comes from, referring to the frames "in between" the keyframes of the animation.

With this old technique, a substantial number of frames needed to be hand-rendered to create the illusion of fluid movement. Thirty seconds of animation might require up to 700 frames. As you can imagine, this required a large staff and a lot of time. Tricks were devised to make hand-drawn animation a little more streamlined. Animators painted their animation on cells, the transparent celluloid sheets used to render each frame. Because cells were transparent, parts of the cell animation that didn't change over a span of frames, could be reused by placing them over or under new cells, thus creating a layer effect. This way, the artist didn't have to duplicate drawings in other cells.

You've probably noticed in old animations where a character may be running against a backdrop of some sort, like mountains or a field. If you've ever examined the animation closely, you would notice that the background loops and repeats itself at some point. It's the same moving backdrop being repeated again and again to create the illusion of a running character.

Computer animation today is more streamlined than the hand-drawn animation of yesterday, but many of the basic rules still apply. Animators always strive for consistency in their animation as well as economizing on visual elements just like in the old days of animation, when the cell technique was used.

Flash offers many ways in which you can economize on the creation of objects. Not only can you reuse parts of already drawn objects with symbols from the library, you also can automatically create the "in between" frames of an animation using tweening animation, which is discussed further in the next chapter. In addition, Flash has layers, which in ways could be viewed as a modern day equivalent to cell animation.

Understand Animation in Relation to Static Graphic Design

Animation is a species apart from static graphics. Static graphics broadcast a message unto themselves. Animated movies combine the passing of time in a limited, linear space to relay the message. Both static and motion graphics need to be designed, but the thought process and method are different. Images displayed in the passing of time create a rhythm regardless of whether sound is added. The frames in an animation can have a beat that can be measured by controlling the delivery time of your frames, much the same way a composer measures the beat of a song. A rock-and-roll, jazz, or Latin beat is measured in four beats to a measure.

In Flash, the frame rate is 12 frames per second. The frame rate can be altered or duplicate images can span more than one frame to redefine the rhythm and mood of the movie. By nature, motion graphics are more entertaining than static graphics, increasing their ability to deliver a subliminal message. People will stare at something moving much longer than a printed piece because they don't have to work as hard as with a printed piece. Hypnotic in its methods, moving graphics can have more impact than print if presented in an engaging way. Motion is a universal language that everyone understands.

Plan Your Movie Before You Begin

It's easy to animate in Flash, but it's not always easy to create a successful animation. It's all too easy for a new animator to create a movie that quickly becomes confusing, busy, or noisy. What's more, professional animators don't become professionals overnight. On large projects, just like in the days of the old Disney movies, professionals work in large teams on a project, the less experienced animators acting as protégés to their more seasoned counterparts.

You don't have to create a full-length feature animation to make a Flash movie. Your animation may last just a few seconds, bringing the viewer to a static page. The beauty of Flash animation is that it can be used for small or large movies, games, e-commerce, or just to add accent to a simple Web page. On either end of the spectrum, you must think like an animator to create a successful animation.

Whether a movie is small or large, video or animation, movies of any sort are generally born in storyboard form, often in conjunction with a written script. Storyboards are much like the cells of a cartoon strip, depicting key movements in the animation sequence and indicating the planned length of time and the mood of the animation. They can be presented to your client on the computer, in print, or both.

Storyboards can be sketched in thumbnail form by hand on any surface, or created on the computer in a drawing program. Designers with a print background often use their favorite drawing program to render storyboard concepts, as shown in Figure 10-1. Because drawing programs are vector-based, revisions and additions are easy to make, and clients are notorious for revising projects at the last minute.

Two of the most widely used drawing programs on both Mac and PC platforms, Macromedia FreeHand and Adobe Illustrator, make it easy to export whole storyboards (or parts of a storyboard) into Flash. FreeHand 9 (and 8) and Illustrator 9 have addressed the need for artists to realize keyframes of their Flash movie on paper before it ever gets to Flash. Both programs enable you to export images and layers into the Flash native format, so art created in these programs can be incorporated into your movie. Because Flash and FreeHand are marketed as a team, FreeHand is even more "Flash-friendly" for making storyboards. When exporting from FreeHand in an SWF format, the Export dialog box offers a Settings button that takes you to a Special Flash Export dialog box (see Figure 10-2).

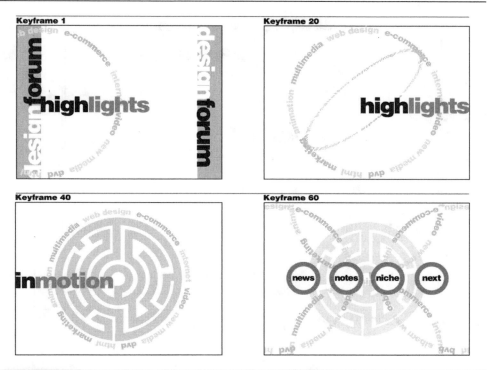

FIGURE 10-1   Storyboard frames rendered in Adobe Illustrator

In this box you can translate pages from FreeHand into layers or frames in Flash, or FreeHand layers into Flash layers. There are many other selections in this box that assist your FreeHand file in blending smoothly into the Flash movie. In addition, when you import a FH file (the FreeHand native file format) into Flash, a FreeHand Import dialog box appears, enabling you to customize your import (see Figure 10-3). Flash assists FreeHand users by offering a streamlined conversion to Flash.

Still other artists may choose to create their storyboards in Flash, because Flash also possesses many drawing features. There are two reasons why Flash authors may choose to render in a program like FreeHand instead. First, some artists are more comfortable with the interface of their favorite drawing program. Second, if additional support pieces are part of a project, like printed material or logos, drawing programs are inherently more print friendly than Flash.

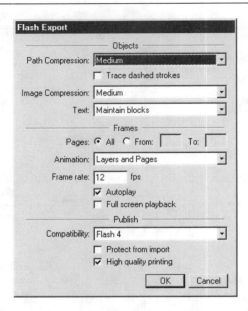

FIGURE 10-2   FreeHand offers a special Flash Export dialog box for SWF file formats being exported to Flash

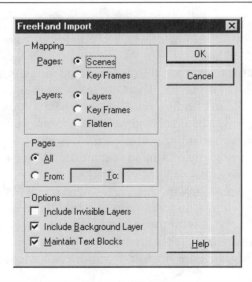

FIGURE 10-3   Flash offers a FreeHand Import dialog box for FreeHand files being imported into Flash

Ultimately, the method you choose to create storyboards is purely subjective and up to the individual.

TIP *If you're planning on importing art from a drawing program into Flash, make certain the document size in the drawing program is reflected in the Movie Properties dialog box of Flash. The latest versions of FreeHand and Illustrator enable you to measure your page in pixels and the Flash measurement system includes inches and picas. If publishing to the Web or multimedia, it's best to measure in pixels, because the measurement system on the Web is pixels.*

Animate on Different Time Sequences

Our ability to maintain and hold a moving object in our vision's brain for a few moments is a quirk of the human makeup. Animation deceives the human eye with the illusion of movement by projecting a series of progressive frames with the passing of time. Video, which is also a series of still pictures, builds 30 entire frames or pictures every second. The images appearing to blend smoothly into movement are based on the speed with which each frame is replaced by the next one in the sequence. Filmed movies are typically shot at a shutter rate of 24 frames per second (fps), creating the illusion of seamless movement to the eye. The ratio for film is then doubled because the flicker rate gives the illusion of doubling the fps . The flicker rate is light being flashed two times through the shutter of the projector.

The default frame rate for Flash animation is 12 fps, about half that for a movie. A small Flash animation can appear pretty smooth in its blending from frame to frame on the Web at 12 fps if your intention was to make the animation appear smooth. You can adjust the frame rate in Flash if you want to slow down or speed up your animation. The frame rate you set is global throughout the Flash movie. There are tricks you can use to give the illusion of slowing down or speeding certain frames in the animation sequence up like adding extra frames or easing in or out on tweening. These methods are covered in the next chapter.

There are two ways to change the frame rate in Flash. Select Modify | Movie from the menu. In the Movie Properties dialog box, highlight the frame rate and type a new rate (see Figure 10-4). You also can double-click the Frame Rate at the bottom of the timeline to access the Movie Properties dialog box. Changing the frame rate should be done with caution if your file is being published to the Web. Your cyberspace audience uses a melange of different configurations, including old, slow, and fast modems and processors. Not everyone will be able to view

10

the new frame rate the way you intended it to look. If you do intend to change the frame rate setting for a movie to be published on the Web, it's not a bad idea to test the movie on a wide range of configurations and browsers after it's put up, to eliminate the prospect of undesirable results.

Animate on Different Layers

Layers are an integral part of moving graphics. If you were directing a real-world movie on a stage, there could be many scenes going on simultaneously. For example, say you were shooting a scene where two people were talking against a bustling city landscape and the conversation they were engaged in was the main focus of the scene. The layers of events occurring simultaneously create a rhythm that balances the main focus of the movie. In effect, the background events, although subliminal to the viewer, augment the two people talking.

Our perceptions of the real world tell us that movement and events occur in the passing of time, as well as simultaneously. Film and video have a sense of real-world spatial relationship on a two-dimensional plane. The equivalent of the real-world spatial relationship in Flash is layers. Layers enable you to have more than one object moving behind and/or in front of one another simultaneously. Layers give a kind of stacking order to animation.

In the previous section, "Think Like an Animator," we discussed the cell sheets used in hand-drawn animation. Because cells were transparent, to save time, certain cells were reused in places where the elements were identical. Flash uses this same concept of a cell as a layer. Layers not only act as a stacking order to

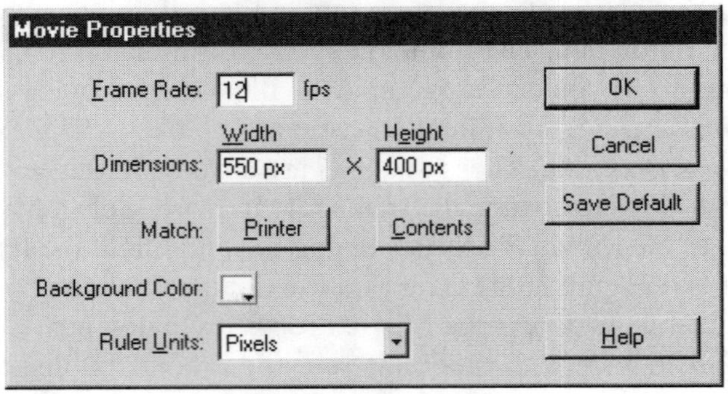

FIGURE 10-4   Change the frame rate of the movie in the Movie Properties dialog box

other layers, they also can extend objects or backgrounds on a layer in linear time to display one layer while something else is going on in another layer.

Let's examine the previous example where a movie was being created with two people chatting against a bustling city backdrop. If this were a Flash animation, the moving cars in the background could continue looping on one layer, and a moving crowd in the background could coexist on another layer while the main scene was running. The ability to layer your animation expands your creative possibilities.

Layers also are useful when making movie clips. Movie clips are reusable symbols that run independently on their own timeline. Flash is so compact, you can have movie clips with their own self-contained layers and frames running on different layers in the main timeline. This allows for endless creative possibilities.

Complex animations in Flash usually have more than one layer. It's not uncommon to create a movie with 35–40 layers or more. A monstrous project requires extensive organization up front to ensure success. Naming layers in a logical manner in the preplanning stage is important too. Like members of a cast, all the elements of your Flash movie should know their place and purpose before production begins (see Figure 10-5).

Layers in Flash default consecutively to the names "Layer 1, Layer 2," and so on. To name a layer, click and drag over the layer name and type the new name. Change the stacking order of the layer by clicking the layer and dragging the layer up or down in the layer row.

Create a new layer by clicking the Insert Layer icon at the bottom of Layer section of the Timeline. Delete a layer by selecting the layer and clicking the Trash icon at the bottom of the Layer section.

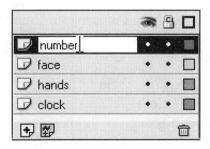

FIGURE 10-5 Name the layers on a timeline by selecting the layer name and typing a new name

Layers are one of the main ingredients in creating basic animation. Beginners often make the mistake of relying on a single layer to do most of their animation. Just like in traditional animation, it's easier to delete a cell, or in this case a layer, than it is to trash a file because it wasn't planned out properly. The other problem you could run into in a one-layer animation is objects erasing one another or connecting when you didn't intend them to. Making use of multiple layers for objects and backdrops is a wise design decision.

Frames in Animation

If layers are a cart, frames are the wheels that make the cart move. Frames reside on layers in the Timeline, and this is where your animation comes alive. There are two major types of frames used to create an animation; the keyframe and the frame. Keyframes indicate key moments in your animation, where the properties of an object change. Keyframes are depicted with black circles in the frame placeholder boxes on the timeline. Frames are a duplicate of the previous keyframe (see Figure 10-6) and are depicted as gray boxes that reside in the placeholder boxes on the Timeline. There are also blank frames and blank keyframes, both of which are used to display a blank frame. For example, if you wanted an object to appear and disappear in a frame sequence, you may use a blank keyframe to do so. There are other variations on frames used when you create a tweening animation, which are discussed in Chapter 11.

Use the Timeline to Add Keyframes

Although a static graphic can call the Timeline its home, timelines are designed to accommodate all facets of animation. Keyframes and frames on selected layers occupy frame placeholders in the Timeline, as depicted in Figure 10-6. Frame numbers depicted in increments of five above the layers act as a time ruler for your frames. Manually play back the animation (or scrub through) by clicking and dragging on the Playhead. Because it's hard to tell which frame your Playhead is sitting on, the current frame is indicated at the bottom of the Timeline too. Because timelines become the framework of your animation structure, it's important to have a well planned out Timeline.

Frame-by-Frame Animation

When learning animation, it's important to understand frame-by-frame animation. Frame-by-frame animation relies on keyframes to indicate changes in the animation sequence. The change in the frame can include a different image or

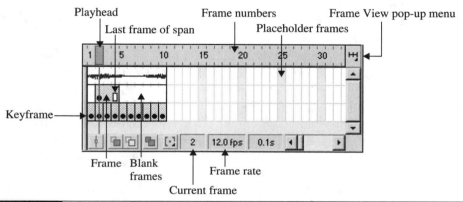

FIGURE 10-6   A Timeline with frames on Layer 1 and keyframes on Layer 2

the same image with the properties of the image changed. This change in frames is known as a "keyframe."

Create a frame-by-frame animation on a new layer by selecting a frame in the layer and drawing the object you want to animate. A keyframe indicated by a black circle will be generated in the first frame of the layer you selected. Create the next frame of the layer by clicking the blank placeholder frame to the right of the keyframe and selecting Insert | Keyframe (F6) from the menu. After the keyframe is created, draw another image. Note that when you select the placeholder frame to the right, the image on the previous keyframe disappears. When you insert another keyframe, it reappears. There must be a keyframe or a frame in a frame placeholder to see the contents of the previous frame.

Continue the process of inserting as many keyframes as is sufficient for your frame-by-frame animation. All keyframes will be duplicates of the previous frame. You can either alter the contents of each frame right after creating each individual keyframe or after you've created a series of identical keyframes. To alter an element in a particular keyframe, click on that keyframe, and change the properties of the element. Properties include, but are not limited to, X and Y position, scale, skew, color, transparency, or a combination of these elements. You can alter each keyframe whenever and as often as you like, each time resulting in a modification of that frame in the animation sequence. The end of an animation sequence is indicated with a white rectangle.

10

TIP *When you import a graphic into Flash, a new layer is created, regardless of whether you want the import to appear on a new layer. If you're importing a graphic that's in an SWF file format, layers created in the other program can be recognized in Flash if the proper settings are selected on import.*

Figure 10-7 depicts a frame-by-frame animation of a clock. On each keyframe, the hand of the clock moves clockwise to the next point on the clock. The clock face, hands, and numbers are all on separate layers. The clock hand is created with an arrowhead line whose center was moved to the bottom of the line (Modify | Transform | Edit Center). A line traditionally will be referenced from the center of the line. In this case, the line around the clock representing the hand of the clock would twirl from the center like a baton, instead of from the end point. Changing the center of the arrowhead line enables you to create this kind of frame-by-frame animation effect where a clock appears to be ticking.

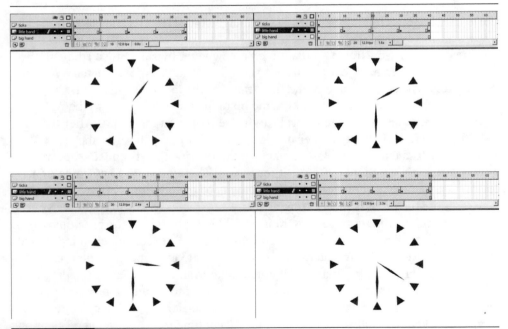

FIGURE 10-7   A few sample frames from an animation of a clock demonstrate the concept of frame-by-frame animation

The importance of layers becomes obvious when creating a frame-by-frame animation. If you have more than one object on a layer but you only want to animate one of the objects, each time you select a keyframe, all objects on the layer become selected, even if this was not your intention. You must deselect all other objects to animate the one object. This is easy if you're only animating a few frames. If there are a lot of frames, it becomes confusing and inaccurate to have to deselect all items on each frame to alter the properties of one object. Consequently, making use of layers to draw different parts of your animation becomes very important to avert a potentially disastrous animation.

To delete a keyframe, click a keyframe to select it. From the menu, select Insert | Clear Keyframe (SHIFT+F6). If the keyframe is in between several frames, this will remove the keyframe and connect the previous frames with the remaining frames, making the animation continuous.

To move an individual keyframe to another place in the timeline, select the keyframe and drag it to its new location. To move a set of keyframes, hold down the SHIFT key while clicking each keyframe. This creates a movable frameset. Drag the selected set to its new location on the Timeline. You also can move an individual keyframe and a frameset to a new layer by dragging them onto the desired layer.

Frame-by-frame animation is relatively easy once you get the feel for it, and it serves as a great technique for animations where rhythm is emphasized.

Insert In-Between Frames in a Frame-by-Frame Animation

Not every frame has to be a keyframe in a frame-by-frame animation. You can insert regular frames next to the keyframes to extend the length of time a keyframe is displayed in an animation. Because changing the frames per second in the movie alters the entire timeline, this enables you to change the length of time on individual elements. To insert a frame in between two keyframes, select the first keyframe and from the menu, select Insert | Frame (F5). A gray rectangle appears in the frame placeholder, representing a regular frame, as shown in Figure 10-8. To add more frames, repeat the process. Adding more frames extends the animation time of the keyframe to the left even more. If your movie is 12 fps and you add 11 frames to the keyframe to bring the frame count to 12 in the Timeline, theoretically, this set of frames will last for one second. In animation time, one second is a considerable amount of time, and you don't always want your animation to move fast. The ability to control the display of frames over time gives the artist more creative flexibility on Flash.

10

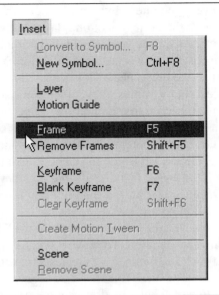

FIGURE 10-8 Insert a frame by selecting Insert | Frame (F5) from the menu

To delete a frame, click on an individual frame while holding down the CTRL/CMD key to select it. From the menu select Insert | Remove Frames (SHIFT+F5).

To move an individual frame to another place in the timeline, select the frame while holding down the CTRL/CMD key, and drag it to its new location. To move a set of frames, hold down the SHIFT+CTRL/SHIFT+CMD key while clicking the frames you want to move. This creates a movable frameset. Drag the selected set to its new location on the timeline. You also can move an individual frame or a frameset to a new layer by dragging it onto the desired layer. Move an already created frameset by clicking the frameset and dragging it to its new position.

Copy and paste frames onto another layer or on the same layer in a different frameset by holding down the SHIFT+CTRL/SHIFT+CMD key to select a frameset. Select Edit | Copy Frames or CTRL+ALT+C/OPTION+CMD+C from the menu. Click the starting frame in the new location. Select Edit | Paste Frames or CTRL+ALT+V/OPTION+CMD+V from the menu. A copy of the frames will now reside in the new frames. Frames also can be cut from their location and pasted into a new location using the same method, by selecting Cut instead of Paste from the Edit menu. Selecting Cut or Copy places a copy in the Clipboard, so multiple copies of the frameset can be pasted in the Timeline if so desired.

The properties of frames also can be altered by right-/CTRL-clicking the frame(s) to display the pop-up Context menu (see Figure 10-9). The options available are the same as in the Insert and Edit menus. You can Insert and Remove Frames and Keyframes, Cut and Copy Frames, Select All, and display the Actions Window and the Frame and Sound Panels quickly by using this method.

Test Your Movie

Previewing a static graphic in a paint or drawing program is a lot easier than previewing a motion graphic. With static art, you only need to look at what's on your screen. Graphics with motion are a different story. To test it, you have to periodically preview it while it's moving. Unless you're psychic, it's impossible to know exactly how long objects should play and when other objects should be introduced on the stage, and animation involves a lot of tweaking before it reaches the ultimate state of perfection. Flash offers many ways to preview your animation, all of which are outlined here.

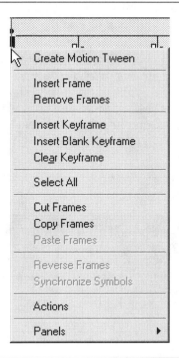

FIGURE 10-9   Right-clicking/CTRL-clicking on frames displays the pop-up Context menu, which offers yet another way to modify frames

10

The quickest way to test your animation is either by manually scrubbing the frames with the Playhead in the Timeline, or by selecting Window | Toolbars | Controller from the menu (Figure 10-10). In Windows, the Controller window can either float independently or dock on the bottom of the toolbar or under the menu. On the Mac, display the Controller by selecting Window | Controller from the menu. The Controller window is used to play back, rewind, and scrub through your animation on the Flash stage. To rewind your animation, press the second button. To play the animation, press the fourth button.

The movie also can be tested as a Flash Player file format (SWF) by selecting Control | Test Movie or CTRL+ENTER/CMD+ENTER. This method creates and displays an SWF file of the movie. The SWF file will be saved in the same folder as your movie. Test the movie as an SWF file when you need to get a better idea of how the movie will appear in its finished state. Sometimes the SWF version will look different from what you expected. One example may be a rectangle used as a background that is intended to bleed off the stage. It may appear as if it bleeds on the Flash stage. However, when you view it as an SWF file, the background may appear chopped off. In a case like this, previewing the SWF file will give you a better idea of what the movie will look like on the Web as opposed to only testing the movie in Flash. A Flash Player (SWF) version of the movie also can be generated by selecting File | Publish Preview | Flash.

You also may want to get an idea of what your movie would look like in a browser. To do this, select File | Publish Preview | HTML. This will generate and embed your SWF file in an HTML page as well as give you an instant preview of the file. This is a wonderful feature because it shows you exactly what your movie looks like when embedded in an HTML document on the particular browser and

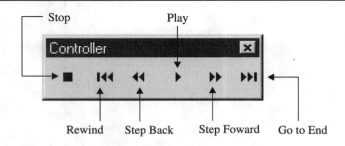

FIGURE 10-10   The Controller enables you to test the playback of your animation in Flash

platform. Flash automatically generates an HTML page and an SWF file, and names them and embeds the SWF file in the HTML page. Both files are automatically saved in the folder that holds the Flash movie you're previewing.

When you preview an animated file, the default action is a looping action. This means the animation plays until you close the file. In Chapter 13, you'll learn how to apply a simple stop action to a frame to make the movie play only once. In Chapters 14 and 15, the looping action is expanded upon to give you even greater control of the way the audience sees your movie.

If you happen to be importing your HTML preview into Macromedia Dreamweaver for further tweaking, Dreamweaver enables you to automatically code options available to embedded Flash Player files. The AutoPlay looping action can be overridden in HTML by deselecting the AutoPlay button in the Properties window. This makes the play of the animation false in the HTML code. In the Properties window you also can change the quality of the Flash file as well as the X and Y position and the scale; you also can add a border and alter the alignment, all of which are generated automatically in HTML (see Figure 10-11).

TIP   *If your viewer doesn't have Flash Player version 5 loaded, he or she will not be able to view the movie on the Web. The latest version of the Flash Player can be downloaded for free from the Macromedia site, www.macromedia.com/software/downloads. It's not a bad idea to put a link on your page to this URL so viewers can easily get the version 5 Player if they don't have it. Your other option is to include a Flash 5 Player detection script directing visitors to an alternative HTML URL if they can't view the Flash file.*

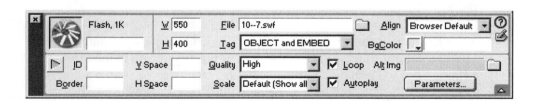

FIGURE 10-11   The Properties window in Dreamweaver enables you to automatically assign HTML-related properties to a Flash Player file (SWF) embedded in an HTML page

Set Onion Skins

When you create a frame-by-frame animation, or any animation for that matter, sometimes it's hard to determine where you want to move the next keyframe in relation to the previous frames. Because you can only see one frame at a time while you're composing the animation, it's impossible to see where the animation has come from to determine where it's going in time. Tweaking an animation by randomly altering objects and playing them back could take hours. Onion Skins come to the rescue and resolve the problem in Flash. The Onion Skin technique is used in animation packages to give you a glimpse of the path of existing frames in your animation. It allows you to see a preview of as many frames as you want at your discretion. This technique is especially useful if you've created a frame-by-frame animation and all your keyframes are identical as a result of hitting the F6 key too many times.

Onion Skins display a selected portion of the animation as translucent ghost images of the original. The term "Onion Skin" comes from the concept of onion-skin paper, a thin, see-through paper artists use to trace over images. How do you move an object from one end of the stage to another in a frame-by-frame animation if the next keyframe keeps jumping back to the original position of the object in the first keyframe? Onion Skins to the rescue.

When you click on any of the Onion Skin buttons at the bottom of the Timeline, an Onion Skin Marker appears as a translucent rounded-corner rectangle over the Frame Numbers in the Timeline. The Onion Skin Marker enables you to customize the span of frames you want previewed. Adjust the Marker by clicking and dragging on the round handles at the beginning and end of the marker. Pick up and move the entire marker by dragging the Playhead to a new location.

The Onion Skin buttons reside at the bottom of the Timeline, and there are four in total. From the left, the Onion Skin buttons perform the following tasks when pressed:

1. The first icon is the Onion Skin button. Click this to view the animation path as a dimmed image. This option does not enable you to modify the Onion Skins on previous frames, as it serves the purpose of indicating the path. Only the current frame can be modified (see Figure 10-12).

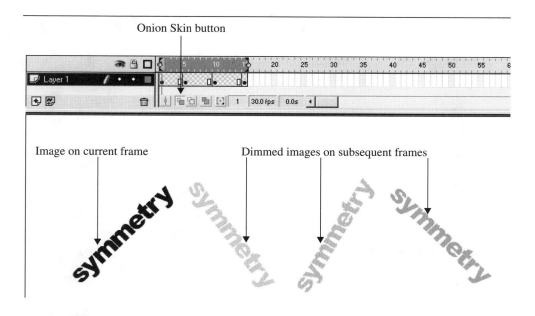

Onion Skin button

Image on current frame

Dimmed images on subsequent frames

FIGURE 10-12   The Onion Skin button turned on. Notice the Onion Skin Marker
spanning a frameset at the top of the Timeline

2. The second icon is the Onion Skin Outlines button (see Figure 10-13).
Click this to display the Onion Skins in outline form. Only the current
frame can be modified with this selection.

3. The third icon is the Edit Multiple Frames button. This displays the Onion
Skins as opaque art and enables you to edit all frames within the confines
of the Onion Skin Marker (see Figure 10-14).

4. The fourth icon is the Modify Onion Markers icon. Click this icon to
display the Onion Skin Modification pop-up menu. The selections from
the menu are as follows:

■ **Always Show Markers** displays a hollowed out Marker even when
Onion Skinning is turned off.

10

- **Anchor Onion** locks the Onion Marker in its current position. Select this to prevent the Onion Skin Marker from moving when you move your Playhead throughout the frames. In regular mode, the Onion Skin Marker follows the path of the Playhead position.

- **Onion 2** displays two frames on either side of the selected frame.

- **Onion 5** displays five frames on either side of the selected frame.

- **Onion All** displays all frames on either side of the selected frame.

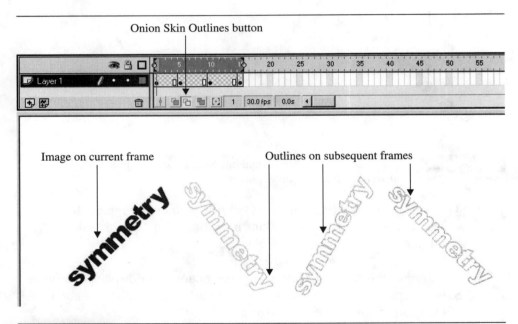

FIGURE 10-13 The Onion Skin Outlines button turned on to depict the path of an animation in outline form

5. Turn off onion skinning by clicking the buttons again. The buttons act as a click on/click off toggle switch.

Locked layers do not display onion skinning.

The Onion Skin feature in Flash enables you to pinpoint the path of your animation. This is an important and time-saving tool in the creation of animation.

Edit Multiple Frames button ⌐   ⌐ Modify Onion Markers button

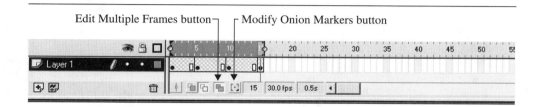

10

FIGURE 10-14   The Edit Multiple Frames button enables you to edit objects on multiple frames

Chapter 11

Use Motion Tweening to Animate Your Flash Movie

How to...

- Make a Simple Motion Tween
- Add and Remove Frames on a Motion Tween
- Tween with Multiple Keyframes
- Change Size, Rotation, Skew, and Color on a Motion Tween
- Control Frames and Framesets in a Motion Tween
- Copy and Paste Frames
- Use the Frames Panel for Motion Tween Settings
- Animate on a Guided Path
- Use a Mask Layer with a Motion Tween

Animation defines the changing of objects from one frame to another to create the illusion of movement. As discussed in Chapter 10, frame-by-frame animation occurs when objects are manually changed on each frame of a movie. Frame-by-frame animation may be time-consuming and inaccurate for certain animations that require smooth movement between keyframes. In this case, tweening animation may be more appropriate. When you tween an object in Flash, the software mathematically generates a series of frames in between two keyframes. The farther apart the keyframes sit, the smoother the movement. In contrast to frame-by-frame animation, tweening takes the guesswork out of the gradual transition of an object between two keyframes. In Flash, you can choose between frame-by-frame or tweening animation, depending upon the requirements of your project.

Motion Versus Shape Tweening

Tweening is a major feature of Flash animation, and it comes in two forms: motion and shape. Although both methods of tweening are based on the same concept, their applications and purposes are very different. In fact, Flash beginners sometimes become puzzled as to which one to use in a movie. In a very simple animation, it may not matter whether you use motion or shape tweening. However, when animations become more sophisticated, your selection will indeed matter. This is why it's important to understand the similarities and differences between the two. This way, you'll know exactly which one to use to optimize the performance of your movie. This chapter focuses on all aspects of motion tweening, and Chapter 12 examines shape tweening.

Understand Motion Tweening

Before learning to make a motion tween, you need to understand some basic rules. A motion tween can only be used on grouped objects, symbols, and text. Shape tweens can only be used on editable objects. Both shape and motion tweens can be used to change the position of an object and the object's color, scale, rotation, and skew. However, to tween color and opacity in a motion tween, the object must be a symbol. Graphic symbols are reviewed in Chapter 8, and buttons and movie clip symbols are discussed in Chapter 13.

Make a Simple Motion Tween

Motion tweening (and shape tweening) is not only fun, it's easy to do. Basically it involves four steps: selecting a group object or symbol; inserting an end keyframe; changing the object on the last frame; and creating the motion tween by selecting a frame in between the two keyframes. Figure 11-1 displays a motion tween created on a grouped object.

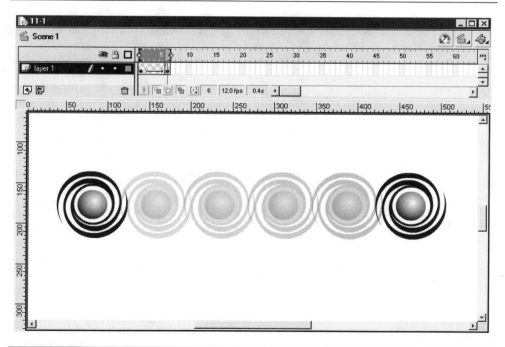

FIGURE 11-1   A simple motion tween spanning six frames

The procedure used on Figure 11-1 is detailed here:

1. Make a new file and create a simple object. By default, a keyframe will appear on Frame 1, Layer 1. This will serve as the first point in the animation you are about to create. If you're working with an existing file, place a keyframe on a frame by right-clicking/CTRL-clicking to display a pop-up menu of features available for that frame (see Figure 11-2). The object must be either grouped or converted into a symbol before applying a motion tween, so click the object and from the menu select Modify | Group or CTRL+G/CMD+G to group it.

2. Select a Frame on Layer 1 where you want the next keyframe to occur. In Figure 11-1, keyframe 6 was selected. With an in-between frame selected, right-click/CTRL-click and select Insert | Keyframe from the pop-up menu (or F6) to create a second keyframe. When you do this, frames are automatically generated between Frames 1 and 5 and are depicted with a light gray fill.

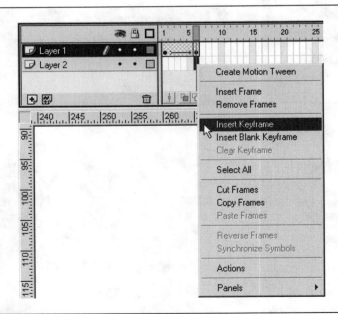

FIGURE 11-2   Display a pop-up menu on a frame by right-clicking/CTRL-clicking on that frame

3. With the last keyframe selected, drag the object to another location on the stage to change its position. Scrub through frames with the Playhead. Between your first and last keyframe, the object will appear to abruptly change position. Tweening will smooth out the in-between frames.

> TIP
>
> *There are three ways to insert and remove frames and keyframes. One way is to select these options from the contextual pop-up menu displayed by right-clicking/CTRL-clicking on a frame or keyframe. Selecting a frame and displaying the Insert Menu options directly from the Modify menu also can display frame options. The third option is to use one of the following shortcut keys: F5 to insert a frame; F6 to insert a keyframe; SHIFT+F5 to remove frames; and SHIFT+F6 to remove keyframes. For a complete list of shortcut keys, refer to Appendix A.*

4. Now that the two keyframes are in place, the tween can be completed. To do so, right-click/CRTL-click between keyframes and select Create Motion Tween. A right-pointing arrow appears on a light blue background on the in-between frames to indicate a motion tween.

5. Scrub through all the frames with the Playhead to see the gradual transition of the object between the two keyframes.

6. If you select the last keyframe to create a motion tween, nothing will happen. Because tweening occurs from left to right in the timeline, the last keyframe is always assumed to be the end of the transformation. The frame to the left of the last keyframe or the last frame (if there is no last keyframe), will display a hollow rectangle, indicating it's the last frame of the span (see Figure 11-3).

Objects that are symbols also can be tweened. In fact, it may often be preferable to motion tween a symbol as opposed to a group because color and opacity can be tweened with a symbol from the Effect panel.

To make an existing object into a symbol, click the object and select Insert | Convert to Symbol (F8). Select the Behavior of the new Symbol (Movie Clip, Button, Graphic) and click OK. The object is now a symbol, stored in the Library. A symbol can be tweened in the same way you tween a grouped object.

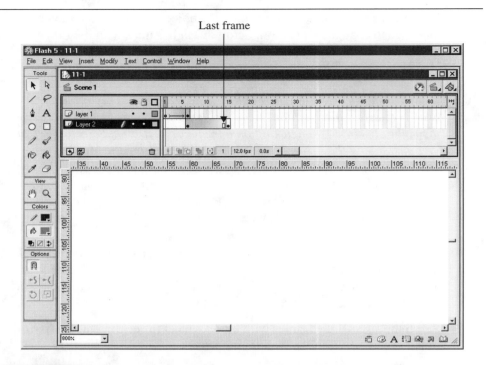

FIGURE 11-3 The last frame of a frameset contains a hollow rectangle

Add and Remove Frames on a Motion Tween

If you play back a movie with six frames, such as the movie in Figure 11-1, you will notice it's a little choppy and moves quickly. It appears this way because only four in-between frames were generated to interpolate the tween and, at 12 frames per second, this animation lasts for less than half a second. This is fine if it's the effect you want to achieve. But let's say you wanted a smoother and longer transition between keyframes. If you add more in-between frames, the movement will appear less choppy.

To add more in-between frames, follow these steps:

1. Press the CTRL/CMD key and select a frame in the middle of the tweened frames. Pressing the CTRL/CMD key enables the selection of just one frame as opposed to grabbing the entire frameset.

2. Once an individual frame is selected, click F5. Each time you click F5, another frame will be added.

In the case of Figure 11-1, if you added frames up to frame 24, the animation sequence would last about two seconds, creating a much smoother animation. Smoothness comes with a hitch, though. The more frames, the larger the file. This is not something to worry about in a simple movie. But, as your movie grows with layers and complex movement, you will need to economize on the movie's growing size. The number of tweened frames may need to be trimmed down to decrease the size of the movie.

To delete frames from your frameset, hold down the CTRL/CMD key and click on an in-between frame. Hold down the SHIFT key while you click F5, or right-click/ CMD+click and select Remove Frames from the pop-up menu. This removes individual frames from the frameset.

> **TIP** *When you click on a keyframe, the single keyframe is selected. When you click a frame or a tweened frameset, the entire frameset is selected. In order to select one frame, hold down the* CTRL/CMD *key. You also can reposition a keyframe on a frameset by clicking and dragging it to a new position.*

Motion Tweening with Multiple Keyframes

In Figure 11-1, the object travels in a single line, from one keyframe to another. This creates limited movement and really isn't very interesting. You can give the object a livelier path by creating additional keyframes on a layer and changing the direction of the object on each keyframe.

In Figure 11-4, the position of an object has been changed several times by adding additional keyframes to the frameset. To add a keyframe to an existing frameset, hold down the CTRL/CMD key and select an in-between frame; then click the F6 key to add the keyframe. To add a keyframe to frame placeholders beyond a frameset, click a frame outside of the frameset and click F6. This extends the length of the current frameset. You also can extend the length of an existing frameset by clicking the last keyframe of the frameset and dragging it to its new position.

Figure 11-4 is actually an alternate version of Figure 11-1, whose last keyframe stops on Frame 6. In the new version, additional keyframes were added (F6) to Frames 12 and 18, and 24. After the frames were added, the tweening process was repeated in between Frames 6–12, 12–18, and 18–24. Once the tweening was set in between the frames, the object on each keyframe was moved to a different position to give the illusion of it bouncing up and down. Turning on an Onion Skin button makes it easy to go back and change the object on any keyframe because you can preview the path of the object. When you're using Onion Skinning for the purpose of viewing an entire path as was done in Figure 11-4, it's important to drag the Onion Skin Markers over the entire frameset. Otherwise you'll only see part of the path on the frameset.

11

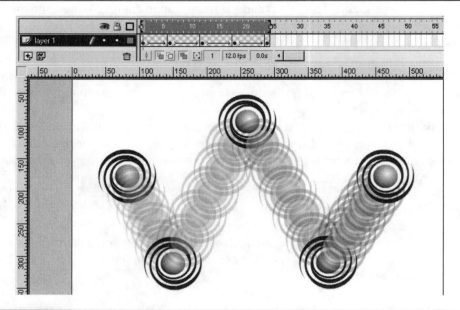

FIGURE 11-4   The object on the stage is tweened with Onion Skinning turned on, and
the object changes position on five keyframes within the frameset

Change Size, Rotation, Skew, and Color on a Motion Tween

In the previous examples, only the position of the object changes. You also can
apply any of the other transformation tools to your object. You also can tween the
size, rotation, and skew of an object. Transformation Tools can be accessed from
the Toolbox, menu (Modify | Transform), or the Transformation panel. To apply
a transformation to a motion tween, select a keyframe. With the object selected,
modify it using one of the transformation tools. Figure 11-5 shows an object
that's position and size are changed. Onion Skinning is turned on to preview the
path. On Frame 6, the scale is changed to 50% of the original. On Frame 18, the
scale is changed to 25% of the original. To scale an object in between keyframes,
click on the keyframe you wish to perform the transformation on. Scale the object
in that keyframe and then apply a tween. The object gradually changes size in
between keyframes.

Multiple transformations can be applied to keyframes. In Figure 11-5, the
object is a graphic symbol that changes position, width, rotation, skew, and height
between five keyframes. The Edit Multiple Frames Onion Skin button is turned on
to view the object on all five keyframes.

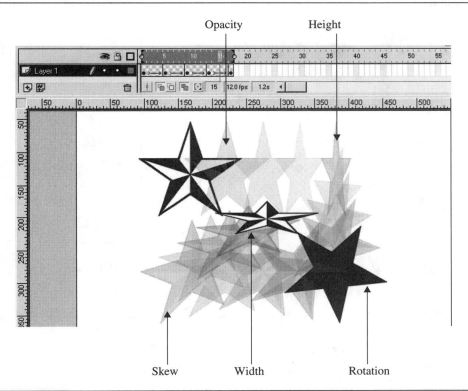

Opacity   Height

Skew   Width   Rotation

FIGURE 11-5	A graphic symbol with a motion tween applied; the position, width, rotation, skew, height, and opacity transform between keyframes

When an object is a symbol, you can tween the color and opacity of the object. In Figure 11-5, the opacity changes from solid color to 20% of the original color on keyframes 19 and 17. The opacity of a symbol (Alpha), as well as the color settings on a symbol, is changed using the Effect panel. Display the Effect panel by selecting Window | Panels | Effect from the menu as shown in Figure 11-6.

To make the Effect panel active, a symbol must be selected on the desired keyframe where you want the color/opacity change to take place. With the symbol selected, click the contextual pop-up menu to modify the brightness, tint, alpha, or customized color settings called "Advanced." Refer to Chapter 8 for a detailed description of settings in the Effect panel. Each individual setting activates customized selections. When you select Brightness or Alpha (opacity), a sliding percentage arrow appears to the right of the selection.

11

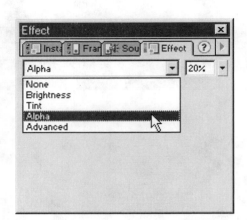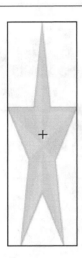

FIGURE 11-6   Use the Effect panel to change the Alpha setting of a symbol

Selecting Tint displays a color mixer bar, tint color box, and RGB sliders where you can input specific RGB percentages. Selecting Advanced enables you to set custom color by adding and multiplying different RBG percentages. Needless to say, the Effect panel enables you to colorize a symbol in virtually any way you can think of.

Motion Tweening Graphic Symbols on Multiple Layers

The possibilities for tweening animation are endless considering that just a few tools give you so many different ways to animate an object. Figure 11-7 is an example of a motion tween on multiple layers with the position and size of a bus and car symbol transformed. There are five graphic symbols on the stage, and each object resides on its own layer. Layers stack upon each other in order of display. For example, the street layer is under the bus and car layer. Examining the movie step by step will help you learn the process of creating a tween animation on multiple layers.

In Figure 11-7, the symbols, layers, and layer stacking order were planned in advance, so the first step was creating, naming all the symbols, and determining the order of the five layers. Layers and symbols are named to reflect the nature of the object that resides on the layer. For example, the car symbol is called "car," as is the layer. When you name symbols and layers in a logical manner, there's no

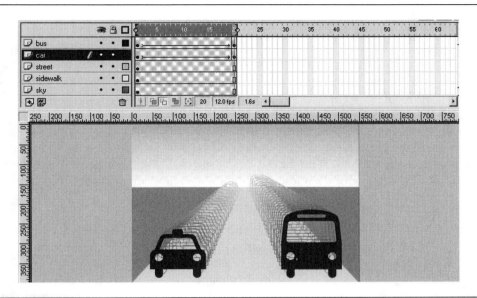

FIGURE 11-7   The positions and sizes of a car and bus are tweened on multiple layers

mistaking the purpose of each layer or its objects. The layers are named in the following order:

- Bus
- Car
- Street
- Sidewalk
- Sky

After the layers were created, the first frame in the sidewalk layer was selected and the sidewalk symbol was dragged from the Library onto the stage. The symbol is a rectangle with a fill and no stroke.

After the sidewalk was in place, Frame 1 of the street layer was selected and the street symbol was dragged from the Library onto the stage. The street was created with a polygon fill.

11

Once the street was created, Frame 1 of the sky was selected and the sky symbol was put in place. The sky is a simple rectangle with a gradient fill.

Frame 1 of the bus layer was selected and the bus symbol was dragged from the Library onto the stage. The bus and the car were drawn with the Pen tool. The process was repeated and the car symbol was positioned on the car layer. The car and the bus symbols are the only objects that animate. The goal was to make the bus and the car appear as if they've moved forward in perspective, on the road. This involved changing the position and the scale of the bus and car symbols.

With all the elements in place, the bus and car were motion tweened. The bus symbol was tweened first. With the bus object selected, a keyframe was inserted on Frame 20. This created the keyframe where the end movement occurs. The process was repeated on the car layer.

To create the tweened frames, the in-between keyframes were selected by right-clicking/CMD-clicking. Create Motion Tween was selected from the pop-up menu. A black arrow with a blue backdrop appears within the frameset to indicate a motion tween.

Finally, the bus and car symbols were changed on Frame 20 on their respective layers. With the bus selected in Frame 20, the bus was moved to the bottom of the stage onto the street. The process was repeated with the car. The path of the bus and car conform to the forward perspective of the street. Enlarging the scale of the two objects creates the illusion of objects moving forward in space. On Frame 20, the scale of the car and bus symbols was enlarged to approximately 400% in the last keyframe of both the bus and car layers. If you were to play back the movie with the Controller, the bus and car appear to move forward in space and time.

NOTE   *The "frameset" refers to a group of frames on a layer.*

Motion tweening on different layers also can be used to make objects appear behind or in front of one another. If you were to transpose the position of the bus and car (refer to Figure 11-7) on Frame 1 of their respective layers (placing the car to the right and the bus to the left), they would cross paths somewhere in the middle of where they tween. Layering also can be used for hiding objects underneath one another during the span of a tween.

TIP   *If you try to tween an editable object, or if the last keyframe in the frameset is missing, a dashed line will appear instead of the arrow in the tweened frames. In this case, the tween won't work.*

Control Frames and Framesets in a Motion Tween

Once you've created a movie with several layers and tweens, there's always a possibility that the movie will need revising. Even the smallest revision can create a domino effect, which could change the entire flow of the movie. Depending on how well you planned out the movie, revising animations can be made into molehills. Flash offers several techniques to make it a little easier to modify framesets and to move keyframes. This is helpful because as often as objects in a movie need to be changed, the actual frames themselves may need to be moved. Sometimes the timing of tweened objects on different layers may need to be revised too. Fortunately, Flash movies are relatively easy to change and test.

Let's return to the Figure 11-7 example of the car and bus movie. There are many ways to modify this movie. For starters, let's suppose your clients thinks the animation is too boring and they want the car to move a split second after the bus. Instead of redoing the entire animation, you could experiment with moving the car frameset up a bit on the Timeline so the car is introduced after the bus. Figure 11-8 shows the revised timeline of this animation with the car frameset moved on its layer to begin at Frame 10. If you played the movie back at this point, all the other elements would disappear from the stage on Frame 20.

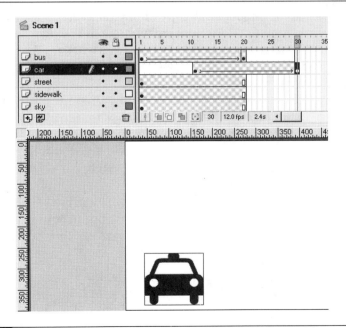

11

FIGURE 11-8   When a frameset is moved, it affects the playback of the movie

To prevent objects from disappearing on the playback when it wasn't intended, you can add frames to all other layers up to Frame 30, where the car frameset now ends. To do so, click Frame 30 of each layer and press the F5 key as many times as needed to fill up the position frames. This fills in the frames to the last frame on the selected layer. On the other tweened layer called "bus," this doesn't work because when you add frames (F5) to Frame 30 on the bus layer, blank frames appear. On a tweened frameset, CTRL-click/CMD-click on the tween and press F5 until you reach Frame 30. This will enable you to control the frames in a tween. To delete tweened frames, blank frames, or regular frames, CTRL-click/CMD-click, hold down the SHIFT key and press F5.

 *Dragging the last keyframe of a frameset to another point in the Timeline also can extend a frameset. If the frameset is tweened, dragging the keyframe to another position will break the tween. Remedy this by redoing the tween.*

Copy and Paste Frames

If you need to copy a keyframe, frame, or frameset to another layer, you can do so easily in Flash. Copying frames leaves the selected frames in place and makes a copy of the frames in the clipboard. A copy of the frameset can be pasted at any time while in the program (until you exit the program or copy/cut another object). In Figure 11-9, the frameset was copied and pasted from keyframe 21 to keyframe 41. Copy a frameset or an individual frame by selecting the frame(s) (or frameset), and right-click/CMD-click to display the contextual pop-up menu. Select Edit | Copy Frames from the menu or CTRL+ALT+C/OPT+CMD+C. Click the first frame you want to paste to, and again right-click/CMD-click to display the contextual pop-up menu. Select Edit | Paste Frames from the menu or CTRL+ALT+V/ OPT+CMD+V. A duplicate of the frameset will appear. If you're selecting a tweened frameset, make certain the last keyframe is in the selection. Otherwise, a dashed line will appear, indicating the tween is broken.

Frames can be cut as well as copied using the same method as Copy, but selecting Cut instead of Copy in the Edit menu. Cutting frames removes the frames and places a copy in the clipboard. The frames can then be pasted as with the Copy Frame command.

Reverse a Frameset   In Figure 11-9, the second frameset was copied, pasted from the first, and then reversed to make the object appear to bounce back and forth. If the frames weren't reversed, copying and pasting would be futile because the movie would look the same as if the second frameset didn't exist because movies

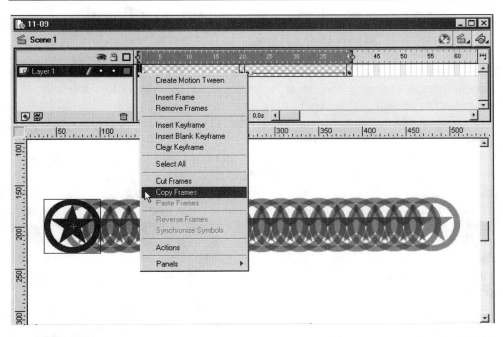

FIGURE 11-9   Copy and paste framesets with the Edit | Copy Frames/Edit | Paste Frames function

automatically loop (Control | Test Movie or CTRL+ENTER/CMD+ENTER). When testing this movie, the object abruptly reappears to the left of the stage at the beginning of each loop. This is because the Playhead always returns to the first keyframe after the last frame is played, unless told to do otherwise by a script.

To make the object appear as if it's bouncing, the second frameset was reversed so it plays in reverse. When the last frame loops back to the first frame, the object on the first frame is now in the same position as the object on the last frame, giving the object the illusion of bouncing back and forth.

To reverse a tweened frameset, select the entire frameset and right-click/ CMD-click to display the contextual pop-up menu. Click Reverse Frames. When you play back the movie, the tween is now reversed. Reverse Frames also can be selected from the menu under Modify | Frames. Note that reversing frames on a motion tween only works if the position of the object is being changed.

The size, rotation, skew, or color can't be reversed on a motion tween. However, you can reverse these elements with a shape tween, which is discussed in Chapter 12.

Adjust Tweened Objects with the Frames Panel

There are additional effects that can be applied to a tween in the Frame panel. Objects can further be customized with rotation effects and easing in and out effects. Rotating in the Frames panel enables you to create special effects like the spinning of an object, and easing lets you control the speed of an object in the beginning or end of a tween.

Rotate in the Frames Panel

When you create a motion tween using the Rotation tool, its capabilities are somewhat limited. If you're creating anything other than a simple rotation, erratic results may occur. Also, if you want an object to spin once and end in the place where it began, or spin continuously, the Rotation tool won't work. In the Frame panel, you can adjust the rotation of an object to create more sophisticated rotations (see Figure 11-10). You can automatically set and customize the rotation of an object so it will appear as if it were spinning. An object can be oriented to a specified path, which is discussed in the next section. This option is only available for motion tweens.

In Figure 11-11, the hand of the clock image spins in position counterclockwise when the Flash Player version of the movie is played. You may remember this clock movie from Chapter 10. In the previous chapter, the clock was created with

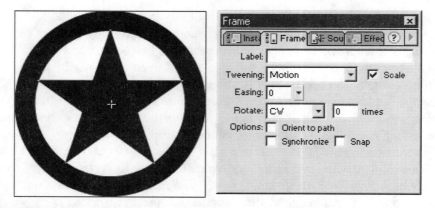

FIGURE 11-10   The Rotation options become accessible in the Frame panel when Motion Tween is selected

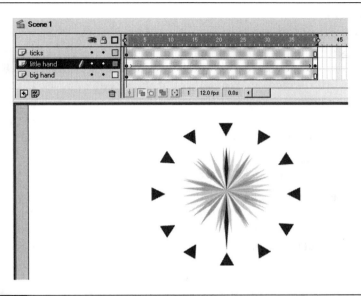

FIGURE 11-11   A movie of a clock with a spinning hand created with the Rotation
option in the Frame panel

a frame-by-frame animation to imply hesitation in the movement between points
on the clock. If you recall, the center reference point on the hand of the clock was
changed from center to bottom center. This made the object rotate from the bottom
of the object. In this updated version, the tweened rotation is smooth, continuous,
and was created with the Frame Panel Rotation options.

The little hand of the clock resides on the hand layer, and the tween ends at
frame 40. To create a similar effect, select the frameset and display the Frame
panel (Window | Panels | Frame). If a motion tween has not yet been applied,
you can select Motion Tween from the Tweening pop-up menu. If a motion
tween already exists, it will be reflected in the Tweening box. When Tweening is
selected, the rotation options become accessible in the panel. On Figure 11-11,
for Rotation, CW was selected and the number 3 was typed in for "times". This
makes the object rotate clockwise three times each time the frameset loops. The
higher the number you type in for Rotation Time, the faster the movie will appear
to rotate. Counterclockwise also can be selected as a rotation direction. If you
modify an object on a keyframe with the Rotation tool, when the Frame panel is
displayed, Rotation will be indicated as Auto.

11

Ease In and Out

Tweening from one keyframe to another doesn't give you much control on the speed of an object as it begins or ends its transformation. Easing in and out from the Frame panel gives you control over the speed of the object. The Easing box is a sliding arrow that goes from -100 at the bottom to +100 at the top (see Figure 11-12).

To make the tween appear as if it starts slow and speeds up at the end, select an increment between -1 and -100. To make the tween appear as if it begins fast and slows down toward the end, select an easing increment between 1 and 100.

Animate on a Guided Path

Motion tweening can easily be done between two or more keyframes. In some instances though, this method of tweening is limited. Sometimes when you do a motion tween, you need the object to follow a complex path that you can't get quite right with a regular motion tween. In this case, Flash offers the ability to have an object follow a predefined path that you create. Figure 11-13 represents a stylized version of a large planet with a smaller planet that rotates around it. The little planet is tweened and follows a motion guide to create a circular movement.

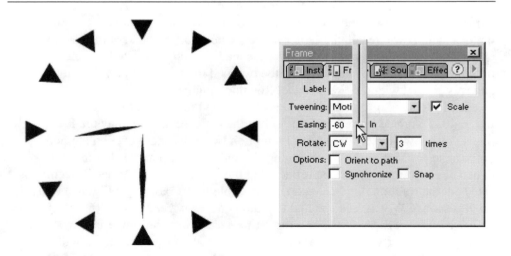

FIGURE 11-12 The Easing selection in the Frame panel eases in from -100 to out at +100

If the little planet was tweened with a frame-by-frame animation, it could take up 100 keyframes or more. Too many frames in a tween could needlessly increase the file size and the task of making it would be very time consuming. The perfect solution is tweening on a motion guide. The little planet in Figure 11-13 was attached to a circular motion guide to create the illusion of the little planet rotating around the big planet.

The first step in tweening on a motion guide is to plan it out first. Make a thumbnail sketch of what path you'd like the motion to take around the object(s). This will make it easier when you draw the motion guide. In creating Figure 11-13, a quick sketch was made to determine the direction of the guide. Then a graphic symbol of a gradient circle was created. This same symbol was used for both the small and big planets. The following section covers the techniques used in Figure 11-13 to create the revolving planet effect.

NOTE   *Motion guides are invisible on playback of the movie.*

11

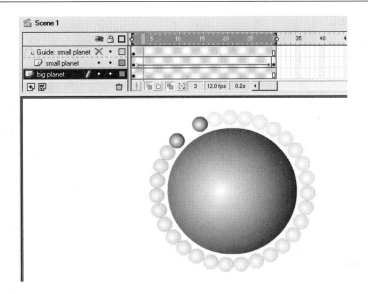

FIGURE 11-13   Symbols resembling planets were used to create this motion guide tween

Create a Motion Guide

A motion guide consists of a path that's drawn on a guide layer. The path can be drawn with the Pen, Pencil, Line, Brush, Circle, or Rectangle tool.

In Figure 11-13, the small planet resides on its own layer, as does the big planet. They are on different layers so they don't cause confusion when the tween takes place. Assuming all your layers and graphics are in place for the tween you are about to create, the motion guide is ready to be made. Select the object that the motion guide will be tweened around and click the Add Guide Layer button at the bottom of the Layer section of the Timeline. A Motion Guide icon will appear on the new layer along with the name of the layer that the guide is attached to (see Figure 11-14). Note that this layer is beneath the Motion Guide layer and indented slightly to the right of the Guide layer.

Select the Motion Guide layer and prepare to draw the guide. In Figure 11-13, the Oval tool was selected for this purpose with a Stroke of blue and a Fill of none. A motion guide can be any stroke color. In fact, you might want to use a contrasting color to make it easy to distinguish. An editable circle was drawn as a guide to extend the parameters of the big planet. A motion guide has to have a beginning and an end so the guided object can attach itself on the keyframes. The oval shape used in Figure 11-13 is a continuous shape, with no beginning or end. To make the oval work as a motion guide, a small piece of the guide circle needs to be erased using the Eraser tool (see Figure 11-15).

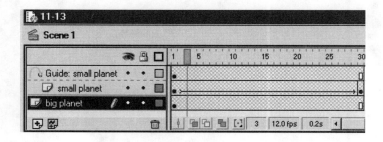

FIGURE 11-14   A Motion Guide layer indents the layers attached to it

The Align panel was also used to align the motion guide to the big planet, so they would be perfectly centered over one another. At this point, the motion guide and big planet layers were extended to Frame 30. This way, none of the elements on the layers disappear while attaching the small planet to the motion guide, when you go past Frame 1. It's a good idea to lock the Motion Guide layer so you don't accidentally grab it while adjusting the small planet to the ends of the guide. Lock the guide by clicking the Lock button on the Motion Guide layer.

Now that all the components are in place, the small planet is ready to be attached to the partial circle on the Motion Guide layer. Click the first keyframe on the Small Planet layer. With the small planet selected toward the center of the object, drag it to the start of the guide. A hollow circle appears in the small planet and it snaps to the start of the circle (see Figure 11-16). Make a keyframe on Frame 30, the last frame. Select the new frameset on the Small Planet layer and right-click/CMD-click to display the pop-up contextual menu. Select Create Motion Tween.

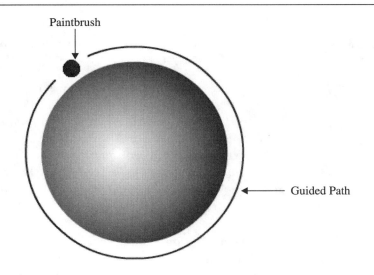

Paintbrush

Guided Path

FIGURE 11-15   A small portion of the circle motion guide was erased so the object that's following it can lock to a beginning point and an endpoint

11

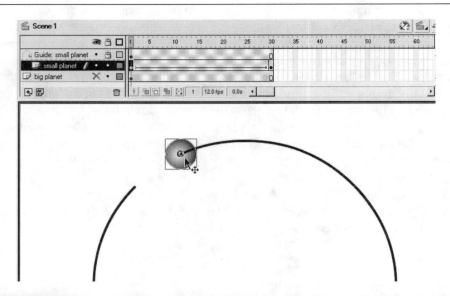

FIGURE 11-16   The small planet snaps to the beginning (and end) of the circle path on a Motion Guide layer

NOTE *Depending on where you grab an object you want to snap-to the beginning or end of a motion guide, the object will reference the snap-to from that point. For example, if you selected the object at its middle left, a hollow circle would appear while you dragged the object, declaring the hollow circle as the reference point. When you play the movie (Control | Test Movie), the motion guide at that point is invisible. You can test the movie without seeing the motion guide by turning off its visibility on the Motion Guide layer.*

Attach Additional Objects to a Motion Guide   More than one layer can be attached to a motion guide. Subsequently, an object on an additional layer can be attached to the same motion guide used by other layers. Figure 11-17 is an expanded upon version of Figure 11-13, of the small planet revolving around the large planet. There is an additional layer with an arrow symbol that revolves in the opposite direction of the small planet. When the movie plays, both objects cross paths in the middle of the guided path. Notice in the Timeline, the new layer, "arrow," is also indented underneath the Motion Layer guide above the Small Planet layer. Any layers attached to a guide are indented.

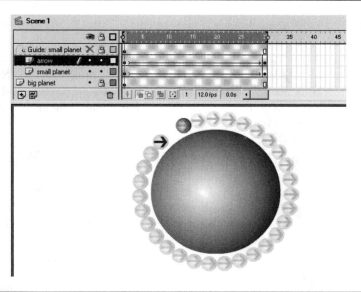

FIGURE 11-17   A small planet and an arrow revolving in different directions around the same circle path on a motion guide layer

To create another layer and attach it to the guide, click the New Layer button at the bottom of the Timeline. Drag the new layer underneath the motion guide layer and place a grouped object or symbol on the layer. The layer becomes indented, indicating an attachment to the motion guide. In Figure 11-17, the arrow revolves in the opposite direction to the small planet. To make this happen, click the center of the new object on the first keyframe and drag it to what is the endpoint of the motion guide (the same guide the small planet uses). Make a new end keyframe and drag the center point of the object to the new endpoint of the motion guide. When you play back the movie, both objects will rotate in opposite directions.

Orient Objects to the Path of a Motion Guide   In Figure 11-17, when the arrow follows the path, it continues to point to the right while following the path. This movement wouldn't make much sense if you were using an arrow because arrows are generally used as a directional device. In static graphics, this is easy to do because you only need one arrow to indicate direction on a path. In an animation, you have to work harder to get the arrow to point in the proper direction. In Flash, you can easily guide an object along a path in a specified direction of the object. Accomplish this by using the Orient to Path option in the Frame panel.

11

In Figure 11-18, the arrow has been rotated and snapped to a point on the circle guide in the first keyframe. When the last keyframe is made, the arrow is rotated slightly to compliment the direction of the circle motion guide endpoint and snapped to this endpoint. A motion tween is then added to the frameset. With the Frames panel displayed, select Options: Orient to Path. Other options include Synchronize and Snap. Select Synchronize if you're using an animated graphic symbol and the total number of frames within the symbol don't equal the number of frames it will occupy on the Timeline. Graphic symbols are discussed in Chapter 8, and animated graphic symbols are discussed in Chapter 13. Checking the Snap button ensures the object will snap to its reference point. Click this option if your object appears to be veering off the path while in motion.

If your guide is complex and long, the object may not follow the path correctly at certain points. In this case, you can add more keyframes at certain intervals on the motion guide path to help the object along in following the path. To do so, click a frame within the frameset where you want to add the new keyframe. Reposition the object on the new keyframe. When the movie plays, the object is re-oriented to the path.

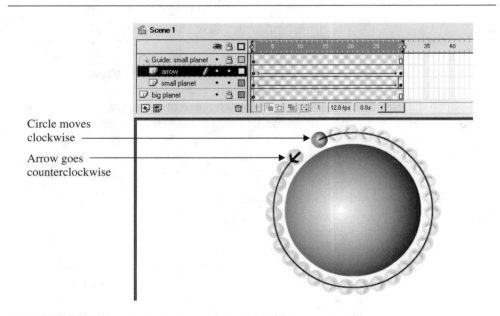

FIGURE 11-18   The arrow rotating around the planet is oriented to the path of the circle motion guide

To unlink a layer to a motion guide path, drag the layer above the motion guide. It then returns to a regular layer.

Use a Mask Layer with a Motion Tween: A Tutorial

The number of effects you can create with tweened objects is endless. In addition to the techniques discussed in this chapter, other effects that have been covered in previous chapters can be combined with motion tweening. In this tutorial, a mask is tweened. This basic recipe can be applied to other projects, generating many interesting results.

In Figure 11-19, a moving mask is used to create the illusion of running water through a word. The word "water" is static on the top layer, which is named text, and a bitmap picture of water moves in a continuous loop from left to right in the background, giving the illusion of a flowing river. A mask in this sense is like looking

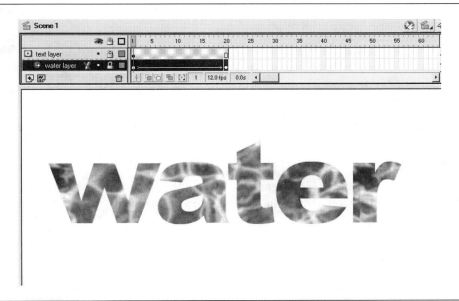

| FIGURE 11-19 | The word "water" is a static layer mask and the water background is masked behind it; in the movie, the water moves continuously to the left |

11

through a porthole, and the porthole creates the shape of the mask. The process for creating a motion tween under a mask such as in the sample is as follows:

1. As always, plan out the movie before you begin. Plan objects, layers, and names. Determine how large you want the movie to be. The Flash default size is 550 x 400 pixels so you can work backwards from this size. Always keep in mind that the bigger the movie, the larger the file.

2. Create and name the first layer and type out a word. This will become the mask layer. The word "water" was typed in 100-point Arial Black because it's very bold, simple, and a good choice for a mask font. Position the word on the stage. Make the text editable by breaking it apart. To do so, click the text and select Modify | Break Apart from the menu or CTRL+B/CMD+B. The text would still work as a mask if you didn't break it apart. However, breaking apart display text that you know won't be further edited is a good idea. You can never be sure that a viewer's fonts will be the same as yours. In an exercise like this, where it's crucial the fonts match, it's best to treat the font as an editable object.

3. Import an image as was done in the sample figure and name the layer. This will be the masked layer, or the layer that is masked out. The water image is a PICT file, but Flash imports many other formats. (Consult Chapter 9, Table 9-1, for a complete list of supported formats.)

4. Convert the imported picture to a bitmap by clicking the image and selecting Modify | Break Apart from the menu. In most cases, this should help reduce the size of the image.

5. Convert the image into a graphic symbol by selecting Insert | Convert to Symbol (F8) from the menu. Now, multiple uses of the symbol will also economize on file size.

NOTE *There are many custom backgrounds you can create right in Flash instead of importing a background from another program. An effect in Flash, such as a gradation that moves or pulsates, creates a nice masked effect, too.*

The water image on the Water layer was tiled three times, so when the masked image loops, it looks like water flowing continuously (see Figure 11-20). To create this effect, drag two more instances of the masked symbol to the masked layer (in this case it's called the Water layer). For the tile effect to work properly, the left side of the picture must mirror the right side so the images begin and end in the

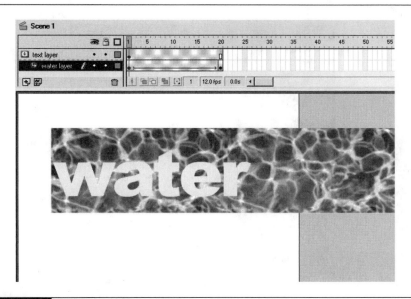

FIGURE 11-20 The water image has been tiled to create a masked effect of continuous movement when the position of the water is tweened

same place and the sum of the tiles should be long enough to accommodate the entire word. Note that the water tile bleeds off the right edge of the stage so a break won't occur in the masked image (water) during the tweening.

To apply the mask, right-click/CMD-click the page icon in the text layer to display the contextual pop-up menu (see Figure 11-21). Select Mask from the menu. The page icon now turns into a down arrow icon (refer to Figure 11-20), indicating the layer containing the mask. Conversely, the Water layer turns into a right-pointing arrow icon indicating the masked layer. The masked layer must always reside under the mask layer.

The masked layer (water image) now needs to be tweened. Remember: The word stays static while the water bitmap moves. Click on a frame to create the second keyframe (F6). In Figure 11-19, Frame 20 is selected. On the text layer, even the frames out to Frame 20 by clicking this frame and pressing F5 (Insert Frame). Reposition the water image in the first and last keyframe so the water appears to move from left to right. You may have to go back and tweak the position of the water after playing back the movie to obtain the desired result. Click on the in-between frames and right-click/CMD-click to display the contextual menu. Select Motion Tween from the menu.

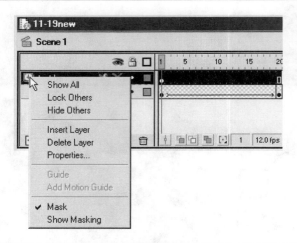

FIGURE 11-21 Display a layer's contextual menu by right-clicking/CMD-clicking the page icon on the layer

Masks don't display in the Flash movie. To test the movie, do one of two things:

- Select Control | Test Movie

- Click the Lock button at the top of the layer section of the Timeline to lock all layers

Locking the layers enables you to see and test the mask with the Controller in the movie or scrub through the Timeline with the Playhead. Remember to unlock the layers again to move the objects.

Once you get the feel for it, motion tweening can produce some awesome results. In the next chapter, shape tweening is discussed. With frame-by-frame, motion and shape tweening, you'll possess a powerful array of tools to satisfy all your animation needs.

Chapter 12

Use Shape Tweening to Animate a Movie

How to...

- Create a Shape Tween
- Shape Tween with Multiple Keyframes
- Modify Properties of a Shape Tween
- Tween on a Multi-Layer Movie
- Morph Between Objects
- Apply Shape Hints
- Set Shape Tween Properties

As discussed in Chapter 11, motion tweening only works on objects that are grouped or symbols. In fact, the very name "motion tween" implies that its primary use is changing the motion of an object over time. In contrast, shape tweening can only be applied on editable objects. A shape tween is primarily used for changing the shape of an object over time.

You can change size, skew, rotation, and color, as well as the position of an object with a motion tween. The same properties can be altered with a shape tween, and often, with a different and unexpected outcome. This is due to the fact that when you change the rotation and skew of an object with a motion tween, the object is addressed as a whole entity. However, the object is perceived as an editable shape instead of a whole entity with a shape tween. The individual edges of the editable shape can transform separately from the object as a whole, causing a shape tween to yield different results from a motion tween. Motion and shape tweening can perform similar functions, but both types of tweening serve different purposes.

Because of the malleable nature of editable objects, shape tweening is used for morphing objects. Morphing occurs when one shape transforms into another shape. In addition, color can be tweened easily on an editable object. This effect won't work with a motion tween unless, of course, the tweened object is a symbol.

Both motion and shape tweening can generate different results. Once you get the feel for tweening, you will better understand when it's appropriate and effective to use a particular method.

Create a Shape Tween

To understand the similarities and differences between making a shape versus a motion tween, it's best to start off by making a simple shape tween. Figure 12-1 is

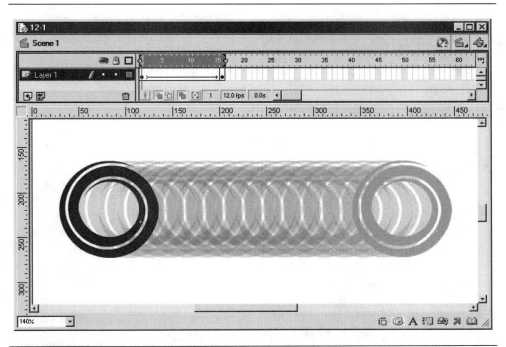

FIGURE 12-1   A representation of a simple shape tween that changes the position of an object

a simple shape tween that changes position. The shape tween object must be editable, so when you select it, the entire object highlights with a pattern as opposed to an outlined bounding box, as is the case with a grouped object or symbol.

Figure 12-1 was created using the following steps:

1. Draw or import an object into Flash. The object used in Figure 12-1 is a single object with one layer. Drawing an object or importing one should automatically generate the first keyframe. In some cases, you may need to make a keyframe before creating the object. If this is the case, press the F6 key to create the missing keyframe, and then draw the object.

2. Select a numerically higher frame to the right and press F6 to create another keyframe (or right-click/CMD-click to display the contextual pop-up menu and select Insert Keyframe). In the second keyframe, move the object to another position on the stage.

12

3. With the in-between frames selected, display the Frame panel. Unlike a motion tween, which can be selected from a contextual menu, a shape tween can only be selected from the Frames panel.

4. In the Frame panel, click Tweening and in the pop-up menu, select Shape. When a shape tween is applied, an arrow appears in the frameset with a light green background. In contrast, when you create a motion tween, an arrow appears in the frameset with a light blue background. This is how you can discern between the two types of tweens on layers.

5. Play the movie back with the Controller (Window | Toolbars | Controller). Only the position of the object was changed in Figure 12-1, and on playback it looks identical to a motion tween.

Let's now do something to this movie that can't be done with a motion tween. Click the last keyframe, and from the Fill color on the toolbar, change the color of the object. Now when you play the movie back, you'll see the color gradually changes with the position of the object. You can't tween color with a grouped motion tween, but you can with a shape tween.

Shape Tween with Multiple Keyframes

Tweening from one keyframe to another can impose a limitation on your creativity. To make an animation come to life, you can expand upon it by adding keyframes to a frameset. Multiple keyframes enable you to change different properties of the object over a series of keyframes.

Unlike motion tweening, a shape tween can't move an object along a guided path. In addition, the rotation options used to spin an object clockwise or counterclockwise aren't available for shape tweens. Despite these restrictions, there are some spectacular effects you can achieve with shape tweening by adding more keyframes.

As was discussed in the last section, shape tweening the position of an object is similar to that of a motion tween. If you wanted to liven up the path of the object in Figure 12-1 to include more keyframes, it can be done easily. In Figure 12-2, four additional keyframes were added to Frames 5, 10, 15, 20, and 25 by holding down the CTRL-click/CMD-click to select each individual frame. Once an individual frame was selected, a keyframe was inserted (F6, or right-click/CTRL-click to access the contextual menu and select Insert Keyframe). With the six keyframes in place, the object was moved to a new position on the stage for each keyframe.

Because the objects in a shape tween are editable, the entire object must be selected in each keyframe before moving it. In Figure 12-2, Onion Skinning was

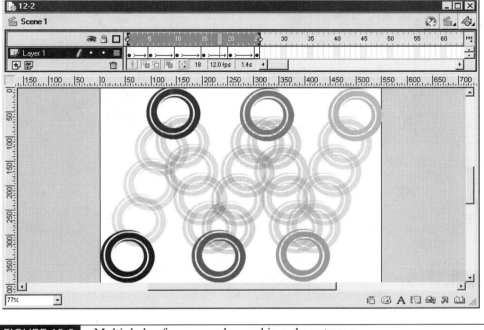

FIGURE 12-2   Multiple keyframes can be used in a shape tween

turned on to determine where the object on each new keyframe would be placed. On playback, you wouldn't be able to determine whether this movie was a motion tween or a shape tween. However, once you depart from the position property, motion and shape tweening begin to take on a different appearance.

Modify Properties in a Shape Tween

In Figure 12-3, the width of the star object is reduced on the middle keyframe, giving the star the illusion of a flat object spinning on a center axis and appearing to move forward and backward in space. The spinning star makes a nice, clean shape tween example.

The star object was imported from Adobe Illustrator. Because objects from drawing programs import as groups, it was ungrouped (Modify | Ungroup) and broken apart (Modify | Break Apart). Once the object was broken apart, a keyframe was added to Frame 20 (F6), the last keyframe of the frameset. A shape tween was created by displaying the Frame panel, selecting an in-between frame, and selecting Shape from the pop-up Tween menu in the Frame panel.

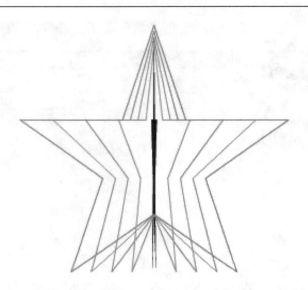

FIGURE 12-3   A star spinning on a center axis gives the illusion of a two-dimensional object spinning on a three-dimensional plane; a shape tween was applied to this star

If you were to play the movie at this point, the star would appear to do nothing because the beginning and end keyframes are identical. To make the star appear as if it's rotating on a full 360-degree center axis, a keyframe was added on Frame 10, the middle frame. The width of the star in the middle frame was made as thin as possible using the Scale tool from the toolbar. Selecting the star on Frame 10 and clicking the Scale tool accomplished this. With the eight scale handles displayed, the middle right handle was dragged left to reduce the width of the star to a razor-thin line (see Figure 12-4).

When you scale an editable object with the Scale tool, it doesn't reference from the center of the object like a symbol does, unless you're using the Scale and Rotate command from the menu (Modify | Transform | Scale and Rotate). It references the object from the point you're dragging on. For example, when you scale the width of the object by dragging on the middle right handle, the object will scale from the middle left as you drag left, as shown in Figure 12-4.

NOTE   *The Scale and Rotate command scales both the width and the height of an object proportionately, so you can't just scale one or the other as was done in Figure 12-4. The Scale and Rotate command does scale from the center point of an object.*

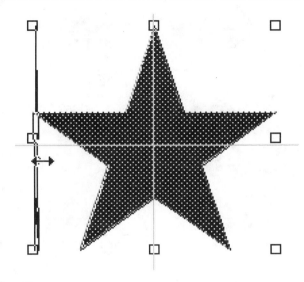

FIGURE 12-4   The width of the object was reduced on the center keyframe by dragging one of the scale handles

In order to give the illusion of spinning on a center axis, the object has to be moved back to the exact same center X and Y position that the first and last frame are on. You can accomplish this in one of several ways. One way would be to use guides on the first keyframe to determine where the center of the object is located.

You can display guides by selecting View | Rulers and View | Guides | Show Guides from the menu. Guides can be dragged from the rulers and positioned in the center of the object for alignment purposes. This way, when you move the object back to the center position in the middle keyframe, you'll know where it was originally located. Another method would be to turn on Onion Skinning to determine where the object on the first and last frame is located. Neither one of these options is the most accurate method.

For pinpoint accuracy, it's best to use the Info panel for positioning. With the Info panel, you can type in the exact center X and Y position of the object on keyframe 10. Display the Info panel by selecting Window | Panels | Info (see Figure 12-5). Take note of the coordinates in the X and Y boxes on the first and last keyframes. After you alter the width of the object, type in the X and Y position of the first keyframe. When the object spins, it will spin on the identical axis throughout.

12

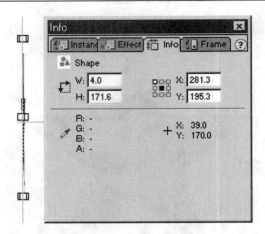

FIGURE 12-5   The Info panel is useful for pinpointing the exact position of an object

NOTE   *When scaling a symbol using the Scale tool, it references from the center. A grouped object being scaled will reference from the handle that's being selected just like an editable object. To make a grouped object reference from the center like a symbol does, select the object and go to Modify | Transform | Edit Center. A crosshair will then appear in the center of the grouped object. When you go to scale the object, it now references from the center.*

Now the star tweens between Frames 1 and 10. Frames 10 and 20 reverse the action on Frames 1–10. When the movie is played back, the star appears to be rotating back and forth in a continuous 360-degree turn from the object's center. A similar effect could be created with a motion tween, too.

The shape changes considerably when you add rotation and skewing to a shape tween. Figure 12-6 shows a shape tween with two keyframes. The beginning and end keyframes are identical (as in Figure 12-3). However, in this movie, the middle keyframe has a rotation and skew applied to it. When played back, the object appears to distort on the in-between frames. In fact, around Frame 7, the object appears as a shapeless blob, momentarily loosing all visual connection to the original object. In this example, you can catch a glimpse of what occurs in morphing, that is, the transformation of one object into another.

The same skewed and rotated object with a motion tween applied to it appears as a two-dimensional object transforming on a three-dimensional plane, as in Figure 12-7. In a motion tween, the object is treated as a whole entity. No matter

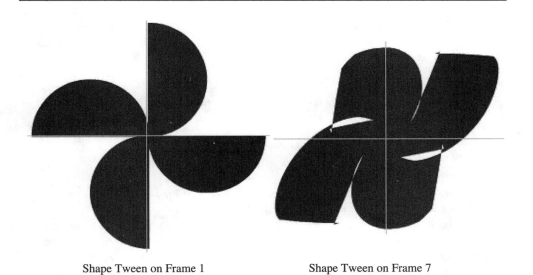

Shape Tween on Frame 1   Shape Tween on Frame 7

FIGURE 12-6   An object that shape tweens with the Rotate and/or Skew tool can distort in an unpredictable manner

Motion Tween on Frame 1   Motion Tween on Frame 7

FIGURE 12-7   Unlike a shape tween, an object that motion tweens with the Rotate and/or Skew tool appears as a whole object

12

what properties are changed, the motion tween always maintains the integrity of the original object. In a shape tween, the same object transforms into another object and sometimes separates into pieces of the original object when a rotation and/or skew is applied.

Shape Tween Versus Motion Tween on a Multi-Layer Movie

So far, the emphasis in this chapter has been on applying shape tweens to simple editable objects residing on one layer. Because editable objects are bitmaps, they often cause editing problems. Bitmaps are created with pixels and don't have a stacking order on mouse release. Changing a portion of an editable object means erasing pixels, which leaves a hole in the place where the pixels were removed. For example, if you created a face and on it were eyes, eyebrows, a nose, and a mouth, and attempted to move an eye by selecting it with the Lasso tool, a hole would be left where the eye once was. Major repair would have to take place to realistically fill in the hole left by the removal of the eye (see Figure 12-8).

Grouped or symbol objects are easy to edit in a motion tween, but they can't perform many of the tricks made available with editable objects in shape tweens.

FIGURE 12-8   A face created with editable objects residing on the same layer is far more difficult to edit than if all the components resided on multi-layers

Placing objects on separate layers can easily resolve the difficulty of editable objects in shape tweens. These elements can be easily edited by going to the appropriate layer the object resides on. Figure 12-9 is a four-layer shape tween. When the in-between frames are examined, shape tweening causes radical transformations on each layer, returning to its original state on the last keyframe.

There are several changes taking place over the course of the shape tween in Figure 12-9. The word "eye" resides on the top layer. The alpha, rotation, and width are changed throughout the tween. Because the word is editable, when paths of the object cross during rotating, it causes the text to almost appear as if it's inside out, as in Frame 27. The same word rotated in a motion tween with almost the identical settings would appear to rotate on a center axis, as in Figure 12-10. Also, the opacity of the color cannot be changed with a grouped motion tween as can be done in the shape tween, as shown in Figure 12-9. In the motion tween in Figure 12-10, the four sections of the masked background rotate from a center axis, unlike on the identical shape tween where the sections separate and distort like the center of a kaleidoscope.

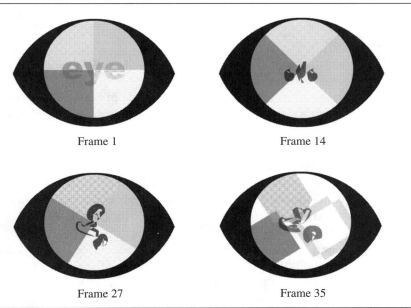

Frame 1   Frame 14

Frame 27   Frame 35

FIGURE 12-9   The editing of a tweened object can be made easier by separating different components of the tween and placing them on separate layers

12

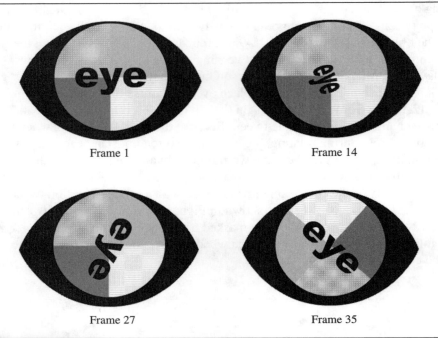

Frame 1   Frame 14

Frame 27   Frame 35

FIGURE 12-10   This figure represents the motion tween equivalent of the previous shape tween; notice how identical frames appear to tween differently

Both movies were created with the same objects, but in Figure 12-9, the moving objects are editable shape tweens and in Figure 12-10 the moving objects are grouped motion tweens. Because the tweening methods are different, the animation in both cases plays back differently. Take notice that the motion tween version has only two keyframes on the mask, as opposed to the shape tween version, which has five keyframes. Because a rotation spin can be applied to a motion tween with the Frames panel, it's not necessary to use the Rotation tool, as it is the case in the shape tween. Shape tweens often require more work because they don't offer many of the automated features that are available to motion tweens.

It's interesting and helpful to compare the two types of tweening to understand the depth of each method. Both methods have their special applications. You also can combine both methods of tweening on different layers in a movie to reap the benefits of both shape and motion tweening.

Deconstruct a Multi-Layer Shape Tween

To better understand shape tweening and the significance of a multi-layer tween, it's helpful to dissect a multi-layer movie in which only shape tweens are used.

Figure 12-9 represents a multi-layer movie on which two of the layers are assigned a shape tween. There is also a mask used in this movie, and the masked object is tweened and conforms to the shape on an eye. Use the following steps to create this movie:

1. Plan out the movie on paper before producing it. Plan the four layers first and add them to the movie. The names and order of the layers are as follows:

    ■ Eye

    ■ Word

    ■ Big circle

    ■ Kaleidoscope

2. Select the eye layer and create an object that resembles the shape of an eye. The object used in this movie that resembles an eye was created and filled with the Bezier Pen tool. The eye provides a framework with a hollowed out pupil, for two overlapping tweens.

3. Next, select the word layer and type out the word **eye** in a sans serif font and center it within the pupil part of the eye on it's own layer. Because these objects reside on separate layers, the editable objects won't get tangled up in one another. The text also needs to be editable to work as a shape tween. So to do this, select the text and break it apart (Modify | Break Apart).

4. Select the big circle layer. This layer contains a circle the size of the pupil in the center of the eye, and it acts as the mask for the last layer, called "kaleidoscope." If the mask didn't exist, the kaleidoscope animation in the background of the pupil would just appear as four rectangles sitting on a layer behind the eye, and as such, would not connect to the pupil. So to create this effect, make a colored circle and use the edge of the pupil on the eye layer to determine the approximate circumference of this circle.

5. The masked layer, kaleidoscope, consists of four identical boxes framed together in the shape of a big rectangle (see Figure 12-11). Each rectangle has a different color, so that during the tween it resembles big pieces of confetti in a kaleidoscope, shifting as the center twirls. To make these boxes, make a rectangle shape and duplicate it by holding down the CTRL+SHIFT/CMD+SHIFT key and dragging right. Align the left side of the new rectangle to the right side of the old rectangle. Select both of these rectangles by holding down the SHIFT key and while again holding down the CTRL/CMD key. The big rectangle is centered over and covers the circumference of the mask (big circle).

12

FIGURE 12-11   The kaleidoscope layer was created with a rectangle duplicated three times and placed together to create a larger rectangle

6. Going back to the big circle layer, select the page icon to the left of the layer to apply a mask to this layer. Apply a mask by right-clicking/ CTRL-clicking and selecting Mask from the pop-up contextual menu. When a mask is applied to a layer, the page icon turns into a down-arrow icon in a circle and the layer underneath becomes the masked layer. Masked layers are represented in the Timeline with an indented, right-arrow circle. The result of this masking effect can be previewed on the stage by clicking the lock at the top of the Timeline in the Layer column.

7. With everything in place, place a keyframe (F6) on Frame 40 of the word and kaleidoscope layers, and place a regular frame (F5) on Frame 40 of the eye layer and the big circle layer.

8. Now, the word and kaleidoscope are all set for tweening. Display the Frame panel (Window | Panels | Frame) and choose an in-between frame on the word layer to select the entire eye frameset. In the Frame panel, choose Shape for Tween type. Repeat this for the kaleidoscope layer.

9. After the shape tweens are established, add keyframes to the word and kaleidoscope layers on Frames 10, 20, and 30. Display guides (View | Rulers-View | Guides) to determine the X and Y position of the center stage because the position of the image is center also. With keyframe 10 selected on the eye layer, reduce the width of the word to approximately 50% and move it back to its center reference point from Frame 1 using the guides.

10. Next, select keyframe 20. Because the keyframes were created before any changes were made to the Timeline, the word object still looks as it originally did on keyframe 1. Rotate the word object 180 degrees in keyframe 20 using the Rotation tool in the toolbar. On keyframe 30, rotate the word object again 90 degrees clockwise. After the word object is rotated on certain keyframes, make it partially transparent on keyframes 1, 10, 30, and 40. Do this by displaying the Mixer panel (Window | Panels | Mixer), selecting the word on the keyframes, and changing the alpha percentage of the object's color.

11. Select the four rectangles on the kaleidoscope layer (with the other layers temporarily locked and made invisible in the Timeline to make the kaleidoscope layer easy to manipulate) and rotate it at different degrees on keyframes 10, 20, 30, and 40 using the Rotation tool from the toolbar. The movie is now complete.

When the movie is played back (Control | Test Movie), instead of the word object and kaleidoscope rotating as objects on their own layers, individual pieces of each shape transform into different shapes while rotating. Some shapes intersect their own paths during the course of the animation, causing an outline effect. The resulting movie (Figure 12-9) looks completely different from its motion tween counterpart, Figure 12-10. The only difference in producing these movies is that the objects in the shape tween are editable, whereas in the motion tween, they aren't.

This comparison will help you understand the difference between shape and motion tweening. When used together on separate layers, you have an impressive range of alternative tweening effects.

Morph Between Objects

Shape tweening is often used to create a morphing effect in an animation. Unlike motion tweens, which treat an object as a whole entity, shape tweens enable you to transform one object into another. A small preview of morphing appeared in Figure 12-9, when the word object and the kaleidoscope completely transformed on certain frames during the tween. However, on the end keyframes, they returned to their original states. When you morph an object, it gradually transforms into another object based on what the first and last objects look like and the properties and settings you change on the in-between frames. Morphing in Flash enables you to tween two entirely separate objects located on different keyframes. What's more, size, rotation, and skew of an object can be added to further distort the morph effect.

12

Figure 12-12 displays a rectangle outline that morphs into a triangle, then into a circle, then into a swirl on Frame 40 and finally disappears, leaving a blank scene for a brief second. On Frame 41 the shapes gradually reappear on stage from left to right reintroducing themselves almost like cast members. On Frame 41, the editable objects are replaced by graphic symbols, and they are motion tweened in steps of five framesets each, one frame apart. This movie plays about four seconds, but packs a powerful impression on its viewer in a short period of time. It's a very simple movie and a good example of how simple images are often more effective than complex images in morphing.

Morphing does involve planning and discretion to work successfully. Otherwise, this technique can produce ugly results when not used correctly.

Deconstruct a Movie Using a Morph Effect

The process of morphing is different from that of an everyday shape or motion tween. A regular tween involves gradually changing the properties of an object from one keyframe to another. Morphing is different because it involves gradually changing one object into another object from one keyframe to another. The position, size, color, rotation, and skew also can vary from one object to a completely different

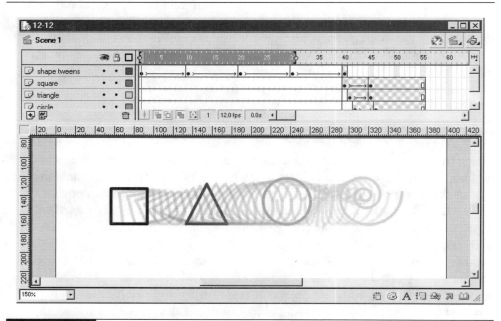

FIGURE 12-12   The morphing of an object goes through three incarnations before ending up a swirl

object. In Figure 12-12, the object changes as well as the position and color of the object on keyframes up to keyframe 30, when the swirl flies off the stage. To thoroughly understand the process of morphing an object with a shape tween, let's examine the steps required to create Figure 12-12.

1. As always, plan your movie before beginning it. No matter how small your movie, its success often depends on good planning up front. Create five layers in the following order:

   ■ Shape tweens

   ■ Square

   ■ Triangle

   ■ Circle

   ■ Swirl

2. Adjust the movie size property to 400 pixels wide by 300 pixels high in the Movie Properties menu (Modify | Movie). Because there's no need for the movie to use up all the stage space of the default size (550 pixels wide by 440 pixels high), you can make it smaller. The smaller the movie, the smaller the final file size.

3. The first layer, shape tweens, contains the majority of the contents of the movie. On keyframe 1, you can set up all four shapes and put them into place. First, a simple rectangle outline was created to the middle left of the stage. It has a stroke of 3 pixels and no fill color. Turn on the snap to grid to make it easy to align and distribute the rest of the shapes on the stage (View | Grid | Snap To Grid). Make a simple triangle outline shape with a stroke of 3 pixels and place it to the right of the first shape. Repeat the process with the creation of a circle outline and a swirl shape sequentially falling to the right of each other (see Figure 12-13). You can use the Align panel if you want to distribute the objects evenly.

4. With all four shapes in place, add a keyframe to Frame 40. Apply a shape tween to the frameset by displaying the Frame panel (Window | Panels | Frame) and selecting Shape in the Tween pop-up menu. Keyframes (F6) were then added to Frames 10, 20, and 30.

5. With all the tweening and elements in place, the movie will begin to take shape when objects are systematically eliminated from each keyframe, creating the illusion of one object morphing into another.

12

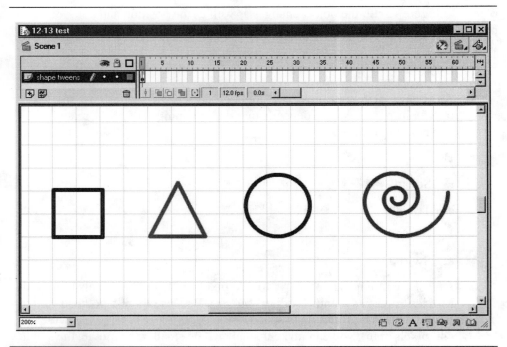

FIGURE 12-13 The objects that will be morphed are in position on the first keyframe of the shape tweens layer

6. Working backward, select keyframe 40 and drag the swirl object off the stage to the upper-right corner. This makes the object fly off the stage after the circle transforms into the swirl. With Frame 40 selected, delete the other three objects to the right (square, triangle, and circle).

7. With keyframe 30 selected, leave the swirl in place and delete the square, triangle, and circle.

8. With keyframe 20 selected, delete the square, triangle, and swirl, leaving this keyframe to highlight the circle as shown in Figure 12-14.

   Repeat the process on keyframe 10 by deleting the swirl, circle, and square and again on keyframe 1, with all objects to the right of the square being deleted.

9. At this point when the movie is played back, each simple shape transforms into another and between keyframes 30 and 40, the swirl flies off the stage.

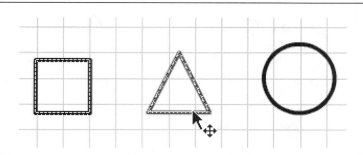

FIGURE 12-14   Objects are being systematically deleted backward from keyframe 40 to create a morphing effect

In the balance of the movie from Frame 40 on, the shapes from layer 1 are eliminated completely. They are replaced by a graphic symbol of a square, triangle, circle, and swirl on their subsequent layers. These graphic symbols are created from the editable shapes that were used on the first layer to create the morph. By Frame 55, all the objects gradually reappear in the identical position from which they were originally morphed from in Frames 1–30 as shown in the Timeline in Figure 12-12.

To create these graphic symbols, click on each shape and select Insert | Convert to Symbol from the menu. A graphic symbol duplicate of these shapes now resides on the movie's Library as shown in Figure 12-15. The shapes give the illusion of gradually reappearing because the outline color goes from none to opaque over a series of five frames. Also, the framesets on each layer are staggered to begin that particular layer's animation one frame after each other to further create a feeling of gradual transition as shown in the Timeline on Figure 12-15. The simple shape tweens blend harmoniously with the motion tweens in this movie.

Apply Shape Hints to Your Morph

When you morph from one object to another, the in-between frames often transform in an unpredictable way. If you were to scrub over each in-between frame, the object would appear to gradually take shape from the first frame to the last. The manner in which objects morph is a default setting in Flash. Shape hints on a morph identify key points on the beginning state of one object and the end state of another object. The shape hints on each object correspond to one another by having an identical letter assigned on each object.

12

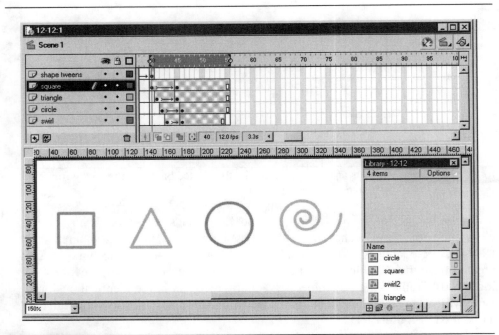

FIGURE 12-15   This part of the Timeline staggers the four motion tweened objects from Frame 40–Frame 55 to create a sense of gradual transition; duplicates of each editable now reside in the Library

The position of these shape hints as key tweening points is crucial to the outcome of the morph. They serve as a road map for the morph, determining what direction the points will travel to arrive at the shapes' final destination. Just like a road map, there are many different ways to get to your destination. Shape hints provide markers to help you get there, and on the way, provide different scenery; depending on which path they take.

You, the designer, can control shape hints. If you don't like the way your shape is morphing in Flash, you can go back in and move the hints until the morph meets your expectations. Shape hints are an important feature when doing serious morphing. The ability to control the hints can mean the difference between frames appearing as shapeless blobs or as a transformation with a clear direction.

Hints are indicated as letters contained in small circles. These letters reside on the object in the first and last keyframes. Figure 12-16 shows a simple shape tween with shape hints applied to the first (visible on the first keyframe as the playhead is on Frame 1) and last keyframes of a morph. The hints in the first keyframe appears as yellow circles, and on the end keyframe, the color turns green. Before a hint is applied, or, when a hint is not sitting directly on an object, the color of the hint is red.

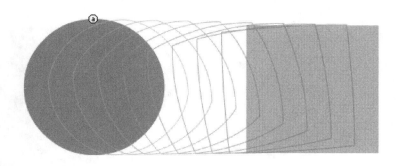

FIGURE 12-16   Applying shape hints to a simple object enables you to see how the hints correspond to one another from one transition to another

To apply shape hints, a shape tween must be made first. In Figure 12-16, a circle is created in keyframe 1. A keyframe is then placed on Frame 10 (F6), and a simple rectangle is created to the right of the circle. A shape tween is then applied by clicking an in-between frame and selecting Shape from the Tweening pop-up menu in the Frame panel.

When the movie is played back, the circle transforms into a square using the Flash default shape hint settings. To control the way the hints tween, click the object in Frame 1 and select Modify | Transform | Add Shape Hint from the menu. A hint letter appears on the stage, and the first hint letter is always the letter "a". Drag the hint to a point on the first object. In this figure, three additional hints were added and positioned on the circle, as in Figure 12-17.

On keyframe 10, the four hints added to keyframe 1 are sitting on top of one another, waiting to be placed on the last object as in Figure 12-18. The hints were positioned to logically correspond to the hints in keyframe 1. When the hints are repositioned on the last frame, the color of the hint changes to green. Concurrently, when revisiting the first keyframe, the hints turn yellow.

Shape hints are most successful if placed in a logical, clockwise order, starting from the top left of the object as a reference point. Otherwise, unpredictable results will occur. In Figure 12-19, a star transforms into a rectangle. The shape hints on the star (a, b, c, d) rotate clockwise from the left around four points of the star. The corresponding shape hints on the rectangle in the last keyframe (a, b, c, d) also rotate clockwise from the upper-left corner, making the star flawlessly morph into a rectangle in the last keyframe.

TIP   *When you move the hints from different points on your object, if Onion Skin Outlines are turned on, you can preview the path of the shape hints within the tween.*

12

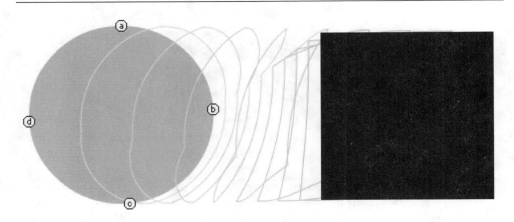

FIGURE 12-17   Additional hints are added to an object in the first keyframe of this movie

Hints also can be removed from an object. To do so, click the object and select Modify | Transform | Remove Shape Hint. All shape hints will disappear.

Shape hints are easy to tweak if they don't meet your expectations. It's simple to go back to the first and last keyframe and reposition the hints. Each time this is done, the morph changes shape. Do this as many times as is necessary to achieve the desired effect. Using simple discretion, like placing the hints in a logical way, helps maintain the integrity of the morph.

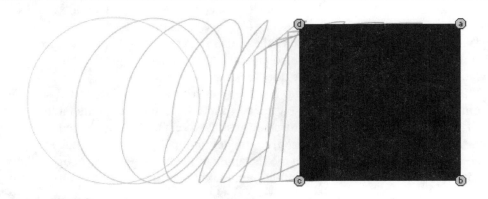

FIGURE 12-18   The hints on the last frame of a movie are green

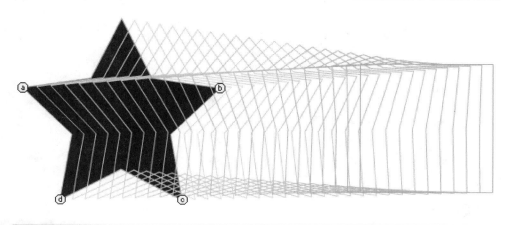

FIGURE 12-19   When shape hints are applied in a logical, clockwise order, the resulting transformation is generally more representational of the original object

Set Shape Tween Properties

Like motion tweens, shape tweens can be assigned parameters. When the in-between frames of a shape tween are selected, the Easing and Blend settings become available in the Frame panel.

The Easing setting is based on the same premise as easing on a motion tween. Tweening from one keyframe to another doesn't give you much control over the speed of an object as it begins or ends its transformation. Easing in and out from the Frame panel gives you control over the speed of the object. The Easing box is a sliding arrow that goes from -100 at the bottom to +100 at the top, as shown in Figure 12-20. To make the tween appear as if it starts slow and speeds up at the end, select an increment between -1 and -100. To make the shape tween appear as if it begins fast and slows down toward the end, select an easing increment between 1 and 100.

The Blend settings become available when Shape is selected in the Frame panel. Select Distributive or Angular from the pop-up Blend menu. When Distributive is chosen, the shape tween will smooth out edges in a tween. When Angular is selected, hard, straight edges and lines will maintain their integrity throughout a tween. Like the Easing parameters, the Blend settings are applied to the in-between frames of a shape tween.

12

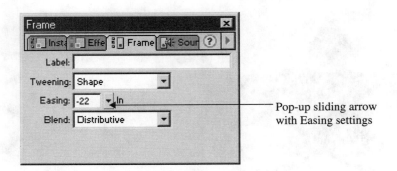

Pop-up sliding arrow
with Easing settings

FIGURE 12-20   The Easing selection in the Frame panel eases in from -100 to out
at +100; the Blend settings enable you to choose from Distributive
or Angular

Shape tweening also can be combined with other types of animation to create
dynamic effects. Good planning always remains a key ingredient with a shape
tween. Shape tweens can cause unpredictable results so planning before you begin
will ensure a successful animation.

Chapter 13

Make Buttons and Movie Clips in Flash

How to...

■ Make a Button

■ Test a Button

■ Add Sound to a Button

■ Add Simple Effects to a Button

■ Make a Movie Clip

■ Add Sound to a Movie Clip

■ Make an Animated Button

Symbols are self-contained elements in Flash that are stored in the current movie's Library. The concept behind the symbol is clever, and if planned correctly, symbols help bring order to the chaos of movie creation. An added benefit of symbols is that they can greatly help reduce file size. The ease of editing symbols and instances helps streamline your workflow in Flash.

Symbols come in three types: graphic, button, and movie clip. Graphic symbols, the simplest kinds of symbols, were discussed in Chapter 8. Graphic symbols can assist you in turning a drawing with a lot of components into a compact, cohesive element. They also enable you to take advantage of the Effect panel, where some exciting color properties can be set on a symbol.

Buttons and movie clips are based on the same concept as graphic symbols. They are compact and can be reused many times in a movie without compromising the file size. In fact, designers often nest graphic symbols in buttons and movie clips to create a well-organized, easy-to-edit movie.

Buttons and movie clips are often used in conjunction with more advanced applications of Flash. In fact, they serve as the gateway to interactivity. In this chapter, the concept behind buttons and movie clips is explored, as well as the mechanics behind their creation. In Chapter 14 you'll learn how to assign scripts to buttons and movie clips, and enter into the world of interactivity. Buttons and movie clips pump up the volume in Flash, and they offer a glimpse at how truly powerful Flash is.

Explore the Power of Buttons and Movie Clips

Buttons and movie clips are a major part of the Flash interactive environment, which is based on the Flash scripting language, ActionScript (discussed in

Chapters 14 and 15). A movie is defined as interactive when a viewer can respond to it. Interactivity encourages the viewer to participate in the ongoing process, thereby making the experience more engaging.

A good example of simple interactivity is hyperlinks. Hyperlinks in an HTML document are interactivity in its simplest form. The process of clicking on an object or text and having it take you to another location demands the viewer interact to experience the site. Although links to HTML documents and SWF files are easy to make, the Flash interface enables you to create far more sophisticated types of interactivity. In Flash, interactivity on an object generally involves buttons, movie clips, or both in some capacity. Therefore, before understanding ActionScript and interactivity, one must have a solid base in buttons and movie clips.

When it comes to interactivity, buttons and movie clips are very powerful. With the click of a button, your viewer can control the properties of a movie clip. For example, on a button press, a movie clip can change size, position, rotation, or color. It can start, stop, or become invisible, as well as many other actions. Buttons also can be nested in movie clips to create special effects for games, e-commerce applications, and killer Web sites.

Movie clips in Flash 5 can be assigned a pretty impressive array of events and actions, many of which were only available for buttons in earlier versions of Flash. In fact, the expanded capabilities of movie clips and ActionScript in Flash 5 have supercharged the program's scripting capabilities, delivering to you, a full- bodied multimedia authoring program.

Make a Button

Buttons are essentially little interactive movies within themselves. When a user creates an event, such as mousing over or clicking on a button, an action can be elicited from the button. The action will be a visual and/or audio change based upon the contents of the three button states. A classic example of a common button when a user rolls over a button and it changes color. Then, when the user presses on the button, it changes appearance again. Theses events are changing the look of the button when a user interacts with it.

As is discussed in Chapter 8, symbols are stored in the Library of your current movie. A symbol can be used many times in Flash without compromising the movie's file size. Because economizing on file size is of major importance on the Web, images are often made into symbols in Flash.

Buttons in Flash can range from simple to sophisticated, only limited by your imagination. They don't all have to look like the classic Web push button seen on so many Web sites. In fact, many buttons in Flash don't look like buttons at all. The rollover and clicking capabilities of buttons make it a viable choice for

13

custom-designed navigation menus that have elements popping out in the movie wherever you want. But starting with the basics is always best in the learning process. Making a simple button in Flash is relatively easy and helps you understand the concept behind all buttons.

Buttons are created on their own four-frame Timeline and can be interactive on this Timeline. The first three frames on the button Timeline enable you to define a button state (Up, Over, Down). The last frame is the Hit frame where the boundaries of the active area within the button are determined.

To create a simple button, select Insert | New Symbol or CTRL+F8/CMD+F8 from the menu. In the Symbol Properties dialog box, check Button for symbol type, name the button in the Name box, and press OK (see Figure 13-1).

You will now enter the Symbol Editing mode where buttons or other symbols can be created or edited. Figure 13-2 represents the metamorphosis of a simple button, named "my_button." When in the Symbol Editing mode, the name of the button and the button icon appear in the upper-left corner of the stage, next to the scene icon. The Timeline in the Symbol Editing mode looks different from the Timeline in the main movie. You can create as many layers as you want, just like on the main Timeline, but unlike the main Timeline, the frames are no longer displayed in numbers. Rather, they are represented in four states: Up, Over, Down, and Hit.

When you first enter the Symbol Editing mode for the button you're about to create, the object you first draw will appear on the Up state. When the movie loads in the viewer's browser, the button will appear the way it does in the Up state. When in the Symbol Editing mode, there is a crosshair in the center of the stage that indicates where the center of the symbol will be. Use this crosshair as a reference to determine where your button elements will appear on each state.

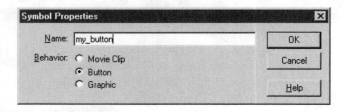

FIGURE 13-1   The Symbol Properties dialog box

FIGURE 13-2   A symbol was dragged from the Library and placed on the Up state of this button

In Figure 13-2, a graphic symbol was added on the Up state and the center reference point of that symbol was aligned to the crosshair in the Editing mode. Your objects can be assembled right on the stage in the Symbol Editing mode, and they can be grouped, editable, or another symbol.

TIP   *If it's important that your object is center aligned precisely with the crosshair in Editing mode, you can display the Info panel and type in an X coordinate of 0 and Y coordinate of 0 with a reference point of center on the object, or use the Align panel. To use this panel, choose the center align horizontal and vertical icons. Note that editable objects don't respond to align options from this panel.*

13

The Over state was clicked and a keyframe (F6) was added. The Over state is the way the button will look on this frame when the user rolls over the button with their mouse. On the Over state in Figure 13-2, the color changes, so when the user mouses over the button, the button changes color. With the object selected, the color was changed in the Effects panel. On the Down state, another keyframe (F6) was added. The Down state is activated when the user mouses down on the button. The button on the Down state was rotated 45 degrees, and the object color was changed again in the Effects panel.

 *If you were changing the color on an editable object, the color can only be changed from the colors in the Toolbar or in the Color panels; not the Effect panel.*

A keyframe (F6) was then added to the Hit state. On the Hit state, a rectangle was drawn over the area where the user would interact with the button. An Alpha was added to a color from the Mixer panel so the button would appear transparent through the rectangle (see Figure 13-3). Any color area or opacity can be used to indicate the hit area as can any shape. Shapes drawn on the Hit state will not be visible on movie playback. The purpose of a Hit state is to declare a certain area surrounding the button as active. It is not absolutely necessary for you to indicate a hit area. If you elect not to do so, Flash assumes the object in the Up state represents the hit area of the button. Indicating a hit area is a good idea when making buttons with unusual shapes where it might be hard for the viewer to select

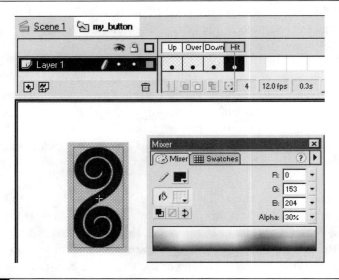

FIGURE 13-3   The rectangle in the Hit state was made transparent so the button could be seen through the rectangle

it, or on disjointed rollovers where an object pops up in a location different from the parent button.

To exit the Symbol Editing mode, click on the Scene icon on the upper-left corner of the menu or select Edit | Edit Movie (CTRL+E/CMD+E). To see the button, open the Library (Window | Library or CTRL+L/CMD+L). The button can be tested in the Library as shown in Figure 13-4. If the button selected in the Library is interactive, an arrow will appear in the bottom-right corner of the Library preview. Click this button to see the changes on the different button states. If you have included a graphic on the Hit state, the graphic will appear in the Library preview. In the next section you'll learn how to test the button without seeing the Hit state.

The button will remain in this Library of the current movie, unless you choose to delete it at some point. Delete the button from the Library by clicking on the button and selecting the trash can icon at the bottom of the window. A dialog box will alert you that the symbol is about to be deleted. Choose Delete to get rid of the symbol, or cancel, if you change your mind and want to keep it. A symbol also can be deleted from the Options pop-up menu in the Library. To delete the button with the Options menu, click the button in the Library, click the Options menu and select Delete. All Library items, including graphics, movie clips, sounds, and bitmaps, can be deleted with this option.

TIP

When you delete a button, your movie size will remain the same unless you do a File | Save As.

13

FIGURE 13-4   Test a button by selecting it in the Library and clicking the right arrow in the Library preview

This button is an example of just one of the many kinds of buttons you can create in Flash. A button doesn't have to change on the Over and Down states. Often you don't need the actual button to be interactive on the Over and Down states. You might just need a clickable button to perform an action on a frame or a movie clip. In a case where you don't want your button to do fancy things, the process would be as follows:

1. Select Insert | New Symbol (CTRL+F8/CMD+F8) from the menu.

2. Check the Button option, give the button a name, and click OK. On the Up state, add or make a graphic. A keyframe will automatically be generated on the Up state when you draw the object. If you want to define the active area, click the Hit state, add a frame (F6), and place a graphic on this frame.

3. Exit the Button Editing mode by either clicking the Scene in the upper-left corner or select Edit | Edit Movie or CTRL+E/CMD+E. The button that now appears in the Library doesn't change when you click the arrow in the Library to preview the button.

NOTE   *With a simple button, you don't have to add frames to the states that are not in use. An image occupying the Up state is sufficient to make a button work. In fact, if you make an object on the main Timeline and use the Insert | Convert to Symbol command to make your button, when you edit the button, you'll notice that it only occupies the Up state in the Symbol Editing mode.*

Sometimes you might want to create an invisible button if you want an area of the stage to be clickable but you don't need an object. When a button is clickable you can assign actions to it (even if there's no button visible). To make an invisible button, create the button as you would a regular button, but leave all states blank except for the Hit state. The Hit state is necessary because the clickable area must be defined for it to work.

Test Your Button

If you drag an instance of a button onto the stage from the Library and click or mouse over it, nothing will happen even if it's supposed to change in the different states. The button probably works, but you can't preview it while in Movie mode. So far, you've only been able to test the interactivity of your button in the Library.

Although the Library is good for quickly catching mistakes on a button, you still need to examine the button further in case it needs adjusting of some sort. Buttons can be further tested in Flash.

There are a few ways to test buttons. Aside from the Library option, buttons can be set to work on the stage. To do this, select Control | Enable Simple Buttons or CTRL+ALT+B/OPT+CMD+B from the menu (see Figure 13-5). Now when you mouse over and/or click on the button, if the button is interactive, it will be displayed on the stage. This menu selection acts as a toggle switch and also disables buttons. When you're finished testing the buttons and want to bring them back to an editable state, select Control | Enable Simple Buttons or CTRL+ALT+B/OPT+CMD+B from the menu again.

When buttons are enabled, your pointer responds to mouse events assigned to buttons. This means you can't move or modify the button the way you ordinarily would if you wanted to edit a movie. To move or modify the button while in Button Editing mode, click on the Arrow tool and drag an invisible marquee around the boundaries of the button to select it without touching it with the pointer. To move the button, use the arrow keys. A button also can become selectable using CRTL+ALT+right-click/CTRL+double-click.

Transform the properties of a button by selecting any of the Transformation options from the menu (Modify | Transform). For example, if you wanted to scale and rotate the button while the button is enabled and selected, display the Scale and Rotate

FIGURE 13-5   Select Control | Enable Simple Buttons from the menu to test buttons in your Flash movie

13

dialog box from the Modify | Transform menu or CTRL+ALT+S/OPT+CMD+S. Type in the new size or rotation and click OK. The button will reflect these modifications.

Although you can edit a button while it's enabled on the stage, it's much easier to edit when buttons are not enabled.

Enabling a button might not work on all buttons. If the button is complex, or has movie clips or animation on frames or layers, it will need to be tested in the Movie or Preview mode, which we will discuss next.

Another way to test a button is to select Control | Test Movie from the menu. This creates an SWF version of the file and stores it in the same folder as your movie. The buttons will be fully active in this mode. The movie can be previewed in a browser by selecting File | Preview | HTML. This also generates an HTML page and an SWF file with the SWF file embedded in the HTML document. The file also is stored in the folder with your movie. Use either one of these options to preview the movie in a manner closer to what the user will experience.

Create Advanced Buttons

You're probably used to looking at the same old kind of radio-like buttons that change color and shape slightly on rollover and mouse down. But in Flash, buttons don't have to be limited to the same old object transforming on different states, as in Figure 13-4. Buttons can be as creative as your imagination allows. Different objects can occupy the button on different states, and you can add sounds, add additional layers, and even incorporate movie clips to add animation to a button. Although the scope of button creation is too broad to cover in this book, let's explore some special effects you can apply to buttons to make them stand out from the ordinary.

Change Objects on Button Hit States   If you're thinking out of the box, there's no reason a button always has to be the same old picture when you roll over or click it. Changing the object on different button states is easy in Flash. Figure 13-6 shows a button in the Up, Over, and Down states and the different shape it takes in each state. The three different objects used on this button are astrology symbols that were made into graphic symbols before being used on the button states. Because they are symbols, the Effect panel can be used to color the objects in the Symbol Editing mode. When the movie loads, the button appears as an image of two fish. When the viewer mouses over the fish, they turn into a goat. When the viewer mouses down on the button, it turns into a man pouring water.

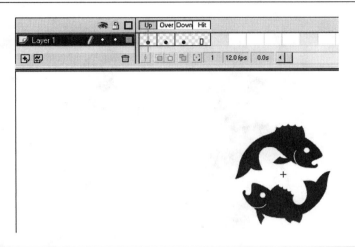

FIGURE 13-6   The image on this button is swapped with other images on the Over
and Down states

To create this button, the images were planned out and made into graphic
symbols. Each object was individually created in the main Timeline. After they
were created, they were selected and converted to graphic symbols (Insert |
Convert to Symbol or F8).

With all the required objects in the Library, Insert | New Symbol or
CTRL+F8/CMD+F8 was selected. In the Symbol Properties dialog box, Button
was checked for the type of symbol and the name "objects" was given to the
button. The Library was displayed (see Figure 13-7) and in the Symbol Editing
mode, the fish symbol was dragged to the stage and centered (on the crosshair)
on the Up state. A keyframe (F6) was added to the Over state, and the goat symbol
was dragged from the Library to the crosshair and centered.

A keyframe was then added to the Down state, and the symbol of the man
was, dragged and centered on the crosshair. Nothing was added to the Hit state
on this button so the live area of the button is defined by the image on the
Up state. The Editing mode was exited and an instance of the button was
dragged onto the stage. To test this button, Control | Enable Simple Buttons or
CTRL+ALT+B/CMD+ALT+B was selected. When the button is tested, the image is
swapped on the Over and Down states.

This technique exhibits a simple form of interactivity because the button
responds to mouse events. You can use this technique of switching images to

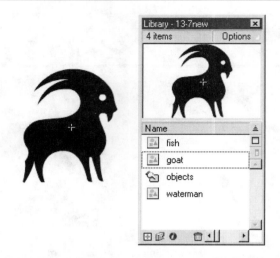

FIGURE 13-7
Symbol instances are dragged from the Library onto the stage; notice the graphic symbols that were used to create Figure 13-6 are also in the Library

add some interesting effects to your button. Although our sample might seem like an unremarkable button in its present state, we expound upon this technique in the next section and substitute animated movie clips for the static objects on the Over and Down states. And then, your buttons do become exciting.

Add Sound to a Button As you would probably agree, making buttons in Flash is pretty easy. Equally as easy is adding sounds to buttons. You can add your own sound or use a wide selection of short sounds offered in the Flash Common Library. Adding a sound can enhance the user experience by making the user more attentive to the flow of the movie. Sound also can be an extra surprise when a user clicks a button, waking the user up from long downloading time on the Web. You can make the button sound like a real click or a beep or anything your imagination can conjure up. Button sounds can be short and small so they don't have much effect on file size, which is a good thing. Sounds in general are notoriously big, so they can make a movie load into a browser slowly. Buttons are a good way to add the impact of audio while still leaving the file size manageable.

Add Sound to a Button from the Sound Library Flash comes jam-packed with a library full of short sounds. Because the sounds are so short, they're perfect for adding to button states. The Sound Library can be found in the menu under Window | Common | Libraries | Sounds, as shown in Figure 13-8. Sound is discussed in detail in Chapter 9.

The Sound Library exists in a file that's located in the Flash program folder on your hard drive. Specifically, it's in the Library | Sounds folder, and its contents can't be tampered with while you're making a movie. You can't add or delete sounds from this Library like you can from the regular Library where your symbols appear. However, when you add a sound to the movie from the Sound Library, a copy of the sound appears in your Library, thus making it easier to organize all symbols and eliminate clutter on the desktop.

The astrology button (Figure 13-6) that was examined in the last section could be jazzed up a little if the user heard a sound when they clicked or rolled over the button. In Figure 13-9, a separate sound has been added on the Over and Down states on this button.

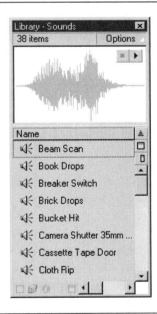

FIGURE 13-8   Sounds can be found in the Common Sounds Library

13

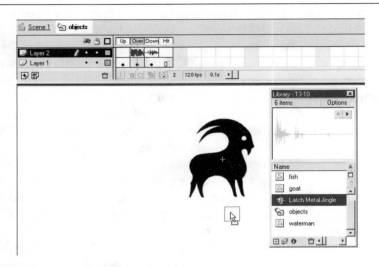

FIGURE 13-9 Sound being added to a button in the Symbol Editing mode

To add sound to a button like this, complete the following steps:

1. Double-click the button in the Library or double-click an instance of the button on the stage to enter the Symbol Editing mode. The name of the layer is superfluous, so name the layer whatever you like. Often Flash authors name a sound layer "sound" for obvious reasons.

NOTE *Although you can place the sound layer above or below the button layer, Flash authors generally place the layer on top of the button layer or close to the top (as they do with frame actions) so it can be easily spotted when making revisions.*

2. Open the Sound Library from the Common Libraries menu, test the sounds, and find two that are suitable for your button. Test the sound by clicking it in the Library and selecting the preview arrow in the right corner of the window. This will enable you to hear the sound before you apply it.

3. On the sound layer, click the Over frame and add a keyframe (F6). Then click the Down frame and add another keyframe. With the Over frame selected, drag a sound onto the stage. Although you won't see anything

on the stage, the frame will depict the sound wave. If you only want a sound on the Over state, your button is ready. However, in this movie a keyframe was added on the Down state to accommodate another sound (you only need a keyframe if you're going to add sound).

4. On the sound layer click the Down frame and drag another sound onto the stage. On the Hit state, you can either add a hit area, leave it blank, or add a keyframe to prevent the sound wave from visually appearing to spill over into the Hit state.

5. Exit the Symbol Editing mode. If you haven't already done so, drag an instance of the button onto the stage and test it using the test methods previously outlined in this chapter.

Add Sound to a Button from an Imported Sound   If you don't find a sound that's appropriate in the Sounds Library, you can add your own. It's easy to find short sound effects and loops on the Internet for free. See Appendix B for audio resources. If you utilize an audio-editing program you can make your own sounds. Either way, if you're looking for special sound and it can't be found in the Flash Library, it's easy to add it yourself.

There are a couple of issues to keep in mind if you plan to import your own sounds for buttons. The sound effects in the Sounds Library last about a fraction of a second, so when a user rolls over or mouses down on a button, the sound is quick. Depending on how long it is, your imported sound will play through until it reaches the end of the audio clip. The user can be long finished mousing over or clicking on the button and that sound will keep on going. What's more, if you put a sound on the Over and Down states, if they're not short enough, they can sound like they're tangled up in one another while the user moves over and clicks, spoiling the whole sound experience altogether. The point is that careful planning needs to be done when using custom imported sounds on buttons. It's okay for a sound to be longer than a fraction of a second as long as you anticipate the ramifications of this design decision in every possible scenario.

To import a sound into Flash and apply it to a button, select File | Import or CTRL+R/CMD+R from the menu. In the Navigate dialog box, navigate to the sound you want to import. On the PC, click the sound and select the Open button. On the Mac, navigate to the sound you want to import, select it, and click the Add button; then click the Import button. The sound will now appear in your Library. Add the sound to a button the same way you add a sound from the Common Library, as was covered in the previous section. When the button is tested, you'll hear the sound.

13

Change the Properties of a Button

If you surf the Web, you've probably noticed that more and more, Flash movies are replacing traditional Web sites. Even if you haven't noticed that Flash sites are increasing in number, you see the Flash logo emblazoned all over the Web and in the media. Because more and more authors build entire sites in Flash, movies often contain some of the static elements used on classic Web pages, like navigational buttons. Creating multiple buttons in this capacity can be time consuming and boring. Flash offers ways to streamline the button production process in the Instance panel.

The Instance panel also is used for graphic symbols and movie clips. Depending on which behavior you've chosen for your symbol, the information in the Instance panel changes to reflect that behavior (see Figure 13-10). Features relating to graphic symbols in the Instance panel are discussed in Chapter 8.

Change the Behavior of a Symbol

When you select a button on the stage and display the Instance panel, the default behavior is that of a button. You can change the behavior on this button instance to a graphic or a movie clip. By changing the behavior of one symbol to another, that instance can have access to the properties associated with the new symbol. For example, by changing the behavior of a button to a graphic symbol, the button instance is no longer clickable. It behaves just like a regular graphic symbol. By changing a button instance to a movie clip, if the button changes on the Over and Down states, the resulting switch to a movie clip will appear animated. If you enter the Symbol Editing mode on this instance, the object is still based on the

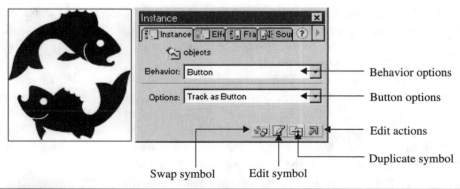

FIGURE 13-10   A button can be edited in many ways from the Instance panel

behavior of the parent symbol in the Library. For example, if you changed the behavior of a button instance to a movie clip, if you revise the instance, the editing stage will reflect that of a button; not the Timeline of a movie clip.

Change the Behavior of a button or any symbol by clicking on the Behavior pop-up menu in the Instance panel. All three types, Graphic, Button, and Movie Clip are listed. Select the new type and the new options in the panel associated with that type.

Under the Behavior type is the Options pop-up menu. For a button, there are two selections:

■ **Track as Button**—This selection is used for a standard, single button, as is the default.

■ **Track as Menu Item**—This selection is used if you're creating pop-up navigational menus that have several clickable selections within a defined area.

At the bottom right of the menu there are four convenient buttons that can instantly perform tasks that might otherwise be time consuming. These buttons are available on all symbol types in the Instance panel:

■ **Swap Symbol**—This is a cool little button that enables you to swap one instance of a symbol with another (see Figure 13-11). For example, let's say you had a sizable movie with many instances of the same button throughout. Your client decides to switch hundreds of buttons with another style of button. Rather than dragging and positioning a new instance on all buttons, you can click an old button and select the new button. Instantly, the symbols are swapped. You can swap different types of symbols also.

■ **Edit Symbol**—This button brings you to the Editing mode of the selected instance.

■ **Duplicate Symbol**—This makes a copy of the selected instance as shown in Figure 13-12. If you needed to make 10 buttons that were almost identical aside from minimal properties changing (like text), you can click this button; make a copy, and then edit the new button by changing the desired properties. This button is a real timesaver for repetitious buttons.

■ **Edit Actions**—This button instantly takes you to the Actions panel where you can add or edit a script on the selected button or movie clip.

13

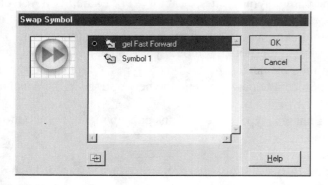

FIGURE 13-11 The Swap Symbol dialog box appears when you slick the Swap Symbol button

Add Simple Effects to a Button

Buttons are very versatile. In the next chapter we will return to the subject of buttons in a different context; that is, assigning ActionScript to buttons. The scope of ActionScript is so broad; entire books are devoted to the subject. Before learning to assign a script to a button there are some issues to consider. When you're new to Flash, it's not always easy to understand how an author constructed a movie, especially movies that use complex ActionScript. If you're dedicated to learning advanced Flash, you have to think like a

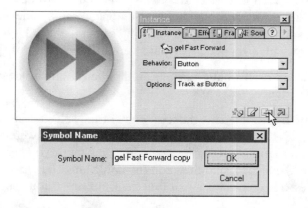

FIGURE 13-12 By clicking the Duplicate Symbol icon, you can make a copy of a symbol

seasoned Flash author. Sometimes, the desired effect and your limited knowledge creates an impasse for your creative juices.

The following is an example of how you might construct a navigational menu in Flash. The buttons in this menu aren't used or constructed as typical buttons on a Web page. This exercise serves as a beginner's primer to thinking out of the box with Flash.

Figure 13-13 shows a linear navigation bar, similar in look to what you might construct on an HTML page. When the user rolls over a topic, "what's new," "archives," "glossary," and "resources," a highlight effect (that looks like a "swish") made from the Paintbrush tool appears in the background. When the user rolls off a topic, the previous topic drops the highlight and the highlight then appears on the current topic. This effect is created with a button that is empty on the Up state. The highlight only shows when the topics are moused over. The following is an account of how to create this effect.

A new movie was opened, and the movie was given the dimensions of 450 pixels wide by 200 pixels high (Modify | Movie | Properties or CTRL+M/CMD+M). Before the navigation bar was created, the layers were planned, as were the assets (symbols and other objects that will be used to construct the movie). Because the navigation bar was planned out thoroughly, it was quick to make because so many symbols were reused and duplicated. In addition, the final SWF file is small in file size.

The maze-like circle to the left of the stage was borrowed from another Flash movie, modified slightly, and made into a graphic symbol. The tab graphic used on each topic on the navigation bar was drawn with the Pen tool and given a stroke of 3 pixels. The tab was also given a curl on the end to complement the maze icon to the left. Lastly, it was converted to a graphic symbol (Insert | Convert to Symbol or F8) and given the name "curly_bracket." The rule that falls under the topics and arches around the maze was created with the Pen tool, given a stroke of 3 pixels, and converted into a graphic symbol. The topic text will be created later as regular text, although this too could be saved as a graphic symbol.

13

FIGURE 13-13   This movie uses a navigation bar similar to bars used on HTML pages

With all the assets organized in the Library and the instances deleted from the stage (except for the text), the layers were then constructed. The layers are set up and named in the following order:

- topics
- static_art
- buttons

On the static art layer, the objects were constructed on the navigation bar. With the Library displayed, an instance of the curly_bracket, graphic_line, and maze was dragged to the stage on the static art layer. The maze and the graphic_line were positioned as per Figure 13-13, and the first curly bracket was butted against the graphic_line instance toward the left where the first topic (what's new) sits. The curly_bracket instance was duplicated three more times by clicking on the object and pressing the SHIFT+CTRL/SHIFT+CMD keys. The instance was duplicated so it could be used for the other three tabs. A reasonable distance was approximated between these duplicate curly_bracket instances, and then they were all aligned and spaced evenly apart as is discussed in the next step. The purpose of holding down the SHIFT key was to constrain the horizontal position of the curly_bracket instance and the CTRL/CMD key duplicated it. Then, all the curly_bracket instances were selected by holding down the SHIFT key while clicking on each bracket. The Align panel (Window | Panels | Align or CTRL+K/CMD+K) was then displayed. With the brackets selected, under Distribute, Distribute Horizontal Center icon (the fifth one from the left) was chosen. The alignment of the curly_bracket instances were made equidistant horizontally.

On the topics layer, the Text tool was selected. On this layer, the words that sit on top of the curly_bracket instances will be typed in. The first word typed was "what's new," which was done in a 13-point san serif font that was stylized bold and italic from the Character panel (Window | Panel | Character or CRTL+T/CMD+T). When creating type, or any objects for that matter, they can be created first and then moved into position and aligned with one another. This is the method that was used for objects on this navigation bar. The text was then dragged into position within the curly bracket and centered horizontally.

The text was duplicated by pressing the SHIFT+CTRL keys and dragging the text horizontally, until the duplicate text was center aligned within the second bracket. The process was repeated until there was text under all four brackets. The purpose of duplicating the text was to make it easy to align many pieces and to avoid having to re-create the text each time. Because the text in each tab is identical except for the wording, this is a very quick way to generate text or objects with similar properties.

With the Text tool selected, on the second text box the word was highlighted and another word was typed in to replace the old text. The process was repeated for the other two text boxes. For this text, the sample movie (Figure 13-13) uses the words "archives", "glossary", and "resources", respectively.

Everything is now in place except for the button that responds to the user's mouse-over. This button was created next. If you recall, when the user mouses over the navigational text, an abstract swish background (or highlight) that looks like a brushstroke appears behind the text and the curly_bracket. Before this button that looks like a brushstroke was constructed, the swish that looks like the brushstroke was made next. The swish was created with the Paintbrush tool using a bold, diagonal brush shape.

The text had to contrast well against this swish, so a light color was selected for the swish. With the button layer and the Paintbrush tool selected, a shape and color were chosen and rendered. To achieve just the right effect, a swish was painted right over some text, using the text as a template. If the brushstroke didn't look right, it was deleted and re-created. When it looked right, it was converted into a graphic symbol. The new swish graphic symbol was deleted from the stage and Insert | New Symbol (CTRL+F8/CMD+F8) was selected. The swish graphic symbol will be used for the art in the button. In the Symbol Properties dialog box, Button was chosen for the type of symbol, and the name given to the button was "button".

A keyframe was added to the Up state, and an instance of the swish graphic symbol was dragged onto the stage and centered over the crosshair. Then the keyframe was dragged to the Over state. The Up state was then blank so when the movie loads, you don't see the button (see Figure 13-14). Another keyframe was added to the Hit state. On the Hit state, a rectangle was drawn over the area to indicate the active area of the button. The Editing mode was exited. The button was then in the Library.

With the button layer selected, an instance of the button was dragged onto the stage and centered over the first topic. Because nothing was in the Up state within the button symbol, the button appeared on the stage as a light blue box. This is where the Hit state is on the button. (This blue box will not show in the actual movie.) The button was duplicated by clicking and pressing the SHIFT+CTRL/SHIFT+CMD and dragging the button so it was centered over the next topic. The process was repeated until there was a button instance over all four topics.

The movie was then tested (Control | Test Movie or CTRL+ENTER/CMD+ENTER). If you mouse over the topics, the button instance (whose layer is under the topic layer) displays the Over state, which was the swish graphic symbol. As the movie stands now, nothing occurs on the Down state, other than the swish graphic still displaying. If this movie were taken a step further, a Load Movie or Get URL

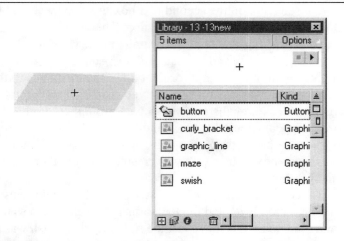

FIGURE 13-14 The swish button in Symbol Editing mode is blank on the Up state

action could be assigned to make the buttons link to another Flash movie or HTML document. Or, an action could be added to each button instructing them to go to another frame or scene in the current movie.

> **TIP** *It's a good idea to archive old Flash movies, even if you don't like or use them. You can always return to old Flash projects and borrow art to use in your new movie (as was done in Figure 13-13) to save time. In Flash, as with most drawing applications, old drawings and parts of old drawings can sometimes be modified to fit into a new movie. One person's design disaster could be another person's treasure.*

The Concept Behind the Movie Clip in Flash

Movie clips are independent movies that run on their own Timelines. Because they are symbols, movie clips possess many of the attributes common to all symbols. For example, movie clip instances can be used as many times as needed in a movie without affecting the file size. What's more, the symbol editing buttons on the bottom of the Instance panel work with movie clips, too.

Just because movie clips are self-contained movies, it doesn't mean that a movie clip must contain animation. A movie clip can be a static graphic and occupy one frame or it can be a full-fledged animation. The obvious question is why would you want to make a movie clip that only occupied one frame as opposed to a graphic symbol or button? The answer is that movie clips are very powerful vehicles for interactivity. In Flash 5, movie clips are so important, they have been assigned their own set of movie clip actions, many being similar to button actions.

Movie clips can be controlled by buttons and frame actions, as well as other movie clips. They can talk to each other and nest inside of one another. Movie clips can be simple or very complex, but they always serve as one of the most important elements in ActionScript. In the section that follows, the basics of making movie clips are covered. Once you understand how to make movie clips, you can move onto more advanced applications, that is, controlling movie clips with interactivity.

Movie clips only occupy one frame on the main Timeline, even if the movie clip contains animation. Animated graphic symbols, on the other hand, need to occupy the same number of frames on the main Timeline as they occupy on the Timeline in the Symbol Editing mode in order to play the whole animation. For example, with movie clips, an animation that uses 20 frames on its own Timeline would only occupy one frame on the main Timeline. The same animated graphic would need to occupy 20 frames on the main Timeline.

Both static and graphic animated symbols can be turned into movie clips. To do so, drag an instance of the graphic symbol onto the stage. With the Instance panel displayed, change the behavior of the graphic symbol to a movie clip. Now the instance of that graphic symbol contains all the properties of a movie clip.

Plan Your Movie Clip

Throughout the book, organization is stressed as a key element in a successful Flash movie. More than any other element, movie clips demand extra planning and attention for movies of a medium to complex nature. As you will see when you start adding actions to movie clips, they can become very confusing.

ActionScript is an object-oriented scripting language. An object-oriented scripting language lends itself to the Flash symbol interface because information is organized into groups known as *classes*. An *object* is a self-contained module that has been architected from various other objects. Movie clips are considered objects within themselves no matter how many elements are contained within a movie clip. All the objects contained on the main Timeline create the structure of a movie. Object-oriented programming makes it easy to deconstruct parts of objects without having to re-create the entire movie if revisions are needed. So when constructing movie clips, think of yourself as an architect who needs to draw up a set of plans, and in some cases, build elements separately before proceeding with the building of the movie.

Instances of movie clips take on a unique role in Flash. If you click a movie clip and display the Instance panel, below the Behavior type, you can enter in a

13

name for the instance, as shown in Figure 13-15. Unlike graphic symbols or buttons, movie clip instances need to be named if you plan on referring to them in a script. Movie clip instances are identified in a script by their instance name in conjunction with absolute or relative paths, or where they are located in relation to the main movie, which is discussed in Chapter 14.

Make a Movie Clip

Basic movie clips are similar to regular objects or animations. The major differences are they are saved as symbols and multiple uses of a movie clip can be identified with an instance name in addition to the movie clip name.

Create an Animated Movie Clip

Animated movie clips are probably the most common type of movie clip. In the following example, Figure 13-16 is a simple animated movie clip of a word that expands and contracts. The creation of this movie clip will be examined step by step. In the next section on animating buttons, this movie clip will be embedded on a button state to create an animated button. Even a simple movie clip like Figure 13-16 needs a bit of planning to eliminate extra work from afterthoughts like "I should have done it this way…". So before we discuss how it was made, let's take a look at what this movie clip does. The phrase "Small Choices" compresses horizontally in a series of five frames, as if it's being pressed between two books. The left and right arrows trail the word as it compresses. There are only three objects in the movie clip, and they are all text. All three objects animate on separate layers on the movie clip's Timeline. You don't have to put

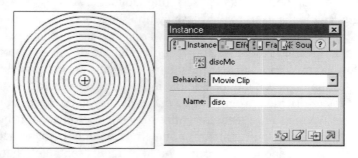

FIGURE 13-15   When a movie clip is selected and the Instance panel is displayed, you can give the instance a name in the Name box

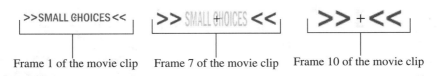

Frame 1 of the movie clip   Frame 7 of the movie clip   Frame 10 of the movie clip

FIGURE 13-16   A movie with an animated movie clip

them on separate layers, but they're easier to control if all elements are on separate layers. With this in mind, let's review how this movie clip was created.

The words "Small Choices" were typed out and separately, double arrows were typed out; one set of arrows pointing left and the other set pointing right, totaling three separate text objects. The font that was used on all three text objects is a 16-point narrow font stylized bold from the Character panel. Each text object was then selected separately and converted into a graphic symbol (Insert | Convert to Symbol or F8). In the corresponding Symbol Properties boxes, the text "Small Choices" was given the name small_txt. The left arrow was given the name "left_arrow" and the right arrow was given the name "right_arrow."

> **NOTE**   *If this button was going to be used on a real Web page, the font might not display correctly on a viewer's system. In that case, it would be best to break the font apart before tweening so no font conflicts would arise.*

With all three objects created and in the Library, the movie clip was ready to be constructed. Insert | Convert to Symbol or F8 was again selected and this time movie clip was selected for the behavior type in the Symbol Properties dialog box. In addition, the movie clip was given a name of "small_mc."

In the Symbol Editing mode, three layers were set up to accommodate all three text objects that are now three separate graphic symbols. The names of the layers correspond to the objects that occupy them. The layers are named in the following order:

- right arrow
- left arrow
- text

The text layer was selected and an instance of the small_txt graphic symbol was dragged onto the stage and centered on the crosshair. Next, the left arrow

13

layer was selected, and an instance of left_arrow was dragged onto the editing stage and positioned to the right of small_txt. The right_arrow layer was selected, and an instance of right_arrow was dragged to the left of small_txt. The Align panel was then used to align and distribute all three graphic symbols equally.

At this point, a keyframe was added to each layer on Frame 10 (F6). To hasten the process, the SHIFT+CTRL/SHIFT+CMD keys was pressed, Frame 10 was clicked on each layer (this selects each frame together), and F6 was pressed to create all three keyframes at once. A motion tween was then applied to the framesets on each layer by selecting each frameset, displaying the Frame panel and selecting Motion for Tweening.

With Frame 10 selected on the text layer, the Scale tool was chosen from the toolbar to compress the type to the point where it's barely visible (see Figure 13-17). Dragging a scale handle horizontally, toward the center of the stage, did this. Because the text was generated from a symbol, when you drag the scale handles in, the text references from the center, so the text doesn't have to be repositioned. The axis stays on the center.

With Frame 10 selected on the right arrow layer, the right_arrow was dragged to the left, almost touching the word on the text layer. The left arrow key was used to constrain the horizontal movement of the arrow and the presses were counted so the distance could be replicated with the left_arrow. The left arrow layer was selected, and the left_arrow object was moved to the right using the same formula as was used on the other arrow symbol (see Figure 13-17).

On Frame 10 of the text layer, the small text object was selected and the Effect panel was displayed. A 20% Alpha was assigned to the text to give it the effect of fading out in addition to compressing. At this point the movie clip is complete and the Editing mode was exited by clicking on the Scene in the upper-left corner. The movie clip then appeared in the Library along with the other symbols.

This movie clip is a multi-layer clip, but you can just as easily make a one-layer movie clip.

When you drag an instance of a movie clip animation onto the stage, it only occupies one frame. Try to test the movie using the Controller or scrubbing over the frame with the playhead and the movie will remain static. To test a movie clip select Control | Test Movie or CTRL+ENTER/CMD+ENTER from the menu. In this mode you will see the full animation of the movie clip.

Control the Way a Movie Clip Loops   When you test a movie clip in the Test Movie mode, you'll notice that just like an animation, it loops continuously, even though you might not want it to. This can be annoying, especially if there's a lot of movement in the movie clip. When a movie clip loops forever, an action tells the

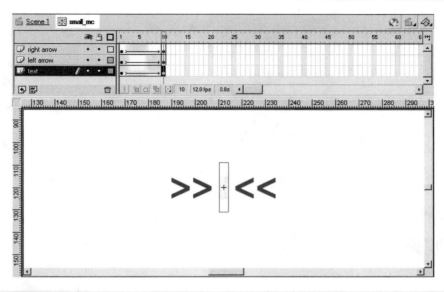

FIGURE 13-17   Frame 10 on the movie clip shows the text scaled horizontally and the arrows moved in to follow the path of the scaled text

clip to keep on returning to Frame 1 after the last frame plays. You can instruct the movie clip to stop by adding a simple Stop action on a frame. This is your first introduction to ActionScript. The movie clip from Figure 13-16 is going to be told to stop playing when it returns to Frame 1. Instead of residing on the main Timeline, this action will be put on the Timeline in the movie clip. Movie clips can have their own set of instructions contained on their own Timelines, separate from the rest of the movie.

To put a Stop action on the movie clip from Figure 13-16, double-click the movie clip to enter the Editing mode. Create a new layer and name it "actions", and drag the layer to the top of the stack so the action can easily be spotted.

Add a keyframe to the first frame and display the Actions panel. The Actions panel can be accessed from the Launcher bar at the bottom right of the stage (second icon from right). You also can access it by right-clicking/CTRL-clicking the layer and selecting Actions from the pop-up menu, or from selecting Window | Actions from the menu. With the keyframe selected, click the plus (+) icon in the upper left of the window. From the pop-up menu select Basic Actions and double-click Stop (see Figure 13-18). This puts a Stop Frame Action on Frame 1. Notice a little letter "a" appears over the keyframe indicating that there's an action

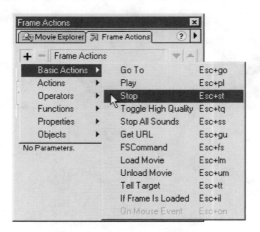

FIGURE 13-18 A Stop action being applied to a frame in the Timeline of a movie clip

on the frame. If you test the movie clip at this point, the clip won't play at all. This is because the Stop action is on the first frame. We want it to play through to Frame 10 and then stop, so drag the keyframe with the little "a" symbol to Frame 10. Now when you test the movie, when the movie clip loads, it plays and stops at Frame 10.

ActionScript is much more complex than this simple Stop frame action, but it gives you an idea of the complete control you can have over every aspect of your movie. Actions also can be applied to objects as well as frames, which is covered next in Chapter 14.

Turn an Animation on the Main Timeline into a Movie Clip

You've probably noticed that the Timeline in the Movie Clip Editing mode looks identical to the Timeline in the main movie. In fact, you can use an already existing animation and turn it into a movie clip easily.

To do so, create an animation or open a movie with an existing animation on the main Timeline. It can be either a motion or shape tween and exist on a single layer or multi-layers. Click and select the first frameset in the Timeline. Clicking the frameset selects the entire frameset. Select Edit | Copy Frames or CTRL+ALT+C/OPT+CMD+C from the menu if you want to retain a copy of the animation on the main Timeline. Select Edit | Cut Frames or CTRL+ALT+X/OPT+CMD+X if you want to eliminate the animation from the main Timeline. Select Insert | New Symbol, check Movie Clip for Behavior, name the movie clip, and click OK. Click the layer and frame you want the frameset to appear on in the movie clip and select Edit | Paste Frames or CTRL+ALT+V/OPT+CMD+V. This pastes the frameset on a layer on the Timeline in the movie clip. To copy and paste additional framesets on other layers, reconstruct the layers in the movie clip and continue to copy (or cut) and paste framesets until the movie clip is reconstructed. When finished, exit the Editing mode and now your movie is a movie clip. Conversely, the frames of a movie clip can be copied and pasted onto the main Timeline or into another movie clip.

Add Sound to a Movie Clip Layer

Adding sound to a movie clip is as easy as adding one to a button. In fact, you add sound to the Timeline of a movie clip the same way you add sound to a layer on the main Timeline. Figure 13-19 shows a two-layer movie clip named discMc and a sound has been added to the first layer named "sound". To add sound to a movie clip, first you must import a sound (or you can use one of the sound effects from the Common Library). For more information about importing sounds into Flash, refer to Chapter 9. If you're editing an existing movie, double-click the movie clip in the Library, or if you're creating a new clip, select Insert | New Symbol from the menu. In the Movie Clip Editing mode, create another layer and name it. The sound will reside on this layer so you might want to name it appropriately. With this in mind, the sound layer on Figure 13-19 is named "sound". With the first frame of the sound layer selected, drag an instance of the sound to the stage. A graphic waveform of the sound now appears on that layer. Exit the Editing mode and drag an instance of the movie clip onto the stage. Test the movie.

Just like sound on a frame in the main Timeline, sound on a movie clip will play forever unless instructed to do otherwise. Sound on a movie clip can be controlled by adding actions to frames or objects in the Movie Clip Editing mode. There might be times when you want a sound to play forever on a movie clip or you might want it to stop once the movie clip gets to the last frame of its own Timeline. If the sound plays continuously on the movie clip, you might need to adjust the synchronization of the sound in the Sound panel (Window | Panels | Sound). For more information about synchronizing sound, refer to Chapter 9.

13

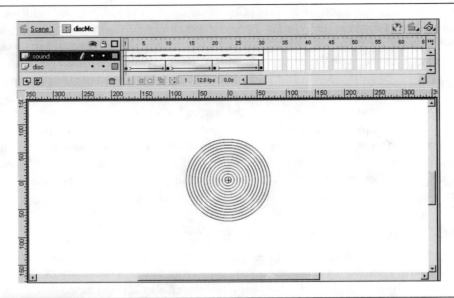

FIGURE 13-19   A movie clip in which a sound is added to a layer in the Editing mode

Make an Animated Button from a Movie Clip

Buttons can be made from vector art, bitmaps, photos, as well as movie clips.
A movie clip instance can be put on the Up, Over, or Down states in the Button
Editing mode. You can create interesting buttons using animated movie clips.
Figure 13-20 depicts a column of four navigation-type buttons, each with
individual titles, the sum of which equals the sentence, "ideas that inspire us".

FIGURE 13-20   When each button is moused over, it displays a unique animated
message; on mouse down, the size and opacity of the animation change

When you mouse over each button, a different animated movie clip plays with a unique message. On click, each movie clip switches back to the first movie clip message (small choices), changes opacity, and grows in size. Using buttons, sound, and movie clips with moving messages can add visual excitement to the movie while delivering a subliminal message. When the first button loads, it says "ideas". On mouse over it again utilizes the movie clip used in Figure 13-16 (small choices) with a sound. On click, the movie clip grows and fades. The production of this simple one frame movie has been streamlined by duplicating instances of graphics, buttons, and movie clips and changing them slightly to create new assets. All the assets are organized neatly in the Library (Figure 13-21), and they were all planned out before being made.

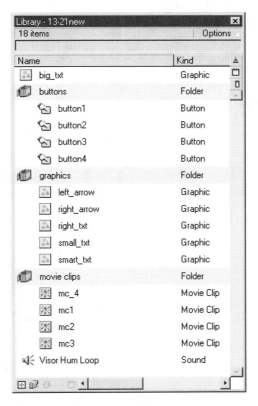

13

FIGURE 13-21   Buttons, movie clips, sound, and graphic symbols are organized neatly in their own windows in this Library

Let's examine this movie a little closer to see how it was structured. On the top level or main Timeline of the movie, there are only four buttons. However, on the Over and Down states of these buttons, there's a movie clip animation nested in the button and therefore twice removed from the main Timeline. In the movie clip animations nested in the buttons, the text is made from graphic symbols. The graphic symbols are in effect three levels removed from the main Timeline. Thus, you begin to see the structure of the movie as well as an introduction to the concept of objects residing on different levels in Flash. Because nesting of symbols is a very important concept with regard to interactivity, it is further explored in Chapter 14.

The following is a synopsis of how the buttons in this movie were constructed.

Because the movie clip already existed, it was brought into the new movie to be reused. File | Open As Shared Library was selected from the menu, and the Figure 13-16 "small choices" movie was opened. With the Libraries from the new and old movie displayed, the old movie clip was dragged into the new Library, and the old movie was closed (see Figure 13-22).

When a symbol is dragged from one Library to another, if there are other symbols nested within the symbols, they copy over too. Notice in Figure 13-22, not only did the movie clip copy over, the three graphic symbols nested in it (left_arrow, right_arrow, small_txt) also were copied over just by selecting the movie clip.

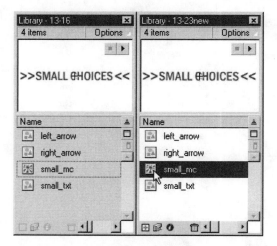

FIGURE 13-22   The Library from Figure 13-16 opened as Shared Library and the movie clip is being dragged from the old Library to the new Library

With one movie clip created, the other three were built starting with the contents of the movie clip. The only element that changes in all four movie clips is the text on mouse over that says "small choices". This text was first created with a graphic symbol. The graphic symbol text "small_txt" was dragged from the Library onto the stage and the Instance panel was displayed. From the Instance panel, the Duplicate icon on the bottom right of the panel was clicked and a new symbol name was given (big_txt). This process was repeated two more times, naming the new copies, consecutively, "smart_txt", and "right_txt", thus duplicating the graphic symbols.

TIP   *You can also duplicate symbols by clicking on the symbol and selecting Duplicate from the Options pop-up menu.*

Now that there are three new copies of the original graphic symbol "small_txt", the text in each one was edited by selecting them one at a time in the Library, double-clicking on each new copy, and entering the Symbol Editing mode for that symbol. The text was edited on the stage in the Editing mode to reflect their names, "Big Choices", "Smart Choices", and "Right Choices". Any symbols lingering on the stage were deleted as they are just being used for set up at this point.

The three new movie clips were made next, using the duplication method as was done on the graphic symbols. The movie clip was duplicated three times and named "mc2", "mc3", and "mc4", accordingly. Again, any lingering symbols were deleted from the main Timeline.

Double-clicking the mc2 movie clip in the Library opened the clip up in Editing mode. On Layer 4 (text) in the movie clip Timeline, the motion tween was removed by clicking the in-between frames and selecting Tweening: None from the Instance panel. All frames on Layer 4 (text) were deleted by selecting the frameset and pressing SHIFT+F5. Layer 4 was the only layer that needed adjusting on all movie clips. A new keyframe was added to Frame 1 (F6) and an instance of the graphic symbol called "big_txt" was dragged onto the stage and centered between the two arrows. The arrows in some cases needed a little horizontal adjusting because the width of the text was different.

A keyframe was then added to Frame 10 and the graphic was compressed with the Scale tool. As with the original clip, the Scale tool was dragged horizontally on one of the ring handles until the symbol was barely visible. This created a compressed effect as in the first clip. The arrows on the left and right arrow layers were moved closer to the text on Frame 10 to give the appearance of shrinking with the text. Now this movie clip is identical to the original clip except the text has changed.

13

NOTE   *If this is confusing, refer to Figures 13-16 and 13-17 for a visual representation of a similar effect.*

A new motion tween was applied to Layer 4 (text) by selecting the frameset and choosing Tweening: Motion from the Frame panel. The Editing mode was then exited by clicking Scene in the upper-left corner.

This process was repeated on the other two movie clips, "mc3" and "mc4", with the appropriate graphic symbol being substituted on Frame 1 of Layer 4 (text) in the movie clip Timelines. Each symbol was given a slightly different treatment on Frame 10, either by rotating or changing the tint in the Effect panel to make all movie clips slightly different.

With the symbols and movie clips in place, the first button was constructed. A new symbol was inserted (Insert | New Symbol), Button was checked for Behavior in the Symbol Properties dialog box, and the button was given the name of "button1". In the Symbol Editing mode, three layers were made in the following order:

- Sound

- Text

- Layer 1

With the Layer 1 Up state selected, a classic button design was made from a simple rectangle with a linear gradient. The first rectangle was grouped. The second rectangle that stacks on top of the first to create a 3-D button effect was duplicated from the first, scaled down, and centered over the first rectangle. The top rectangle was then edited so the direction of the gradient was in the opposite direction to imply a push-button effect (see Figure 13-23). A keyframe was added to the Over state (F6) and an instance of the movie clip called "small_txt" was aligned center stage. The rectangle button was deleted in the Over state. On the Down state a keypress was added, and the movie clip was scaled up 125% (CTRL+ALT+S/OPTION+CMD+S).

On the sound layer, a keyframe (F6) was added to the Over state and a sound from the Common Library was dragged onto the stage (Visor Hum Loop). The last layer is the text layer. On this layer the word "ideas" was added in a bold serif font on the Up state, giving the appearance of sitting on top of the rectangle button. On the Hit frame a rectangle was added to indicate the area that would be active for the user. It's a good idea to add a Hit state on an animated button because if the Over or Down state is animated, they can be hard to click with because they are moving objects.

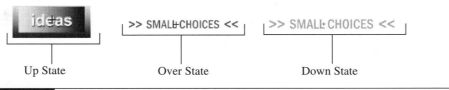

| Up State | Over State | Down State |

FIGURE 13-23   The Up, Over, and Down states of button 1

The process used for making this button was replicated for buttons 2–4, with the appropriate movie clips being substituted on the Over states on the text layer. Again, the Down state was left the same as it was in the original button. The text on the text layer of each button was also changed from "ideas" on button 1 to "that", "inspire", and "us", accordingly. Only Frame 1 of the text layer contains the name of the button. The rest of the frames on this layer are blank. The sound layer was left untouched.

With all the assets organized in the Library, the only thing left to do was to construct the actual movie. That involved dragging all four movie clips onto the stage and then stacking and aligning them.

The completed movie only occupies one frame on the main Timeline, yet in the buttons there are four separate animated movie clips all running on their own Timelines. However, the animation can only be seen if the user interacts with the buttons. Thus, you have nested graphic symbols in movie clips and in the movie clips button.

In the next chapter, interactivity on buttons and movie clips is explored further. We will assign ActionScript to buttons and movie clips to give the user control over the way a movie plays. We also examine ActionScript in terms of what it is and how it works.

13

Part IV

Building Interactive Movies

Chapter 14

Assign ActionScript to Movie Clips, Buttons, and Frames

How to...

- Understand Object-Oriented Programming
- Navigate the Actions Panel
- Assign an Action to a Frame
- Control Frames on the Main Timeline with Buttons
- Assign Scripts on Buttons
- Control the Behavior of a Movie Clip with a Button Event Handler
- Understand Nested Movie Clips
- Understand Absolute Versus Relative Paths
- Use Dot and Slash Syntax
- Use Movie Clip Event Handlers

ActionScript is a scripting language that is the power behind Flash interactivity. In Flash 5, ActionScript has taken on a more dominant role than earlier versions of the language. With release 5, it has been re-engineered and transformed into a mature object-oriented scripting language.

Flash possesses great animation capabilities, but interactivity is one of the more important aspects of advanced Flash utilization. ActionScript can be assigned to frames, buttons, and movie clips. These elements can respond to a user mousing over itself or another object, typing something in a text field, clicking or releasing the mouse, dragging and dropping an object, frames themselves, as well as many other exciting things. You, as the author, give your objects intelligence so the audience can interact with them.

Before you work with ActionScript, it's important to understand a little more about what interactivity is and how it relates to ActionScript. Also it's a wise idea to grasp the basics of how ActionScript works. So before you start generating scripts, let's examine what ActionScript is and how it works.

Interactivity and ActionScript

When a movie is interactive, the user controls the flow or the direction the movie will take based on his or her selections, movements, or interactions. There can be a million different ways a viewer can determine the outcome of a movie depending upon the selections he or she chooses. As a result of having a million different choices and variations to choose from, everyone will have a unique experience because it's based on the viewer's perceptual selection. This is the core of interactivity and the genius behind ActionScript.

Interactive media surrounds us these days, and the Web appears to be at the forefront of the movement. The Web is now accessible from home television and cell phones. Gaming applications have always involved interactivity, as do ATM bank transactions at kiosks found almost everywhere nowadays. Supermarket and department stores are equipped with interactive computer stations attempting to personalize the selling of a product. Interactivity customizes a user's experience to that particular user. Interactivity will eventually become an assumed reality in our daily routines in the new millennium.

Understand Object-Oriented Programming

Before studying the basics of ActionScript, it's important to gain an understanding of what it is and how it works.

ActionScript is an object-oriented scripting language based on object-oriented programming (OPP). In OOP languages, emphasis is placed on objects that can be created, modified, defined, and cloned as instances.

Organization is the main building block of OPP languages. JavaScript is also an OPP language, and Flash is very similar to the JavaScript language. In fact, ActionScript is based on ECMA-262 specifications. ECMA-262 is a document that defines the rules and parameters of the JavaScript language. If you're familiar with JavaScript, learning ActionScript will be a breeze.

The gathering of information and the storing of it in a group characterizes an OOP language. This group is referred to as a *class* and a class defines everything there is to know about an object. Within a class, you can create an object by defining its properties, methods, and event handlers. The properties of an object are its characteristics like height, color, size, and so on. The methods of an object are what an object does and how it behaves. Things that cause the object to react like a mouse click are event handlers.

14

A class can generate many instances or objects, and all objects have a unique identification. When they are called on to change or do things in ActionScript, the identification name is what makes them unique. For example, let's say a bottle is a class. You can have several objects (instances) of this class. The properties of the bottle can be changed (size, color, and so on), the methods can change (the bottle can pour or break), and the event can change (when the user picks up the bottle and puts it to his mouth, liquid pours out of the bottle).

You also can define the properties and methods of a class by creating a "constructor function." A constructor function enables you to create a task for a class, and that information can be returned on a particular object. For example, let's say you want the numerical value of a movie clip's exact X, Y position on the stage returned to you every time a person clicks a button. This task can be easily accomplished by creating a constructor function. Functions also are reusable within the movie.

Every element in a Flash movie is an object of some sort including the movie itself, frames, layers, text boxes, and other things. As such, you can change the properties of these objects too. When you change the movie size or the frame rate, you're changing the properties of these predefined objects.

Not only do objects have unique names by which they are identified, but they also are referenced by their location on a particular level. All objects exist on a particular hierarchy in a movie. They are called on to do things by identifying their location in the movie as well as their identification names. This concept is quite logical considering objects can be made with parts of other objects, making ActionScript modular in its application. For example, if you had an instance of a movie clip nested inside another movie clip instance, both movie clips would be on different levels, away from the main movie and the nesting order would determine their location in the movie. To instruct the nested movie clip to do something or change from the main Timeline, you would have to reference not only its unique name (instance name) but also its hierarchical location within the movie. The concept of addressing these levels is discussed later in this chapter, but it's important for the ActionScript beginner to understand this hierarchical concept and its importance in generating a successful script.

> **NOTE** *Additional movies can be loaded into your movie on different levels using the loadMovie action. The level property is a property used in conjunction with the loadMovie action that can be set to determine how the movies will stack on top of one another. Level 0, the base level, defines movie properties such as background color. Level 1 would be the next layer, and so on. Use the loadMovie action when you want another SWF movie to load from the current movie either in its own window (level) or a movie clip (target).*

With ActionScript, objects can talk to one another when a script commands them to do so. This is just another example of the complexity of ActionScript. Flash authors and programmers study languages like this for years and still learn new things about them every day. Even seasoned ActionScript users aren't always aware of the full spectrum of its capabilities. This is why it's important to start with a solid understanding of the basics of ActionScript, learn it the right way, and grow from there.

Although the basic actions haven't changed much from version 4, ActionScript has been re-engineered in version 5. If you are experienced in writing scripts in Flash 4, you need to take a new look at ActionScript in Flash 5. There are a lot of new actions, as well as new standards for movie clips, which now have their own event handlers just like buttons. Also some commonly used actions you might be familiar with from Flash 4 have been deprecated in Flash 5. When code is deprecated, it can still be used, but it will become obsolete at a future date. Generally when a code is deprecated, the next version of the software will not include the deprecated code. In this chapter, we discuss deprecated code and its replacement code further.

ActionScript is much more complex than what is covered here in a few brief paragraphs, but more will be covered by example as we go along.

Navigate the Actions Panel

Use the Actions panel in Flash to attach a script to a frame, button, or movie clip. The ActionScript interface in version 5 is easy for beginners and experts alike. Beginners can use actions with a point and click simplicity with the Normal mode, while more advanced users can take advantage of the Expert mode, which enables them to type in the script directly. This is great news for the new user because the repetitive clicking on actions often causes the user to absorb code subliminally. Little by little, you'll find yourself recognizing and understanding actions and syntax as you go along.

The Actions panel can be accessed from several different locations in Flash:

- From the menu select Window | Panel | Actions

- CTRL+ALT+A/OPT+CMD+A

- The Launcher (second icon from the right that resembles a diagonally-pointing arrow)

- By right-clicking/CTRL-clicking on frames, buttons, or movie clips to display the contextual menu

14

> TIP *In the Actions panel Toolbox list, codes that are deprecated are highlighted in green.*

Figure 14-1 shows a sample of the Object Actions panel in use. When you select an object and add a script (button or a movie clip), the tab in the upper-left corner is labeled "Object Actions," indicating the script will be on an object. When you select a frame to write a script on, the upper-left corner will indicate "Frame

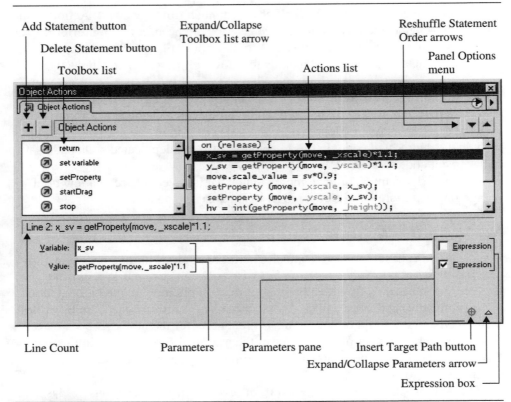

Add Statement button

Delete Statement button

Toolbox list

Expand/Collapse
Toolbox list arrow

Actions list

Reshuffle Statement
Order arrows

Panel Options
menu

Line Count

Parameters

Parameters pane

Insert Target Path button

Expand/Collapse Parameters arrow

Expression box

FIGURE 14-1   The Object Actions/Frames panel

Actions." This is a good way of keeping track of whether the code is on an object or a frame. Object actions are always assigned to buttons and movie clips, either to manipulate them or to tell them to manipulate another movie clip. Frame actions are always assigned to frames. We will be assigning both frame and object actions throughout the next two chapters as they are both widely used methods.

NOTE   *Not all actions work with both frames and objects. Actions that aren't applicable to what you're currently selecting appear dimmed in the Toolbox list of the Actions panel. If an object or a frame is not selected, the actions also are dimmed.*

As mentioned before, ActionScript code can be generated in either Normal or Expert mode. Normal mode is the default as it is assumed most people are not experts in ActionScript. When you are scripting in Normal mode, you select Actions from the Toolbox list or the Add Statement button, as shown in Figure 14-1.

The Actions list can be expanded and collapsed by clicking on the arrow in between the Toolbox list and the Actions list. Collapse this panel if you prefer to use the Add Statement button instead of the Toolbox list. Both the Toolbox list and the Add Statement button contain the same list of actions. The only difference is the Toolbox list provides a navigation style list, whereas the Add Statement list is a classic pop-up menu style with secondary pop-up lists for major categories like Actions, Functions, and so on.

To assign an action to an object or frame from the Add Action list, double-click on the "+" button (Add Statement) and select an action. The selected action then appears in the Actions list to the right of the panel. To delete a statement in the Actions list, select the statement and click the "-" button (Delete Statement) or select a line of script in the Actions list and use the BACKSPACE/DELETE key.

Actions can be assigned from the Toolbox list in one of two ways. The first way is to select the action from the Toolbox list and double-click the action. It then appears in the Actions list. The second way is to navigate the list, expand the category you want an action from, and select the desired action. Click and drag the action into the Actions list. Neither one of these methods is superior to the other. Selecting a method is just a matter of personal choice. The Add Statement button works in a similar manner to the Action list in Flash 4, so old users might prefer this interface. Because the most commonly used method is the Toolbox list, this is the standard that will be referenced when displaying code in this chapter and Chapter 15.

The Panel Options menu in the upper-right corner is a pop-up menu with several convenient utilities. The contents in this pop-up menu are as follows:

- **Normal mode**—This mode is for beginner/intermediate users of ActionScript. Normal mode enables selection from the Toolbox list and Add Statement button only. Flash authors can't type in the Actions list in this mode. Normal mode also activates the Parameters pane for certain actions when the script needs to be further defined. You can switch from Normal mode to Expert mode and maintain formatting and indentations within the script. If a mistake is made in the Expert mode, you can't return to Normal until the mistake is corrected.

14

■ **Expert mode**—This mode enables you to type code in by hand. You also can use the Add Statement button and the Toolbox list in conjunction with the Expert mode. However, you do not have access to the Parameters pane when in this mode. Switching from Expert mode to Normal mode removes white space and indentations and if there are errors in the Expert mode script, the conversion to Normal mode will not work.

> **TIP** *The default setting in Flash is Normal mode. If you prefer to always work in Expert mode, this can be changed in the Preferences menu. Do this by selecting Edit | Preferences | General from the menu. In the General Preferences dialog box under Actions Panel, switch the mode from Normal to Export.*

■ **Go To Line**—This selection takes you to a particular line of code. The line count in the middle of the box keeps track of what line you're currently on, but you can indicate a new number in the Go To Line dialog box.

■ **Find/Replace**—This finds a word of code or statement. Replace will replace the code with whatever you type in the Replace With text box.

■ **Check Syntax**—Use Check Syntax to check for errors in your code. This dialog box will spot errors, give you an idea of what the problem is, and tell you what line the error is on so you can go to that line and fix it.

■ **Import From/Export As File**—You can import code from another Flash file and export code to other Flash files from these dialog boxes. The code is saved separately with an ".as" extension. You also can copy and paste script from one file to another.

■ **Colored Syntax**—Select Colored Syntax if you want to easily distinguish between actions and text in the script that isn't an action such as instances, file names, variables, properties, and so on. The Syntax default color is blue.

■ **Show Deprecated Syntax**—Check this if you want the deprecated code to be highlighted in the script. Use this if you're uncertain of which actions are deprecated.

■ **Font Size: Small, Medium, and Large**—The default display size in the Actions list is Small. If you need to view the code bigger, change it here. Small, Medium, and Large are in a submenu of the Font Size.

When the contents of the Toolbox list and Add/Delete Statement pop-up menu is mentioned, they are referred to as actions in this book. Although the contents of these lists/menus are a combination of actions, properties, methods, functions, operators, and so on, they're globally referred to as actions or statements.

The Reshuffle Statement Order Arrows enable you to select a line of code and move the code up and down within the list without destroying the basic structure of the script. ActionScript has to be written in a logical order and in a certain way. Otherwise, a scripting error will occur. This is especially useful for beginners who don't feel confident enough to go into Expert mode and move lines of script if required.

The Parameters pane appears when you select a line of code in the Actions list and the code needs additional information typed in. In this sense, the ActionScript interface is almost like a fill-in-the-blanks format. For example, in Figure 14-2, a Go to and Play frame action is applied to Frame 9 on the first layer of this movie.

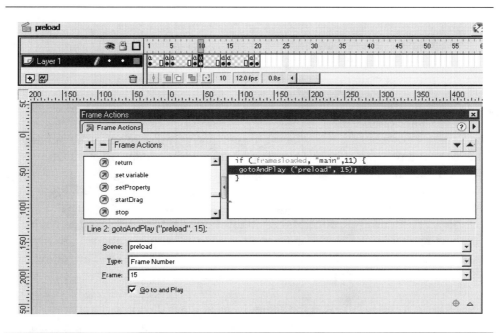

14

FIGURE 14-2   When a Go to and Play action is assigned to a frame, the Parameters pane in the Action panel becomes active

When the line of code is selected, the Parameters pane prompts you for additional information. Because the Go to and Play is an action, it needs to know exactly where and what it needs to go to and play. On this action, you need to indicate a Scene, Type, and Frame.

Some of the parameters contain pop-up lists to the right of the text box. These lists enable you to type in the parameter or select one from the pop-up list. The pop-up will list information relevant to that object. The Scene prompts you for a scene name, the Type prompts you for what type of a frame are you referencing like the number or label, and the Frame prompts you for a frame number, sequence, or frame label name. On this particular statement, there is an additional selection box at the bottom. If Go to and Play is checked, the Actions list will reflect this. If it is deselected, the statement will change to Go to and Stop.

When you become more experienced in scripting, you will become familiar with frequently used actions and the parameters attached with them. The Parameter pane is a great help when learning ActionScript.

The Insert Target Path button displays the Target Path dialog box. Use this dialog box to target the path of an object (instance) that you want to address an action to. If you're not familiar with where objects are located in relation to the main Timeline, you can use this dialog box to find the path of an object and select it.

The Expand/Collapse Parameters Arrow enables you to close the Parameters pane. If you have a small monitor, the pane might take up too much room so you can close it if not needed.

Examine the Toolbox List in the Actions Panel

The Toolbox contains the list of all of the currently available actions, operators, functions, and properties in Flash 5. They are listed in collapsible navigation folders. When an action is depicted as a rectangle icon with a diagonal arrow (the diagonal arrow icon always represents ActionScript in Flash), the folder contains more selections. When the folder is expanded, the icon appears as an open book. The icons for subcategories in this book icon are displayed as circles with the diagonal arrow. Notice actions are contained within groupings. Actions are organized so that simple actions are listed in descending order. The following elements are available in the Toolbox list:

- ■ **Basic Actions**—This is the same list as in Flash 4 so it will look familiar to old users. The basic actions include simple code that can be assigned to buttons or frames, such as Stop, Stop Sound, Get URL, and so on.

■ **Actions**—Actions include code from the Basic Actions list but expand upon the Basic Actions list with many other actions.

■ **Operators**—These are used for performing calculations or comparing objects. Some of these elements include the following signs: +, =, >=, *, +, as well as many others.

■ **Functions**—Functions receive values, evaluate the value, and return a result. Often these are referred to as methods and the user defines the parameters on these methods. Some commonly used functions are True, False, Get Property, Scroll, Maxscroll, and Number.

■ **Properties**—These elements relate to the characteristics that describe an object. Some properties can be assigned to the entire movie, and others can be assigned to a particular object or a part of an object (movie clips). Properties list with an underline before the property. Some commonly used properties in the list include _xscale, _yscale, _width, _height, _droptarget, and _visible.

■ **Objects**—These represent instances of a class that have their own predefined methods. Some of the more commonly used objects include Numbers, MovieClip, Color, Date, and Mouse. Each object has a subset of actions in the Toolbox list relating to that particular object.

Up and Running with ActionScript

ActionScript can be simple if approached in a logical manner. The remainder of this chapter as well as Chapter 15 will be devoted to presenting ActionScript in a simple, concise way to get you up and running with some commonly used techniques. All actions associated with ActionScript are not covered in this book because the scope is too broad to cover. However, the most commonly used actions are reviewed in detail, which serves as a good introduction to the language. From here, your knowledge base can spring you to the next level if you decide to study ActionScript further. This chapter proves that even a beginner can start scripting right away.

14

Assign an Action to a Frame

In Chapter 13, you assigned a simple Stop action to a frame on a Timeline to stop the frame from looping continuously. This involved selecting a keyframe. Then from the Actions panel | Toolbox | Basic Actions, the Stop action was selected. It was fairly simple to do and very logical. When a Stop action is assigned to a frame, it is considered a Frame action. Figure 14-3 depicts a simple animation on the main Timeline with a frame action on it. Notice the Actions panel in this figure reflects the type of action that was assigned; that is, a Frame action.

When a Frame action is applied, the action is represented on the frame with the letter "a". The Frame action in this figure appears on the last frame in the Timeline. If you recall, in the last chapter when you double-clicked the word Stop, the "a" landed on the first frame of the layer. No matter which frame you select on a layer to add an action to, the action will always appear on the next available frame. In Figure 14-3, if the Stop action remained on Frame 1, when the movie loaded,

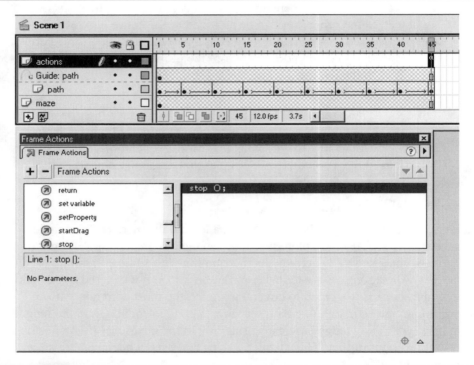

FIGURE 14-3   When a Stop action is applied to a Frame in an animation on the main Timeline, the tab and the panel names change to Frame actions

the animation wouldn't play. When the Stop action is moved to Frame 45 (the last frame), the movie plays when it loads and it stops on the last frame, causing the animation to only play once.

What if the viewer wanted to see the movie again or turn it on and off at will? You can add interactive buttons and movie clips to do this. This is interactivity in its most basic state. In the next section you'll learn how to supply the user with the means to control this movie.

Events on Buttons

As you learned in the last chapter, buttons possess their own interactivity of sorts. A button can change its properties when a user clicks or rolls over it. With ActionScript, a script can be assigned to a button and an event assigned to the button can determine when the action defined in the script will be executed. All button events are performed by the user with a mouse. In other words, when the user does things with a mouse (the event—like roll over), a response (action) will occur in the movie. When you assign an action to a button, you can select from the following events in the Parameter pane (see Figure 14-4):

- **Press/Release**—This refers to the pressing down/releasing of the mouse on a button. If Release is chosen as the mouse event, a user can deactivate the event and action by dragging off the button before releasing the mouse.

- **Release Outside**—Unlike the Release event, when this is chosen, the user presses the button, releases the button outside of the hit area of the button, and the action still takes place.

- **Key Press**—The event occurs when the user presses a key, which is assigned by you, the author of the movie.

- **Roll Over/Roll Out**—These mouse events involve either rolling over or over and off the active hit area of the button.

- **Drag Over/Drag Out**—These events work when the user clicks and drags on and off the hit area, almost like a rollover/out but with the mouse depressed.

14

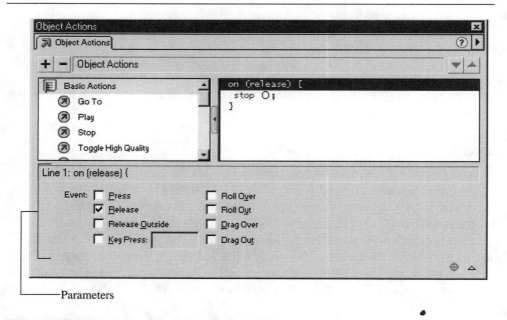

Parameters

FIGURE 14-4   When you apply actions to a button on a mouse event, the Parameters
pane in the Actions panel becomes activated

Control Frames on the Main Timeline with Buttons

Buttons were used in Flash 4 to control movie clips and events on the main
Timeline. They still are very useful in Flash 5 and are probably here to stay
throughout the life of Flash. Scripts on buttons can control frames in a movie
and movie clip as well as interact with other scripts on frames. Both of these
concepts are demonstrated in the following section. In the first scenario, there
is a script only on the buttons that control the movie. In the second scenario,
there are actions on two frames on a layer and the script on the buttons controls
the frames in the movie.

Assign Scripts on Buttons

All of the actions in the Basic Actions panel are available to be used on buttons
and movie clips, with the exception of On Mouse Event, which is reserved
exclusively for movie clips. Figure 14-5 represents a maze similar to the maze
movie in Chapter 13, but with a different twist. This maze has an animated marble
that follows the maze path. The path is a motion guide. There are two buttons on
either side of this maze. One says "stop" and the other says "go." These buttons

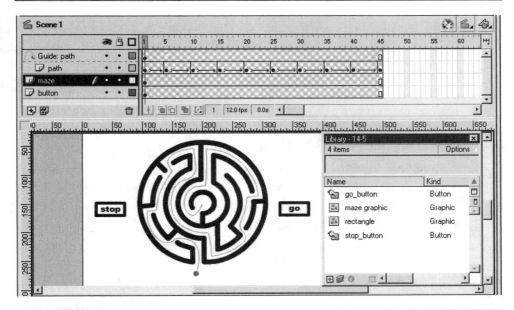

FIGURE 14-5   The marble in the maze figure is controlled by the user with Stop and Go buttons

enable the user to control the animation of the marble through the maze using a button event. The event is "On" Release. This means that when the user clicks and releases each button, the animation will start or stop according to the label on the button.

Let's examine how this movie was made:

1. Layers were created in the following order:

    ■ Guide: path (motion guide to the path layer—explained in step 3)

    ■ path

    ■ maze

    ■ button

2. A maze graphic symbol was created and placed on the maze layer. An animated marble was created along a motion guide on the path layer and a path that follows the maze was created on the guide layer (Guide: path). The marble on the path was motion tweened along the guide on the path layer.

3. A button was then created and labeled "stop_button" in the Properties dialog box. Two layers were created in the button's Symbol Editing mode; one called "text" and the other called "Layer 1". The text named "button" resides on the text layer. The button remains the same on all states and its sole purpose is to control the movement of the marble in the maze. Choosing the Stop button in the Library and then selecting Duplicate from the pop-up options menu made a duplicate of this button. The duplicate button was named "go" in the Symbol Properties dialog box and the text "stop" on the text layer of the button was edited to say "go".

4. Both buttons were dragged from the Library to the main Timeline onto the layer named Buttons and aligned on either side of the maze. Now the script was generated on both buttons.

5. The Actions panel was displayed (CTRL+ALT+A/CMD+OPT+A) and the Stop button was selected, and in the Toolbar list section of the panel, the Basic Actions were expanded (see Figure 14-6). The word "Stop" was then double-clicked causing three lines of code to appear in the Actions List:

```
on (release) {
    stop ();
}
```

6. On Line 1, the word "on" is the beginning of the statement and the word between the parentheses (release) is the event. The curly brackets are always present in ActionScript and they serve as the container for the release event associated with this button. When you add script to a button, the Actions panel and tab is titled "Object Actions".

TIP   *Notice when you select a line of code that the line number you're currently selecting is indicated in the middle of the Actions panel.*

7. The "go" button was selected and with the Actions panel displayed, in the Basic Actions list, "Play" was dragged over and dropped in the Actions list. Note you can double-click an action or drag and drop it in the Actions list. The script now reads

```
    on (release) {
play ();
}
```

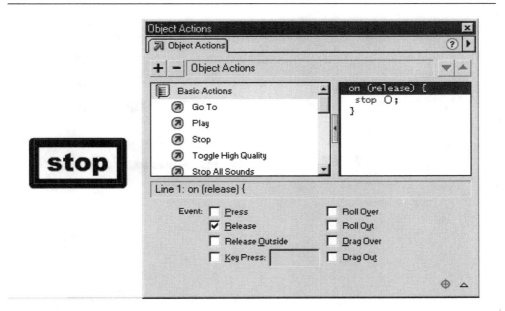

FIGURE 14-6   The script on the Stop button in the Actions panel

Now when the user clicks the Stop and Go buttons, the movie stops and starts on the frame that the playhead is sitting on at the moment of release. Thus, the movie is interactive. At this point you might want to experiment with another event on either the Stop or Go button. Try rollover or keypress. It's fun to experiment with different events to see what the outcomes will be.

You also can add multiple actions to the same button event. On Figure 14-7, a sound layer was added to the maze graphic. A sound was imported into the Library and added to this new layer. Additional script was added to the Stop button to stop the sound that loops continuously when the movie loads.

With the Actions panel displayed and Line 2 of the Stop button script selected (stop();), Stop All Sounds was double-clicked in the Basic Actions List. Now when the Stop button is released, it performs two actions. It stops the animation on the main Timeline and stops the sound.

14

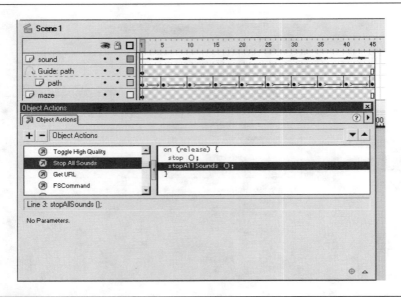

FIGURE 14-7 The Stop button now controls the playing of sound as well as stopping on a frame

Assign Script on Frames and Buttons

In the last section, we added a script to buttons to control the play of frames in the main Timeline. Figure 14-8 is a variation of the Figure 14-5 maze movie, but it utilizes different actions and frame labels. The outcome of the new movie is a different experience than the previous version. When the new movie loads, the animation is static because the movie has a Stop action on Frame 1. When the user rolls over the Go button with their mouse, the movie plays, but only from Frame 6. When the user then presses the Stop button, the movie stops on the frame it's currently on. Then again, if the user clicks the Go button, the playhead always returns to Frame 6 in the Timeline. On the Actions layer, two actions have been assigned and given labels so the script on the Go button identifies the frame by its label as opposed to its frame number. Let's examine how this script variation of the maze movie works.

There are two scripts on a new action layer, which was added to the top of the Timeline (see Figure 14-8). After the action layer was created, a keyframe was added to the first frame and Stop was chosen from the Actions panel Toolbox list (from Basic Actions). A keyframe was added to the second frame and a Play

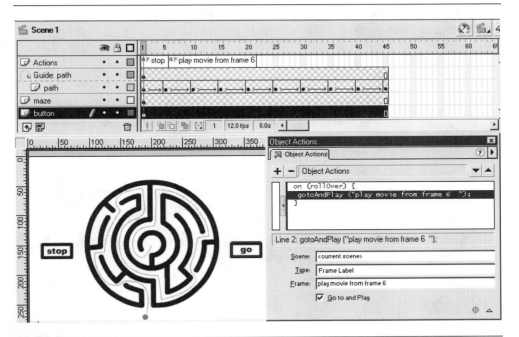

FIGURE 14-8   Buttons control the actions on two frames that are addressed by their frame names

action was chosen from the Actions panel Toolbox list (from Basic Actions). The second action was then moved to Frame 6. Labels were then added to each of these actions by displaying the Frame panel. In the Frame panel, you can give names to your frames. With the first action selected, in the Frame panel the following label was typed: "stop." The second frame was selected and with the Frame panel displayed, a label was given to this action called "play movie from Frame 6." Actions can be called from frames using their number, position, or label. Labeling frames often is a good idea because it can help you keep track of the flow of the movie.

NOTE   *If there is only one frame on a layer with a frame label, the label might not be visible because the text used for the label is generally longer than the span of one frame. If this occurs, click on the next frame to the right of the action and add enough blank frames (F5) for the label to become visible.*

14

On the Stop button, the script is as follows (the script on this button has not been changed from the way it was in Figure 14-5):

```
    on (release) {
stop ();
}
```

The script on the Go button needed to be revised from its previous state in Figure 14-5 in order to control the location of the playhead, so the old script was deleted by clicking on Line 1 and selecting " " on the Delete Statement button. In this version of the movie, when the Go button is pressed, the movie jumps to Frame 6 on the main Timeline and performs the action applied to that frame. If you recall, in the previous paragraph we put a Play action on Frame 6 from the Basic Actions list.

With the Go button selected, Go To was selected from the Basic Actions list in the Actions panel. At this point, the script read:

```
on (release) {
gotoAndPlay ();
}
```

On the Go button, instead of the action occurring on mouse release, it was changed to Roll Over. With Line 1 selected, in the Parameters pane, Release was deselected and Roll Over was checked.

Line 2 of this script (gotoAndPlay ();) is incomplete. The action needs to know where it has to go to. This information will appear in between the empty parenthesis after the parameters are set. Line 2 was chosen and the Parameters pane then became active. The following information was typed in or selected from the pop-up menus next to the input text boxes:

```
Scene: <current scene>
Type: Frame Label
Frame: play movie from frame 6
```

Make sure Go to and Play is checked. When the type is Frame Label, you can target a frame using the label name you assigned in the Frame panel. The Frame can then reference a frame label as opposed to a frame number. The playhead will jump to one of the labeled frames when the user releases the Go button. The script on the Go button now looks like this:

```
on (rollOver) {
gotoAndPlay ("play movie from frame 6");
}
```

When the movie is tested and the Go button is clicked, the playhead always returns to Frame 6, which has the frame label of "play movie from Frame 6."

In summary, scripts can be added to both frames and buttons. Labeling frames sometimes makes it easier for you to spot an action on a frame or get a quick synopsis of the flow of the movie. The scripts in the maze movie are simple, but give you a solid structure on which to build your knowledge of ActionScript. You experimented with controlling the playback of frames using actions from the Basic Actions Toolbox list. Buttons also are capable of doing far more sophisticated things. In the next section, you'll learn how to control a movie clip that's on the main Timeline.

Control the Behavior of a Movie Clip with a Button Event Handler

ActionScript really starts getting fun when you start mixing buttons with movie clips. When you understand the concept of controlling movie clips with buttons, you'll be well on your way to understanding the concept behind ActionScript.

Because ActionScript is modular, once you become comfortable with 10–15 simple scripts, you'll feel confident enough to start experimenting with different combinations, substituting different objects and instances with one another to create different forms of interactivity.

Let's return to the movie clip from an earlier chapter. Figure 14-9 represents a ticking clock that was examined in Chapter 10 (Figure 10-7 in Chapter 10). In that chapter, the clock was animated with a frame-by-frame animation on the main Timeline so that the big hand would move clockwise, stopping at each tick mark, creating a ticking effect. The clock looped continuously and the user had no control over it. In this chapter, the clock has been removed from the main Timeline and made into a movie clip. The animation in the new movie clip is identical to the previous version except the clock now resides on a movie clip Timeline and is controlled by buttons on the main Timeline.

14

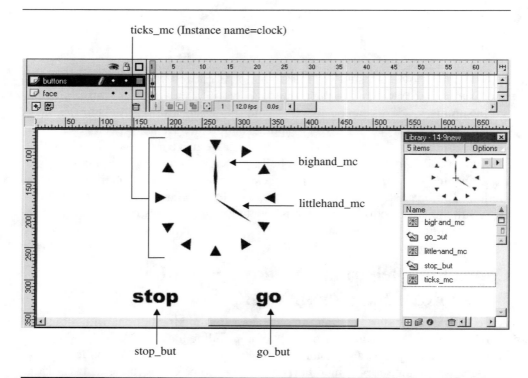

ticks_mc (Instance name=clock)

bighand_mc

littlehand_mc

stop_but

go_but

FIGURE 14-9   A clock movie clip that's passing of time is controlled on a button event

Just like the maze movie example (Figure 14-5) the Stop and Go buttons have scripts attached to them, but the new buttons control the stop and play actions on a movie clip instead of on frames on the main Timeline. Actually they're controlling stop and play actions on the movie clip's Timeline. This is an important concept in Flash as it demonstrates how powerful movie clips are. Let's examine how this movie was created:

A new movie was created and the objects that make up the clock were borrowed from the original clock movie from Chapter 10. The big hand (bighand_mc) and little hand (littlehand_mc) of the clock and the tick marks depicting the clock face (ticks_mc) were converted into three separate movie clips and stored in the new Library. The littlehand_mc and the ticks_mc remain as static movie clips, whereas the big hand is animated so it rotates around the clock face. The static movie clips could have both been made into graphic symbols instead, but because we expand upon the clock exercise in the next section, the movie clip was a better choice for this exercise. For interactivity, movie clips are far more versatile than regular graphic symbols.

Two buttons were also created for this movie. One is called "stop" and the other is named "go." You also can use buttons from the Common Library instead of making your own.

The movie clip named ticks_mc was then edited because all the animation in this movie takes place within this movie clip. Because a movie clip is a self-contained movie, the ticks_mc movie clip was planned out just like any other movie. It was given three layers named in the following order (see Figure 14-10):

- bighand

- littlehand

- face

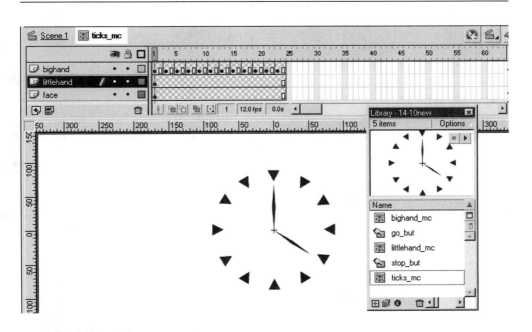

FIGURE 14-10 The tick_mc Movie Clip Editing mode

14

The tick marks in this movie clip were placed on the layer named "face". Because the big hand's animation in the ticks_mc movie clip plays out to Frame 24 on this Timeline, a frame was placed on the face layer (F5) on Frame 24 so it won't disappear when the big hand rotates around the ticks.

An instance of the bighand_mc was dragged onto the bighand layer and an instance of the littlehand_mc was dragged onto the littlehand layer. Because both of these objects reference from the center (indicated with a cross), their reference point was changed from dead center to the bottom center on the bighand_mc movie clip and top center on the littlehand_mc movie clip (Modify | Transform | Edit Center). The crosshairs on both movie clips were dragged to their new location and they were aligned with the crosshair on the stage. The bighand_mc was created to start out on what would be the 12:00 tick on a real clock. The littlehand_mc was created to point to what would be 4:00 tick on a real clock by rotating it slightly from its top axis so the top center stays on the center crosshair while the bottom changes position.

Because the movie clip plays out to Frame 24, a frame was placed on the littlehand layer (F5) on Frame 24. The bighand_mc and the littlehand_mc have now become nested within the parent movie clip, called the ticks_mc.

The only object that moves in this movie clip is the big hand, so the bighand_mc was selected and a keyframe was placed on Frame 3 of the bighand layer. Keeping the center axis on the bighand_mc on the stage crosshair, the bottom of the bighand_mc was rotated clockwise to the next tick mark. This was done with the Rotate tool from the Toolbox. A keyframe was then placed on Frame 5 and the bighand was rotated again to the next tick mark. This process was repeated on every other frame until Frame 23, which is at 11:00. A regular frame was placed on Frame 24.

The movie clip is now finished so the Editing mode was exited. On the main Timeline two layers were created in the following order:

- buttons

- face

With the face layer selected, an instance of the tick_mc was dragged from the Library to the stage and centered. With the Instance panel selected, the movie clip (tick_mc) was given an instance name of "clock." When a button talks to a movie clip, movie clips are always referenced by their instance name. If you don't give a movie clip an instance name, it can't be recognized in a script. The two movie clips nested within the tick_mc movie clip don't have instance names because they haven't been given any instructions to do anything. The script will relate to the Timeline of the parent movie clip, ticks_mc. In the next section, the nested littlehand_mc movie clip also is given an instance name and instructed to do something from the buttons on the main Timeline.

With the Buttons layer selected on the main Timeline, the Stop and Go buttons were dragged onto the stage and placed underneath the clock movie clip. With all elements in place the script was then ready to be generated.

With the Stop button selected and the Actions panel displayed, the Actions list was expanded (underneath Basic Actions). The "with" action was chosen and then appeared in the Actions list. The Actions list then looked like this (see Figure 14-11):

```
on (release) {
    with (<not set yet>) {
        }
}
```

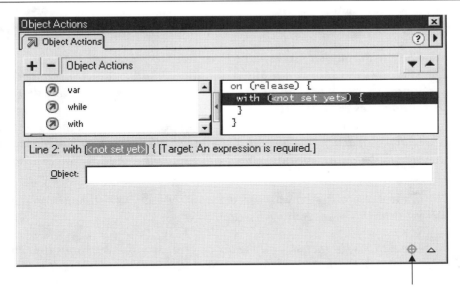

Insert Target Path Button

FIGURE 14-11   The script on the Stop button that controls the movie clip called tick_mc

14

The (<not set yet>) on Line 2 is highlighted in red to alert you to the fact that you need to fill in the blanks. When you choose the "with" action, you are temporarily changing the target path of a movie clip to evaluate an action. After the "with" action happens, the clip returns to its original state. When Line 2 of the code is selected in the Actions list, the Parameters pane prompts you for an Object name. It wants to know what object (instance) you want to talk to. You can type the name in manually but for beginners, the Insert Target Path button assists you in making a foolproof selection. Using this button eliminates syntax problems for beginners.

To review what happens in the movie, the tick_mc movie clip plays immediately when the movie loads. When the Stop button is clicked, the tick_mc movie clip needs to be told to stop playing, wherever the playhead happens to be at that moment. With Line 2 of the script selected (with (<not set yet>) {), the Object box in the Parameter pane was clicked and then the Insert Target Path button on the bottom right of the panel was selected. In the Insert Target Path dialog box, Relative mode was checked and "clock" was clicked as the Target. If you recall, clock was the instance name given to the tick_mc. Only an instance of the movie clip can be controlled, not the actual movie clip symbol. The dialog box was then closed.

TIP
The "with" action has replaced the Tell Target action in Flash 5. The Tell Target action is still available in the Basic Actions and Actions lists and performs the same basic function. However, that action uses the old slash syntax. Notice in the Toolbox list portion of the Actions panel, "Tell Target" is highlighted in green, the color that indicates a deprecated action. You can use the Tell Target action instead of with, but Macromedia recommends using the "with" action instead.

With Line 2 selected, stop was selected from the Actions list. Stop also could be selected from the Basic Actions list, too.

NOTE
The Actions list includes all the actions from the Basic Actions list. This is because Flash 4 only offered Basic Actions in a list format. If you're familiar with Flash 4, the new ActionScript won't look totally foreign to you and you can gradually wean yourself off the old interface.

The final script on the Stop button looks like this:

```
on (release) {
    with (clock) {
        stop ();
    }
}
```

With the Stop button script complete, the final script was written on the Go button. With this button selected and the Actions panel displayed, the following script was generated:

```
on (release) {
    with (clock) {
        play ();
    }
}
```

The script is almost identical to the script on the Stop button except for Line 3 where play was selected instead of stop. Now when the play button is released, the tick_mc will start to play.

The previous example demonstrates some important basics in ActionScript. First, buttons can control movie clip instances, but the movie clip must be referenced by an instance name. Second, although an instance of the movie clip is on the main Timeline, the button is controlling the movie clip on the movie clip's Timeline. This means you can control several movies simultaneously instead of just on the main Timeline. Third, movie clips can have other movie clips nested within them. And nested movie clips can have additional movie clips nested within them, creating a level hierarchy of sorts. Finally, you have added a new action to your ActionScript knowledge base—the "with" action.

In the next section you'll take this nesting concept a step further and control a movie clip nested within a movie clip from the main Timeline.

Understand Nested Movie Clips

The finished clock movie (Figure 14-9) is controlled with simple stop and go actions attached to buttons. The only hand that moves is the big hand while the little hand remains static. There are many ways in which you could dress up this animation.

14

In Figure 14-12, the clock movie now has another function added to it. When the user presses down any key on the keyboard, the little hand on the clock face moves clockwise to the next tick mark and stops until a key is pressed again. If you recall, the hands of the clock are independent movie clips residing within the parent movie clip called tick_mc. The keypress action is attached to a new movie clip called "littlehand_press." This new movie behaves like a button because the keypress action is associated with this movie clip. But because movie clips aren't clickable, you don't have to press directly on the movie clip object to make it work. To create this effect, it's important to know how to address the instance of littlehand_press so the script can find a nested instance from the main Timeline. Later in this chapter we'll deconstruct how this button was made, but it's important to first understand the concept of nesting movie clips and how to address them in a script.

littlehand_press movie clip

FIGURE 14-12   The clock movie now has an additional button called "little hand_press" that controls the little hand nested in the clock movie clip

Understand Absolute Versus Relative Paths   Movie clips are perhaps one of the most versatile objects in ActionScript. Imagine the ability to control another movie clip from a movie clip within a movie clip and so on with any number of actions. So far in this chapter we've dwelled on the simplest of actions relating to the playing and stopping of user controlled frames: Stop, Go, Go to and Play, Go to and Stop, and the With action. In Chapter 15, you'll learn more complex actions, but the simple actions are a good place to start to understand the hierarchy concept in ActionScript. If you're familiar with HTML, you probably know about absolute addressing versus relative addressing. Addressing in HTML relates to an HTML page being capable of locating an HTML page from its current or remote location. In other words, the path of the page must be made clear before a page can display. In ActionScript, movie clips have a hierarchy too. If you tell a nested movie clip to do something, the action won't work if the movie clip instance can't be located. So Flash, like in HTML, uses absolute and relative addressing (or paths) to solve the problem of locating the path of an instance within a movie.

If you recall, when the Target Path dialog box was displayed in the last section, you needed to check one of two buttons in the box: Absolute or Relative. In Figure 14-13, there is a movie clip called moonMC with an instance name of mainmoonMc. This movie clip has a movie clip nested in it that's been given an instance name of face. To give a nested movie clip an instance name, select the Instance panel from the Window menu and type in the new name.

The face instance has another movie clip instance named lefteye. This instance is three levels from the root, or top level of the movie clip. To talk to a movie clip instance nested three levels deep within the mainmoonMc, you need to specify where the instance is located within the hierarchy of the main movie clip. The Target Path dialog box helps you to identify the location of a movie clip instance within the hierarchy.

In Figure 14-13, when the Absolute button is checked, the top level is indicated as the _root. Underneath the _root is what's nested within the movie clip in hierarchical order. The "+" indicates an expandable list of instances and a "-" indicates the absence of additional instances within that level. If you click on the Relative button, the list looks identical except instead of _root it now says "this" (see Figure 14-14) because you are addressing the object from the current Timeline as opposed to returning all the way to the root level and looking down.

With an absolute path, the path always goes to the root level of the movie. Absolute paths always look the same and are consistent no matter where they're referenced.

14

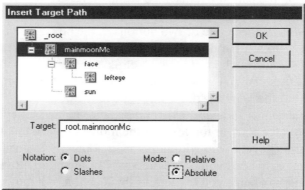

FIGURE 14-13   The Target Path dialog box (displaying Absolute addressing) from
a movie clip with movie clips nested three levels deep

As you can see in Figures 14-13 and 14-14, absolute and relative paths are
almost identical. Often it doesn't matter which one you use to address a movie
clip. They only become important when you are referencing movie clips from
other nested items. For example, if you had a button nested inside a movie clip
and you wanted to control another movie clip instance from the button nested in
a movie clip instance, you would need to use absolute addressing.

Use Dot and Slash Syntax   In the Target Path dialog boxes depicted in Figures
14-12 and 14-13, you'll notice in the bottom left you can select a Notation of
either Dot or Slash. Dot syntax is new in Flash 5 ActionScript and is the default

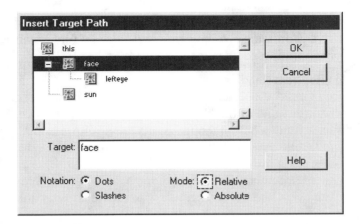

FIGURE 14-14 When Relative is checked in the Target Path dialog box, the top-level movie clip is referred to as "this"

syntax. Slash syntax was used in Flash 4. Dot syntax delineates the levels of a path with a dot, whereas slash syntax uses the slash as in URL addressing. For example, in the Figure 14-13 Moon movie, if you target the instance called "lefteye" that's buried three levels deep within the hierarchy of the movie, with absolute and dot syntax selected, the path would look like this in ActionScript:

```
_root.mainmoonMc.face.lefteye
```

When you target the same path with slash syntax, it looks like this:

```
mainmoonMc/face/lefteye
```

The slashes are the same as the dots; they determine the path of the movie clip. Slash syntax also has a different way of addressing absolute and relative paths. Because slash syntax has been deprecated, there is no point in elaborating on its structure. Suffice to say, dot syntax serves the same purpose for both absolute and relative addressing and replaces slash as the standard.

Dot syntax also is used to tell a movie clip instance to change the property on a particular movie clip instance. For example, if you wanted to drag a movie clip instance on a clip event, the script might look like this:

```
onClipEvent (load)
this.startDrag (lockCenter, 100, 100, 200 500) ();
```

14

Movie clips talking to other movie clips from different parts of a movie can become quite confusing. The purpose of dot syntax used in conjunction with either absolute or relative addressing is to help you organize and find instances that could otherwise become buried beneath a lost movie clip.

Examine Movie Clip Event Handlers   If you recall, in Figure 14-12, a movie clip called "little hand_press" (press a key to make the little hand move) controls the movement of the little hand of the clock when the user presses a key. The new element in this case is not a button though. It's a movie clip. Flash 5 contains what are known as movie clip event handlers. Just like buttons, you can have a movie clip talk to another using movie clip events.

Although named differently, movie clip events are very similar event-wise, to button events. The event handlers associated with movie clips are the following:

- **Load/Unload**—This movie clip event is associated with a movie loading into the first frame. The action is triggered when the movie loads, or unloads depending upon which one you selected.

- **Enter Frame**—The action on this movie clip event occurs when each frame of the movie clip loads.

- **Mouse Down/Mouse Up**—Similar to Press/Release on a button event, a script becomes activated when the user clicks or releases the mouse anywhere on the stage.

- **Mouse Move**—Similar to Roll Over/Roll Out on a button event, this event calls a script when the user moves the mouse while the movie clip is being displayed.

- **Key Down/Key Up**—This event calls a script when a key on the keyboard is pressed when a frame that contains the movie clip is displayed in the movie.

- **Data**—This event becomes active when a script from another movie passes information to this movie.

The major difference between button events and movie clip events is that movie clips aren't clickable like buttons are. Movie clips don't have those nifty little Up/Over/Down states in their Timeline like buttons. Rather, the movie clip Timeline looks just like the Timeline in the main movie. So when you attach an event to a movie clip, like a release event (which is called Mouse up), just the act of releasing the mouse anywhere on the stage will invoke the action(s) contained in your script.

In a movie that uses a button event and an equivalent movie clip event, a conflict can exist between these two events. For example, because the On release event from a button is identical to the Mouse up event on a movie clip, the act of releasing the mouse will choose one event over the other. Because of this, when using similar event handlers for a movie clip and button on the same movie, you must pay careful attention to which event will take command in the movie. The movie clip event always will take precedence over the button event.

Because you often nest movie clips and buttons within one another, it's important to consider how each object will react if similar event handlers are used. A movie clip's event handlers take priority over a button if a button is nested within a movie clip. However, if a movie clip is nested within a button, the events and actions associated with that instance will be ignored as if they didn't exist.

With regard to Key events, the movie clip can be assigned a Key up/Key down event, whereas the button event Key press, involves assigning a specific key. In the case where you have a Key event assigned to a button and a movie clip, the movie clip Key event will activate the movie clip event over the button event.

In short, careful planning has to be done when you use similar button and movie clip events in a movie, because the movie clip event might cancel out the button event if they reside on the same frame.

Control a Nested Movie Clip with a Movie Clip Event Handler   Now that you understand the concept of paths within movie clips and how to address them, let's return to Figure 14-12. This figure is an information-packed movie for ActionScript beginners because it combines both button and movie clip events in the same movie. In addition, it targets the little hand instance (little) of the clock movie clip instance (ticks_mc) and the little hand instance is nested in this clock movie clip. Finally, the main Timeline on which the clock movie clip (ticks_mc) resides is sparsely populated with only two layers with one frame each. This is because the majority of work is contained within the movie clips. This serves as yet another example of how self-contained and modular ActionScript is.

If you recall the Stop and Go buttons in this movie tell the user how to make the clock stop and go. The new text to the right of go is a movie clip called littlehand_press. It explains the following: "press a key to make the little hand move." A Key down event was assigned to this movie clip. Each time the user presses any key down on the keyboard, the little hand movie clip instance nested in the clock movie clip instance advances one tick mark at a time on the clock face. If the little hand_press movie clip was assigned a Mouse up event, it would have cancelled out the Release on the Stop and Go buttons because, as we learned in the last section, mouse events take precedence over button events of a similar

14

nature. Also if a Mouse down event was assigned to this movie clip, the user could click anywhere on the stage and the action would execute because the movie clip event is not contained within an object like a button event.

Let's examine the way this movie was made. Obviously, the basic structure, buttons, and the script on the buttons are still intact from Figure 14-9, which was an earlier and simpler incarnation of the new figure.

Figure 14-9 contains a clock movie clip called ticks_mc. Within this movie clip, there are tick marks that indicate the circumference of a clock face. If you recall, the hands on the clock face of this movie clip were made from two previously created movie clip instances named littlehand_mc and bighand_mc. In their current state (as in Figure 14-9) these hands don't have instance names. They are not needed in this figure because they don't need to be referred to in that script. The buttons on the main Timeline only control the instance of the movie clip called ticks_mc. The script on the buttons plays and stops the ticks_mc movie clip and it is targeted using its instance name, which happens to be "clock." Now that you've refreshed your memory on the history of this movie, let's forge ahead and examine the added interactivity in Figure 14-12.

An additional movie clip was created for this movie and named littlehand_press. The content of this movie clip is simply the following instructional text on one frame: "press a key to make the little hand move." The movie clip does nothing more than instruct the user what to do as well as act as a placeholder for the movie clip event attached to it. After it was made, this movie clip was dragged to the stage to the right of the button called go.

With everything in place, there are a few things that still need to be done. The movie clip called littlehand_mc needs to be animated on its own Timeline and scripting needs to be added to each frame on this movie clip. The user needs to be able to press a key on the keyboard and each time he or she does, the little hand_mc movie clip will rotate clockwise to the next tick mark on the clock face. This was done by creating a frame-by-frame animation on the movie clip's own Timeline. A Stop action resides in each frame on the Timeline and forces the rotation to stop on each frame. The littlehand_mc movie clip was previously nested in the ticks_mc movie clip and it remains in this place throughout the creation of the movie. In contrast to the littlehand_mc, the frame-by-frame animation on the bighand_mc resides on the Timeline of its parent movie clip, ticks_mc, instead of on its own Timeline. The next step was adding animation to the littlehand_mc movie clip.

To do this, the Editing mode of the littlehand_mc movie clip was entered by first entering the editing mode of the ticks_mc movie clip. To do so, double-click ticks_mc from the Library. From the ticks_mc movie clip editing mode, double click the littlehand_mc. The parent movie clip (ticks_mc) is dimmed in the background and the littlehand_mc is now the current selection. Figure 14-15 depicts the Editing mode for littlehand_mc. Notice the hierarchy of the movie in the upper-left corner of the stage.

If you recall when the movie clip called littlehand_mc was created way back in Figure 14-9, it was a static movie clip and as such, occupied only one frame on its own Timeline. In Figure 14-15, the movie clip now has two layers on its Timeline and the frames have been greatly expanded upon. The layers in the littlehand_mc are now in the following order:

- actions

- layer 1

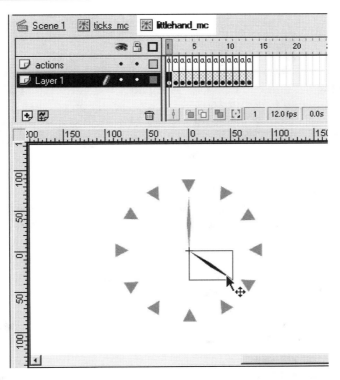

FIGURE 14-15   The movie clip Editing mode for the littlehand_mc movie clip

14

The littlehand object resides on Layer 1. A frame-by-frame animation has been added to the little hand to coincide with the ticks on the ticks_mc movie clip. The rotation is done in much the same way the bighand_mc movie clip was rotated earlier. That is, the center reference point was changed to either the top or bottom of the object, the new center point was aligned to the center crosshair on the movie clip's stage, and then the object was rotated. The littlehand_mc is a little different in that it needs to be rotated clockwise on each keyframe to the next tick mark on the parent movie clip, ticks_mc until it turns a full 360 degrees. It also needs to stop on each frame of its own Timeline so the animation doesn't keep going. Making the rotation of the littlehand_mc correspond with the ticks on the ticks_mc movie clip is easy because you can use the dimmed parent movie clip, ticks_mc, as a guide for the placement of the tip of the littlehand_mc.

If you recall, on the earlier version of the littlehand_mc, the center reference point was moved to the top center of the object so it would rotate around the clock from the top of the object. This was done by selecting the object and choosing Modify | Transform | Edit Center. The crosshair of the object was then moved to the top center of the object and the new crosshair position was aligned with the crosshair on the stage.

A keyframe was then added to each frame on Layer 1 (where the little hand object resides) up to Frame 13. On each keyframe, the hand was rotated to the next tick mark, using the dimmed ticks_mc as a guide. The last rotation stops one tick mark short of the first for a full 360-degree representation of a hand turning. If the Editing mode was exited at this point and the movie tested, the littlehand_mc would just go along ticking forever in its own frame-by-frame movie as it did in Figure 14-9. The desired effect is for the user to be able to control this ticking movement with a movie clip event. Now, an action has to be added to each frame to make the frames stop so the user can control them.

On the actions layer, a keyframe was added to each frame and a Stop action was applied from the Actions panel, up to Frame 13, the last frame. The Stop action can be accessed either from the Basic Actions list or the Actions list. The Stop action prevents the playhead from looping unless told to do otherwise as will be done with the movie clip event on the littlehand_press movie clip. On keyframe 13 the Go to action was selected from the Actions list. The Go to action makes the playhead return to the first frame. Otherwise, because of the Stop actions on the other frames, when the user presses the key to move the little hand around the clock, he or she could only turn the hand around once in 360 degrees (see Figure 14-16). When Go to is selected, the Parameters pane is activated and prompts you for a Scene, Type, and Frame. The scene is relevant if you have used more than one scene in your movie. Otherwise the default is the current scene. The type

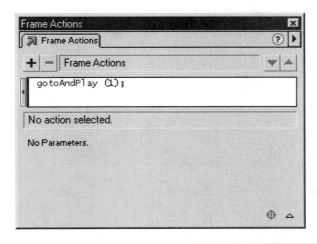

FIGURE 14-16   The script on Frame 13 of the Actions layer has a Go to action
applied to it

refers to what kind of frame you're targeting. In this case a frame number is being
used. Frame refers to the frame number if you're targeting a frame and of course,
Go to and Play is checked, because we want a Play action on this frame.

The Editing mode was exited and the last thing left to do in this movie was to
apply the script to the movie clip called littlehand_press and give an instance name
to the littlehand_mc movie clip. To control the movie clip littlehand_mc that's nested
in the ticks_mc movie clip, it needed to have an instance name assigned on the
ticks_mc Timeline. Otherwise when the script was generated on the littlehand_press
movie clip, you wouldn't be able to locate the movie clip called littlehand_press
or the littlehand_mc. Also important is the fact that the ticks_mc movie clip has
an instance name of "clock" from its previous state. Because this is the parent
movie clip, it too must have an instance name for the movies to communicate
with one another.

An instance name was added to the littlehand_mc by entering the Editing mode
of the ticks_mc movie clip and clicking the littlehand_mc (see Figure 14-17).
From the Frame panel, an instance name of "little" was assigned to this movie clip
and the Editing mode was then exited.

On the main Timeline, the littlehand_press movie clip was selected and the
Actions panel displayed. With most of the script having been generated on the
littlehand_mc Timeline, the script on this movie clip was easy. Littlehand_press
doesn't need an instance name because its only purpose is to tell the littlehand_mc
what to do.

14

FIGURE 14-17   An instance name was given to the littlehand_mc of "little" in the Editing mode of the parent movie clip, ticks_mc

In the Toobox list, Actions was expanded and "with" was selected. The script in the Actions list looks like this:

```
onClipEvent (load) {
    with (<not set yet>) {
    }
}
```

All that needs to be done is to fill in the blanks on the script. With Line 1 selected, in the Parameters portion of the panel the key down selection was checked. With Line 2 selected, the Object box in the Parameters pane was clicked on and the Target Path button was clicked. In the Target Path dialog box, Absolute mode was selected and the "+" sign was clicked to expand the hierarchy of the movie clips. "Little" was checked and on the bottom of the dialog box the Target reads _root.clock.little. The "little" if you recall, was the instance name given to the littlehand_mc that was nested in the ticks_mc movie clip.

   *When you use the "with" action on a button, the top line of script reads "on (release)." ActionScript recognizes this object as a movie clip so it calls a move clip event (onClipEvent), and Load is the default event.*

The littlehand_press movie clip needs to know what to do with the "little" instance now that it's targeted it using the "with" action. With Line 2 selected,

Go to was chosen from the Actions list. In the Parameters pane, the following information was selected from the pop-up menus in the Scene, Type, and Frame boxes:

- Scene: <current scene> (the default setting)

- Type: Next Frame

- Frame: (Not applicable)

The finished script on the movie clip looks like this:

```
onClipEvent (keyDown) {
    with (_root.clock.little) {
        nextFrame ();
    }
}
```

When the movie is played, and the user presses any key, the little hand will rotate ahead one tick each time a key is pressed.

ActionScript is a lot more powerful than just making frames play with buttons and movie clips. Once you understand the basics of ActionScript, you can perform many exciting interactive tasks. Because the scope of ActionScript is far too broad a subject to cover in this book, the next chapter will examine some common ActionScript routines that will help expand your knowledge base of the language.

14

Chapter 15

Learn the Full Power of ActionScript

How to...

- Work with Variables
- Create a Drag-and-Drop Effect
- Set the Position of a Movie Clip
- Make Objects Collide
- Use Conditional Statements (If/Else)
- Use the getProperty Function
- Use Smart Clips
- Create a Basic Preloader

In the last chapter, the basics of ActionScript were covered; specifically what it is and how it works. You examined interactivity of buttons, frames, and movie clips. The focus was mainly on movie clips and frames, using the With, Go To, Stop, and Go actions. These actions barely touch the scope of ActionScript.

In this chapter, the focus is on the conceptual aspects of ActionScript. With scripting alone, you can change and manipulate the properties of movie clips, drag and drop movie clips, return information on a movie clip, define and change the function of a movie clip, and many more interactive tasks. Some Flash authors create almost their entire movie using only ActionScript, including the creation of objects and their properties.

To further understand ActionScript, we'll cover some advanced scripting concepts in this chapter. Advanced ActionScript pumps up the interactivity in your movie by further customizing the audience's experience.

Understand the Concept of Variables

If you recall, in Chapter 5 a simple Text Input field was created that used a variable. The variable name assigned to that text field was repeated in another text field. When the user typed his or her name in the first text field, the name was automatically generated in the second text field with the same variable. This was an elementary example of how a variable works. The name that was typed would vary depending on who typed it in.

Variables are recognized in a script by the name that's assigned to them, and as the name implies, variables change. Variables store groups of data, all of which have different values assigned to them, and as such, values can change over time. For example, if you were using a text field variable to display the current position of your cursor, the value in the text field would change each time the cursor moved. The value of a variable can contain other actions, properties, methods, and functions. There is no end to what you can do with variables.

Variables are a common component in most programming languages, although they work differently from language to language. In ActionScript, they serve as a container for information that is determined by the author of the movie. Variable data can be numbers, strings, objects, or movie clips. When you name a variable, it must be contained in a single string with no spaces, and case sensitivity is not an issue.

Careful consideration should be given to the names you select for your variables. As with naming all elements in your Flash movie, it's good practice to name variables in a logical format, relating to the variable you're declaring. You also don't want to use words that are already reserved as code in ActionScript. This is true for any extraneous elements you're naming, whether they are layers, instances, and so on.

Scope of a Variable

The scope of a variable can be either global or local. Will a variable be recognized on the click of a button, or will it be recognized throughout the entire movie in every frame and scene? The scope refers to the extent of which a variable you assign will be recognized.

A local variable is referenced in its own block of curly brackets within a statement. When a local variable is used, once the script is played, the variable no longer exists. The local variable (var) is found in the Action List of the Actions panel.

A global variable is constant. If a text field variable is set once in a movie, that variable will be recognized throughout the entire movie. The global variable found in the Actions List (setVariables) is used to declare a global variable. Because a global variable is the most commonly used for ActionScript beginners, you'll be experimenting with the setVariable action in this chapter.

Understand Strings and Expressions

Before you declare variables in ActionScript, because you're essentially learning to speak a new language, all the rules need to be understood before using it. In

15

Chapter 14, absolute and relative paths were discussed. Paths are an important concept to keep in mind with variables too. You'll often be declaring variables on elements that need to be referenced from a different Timelines within the movie. Incorrect addressing often causes scripting errors.

The other concept you need to familiarize yourself with is the difference between strings and expressions. When you declare a variable in a script, the Parameters pane prompts you for a variable, a value, and whether or not the statement is an expression.

The Expression check box is checked on the value in Figure 15-1. When the Expression box is checked, a value can be returned on that expression, based on the logic of the script. Expressions can contain more that one element (examples to follow) as well as functions and operators. For example, a variable might be something like the following example, which is a two line script written for a button.

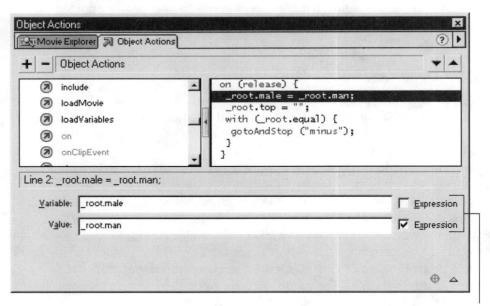

Expression check boxes

FIGURE 15-1   The Actions panel displayed from a movie clip with two variables from text fields set on a movie clip event

The word "top" is the variable and "top add 8" is the value. Note the value in this case is more than one element. It's the adding of a variable to a number.

```
top = top add 8;
```

"_root.total" in this case is the variable and "Number(_root.bottom) + Number(_root.top)" is the value.

```
_root.total = Number(_root.bottom) + Number(_root.top);
```

 NOTE *When you see "//" with text following it in a script or frames, it always indicates author's comments The script ignores the text that follows the "//" until the next paragraph.*

Variables always contain an equal sign (=) that bridges the next part of the statement to the right of the "=", which is the value. When a variable or value is numeric, it is considered an expression. A returned value doesn't necessarily have to be a number, just as a number doesn't have to be numeric as in a math function. A number can just represent text, in which case it's a string.

Strings are words or text that represent a concept. The Expression box is not checked for text that represents strings, and strings, in some cases, are contained in parenthesis. A variable with a string value might be

```
Rectangle="big"
```

If the text is meant to return a value, it's an expression. Whether the Expression box is checked determines if your script will play out the right way. When troubleshooting a script, add this on your list of potential reasons why the script won't work.

NOTE *When you work in Expert mode, you evaluate your own expressions because the Parameters pane in the Actions panel isn't there to help you as it is in Normal mode.*

When a value is a string, parenthesis appear around that element. When two strings are joined together into one element, they are concatenated. For example, if you had a value of "big" + "man", this string would be concatenated. The result of this string would be "bigman". Note these strings are joined together with a plus (+) sign. When the plus sign is used to join strings together, it's known as a *string operator*. The value returned joins two elements together instead of performing a mathematical calculation on them. Additional string operators can be used from the Operator list (in the Toolbox list) as well as from the String Operator list. Take note, however, that the operators in the String Operator list have been deprecated in version 5.

Math operations performed on numbers are called *numeric operators*. These operators perform functions such as addition, subtraction, multiplication, increment, greater than, equal to, and many more. Math operations are also located in the Operator list in the Toolbox list. You will notice, some of these have been deprecated also.

> **NOTE**　*The Expression box in Normal mode also becomes a selectable option for other actions and functions like the setProperty action and getProperty function, both of which are discussed later in this chapter.*

Create a Simple Variable

Figure 15-2 represents a simple two-frame movie that prompts the user for a first name and last name, the sum of which is represented in Frame 2. After the user fills out her first and last name, she presses an arrow button to enter Frame 2. On Frame 2, there is a personalized greeting and a question regarding marbles. In its present state, Frame 2 doesn't make a lot of sense, but the purpose of the movie becomes clearer as the movie progresses in the section that follows.

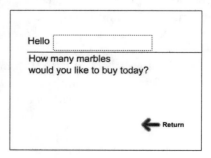

Frame 1　　　　　　　　　　Frame 2

FIGURE 15-2　Frame 1 and Frame 2 of a movie that utilizes global variables

This is a simple movie that utilizes several of the concepts we've discussed so far in this chapter. Variables have been set on three text input fields in two separate frames of this movie and because the variables are global, they are active throughout the entire movie. An expression and an operator are also used in the script. The following explains how the movie was made and the purpose of the variables in the movie:

This movie was given two layers in the following order:

■ **actions**—This layer sets some global variables and Stop actions.

■ **variables/button**—This layer contains all the static instructional text ("Last Name" and "First Name", "Press the arrow to enter the site"), text fields, and scripted arrow buttons.

On Frame 1 of the variables/button layer, an arrow button was added to the bottom right of the stage, to the right of the text ("Press the arrow to enter the site").

Four blocks of static text were added to frame 1 of the variables/button layer. The purpose of this text is to tell the user what to do. The first text in the upper-left corner says "Please enter your name". Under this block of text are the words "First Name:" and "Last Name:". Next to the arrow in the bottom right is a static text statement that says "Press the arrow to enter the site." This text instructs the user to press the arrow after they've typed in the necessary information. Now that all the instructional text is input, the text input fields that the user fills out need to be created.

On the same layer and frame, a text input field (selected as a choice from the Text Options panel) was drawn on the stage, to the right of "First Name". This input field will be where the user types his first name. The text field was then duplicated (CTRL+SHIFT/OPTION+SHIFT), dragged down, and aligned with "Last Name". The top box was selected and given a Variable name of "first" in the Text Options panel and the second box was selected and given a variable name of "last".

A keyframe was then added to Frame 2 on the variables/button layer and all the text on this frame was revised to respond to the name prompt the user types in on Frame 1 in the "first" and "last" text input fields. When a keyframe is added, the previous frame becomes duplicated in the next frame. Because the contents of Frame 2 need to be different in this frame, one of the variable text fields and static text boxes was deleted and the remaining text boxes were revised. The left-over arrow button was rotated 180 degrees to point backward to direct the user back to Frame 1; so when a script is added, they press on this button to return to Frame 1. The left over text variable field in Frame 2 was selected and given the new

15

variable name (from the Text Options panel) "fullname". The static text that was left over from Frame 1 was revised to read, "Hello". A personalized greeting that includes the name and user input will appear on this text field next to the word "Hello". This will occur after the user enters her first and last name in Frame 1, and then pushes the button that takes her to Frame 2.

If you were to test the movie at this point, it would loop. This movie is not about animation. It's about interactivity. It needs to pause on each frame until the user clicks a button to go to the next frame or return to the first frame. So a Stop Frame action was added on Frames 1 and 2 of the Actions layer to stop the movie on both frames (to refresh your memory, you need to make a keyframe (F6) before you add the action).

On Frame 2, actions layer, under the Stop action, another action was set. With Line 1 selected, in the Actions list, set variable was selected. In the Parameters pane, for Variable, "fullname" was typed in. For Value, "first + " " + last" was typed in as shown in Figure 15-3. Note the quotes with a space between them in the script. This variable could have been set on a button instead of a frame because it's a global variable. So the location of the variable in the movie is your choice. The script on Frame 2 now reads

```
stop();
Fullname=first+" "+last;
```

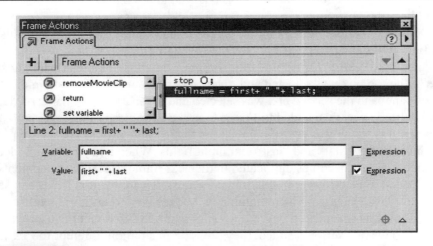

FIGURE 15-3   The Frame Actions panel on Frame 2 of the movie has a Stop and a Set Variable action assigned to it

If you recall, "first" and "last" are the variables for two text fields in Frame 1. "Fullname" is the variable for the text field in Frame 2. The variable states that the value of "fullname" is first+ " " +last. This is the sum of the two text variables plus a space (delineated by the empty quotes) after the first name and before the last name in Frame 1. If the space wasn't there when the user typed their full name in, it would run together with no space in between. The space between the two quotes tells the script to add a blank space between the two variables that are joined together. The Expression box is also checked next to the Value. This means a value will be returned instead of a string and as such there are no quotes around the first and last. There are only quotes where the blank space is required. The operator in this case is the plus sign (+).

> **NOTE**
>
> *If Expression box is not checked for Value in this exercise, the variable (wholename) regards the value ("first+ " " + last," which would read "first+ " " last") as a string operator. The wholename variable would literally equal the words "first + " " +last" and this is the text that would appear in the wholename text field, instead of the name typed in by the user.*

The remainder of work involves a script on both buttons. The button scripts navigate from one frame to another at the user's discretion. On the arrow button on Frame 2, the script is a simple Go To action from the Action (or Basic Action) list that takes the user back to Frame 1. The script now reads

```
    on (release) {
gotoAndPlay (1);
}
```

The arrow button on Frame 1 contains the majority the script that makes the movie interactive. With the arrow button selected, a Go To Action was applied, instructing the playhead to go to Frame 2. The script looks like this:

```
on (release) {
gotoAndPlay (2);
}
```

Notice this script is identical to the script on the other button except for the frame number.

15

The movie is now complete. Now, when the user types her first and last name in Frame 1 and clicks the button to go to Frame 2, she sees her first and last names combined in the whole name text field (see Figure 15-4).

Use a Button Event to Indicate the Value of a Variable

Variables can be set on buttons as well as frames. In Figure 15-5, a variable is set on a button, which returns a value to the text field to the right of the arrow button on which another value is set. On Frame 2 of this new version of the previous movie in Figure 15-2, the user can select the number of marbles she wants to buy by clicking another button. This involves setting up more variables and using a numerical operator.

Figure 15-5 introduces a new arrow button on Frame 2 under "How many marbles would you like to buy today?" There's also a new static instructional text block that says "Click a button to select a number". To the right of this text block there's a button. To the right of the new arrow button, there's a new text input field with a variable name of "total". The user can click the button and stop clicking until she reaches the number of marbles she wants to purchase.

In addition to the new instructional text, a new button was needed on Frame 2, which in this case was borrowed from the Common Library. With the new button selected on Frame 2, Set Variable was chosen in the Actions panel. For Variable, *total* was entered (the name of the new text input field). For Value, "total + 1" was

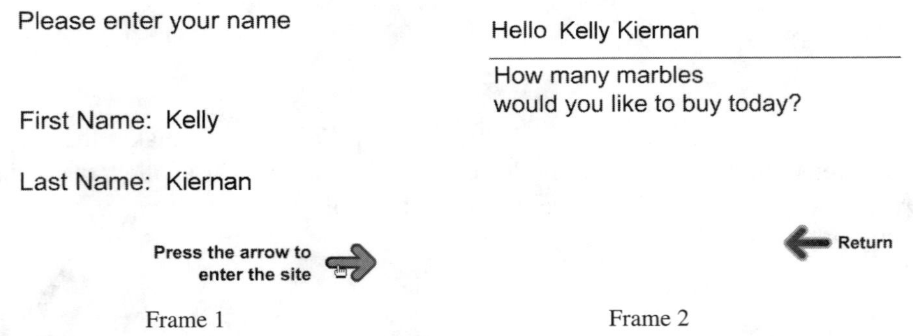

Please enter your name

Hello Kelly Kiernan

How many marbles
would you like to buy today?

First Name: Kelly

Last Name: Kiernan

⬅ Return

Press the arrow to
enter the site ➡

Frame 1

Frame 2

FIGURE 15-4   When a user inputs their first and last name and presses the arrow, his/her name appears in one box in the text field on Frame 2

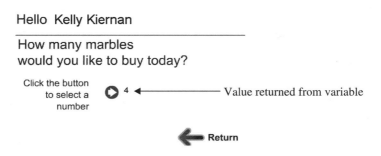

Hello Kelly Kiernan

How many marbles
would you like to buy today?

Click the button
to select a
number

4 ◄─────────── Value returned from variable

◄═ Return

FIGURE 15-5   A variable is set on a button in this movie that returns a value to a
text field

entered (the text field variable plus the number 1). The Expression box was checked
for Value. The script on the new button looks like this (see Figure 15-6):

```
on (release) {
    total = total +1;
}
```

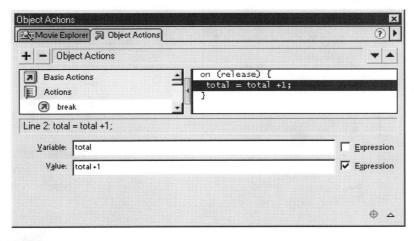

FIGURE 15-6   The Actions panel for the text field whose variable name is total

Each time the button is pressed, a number, starting with the number 1, is added to the text input field called "total". Each time the button is clicked the number increases +1. Total+1 acts as a numerical operator by increasing the number in the total text field by 1 each time the user clicks the button. So, if the user clicked the button six times, the number in the text field would be 6.

Variables can be set on either frames or buttons as long as the script follows a logical order. In this example, it's logical for the variables to be set on a button because it is the button event (on release) that causes the variable to display in the text field. This is also a good example of the changing nature of variables. Each time the user clicks the button, the output in total text field varies.

Set Multiple Variables on a Button

Variables are incredibly flexible. You can set as many variables as you want on the same button or frame. In Figure 15-7, Frame 2, an additional text field has been added to the movie we've been working on. The new text field has a variable name of "price". To the left of this new text field, there is new static instructional text that says, "Price @ $3.00 each". Each time the user clicks the mouse to select the number of marbles she wants to buy, the price text field calculates the price of the marbles based on the other variable that has been set by the user (the total

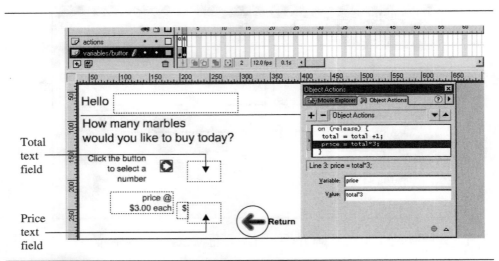

Total text field

Price text field

FIGURE 15-7 A new variable has been added to a button to return the price of the total marbles the user selects

marbles gotten by the user clicking the arrow button). A dollar sign ($) was placed next to the text input field so it would appear to the user as if the price was represented in dollars.

Aside from the addition of a couple of static text fields and a text input field with a variable name of "price", the only extra component of the movie is additional script on the existing arrow button that's clicked to view the total number of marbles. If you recall, the script on this button currently reads

```
on (release) {
    total = total +1;
}
```

With Line 2 of the script selected, Set Variable was chosen again from the Actions list creating Line 3. This time, for Variable, "price" was typed in. This is the name of the new text field. For Value, "total" was typed in. With the cursor still in the Value box, from the Operators List * (multiply) was chosen. You could also type in this sign manually if searching through the Operators list is too time-consuming. The number 3 was typed in to the right of the multiplication sign (*). (In this case the number 3 was arbitrarily chosen to perform a calculation.) Because this value is a numerical operator, the Expression box is checked for Value. The script on this button now reads

```
on (release) {
    total = total +1;
    price = total*3;
}
```

NOTE *Although it is checked, the Expression box in Figure 15-7 is not visible. The Actions panel was collapsed to minimize space.*

15

Create a Drag-and-Drop Effect

Drag-and-drop actions are used for many functions. On the Internet, you can drag and drop items into shopping carts. You also see this technique used for games and puzzles. There's a Web site where you can create your own art for custom refrigerator magnets by dragging things like moustaches, eyebrows, and funny hats over pictures you've downloaded of friends or family. Your imagination is the only thing holding you back with drag and drop. The more you surf the Web, the more you'll discover how creative Flash authors really are with ActionScript and the drag-and-drop action is no exception.

In this section we'll start with a simple drag-and-drop technique and continue to expand upon it to create some interesting interactive effects. The sample movies used to demonstrate different techniques can be modified, mixed with other scripts, and applied to your own movies. Once you understand the processes involved for each action and how it relates to ActionScript as a whole, your sites will be interactive in no time.

The most efficient way to do a drag and drop is to insert a button instance into a movie clip and place the script on the button in the movie clip. Because movie clips are dragable and buttons are clickable, together, they make a dynamic duo for a drag-and drop-effect.

NOTE   *You also can perform a drag and drop on a movie clip event onClipEvent (mouseDown). However, this might not be the most efficient way to create a drag-and-drop effect for your project. Unless you're experienced in ActionScript and know its limitations, for now, stick with the simple methods outlined in this chapter.*

After you get the hang of it, drag and drops are easy to make. Figure 15-8 represents a very simple one frame, one layer drag-and drop-movie. There are four movie clips on the stage: a circle, polygon, star, and swirl. The objects can be clicked and dragged by the viewer. Your mouse can pick up objects, much like a cursor moves an object in a drawing program. When the mouse is released, the object also is released.

To create this simple effect, four buttons were created that represent each one of the four objects portrayed in Figure 15-8. The buttons were named circle_button, star_button, poly_button, and swirl_button. Then, four movie clips were made to correspond to each one of the four buttons. The movie clips were named the following: circle_mc, star_mc, poly_mc, and swirl_mc.

TIP   *The names of the buttons and movie clips are suggestive of the objects themselves.*

In the Editing mode of each movie clip, each corresponding button was nested in the first frame on the Timeline of each corresponding movie clip. Then the Editing mode for that particular movie clip was exited, and the next movie clip was created, until all four were complete.

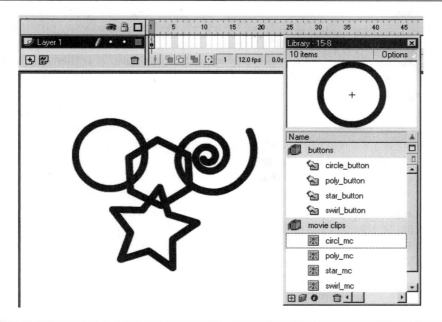

FIGURE 15-8   A simple drag-and-drop action is attached to each one of these four objects

> *There are other ways to make the movie clips. For example, you could make a movie clip, drag a graphic symbol into the Movie Clip Editing mode, and change the object's behavior to a button from the Instance panel. But, for the sake of understanding the process in whole, the exercise is approached on a step-by-step basis.*

TIP

An instance of each movie clip was dragged to the stage. In the Instance panel, each movie clip was given the following instance names to correspond with their shape, button and movie clip names: poly, swirl, star, and circle.

In this movie, the script on each movie clip is located on the buttons in the movie clip Timelines. With this in mind, the circle was the first movie clip instance to be assigned a script. The circle_mc was double-clicked in the Library. In the Editing mode, the circle is a nested button. So the script will reside on the button in the movie clip. However, it's the movie clip instance that's being talked to (circle). So the script must make reference to the movie clip instance that resides on the main Timeline.

15

With the circle button selected, the Actions panel was displayed. In the Actions list, startDrag was chosen. With Line 2 selected, the Parameters pane prompts you for a Target. The Target refers to the instance you want to start dragging. The Target box was clicked and the Target Path button was chosen. Either Absolute or Relative can be used for this object. Relative was checked, and the Target Path dialog box was then closed. The Expression box was checked also. With Line 3 selected in the script (a line was skipped to create the container for the new action), Line 4 was created and stopDrag was selected from the Actions List. Line 1 was then selected and Press was checked for the Event from the Parameters pane. If the Press Event isn't chosen, nothing will happen. Release was selected for the Event on Line 4. The default event for both startDrag and stopDrag is Release. To make the drag and drop work properly, you have to make the drag event a Press and the drop event a Release (see Figure 15-9).

This process was repeated for the other three objects (polygon, swirl, star), substituting the appropriate button in the movie clip and targeting the appropriate movie clip instance for each movie clip. When the movie is tested, each object can be picked up, moved, and dropped.

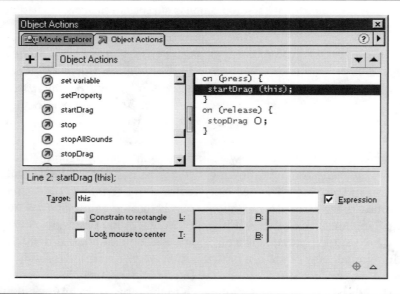

FIGURE 15-9   The script on the circle button nested in the circle movie clip

You probably noticed that when Line 2 was selected in the Parameters pane, there were additional selections:

- **Constrain to rectangle and L, T, R, B**—When Constrain to Rectangle is checked, you can specify the exact coordinates that you want an object to be constrained within. The L, T, R, and B refer to the left, top, right, and bottom borders the object will be constrained within. The L, T, R, B only highlight when Constrain to Rectangle is checked. When you do select this option, the coordinates are reflected in the script.

- **Lock mouse to center**—When this is checked, the mouse becomes locked to the center of the object until you select another object or exit the movie.

It's a good idea to play with these settings to get an idea of how they work. Sometimes the experience makes more sense than the verbal explanation. Now that you understand the basic drag-and-drop concept, let's build on this action by making the movie a little more meaningful.

Use the Set Property Action to Set the Position of a Movie Clip

In Figure 15-8, the movie clip objects moved around and the viewer could drop them at will. Although drag and drop is an amusing effect, without a purpose, dragging and dropping those movie clips all around the stage just seems senseless. So in Figure 15-10, a shopping bag has been introduced into the movie, along with a Reset button and instructions for the viewer to place his object in the shopping bag. Although it has shopping overtones, this movie is still miles away from a shopping cart function. As the movie progresses in content, you will begin to get a sense of how you might go about building a shopping cart function or a game using a combination of advanced actions.

In Figure 15-10, the movie assumes more goal-oriented purpose than in its first incarnation. The viewer now has something to do with his toys; that is, stuff them in a bag and click the Reset button to get them to return to their original place if he changes his mind. You would logically assume that the shopping bag is created on a higher layer than the objects, so when the viewer drags the objects into the bag, they appear to drop in. The only problem is this bag has a quasi-3D design, so if you merely put the shopping bag on a higher layer, when dragged and dropped, the objects appear to go behind the bag instead of inside it.

Even for this simple movie there is planning that was done up front. Otherwise unpredictable problems can arise that force you to go back and start from scratch.

15

FIGURE 15-10   In this movie, the objects can be dragged and dropped into a shopping bag

Figuring out solutions to potential problems before the project begins saves a lot of time in the long run.

The desired drag-and-drop effect in this movie is for the objects to appear as if they've been dropped inside the bag. So to do this, the shopping bag was created as two separate movie clips; the front portion (frontBag_mc) and the back portion (backBag_mc) as shown in Figure 15-11. Each part of the shopping bag was placed on two separate layers so the top portion would sit in the back layer, and the front of the bag sits on a higher layer. The objects, which will be dragged in between these two layers, were placed on layers in between the front and the back of the shopping bag. Unlike the last movie, each draggable movie clip has been

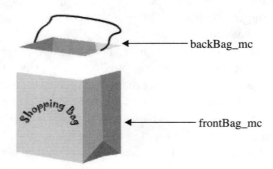

FIGURE 15-11   The shopping bag object in Figure 15-10 is made by joining these two movie clips together to take advantage of their stacking order

put on its own layer. They could have remained on the same layer, but putting each object on its own layer gives you more control over the stacking order of these objects. You know right away which one will stack first by looking at the layer order. The layers were named in the following order: front bag, swirl, circle, star, polygon, and back bag misc.

The final issue with this movie is that if the viewer puts any of the objects deep in the bag so they're no longer visible, how does the viewer take them out? As a side note, when a user mouses near a clickable object (as are the movie clips in this movie because a button is embedded in them), the cursor turns to a hand where the area is active (the area where you've indicated a hit state on the button). So even if one of these objects becomes invisible because of stacking order, you could locate it in the bag by finding the hit area of the button (the cursor hand) on the bag.

Now your viewer probably doesn't know the hand represents the active area of the button. This problem could be resolved if you place a Reset button in the movie so all the objects can return to their original position if the user so chooses. This way, the objects never get lost on the stage. In Figure 15-10, the new button in the bottom-right corner, which resides on the back bag/misc layer, is called "Reset" to indicate to the viewer its purpose. The Reset button has a script on it that returns each object to its original position. This was done with the setProperty action.

Let's examine how the setProperty action works on this button. As you recall from the original movie (Figure 15-8), the dragable movie clips are created from buttons nested in the clips. The movie clips on the main Timeline have instance names to logically correspond with each object. To refresh your memory so you'll understand their reference in the script on the Reset button, the instance names on the objects are as follows: poly, swirl, star, and circle.

To have all four movie clips return to their original position, it has to be determined where their original position is located. The position of an object is its X, Y coordinate. You can identify the exact location of each object by clicking it and viewing the coordinates in the Info panel. With the four objects, the X, Y coordinates in this movie are as follows:

	X	Y
poly	260	45
swirl	310	110
star	330	185
circle	265	250

These coordinates were recorded by selecting each object in their starting position and viewing the Info panel before the script was written. If you keep the X, Y coordinates simple and round them out, it makes it easier to type them in later.

With the instance names and the X, Y coordinates all lined up, the next step was to write the script on the Reset button. With the Reset button selected, the Actions panel was displayed. In the Actions list, setProperty was chosen. The script on the first two lines now reads

```
on (release) {
setProperty ("",<not set yet>, "");
}
```

The properties of the objects will be scripted in the order that they appear in the layers (which is also the order that we've been discussing them in). Each property (X, Y for each instance) will be set line by line in this example.

Line 1 was selected, Press was checked, and Release was deselected. With Line 2 selected, the following parameters were typed in:

- Property: **_x** (X position)—This can be selected from the pop-up Properties menu or typed in.

- Target: **poly**—The instance being targeted. This can either be typed in or the Target Path button can be clicked and the Target Path dialog box can be used. Either Relative or Absolute can be checked. In this script, Relative addressing is used. The Expression box was also checked.

- Value: **260**—The Expression box was also checked. This was the number of the X position recorded from the Info panel.

With Line 2 selected, setProperty was chosen again, generating the same fill-in-the-blanks template for the Parameters pane. For Line 3, the following parameters were input:

- Property: **_y** (Y position)—This indicates the Y position of the object.

- Target: **poly**—The instance being targeted. The Expression box was also checked.

- Value: **45**—This indicates the exact coordinate of the Y position. The Expression box was also checked.

This process was repeated for the remaining three objects. The final script on the Reset button looks like this (see Figure 15-12):

```
on (press) {
    setProperty (poly, _x, 260);
    setProperty (poly, _y, 45);
    setProperty (swirl, _x, 310);
    setProperty (swirl, _y, 110);
    setProperty (star, _x, 330);
    setProperty (star, _y, 185);
    setProperty (circle, _x, 265);
    setProperty (circle, _y, 250);
}
```

Now when the movie is tested and the objects are moved around, when the Reset button is clicked, the objects always return to their original position.

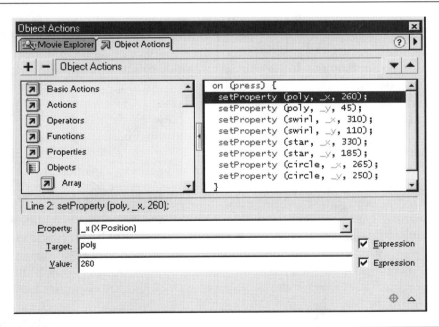

15

FIGURE 15-12   The script on the Reset button of the current movie

The setProperty action is a very powerful. You can change many of the properties of a movie clip with a setProperty action. The list of available properties can be previewed in the pop-up Properties menu that appears if you click the arrow in the Parameter pane in this movie. Some of the changable properties include alpha, visibility, rotation, size, and scale.

Use the hitTest Function

There are many ways to use a collision detection effect in Flash. Often they are used for games that require some sort of skill from the player. In Flash, there's sample movie under Help | Samples called Mosquito Killer that uses collision detection on a mosquito movie clip. If a movie clip (mosquitos) collides with the hit area of the of a fly swatter movie clip (that substitutes for the cursor), the mosquito gets crushed and a "squish" sound is emitted. If you examine the script and functions in this movie, you might be a little overwhelmed, so for now, concentrate on the concept of collision detection; that is, an action occurring as a result of an object coming in contact with another and you as the author, decide the outcome.

The function used to detect a collision is hitTest. The hitTest is a movie clip method and as such, can only be used to detect colliding movie clips.

In Figure 15-13, when a user drags the swirl, star, and circle movie clips into the shopping bag, each object responds differently when the target is hit, which happens to be the shopping bag movie clip. If you recall, the front of the shopping bag is a movie clip as are the objects. If the objects are dragged anywhere else in the movie, nothing happens.

Lets review how the objects respond when they collide with the bag. When the polygon hits the target, it doubles in size and a text message displays under the shopping bag that says "Woops! Too big!" This was accomplished by adding a script on the polygon movie clip telling the polygon to go to another movie clip (with a text message) and play Frame 2 of this movie clip. The new movie clip, called "woops_mc" contains text that starts on Frame 2 and ends on Frame 40 on its own Timeline. On Frame 41, the text disappears. Now, in addition to being able to be dragged and dropped, the script tells the polygon movie clip to change its width, height, and play a frame of another movie clip "woops_mc", when it hits the shopping bag. The size of the polygon was altered by adding a setProperty action to change the width and height of the object similar to what was done on the Reset button.

When the star object hits the same target (shopping bag), a movie clip instance that has a sound nested in it called "zoom," plays. Also, hitting the target with the star makes the polygon movie clip instance become invisible. The polygon is not seen again until the Reset button is pressed.

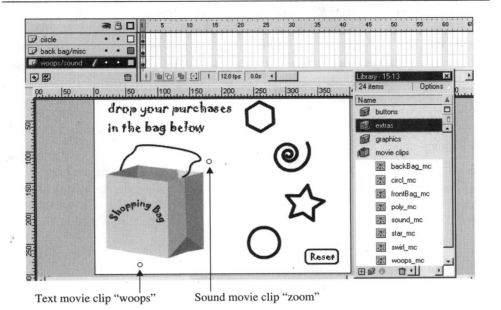

Text movie clip "woops"   Sound movie clip "zoom"

FIGURE 15-13   When the swirl and the star movie clips are dragged into the shopping bag, they respond in a different ways as a result of colliding with the shopping bag

The polygon stays visible unless the star movie clip hits the target, in which case, the polygon disappears. The circle does nothing for now but remains dragable as it was before. A conditional statement (If/Else) will be added to the circle later in this chapter.

The script on the Reset button has a few additional statements added to the end. If the swirl movie clip instance hits the shopping bag, it grows twice the size. So when it returns to its origin by clicking the Reset button, the size has to be adjusted back to normal. The visibility of the polygon also has to be returned to normal (True) when the user clicks Reset because if the star hits the shopping bag, it becomes invisible.

Although this movie might seem complex, what's happening is really very simple. A hitTest is changing properties of three of the four movie clips. All the properties that are changing are properties that have been used before. They are, however, being used in a different context. They only change if each object hits a target, that is, the shopping bag.

15

Use the If Action to Evaluate a hitTest   The if action is used in ActionScript when a statement needs to be evaluated as true or false. In the case of Figure 15-13, the if action evaluates a condition, which in this case is a movie clip instance (swirl or star) colliding with another movie clip instance (shopping bag). If the condition is true, it runs the next statement, which happens to be different on each movie clip. This is often used in conjunction with the else statement. The else statement changes the condition of the previous statement if the statement is returned as false. The else statement also is used later on in this chapter. As you will see, the if action helps makes a logical statement out of the hitTest action.

Make Objects Collide   Many of the components of Figure 15-13 have already been created but there are two additional movie clips that need to be added to the Library to make this scenario work. They include a movie clip for the swirl that says "Woops! Too big!", and a movie clip with a sound nested in it (zoom) that will play when the star collides with the shopping bag.

Let's examine the movie, its new components, and how it works: The basic structure of Figure 15-10 is still intact with Reset button and all. A new layer was added to the bottom of the main Timeline and named "woops/sound". The woops movie clip instance that plays when the swirl hits the shopping bag and the sound movie clip that plays when the star hits the shopping bag will be placed on this layer.

The new movie clips were made starting with "woops_mc" (see Figure 15-14). This movie clip has two layers: action and text. On the text layer the following text was typed: "Woops! Too big!" a frame was put on Frame 40 of this layer to extend the length time the text will display after the collision that activates this movie clip occurs. The first frame of the text layer was moved to Frame 2. So when the movie loads, this movie clip will be invisible.

A Stop action was put on Frame 1 of the actions layer so the movie clip stops when it loads until told to play on Frame 2 where the text appears (this movie clip is invisible on load). A Go To action was assigned to a keyframe next to the Stop action and it was dragged to Frame 41 (see Figure 15-15). This action goes to and stops the movie on Frame 41, which is a blank frame. So, the text disappears once it hits Frame 41. To accomplish this, the following parameters were input:

- Scene: **\<current scene\>**

- Type: **Frame Number**

- Frame: **41**

- Go To And Play was deselected so it now reads Go To And Stop

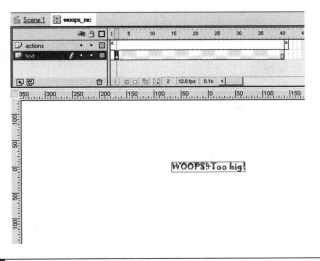

FIGURE 15-14 The woops movie clip Timeline

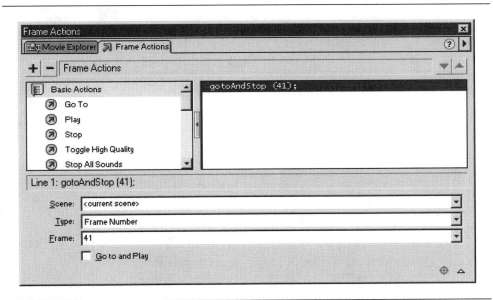

FIGURE 15-15 The script on the woops movie clip, Frame 41

The Editing mode of this movie clip was then exited and an instance of the woops movie clip was placed on the bottom left of the stage on the woop/sound layer (refer to Figure 15-13). The instance was named "woops". The instance name is what will be targeted when the hitTest is evaluated. The sound movie clip was then constructed. A new movie clip was created and named sound_mc. Two layers were created in this movie clip: actions and Layer 1.

In the movie clips' Editing mode, a keyframe was created on Frame 1 (F6), Layer 1, and a sound from the Common Library was dragged to the Timeline of the movie clip. In this case the sound called "Book Drops" was used. The keyframe was then dragged to Frame 2 (see Figure 15-16). A keyframe was added to Frame 1 of the actions layer and a Stop action was assigned. A keyframe was then added to Frame 2 and a Play action was assigned. When the movie loads, the sound instance is prevented from playing because of the Stop action on Frame 1. However, when the star movie clip instance hits the shopping bag, the script on the star tells Frame 2 of the sound_mc Timeline to play, thus activating the sound. Because audio is not visible on the stage, the movie clip will appear blank too,

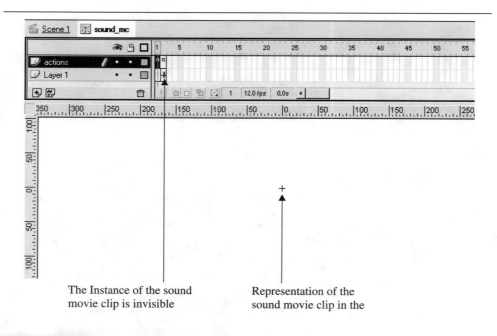

The Instance of the sound movie clip is invisible

Representation of the sound movie clip in the

FIGURE 15-16   The Timeline of the sound_mc movie clip

except for a little circle indicating its presence on the stage. An instance of the sound_mc was dropped on the stage to the top right of the shopping bag cord (refer to Figure 15-13) on the woops/sound layer in the main Timeline and the instance was named zoom.

With the new layer, woops/sound intact and the two new movie clip instances "woops" and "zoom" in place on the stage, the script was ready to be generated. The swirl instance was done first. Double-clicking the movie clip in the Library (or the instance on the stage), displayed the editing mode for this clip. The Actions panel was displayed with the last line of script (Line 5) reading: stopDrag (); With Line 5 selected, in the Actions list, the if action was selected. The Parameters pane then prompted for a Condition. With the Condition box selected, the Target Path button was clicked. With Absolute checked, swirl was selected. With the cursor at the end of this statement in the Condition box, in the Actions panel, Object | Movie Clip | hitTest was selected. Placing the cursor in between the parenthesis (), the Target Path button was selected again, and with Absolute checked, bag was selected. Line 6 now reads

```
if (_root.swirl.hitTest(_root.bag)) {
```

With Line 6 selected, in the Actions list, setProperty was selected and Line 7 was generated. The following information was entered in the Parameters pane:

- Property: **_width** (Width)
- Target: **This**
- Value: **100**

This is relative addressing, that is, addressing the object that's setting the property. Absolute addressing could be used instead. Expression box is also checked. This will make the movie clip 100 pixels wide when the target is hit. Expression box is also checked. Line 7 now reads

```
setProperty (this, _width, 100);
```

With Line 7 selected, in the Actions list, setProperty was chosen again and Line 8 was generated. This time the following parameters were entered and the Expression box was checked:

- Property: **_height** (Height)

■ Target: **This**

■ Value: **100**

This will make the movie clip 100 pixels high when the target is hit. The Expression box was checked.

With Line 8 selected, in the Actions list, the with action was selected and Line 9 was generated. In the Parameters pane, for Object, the Target Path button was selected and (Absolute) woops was chosen. Woops, if you recall is the new text movie clip instance. With Line 9 selected, in the Actions list, Go To was selected and Line 10 was generated. In the Parameters pane, the following information was input:

■ Scene: **<current frame>**

■ Type: **Frame Number**

■ Frame: **2**

Go To And Play remained checked. The finished script now read as follows: (see Figure 15-17):

```
on (press) {
    startDrag (_root.swirl);
}
on (release) {
    stopDrag ();
    if (_root.swirl.hitTest(_root.bag)) {
        setProperty (this, _width, 100);
        setProperty (this, _height, 100);
        with (_root.woops) {
            gotoAndPlay (2);
        }
    }
}
```

The script (after the drag and drop) states that if the swirl instance hits the bag instance, the property of the swirl will change to a width and height of 100 pixels. In addition, Frame 2 of the instance called woops will play. The script on the swirl movie clip is now complete and the editing mode was exited.

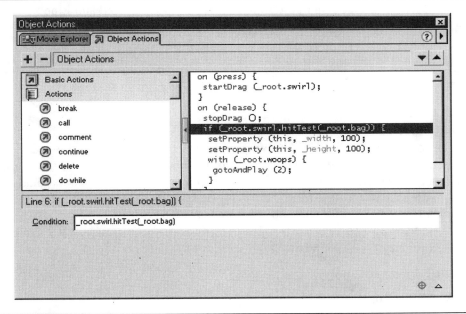

FIGURE 15-17   The script on the swirl movie clip

The next script to be generated is that on the star movie clip. This movie clip was double-clicked either in the Library or on the stage and the following script was generated under the last line of existing code

```
(stopDrag ()):
```

With Line 5 selected (stopDrag), the if action was selected from the Actions list. Just like on the last movie clip, a condition had to be entered in the Parameters pane. Using the Target Path button and the methods used on the last example, the following code was generated on Line 6, targeting the bag again:

```
if (this.hitTest(_root.bag)) {
```

With Line 6 selected, in the Actions list, the with action was selected and Line 7 was generated. For object in the Parameters pane, _root.zoom (the sound movie clip instance) was typed in. The sound can either be typed in or selected from the Target Path button.

15

With Line 7 selected, in the Actions list, Go To was selected and Line 8 was generated. The following information was input:

- Scene: **<current scene>**
- Type: **Frame Number**
- Frame: **2**

Go To And Play was checked. With Line 8 selected, the with Action was selected again and Line 9 was generated. For the object, this was typed in (or you can choose Absolute addressing, that is, star from the Target Path button dialog box). With Line 9 selected, from the Actions list, setProperty was selected. In the Parameters panel, the following information was typed in:

- Property: **_visible** (Visibility)
- Target: **_root.poly**
- Value: **false**

The target can be selected from the Target Path button or input manually. The Expression box was checked. The final script reads as follows (see Figure 15-18):

```
on (press) {
    startDrag (this);
}
on (release) {
    stopDrag ();
    if (this.hitTest(_root.bag)) {
        with (_root.zoom) {
            gotoAndPlay (2);
            with (this) {
                setProperty (_root.poly, _visible, false);
            }
        }
    }
}
```

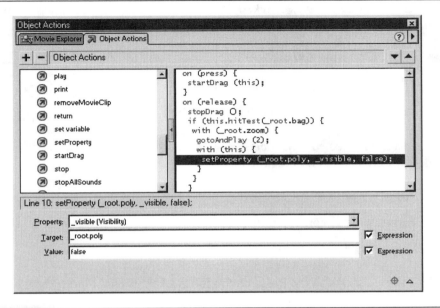

FIGURE 15-18   The script on the star movie clip

After the script is given dragging instructions, it's told that if the star movie clip instance hits the bag movie clip instance, Frame 2 of the zoom movie clip instance will play. In addition, the polygon movie clip instance will become visible. These are the conditions that will take place if the two movie clips collide.

The last script to be adjusted in this movie is the script on the Reset button. Because the properties of the swirl and star will change if a collision occurs, they have to be set back to their original properties on this button. With the Reset button selected on the main Timeline, Line 9 was selected and from the Actions list, setProperty was selected, and Line 10 was generated. The following parameters were entered:

- Property: **_width** (Width)
- Target: **swirl**
- Value: **53**

15

The Expressions box was checked. With Line 10 selected, setProperty was chosen again and the following parameters were entered on the new Line 11:

- Property: **_height** (Height)
- Target: **swirl** (Expression box checked)
- Value: **44** (Original height; Expression box checked)

With Line 11 selected, setProperty was selected again and the following parameters were entered on the new Line 12:

- Property: **_visible** (Visibility)
- Target: **poly** (Expression box checked)
- Value: **True** (Expression box checked)

The finished script on the Reset button looks like this (see Figure15-19)

```
on (press) {
    setProperty (poly, _x, 260);
    setProperty (poly, _y, 45);
    setProperty (swirl, _x, 310);
    setProperty (swirl, _y, 110);
    setProperty (star, _x, 330);
    setProperty (star, _y, 185);
    setProperty (circle, _x, 265);
    setProperty (circle, _y, 250);
    setProperty (swirl, _width, 53);
    setProperty (swirl, _height, 44);
    setProperty (poly, _visible, true);
}
```

When clicked, the Reset button returns all four movie clips (polygon, swirl, star, circle) to their original state and position.

Use the If and Else Statements to Evaluate a Condition   The if statement is used on the movie clips in the shopping bag movie we've been working on. In this movie, the If statement is used in conjunction with the hitTest function to alter the circle, and it also can be used in a plethora of other ways. To review, the way this movie

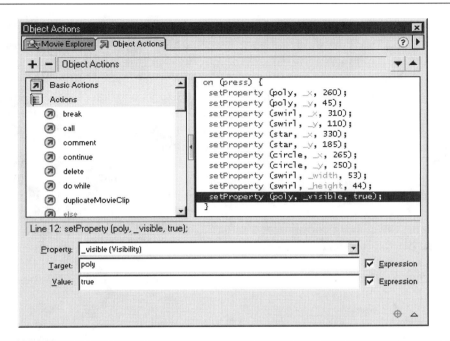

The completed script on the Reset button

works is if the hitTest condition returns as true, various parameters of the movie clips are changed, as per each individual script. If an else statement is added to one of the movie clips, when the if statement returns as false, the statement attached to the else statement will occur.

In the shopping bag movie, the script on the button nested in the circle_mc movie clip currently reads:

```
on (press) {
    startDrag (this);
}
on (release) {
    stopDrag ();
    if (this.hitTest(_root.bag )) {
        _root.silly.gotoAndPlay( 2 );
    }
}
```

15

If you recall, when the circle movie clip instance is dragged and collides with the shopping bag, a sound that's nested in the sound movie clip plays. If the clip doesn't collide with the shopping bag, it drops where the mouse has currently dragged it and nothing else occurs. So to introduce an Else statement, you need to create an alternate condition. Let's make the new condition that if the clip doesn't hit the target (the shopping bag), it will snap back to its original place. The else statement introduces yet another condition into the script, which in this case will be an alternate position. The if and else statements are often used in conjunction with one another to generate a combination of different outcomes.

In Figure 15-20, the script on the button nested in the circle_mc movie clip has been augmented to include an else statement. As discussed before, if the collision doesn't occur between the circle_mc instance and the shopping bag, the circle_mc instance will return to its original position, or X, Y coordinate. To indicate in the script what the starting coordinates are for the circle_mc, they had to be recorded first. As per the Info panel, the starting X position is 260 and the Y position is 250 (center reference point).

With the circle_mc movie clip Editing mode displayed and the circle button selected, the additional script was added.

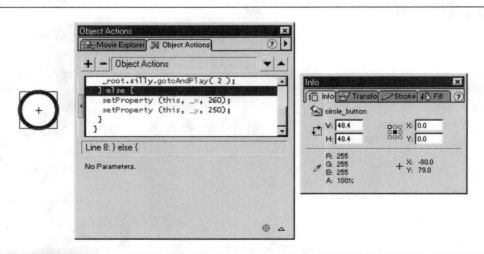

FIGURE 15-20   The script on the button in the circle_mc movie clip now includes an else statement

With Line 7 selected, in the Actions list, else was selected, which generated a new Line 8. With Line 8 selected, from the Actions list, setProperty was chosen and the following parameters were entered:

- Property: _x (X Position)
- Target: **this** (Expression box checked)
- Value: **260** (Expression box checked)

With Line 9 selected, from the Actions list, setProperty was chosen again and the following parameters were entered:

- Property: _y (Y Position)
- Target: **this** (Expression box checked)
- Value: **250** (Expression box checked)

The final script on this button/movie clip now reads

```
on (press) {
    startDrag (this);
}
on (release) {
    stopDrag ();
    if (this.hitTest(_root.bag )) {
        _root.silly.gotoAndPlay( 2 );
    } else {
        setProperty (this, _x, 260);
        setProperty (this, _y, 250);
    }
}
```

The else statement returns the circle_mc movie clip instance to its place of origin if the conditions outlined in the if statement aren't met. There are many different variations that can be used with if and else statements. You can create and combine many if/else alternates in the same script. This is particularly useful for complex navigational sites, gaming software, or whatever your imagination can conjure up.

15

This movie serves as a good example of the incredible diversity of ActionScript. With a little knowledge of how to mix and match actions with properties, the possibilities are endless for interactivity.

Use the getProperty Function in a Script

In the previous section, the setProperty action was examined in detail. SetProperty is used to change the properties of a movie clip during the course of a movie. They can occur on button, movie clip, or frame events. The target can be either the object that is currently selected or another object in the movie.

In contrast, the getProperty action is a predefined function. A *function* is a block of code that can be used globally throughout the movie. Functions are given arguments of an instance name and property. The getProperty function returns the value of the specific property of a movie clip instance. The script for a getProperty function is different from the script on the setProperty action. However the two can be used together in the same statement as is demonstrated in the following example.

In Figure 15-21, setProperty and getProperty are used on the same button script to rotate a movie clip instance named "slice". First, the property is set on the button. If you recall, in a setProperty action, three elements must be defined: the

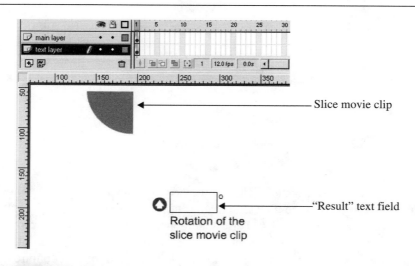

FIGURE 15-21   The main Timeline of a movie where the getProperty function and the setProperty action are to rotate a movie clip

Property, which in this case is rotation; the Target, which in this case is the "slice" movie clip instance; and the Value, which in this case is the getProperty function.

Because getProperty is a function, an additional argument needs to be defined. The argument is the name and property of the movie clip, "slice". The argument appears in between parenthesis. In ActionScript, when a function is defined or called, the argument can appear within parenthesis. The Value of the equation is the number –20, which represents the degree amount the movie clip instance rotates each time the button is pressed. As a final note on this script, a setVariable action is used to return the value that the getProperty has gathered in a text field whose variable name is "result". And again, the getProperty function defines the rotation of the movie clip instance "slice".

Now that you understand how the getProperty function works in this movie, let's examine how the movie was made:

Figure 15-21 is comprised of one movie clip, one button, one text field, and some miscellaneous static text that tells the user what to do. There are two layers on the main Timeline; one layer for the miscellaneous static text and another layer for all the other elements. They are named in the following order: main layer, text layer.

You will notice the more script-intensive your movies become, the less action you'll see on the main Timeline, because most of the animation and scripting takes place on movie clips, frames, and buttons. Or often the actions, variables, or functions will be defined on a frame in the main Timeline.

Once the layers were defined, the symbols were created. A button was chosen from the Button Common Library and a movie clip was made. The name that was given to the movie clip was "sliceMc". Within the movie clip is one quarter of a full circle that resembles a Pac-Man like image.

The movie clip has no animation on it. It's just a one frame, one-layer movie. An instance of this movie clip was dragged onto the main layer and an instance name of "slice" was given to it.

On the main layer, a Text Input field was created and placed in the bottom right of the stage. Using the Text Options panel, the Text Input field was given a variable name of "result". An instance of a button was dragged on the main layer to the left of the Text Input field.

On the text layer, static text was typed under the text field explaining what the text field is. The text field will display the rotation property of the slice movie clip instance. The static text displays the following information: "Rotation of the slice movie clip". You can rotate from 0–360 degrees clockwise or counterclockwise (minus or plus); but because this movie clip enables you to control the rotation in little increments, a small increment is used in the script.

15

Now that all the pieces are in place, the script is ready to be generated on the button. With the button selected and the Actions panel displayed, setProperty was selected from the Actions list. The following parameters were typed in:

- Property: **_rotation** (Rotation)—This can be selected from the pop-up menu.

- Target: **slice**—This is the instance name given to the movie clip. You can either type the name of the instance in manually or click the Target Path button to display the Target Path dialog box and select it there. Check the Expression box.

- Value: **getProperty(slice,_rotation)-20**—This can either be typed in manually or you can use the Toolbox list to assist you in generating this statement. To use the Toolbox List, with the cursor in the Value box, select Functions | getProperty. When you do this, the following displays in the Value box:

  - getProperty (target, property)

  - For Target, type in slice, or access the instance name from the Target Path dialog box.

  - For Property, type in _rotation, or select it from the Properties list. Check the Expression box.

Line 2 now reads

```
setProperty (slice, _rotation, getProperty(slice, _rotation)-20);
```

The number, "-20" can be any number. This is the incremental degrees the movie clip will rotate.

With Line 2 selected, from the Actions list, setVariable was chosen, which generated Line 3. The following parameters were input:

- Variable: **result**—This is the text field variable.

- Value: **getProperty(slice, _rotation)**—The getProperty function can be selected from the Functions list or input manually and the (target, property) can be highlighted and replaced with the proper information. Check the Expression box.

The final script on the button reads as follows (see Figure 15-22):

```
on (release) {
    setProperty (slice, _rotation, getProperty(slice,
    _rotation)-20);
    result = getProperty(slice, _rotation);
}
```

When the movie is tested, the slice movie clip instance rotates -20 degrees each time the button is clicked. This same formula can be used on other buttons to set and return properties on an object. You could also create a button that alternately tracks the clockwise movement of the slice by duplicating the script above on another button and substituting +20 for -20 for the number of increments the slice rotates.

Use setProperty and getProperty to Return the Value of the X, Y Position of a Movie Clip

Now that the formula makes a little more sense, let's apply a similar recipe and create a button that will track the X, Y position of the slice movie clip on a button event, and return its numerical position in a text field.

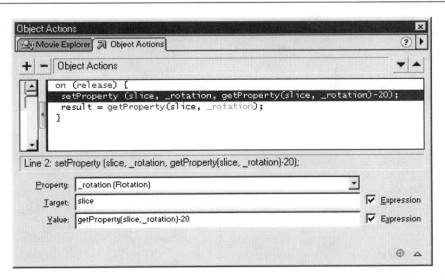

FIGURE 15-22 The script used on the button that controls the rotation of the movie clip

To make life easy, the button, Text Input field, and the description text were duplicated twice (from the existing pieces) and dragged to the left of the stage by SHIFT-selecting the items and SHIFT+CTRL/SHIFT+OPT-dragging the objects to duplicate them in position (see Figure 15-23). The description text under both text fields was changed to indicate the new buttons function. The static text field on the top left now reads "X position of the movie clip", and the bottom static text box now reads "Y position of the movie clip".

The script on the duplicate buttons is still intact from the old button, so all that's left to do is to go in and modify the script on each button to reflect its new purpose. Also the names of the text field variables have to be changed so when they're targeted, they will know what data to display.

First, the text variables were changed. With the top text field on the left selected (X position), a new variable name was given of "Xslice" in the Text Options panel. The second text field (Y position) was given a variable name of "Yslice".

Next, the script on the top left button was changed (X position). To review, each time the button is clicked, the numerical value of the X position will appear in the text field named "Xslice". With the button selected and the Actions panel displayed, the following script was revised, changing only the parameters and the text field variable (on Line 3) from the other script (see Figure 15-24).

```
on (release) {
    setProperty (slice, _x, getProperty(slice, _x)-20);
    Xslice = getProperty(slice, _x);
}
```

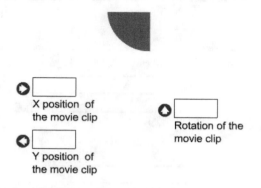

X position of
the movie clip

Y position of
the movie clip

Rotation of the
movie clip

FIGURE 15-23   The button, static text, and text field on the bottom right that are used to rotate the slice were duplicated two times on the left of the stage to perform other functions

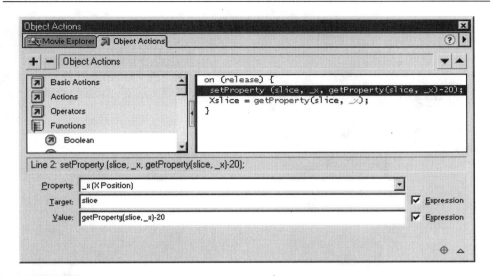

FIGURE 15-24 The script on the button that controls the X position of the slice movie clip and displays the X position in the Xslice text field

The script for the bottom button (Yslice) was then revised, again only changing the parameters and the text field variable (on Line 3), as in Figure 15-25:

```
on (release) {
    setProperty (slice, _y, getProperty(slice, _y)-20);
    Yslice = getProperty(slice, _y);
}
```

If you test these buttons, you'll notice they only go in one direction. Once the slice travels off the stage as a result of the user clicking it and its X, Y position only travel in one direction, the slice is gone. Therefore, if you actually used this function in a game, you would probably want to include additional buttons that move the position of the slice forward and backward. Do this by duplicating the button with the script on it and changing the value on Line 2 from a minus (–20) to a plus (+20).

Make a Customized Function

So far, the functions that have been used in this chapter have been predefined. In ActionScript, you also can create and define your own functions. Similar to a

15

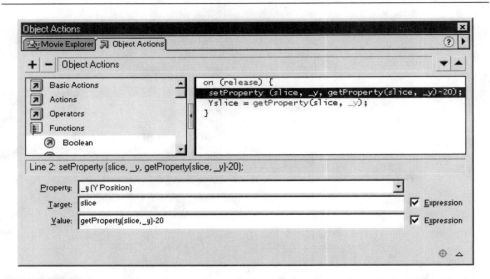

FIGURE 15-25   The script on the button that controls the Y position of the slice movie clip and displays the Y position in the Yslice text field

variable, once a function is set within a movie, it can be recognized by any Timeline within that movie.

You can create as many functions as you can dream up in ActionScript, all defined by you-the user. Figure 15-26 is a simple example of a customized function. The movie consists of a button, instructions on what the button is, and a Text Input field with a variable name of myPrice that will display the results of clicking the button.

The movie itself is unremarkable but the concept behind it—a custom function— is quite powerful. All that occurs in the movie is the user clicks the button and a

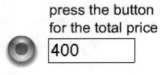

FIGURE 15-26   A button and text field variable that use a customized function

text field gets a number based on a defined function called "getPrice". In fact, it looks similar to the buttons and text fields with variables that have been created throughout this chapter.

The significant aspect of this movie is that the script has been created completely with a user-defined function. Nothing in this script (other than the "function" action and the button event) can be found in the Toolbox list.

Lets examine the script on this simple movie to see how the function was created: This movie has two layers. The first layer is the actions layer where the function is defined. The second layer, movie, is where the button, text field, and the static instructional text reside.

After a button was added to the stage, a description of what to do ("press the button for the total price") was generated in a static text field, and a Text Input field was created and given the variable name of "myPrice".

A keyframe was then added to the first frame in the Timeline. With the Actions panel displayed, the Expert mode was chosen from the pop-up menu and the following script was typed (see Figure 15-27).

```
function getPrice(total){
myPrice=total;
}
```

NOTE   *In the Actions panel, the word "function" is highlighted in blue in the script because function is predefined in ActionScript.*

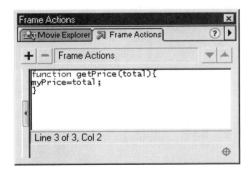

FIGURE 15-27   The script on Frame 1 defines a function

The function is called "getPrice". The argument is "total". The variable named myPrice (the text field) is declared equal to the argument (getPrice). With this now established, a script is needed on the button in order to see the results.

With the button selected, the following script was typed in Expert mode (see Figure 15-28).

```
on (release) {
getPrice (400)
}
```

When the button is released, the user-defined function, getPrice, performs its function, which in this case is to display the number 400.

User-defined functions can be powerful and elaborate. If you examine the movie in Flash Help | Samples | Mosquito Killer, you'll notice that several used-defined functions were set on a layer named "functions". This movie serves as a good example of the how powerful and diverse functions can be.

Use Smart Clips

Smart Clips are a new feature in Flash 5. These are movie clip symbols that have predefined parameters. You can drag a Smart Clip from the Common Libraries window and fill in the blanks for a quick and dirty script. You can create your own Smart Clips or use third-party extensions of which there is an abundance of on the Web. See Appendix B for more information about third-party extensions (that include Smart Clips) for use in Flash and how to load them.

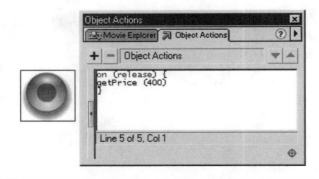

FIGURE 15-28   The script on this button calls the function on Frame 1

Creating your own Smart Clips requires a fairly advanced understanding of ActionScript because their purpose is to eliminate having to rewrite complex repetitive scripts. Because they are rather complex to create, the purpose of this section is to explain what a Smart Clip is and how to access ready-made clips for those who find them useful.

The future popularity of Smart Clip technology is based on the premise that programmers will provide the complex scripting and artists can sculpt the script into a creative movie. On their Web site (Appendix B), Macromedia offers hundreds of Smart Clips under the Extensions category. Extensions are developed by programmers and they have been tested and rated by Macromedia. Extensions include Smart Clips as well as small tutorials, clip art, source files, and ActionScript code samples. Flash 5 ships with a few examples of Smart Clips that aren't incredibly exciting, but they are sufficient enough to get the feel for what the technology is all about.

Smart Clips are located in the Window | Common Libraries, as shown in Figure 15-29. As you load more Smart Clips into Flash, using the Macromedia Extensions Manager, they will appear in the Common Libraries menu by name.

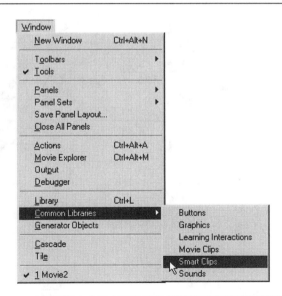

15

FIGURE 15-29   Smart Clips are found in Window | Common Libraries in Flash

Because Smart Clips are made from movie clips, you access them like movie clip instances. To use a Smart Clip, drag it to the stage from the Smart Clip Library and then define the parameters in the Clip Parameters panel. Let's take a look at a couple of Smart Clips in the Smart Clip Library to see how they work.

The RadioButton Smart Clip as shown in Figure 15-30, is a simple button with a label and a check box. If you dissect the clip in the editing mode, you'll discover it's made from a movie clip nested in a movie clip. There's a text field variable in the movie clip named "label" and nested movie clip called "RadioButton assets".

Assuming you don't know much about ActionScript and you want to make use of this button in a movie, you could drag it to the stage from the Common Libraries and display Window | Panels | Clip Parameters. In this window, the various elements of Smart Clips can be customized. Figure 15-31 shows another Smart Clip, the Menu Smart Clip, and the Clip Parameters panel. Depending on the parameters and values required to define each Smart Clip, the fill-in-the-blanks information appearing in the Clip Parameters panel changes.

To customize this Smart Clip, the values that appear in the pop-up menu need to be defined. These are the values the user will select when she presses the menu. When the user scrolls down and selects a value, the new value appears at the top of the list (see Figure 15-32).

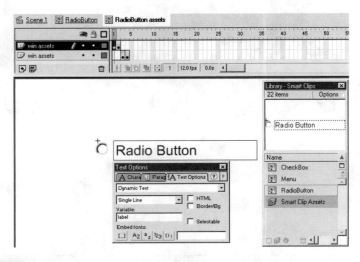

FIGURE 15-30   If the RadioButton Smart Clip is examined, you can see it's a movie clip nested in a movie clip with a text field

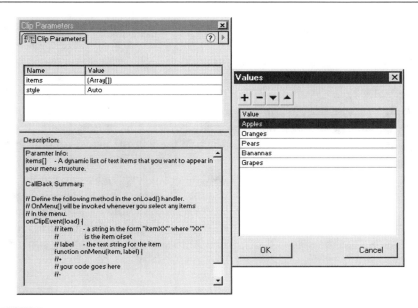

FIGURE 15-31   When a Smart Clip is selected, the values and parameters of the clip can be adjusted in the Clip Parameters panel

NOTE   *The interface for Smart Clips varies in the Clip Parameters panel depending on its function and the developer, so they will not all look like the Menu Smart Clip in Figure 15-32. Because Smart Clips are written for non-programmers, it's usually pretty easy to figure out how to use them.*

If you click an instance of the Menu Smart Clip and display the Parameters panel, a description of how the clip works and what your options are appears in the Description section of the panel on the bottom. A two-column table appears at the

FIGURE 15-32   When the Menu Smart Clip is tested, the values you selected are represented in the pop-up portion of the menu

top with the headings of Name and Value. In the Value column, if you double-click on the word (Array[]), a Values panel appears (refer to Figure 15-31). The Values panel is where you type in your data. To do this you simply double-click the first entry and type. Continue down the column, double-click, and type on each entry until you're done.

In the Values panel you can reshuffle the order of your values, add values, or delete them by using the plus, minus, arrow down, and arrow up buttons on the top left of the panel. The plus button adds a value; the minus button deletes a value; the arrow down button moves a value down in the list; the arrow up button moves a value up the list.

In the main Clip Parameters panel, you also can select a style from the pop-up menu under Auto: Default, Windows/Macintosh. This refers to the style in which the menu will display. If you select Windows, the menu items will highlight when you select them. If you select Macintosh, when you select a menu item, a check box appears next to the selected item. The Auto setting is the default setting so an individual's computer decides how it displays.

> **NOTE** *The icons for Smart Clips in the Library are slightly different from the movie clip icon, making it easy to distinguish between the two.*

Smart Clips might be useful, especially for repetitive tasks you might not feel like making yourself. You can find tons of Smart Clips for preloaders, counters, scrolling effects, and navigation bars, and the list goes on. However, once you become comfortable with ActionScript, you might find you prefer making your own scripts and customizing them for your particular needs.

After you select a Smart Clip, you need to read the instructions on how to use it in the Description portion of the Clip Parameters panel (refer to Figure 15-31). The Menu Smart Clip that ships with Flash 5 is a rather ironic example of a clip because the instructions won't make much sense unless you have some knowledge of ActionScript. The instructions as such are a bit cryptic for a beginner. Fortunately, the instructions for many extensions/Smart Clips are very easy and you can choose to ignore the complex ones if they're intimidating.

Getting back to the Menu Smart Clip description, the "//" is used for comments in the Description box and a set is placed before the comments are made. The text after the // won't appear in the script. Most scripting languages enable you to post comments throughout a script, and ActionScript is no exception.

In the Menu description, the CallBack Summary explains step by step how to make this clip work. The menu is a method and it works with an onLoad event. To

use this menu, select the clip on the stage and display the Actions panel. As per
the directions in the Clip Parameters panel you need to create a custom function
(using functions from the Actions list or type the word "function") and in the
Parameters pane, the function is to be named "onMenu". The Parameters are "item,
label". That's it. The clip is now ready to be used in a movie. So on the Smart
Clip, the script you create will read

```
onClipEvent (load){
function onMenu (item, label){}
```

You would need to dress up the movie around this menu item. Obviously the
menu selection would need to be a selection based on a response to a question. The
menu provides the response selection, but you must also provide the question from
which the viewer is making their selection.

Figure 15-33 displays a third-party Smart Clip called FPS Tester. This clip tests
the frame rate of your movie and displays the results. You can find this clip on the
Macromedia Extensions page. Notice that the Clip Parameters panel on this clip is
very simple as compared to the Menu Smart Clip. To change the parameters of this
clip, click arrows or buttons. Additional directions are provided on the Macromedia
site for each extension.

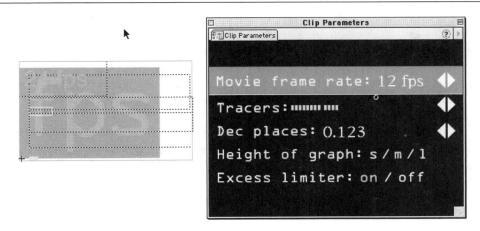

15

FIGURE 15-33   A Smart Clip called FPS Tester

Whether you choose to use Smart Clips or not is a matter of subjective preference. However, for the curious, it's fun to check out the different varieties that are offered on the Web. More and more are uploaded all the time.

Create a Simple Preloader with the ifFrames Loaded Action

Often, when a Flash movie loads in your browser, while you're waiting, a message appears indicating that the movie is loading. Sometimes it asks you to "please wait". Other times, the preloader might be quite elaborate, with elements that entertain you while you wait. Using a preloader is always a good idea for movies that load slowly. If your movie contains sound loops, bitmaps, QuickTime video, or anything that creates a sizable file, preloaders are a must.

Aside from being graphically appealing and easy to navigate, another key factor in making a successful movie is the loading time factor. A movie that loads fast will keep your audience more interested. Often, movies get out of hand and end up bigger than they should be and as a result take a long time to load. Sometimes big movies can even crash a users system. So it's a good idea to be prepared for an impatient audience and plan to create preloaders for movies that tip the scales in file size. This way the audience has entertainment while they wait.

Too understand preloaders, it's important to understand how Flash movies are viewed by your audience on the Web. Flash movies stream. This means that as soon as the information for each individual frame is loaded, it plays. Ideally, the playback and download ratio would be equal, or, at least the playback would be slower than the download. Because your Web audience possesses a wide range of bandwidths, this perfect ratio is rarely achieved. When the playback is faster than the download, choppiness can occur, audio can begin to sound like nonsense, and the results can be disastrous. What's worse is you have no control over how your audience is experiencing the movie. Preloaders can often save your movie from looking foolish.

With a simple preloader, you're setting a frame action on a movie that checks to make sure a particular frame that you designate is loaded before the remainder of the movie is played. In Chapter 16, you'll learn how to test your movie before it premieres in cyberspace. Testing your movie helps eliminate potential erratic playback. Because preloaders are checking for frames loaded, the preloader must be tested in a special way. This will be discussed after we examine the creation of a basic preloader.

Creating a basic preloader is actually quite simple. Figure 15-34 is a movie with just a bitmap photo that animates. Because it's a bitmap, the movie takes a

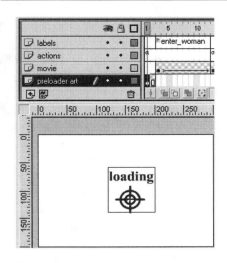 

Frame 1   Frame 3

FIGURE 15-34   The preloader on this movie is an animated movie clip that pulsates a registration mark and the word "loading"

considerable amount of time to load. When you experiment with this exercise, you can add audio or bitmaps to pump up the size/loading time of your movie for experimenting purposes.

When you finish a movie that needs a preloader, the first task is to actually create a preloader. Preloaders are usually made from movie clips, but you can use any graphics. You're only limited by your creativity.

Some Flash sites have tremendously elaborate preloaders and it's a good idea to familiarize yourself with what other authors are doing. So look around on other Flash sites to get your creative juices flowing for preloader ideas. Some sites are painfully simple yet tasteful. The point is, a preloader can be anything you want, but it must always act as a device to tell the audience that the site is in the process of loading. Otherwise they might think the link is bad or their Internet connection has crashed. They could come to any number of conclusions that result in them leaving your site. So the preloaders main purpose is to keep the audience at your site.

Now that you understand the basic concept of why you would use a preloader, let's talk about how to make one. Figure 15-34 has a preloader in the first two frames of the movie and it resides on the last layer of the movie called "preloader art". The preloader art is a movie clip called preloader_mc. The actual animated bitmap movie is only on one layer (called "movie"), which is the second to last layer. If

15

you examine the Timeline, you'll notice that the movie plays from Frame 3 to Frame 13. The other two layers, labels and actions, hold a frame label and some actions accordingly.

With the preloader in place on the Frames 1 and 2 (preloader art) and the movie beginning on Frame 3 of the movie layer, the Frame Label was generated on the labels layer. To do this, the Frames panel was displayed and a keyframe was put on Frame 1 in the labels layer. In the Frame panel, the label of "enter_woman" was given. Then, the keyframe was dragged to Frame 3. Labels if you recall, serve two purposes in a Timeline. First, they help you identify events that are taking place in your movie, such as when certain elements are being introduced on a particular frame. In other words, it provides a visual roadmap of instructions on a Timeline of events that have yet to occur. Labels are also used to call frames in a script with a label instead of a number. As your movies become more complex, labels (as opposed to numbers) often make it easier to track multiple events on a Timeline.

The "enter_woman" label announces the introduction of a bitmap image of a woman on the movie layer that again spans from Frames 3-13. This label will be referenced in the script.

On the Actions layer, a keyframe was placed on Frame 1 and the Actions panel was displayed. In the Actions list, the if action was selected. With Line 1 of the script selected, in the Parameters panel, the Condition box was selected and in the Properties list, the _framesloaded property was selected. The script now reads

```
if (_framesloaded) {
}
```

With the cursor at the end of _framesloaded in the Condition box, in the Operators list, ">=" was chosen. This operator will evaluate whether one property is greater than or equal to another. The script now reads

```
if (_framesloaded>=) {
}
```

The cursor was again placed at the end of the Condition box and from the Properties list, _totalframes was selected. Line 1 now reads

```
if (_framesloaded>=_totalframes) {
}
```

With Line 1 selected, in the Actions list, Go To was selected. In the Parameters pane, the following settings were chosen:

- Scene: **\<current scene\>**

- Type: **Frame Label**

- Frame: **enter_woman**

- Go To And Play remains checked

As a final touch, on the actions layer, another keyframe was added to Frame 2 and a stop action was applied. The stop action keyframe was then dragged to Frame 13, the last frame. This way, the movie doesn't loop: it stops on Frame 13. The final script on Frame 1 reads as follows (see Figure 15-35):

```
if (_framesloaded>=_totalframes) {
    gotoAndPlay ("enter_woman ");
}
```

Now when the movie loads, the "enter_woman" label (which starts on Frame 3) will begin to play once all frames are loaded. So the preloader, which is on Frames 1 and 2, will play until the balance of frames load.

There are two properties used in this movie, _framesloaded and _totalframes. _framesloaded reads the number of frames that are being loaded as it streams. It keeps watch over the frames in the background. The _totalframes property reads the total number of frames in a movie. In the argument "if (_framesloaded>=_totalframes)", if the number of frames that have loaded are equal to or greater than the total number of frames, the bulk of the movie which is on Frame 3 starts playing. There are other variations on this same script. For example, for Line 1, the script could also read

```
if (_framesloaded==13)
```

This equation is similar to the original first line, that is, if the frames loaded = 13, go to Frame 3 and play the movie. The ifFrameLoaded action located in the Actions list also can be used for this purpose. The equivalent script using this action would read

```
ifFrameLoaded (13) {
    gotoAndPlay ("enter_woman");
}
```

15

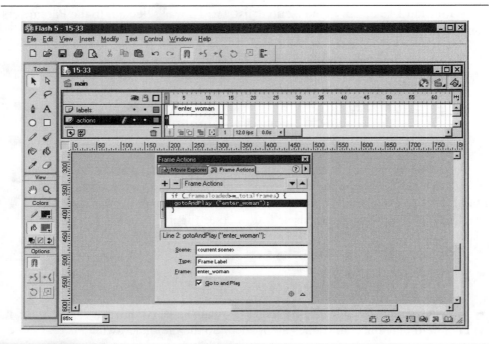

The final script on the first frame of the preloader movie

Notice on this script, ifFrameLoaded is the action instead of "if". IfFrameLoaded has been deprecated in Flash 5. Although you can still use it, Macromedia recommends using the _framesloaded property instead.

TIP

Preloaders also can be set up on different scenes in Flash instead of on the main Timeline. If the Timeline is very intricate and it's getting confusing, you might want to consider another scene for the preloader. However, if you put it in another scene, make certain the scene with the preloader is the first scene to load. Do this by stacking the preloader scene on top of the main movie in the Scene panel. Access the Scene panel by selecting Window | Panels | Scene from the menu.

When you test a movie with a preloader in it like the movie in Figure 15-34, you won't see the preloader in action. Testing a movie in Flash doesn't display streaming. In order to see the preloader the way it will appear to your audience, you have to be able to experience the streaming. So after you select Control | Test Movie in the Player Window, select View | Show Streaming (CTRL+ENTER/CMD+ENTER). When streaming is activated, you can see how the entire movie plays out.

When you finish building your movie, preloaders become an important consideration in the final packaging and delivery of your movie. When the movie is complete, extensive testing is required to make certain the movie will live up to everyone's expectations. In Chapter 16, we move on to the final process in Flash movie making: testing and publishing the finished movie.

15

Chapter 16

Test and Publish Your Flash Movies

How to...

- Optimize Your Movie
- Test Your Movies in Flash
- Use the Flash Player
- Interpret the Bandwidth Profiler
- Test with Different Baud Rates
- Debug a Movie
- Test in Different File Formats
- Export Your Movie
- Publish Your Movie
- Use Projector Files
- Evaluate Your Movie

Once your Flash movie is finished, you need to get it ready for your audience. This is when the real test begins. Flash 5 authors always have a common goal: to marry efficient playback with good design in their Flash movie. To do this the author must step back, critically view, assess, test, and debug his work before presenting it to the audience.

Think of this as the dress rehearsal before opening night of a theatrical performance. Just as actors need to be sure that their dialogue is delivered timely and accurately and that everything is choreographed with synchronicity before the actual performance, so should your Flash movie be tested.

To perform this test dress rehearsal, to be sure every action, event, sound, and movement is correct, your Flash movie must be examined thoroughly. This is done by first double-checking to make certain all the players (objects, bitmaps, sound, movie clips) will download quickly and that they are as small as possible. Second, the movie must be prepared for export. This includes decisions about how it's going to be seen by the audience. Will it be a Web site or a stand-alone projector file that's distributed on a CD or disk? Or perhaps it will be a stand-alone player that's distributed via e-mail. First the movie must be tested, and then the movie is published so it can be ported to its final destination. In this chapter, all facets of the final phases of movie delivery are examined. The aspect of movie making, the actual delivery of the movie, is perhaps the most exciting and crucial part of Flash production.

Optimize the Movie Elements

When a Flash movie is published or exported (which we discuss later in the chapter), movies and their various components are optimized to make certain the movie will compress to as small a size as possible. However, the onus still falls on you, the author, to make sure all elements in a movie are as compact as possible before getting to this point. Adding sound and bitmaps to a movie can automatically tip the scale size. There are a myriad of other issues you might not even be aware of that can contribute to a larger file size. The following is a checklist of issues you want to make yourself aware of to help keep the file sizes down:

- Grouping objects together helps keep file sizes down because they are then addressed as one object as opposed to several elements.

- Animation can take up a lot of frames, which means bigger file sizes. Tweening can help keep files smaller as opposed to frame-by-frame animations that use many keyframes. Also with animations, movie clips are more compact than graphic symbols.

- As mentioned throughout this book, using symbols for repetitious graphics is a very efficient method for keeping file sizes down. Symbol data is stored in the first frame on which it appears. Any other instances of that symbol are linked to the first. Thus, the bulk of the data on the symbol only loads once, resulting in a smaller movie. Also colorizing symbols with the Effect panel adds color without compromising file size.

- Bitmaps should not be animated or if necessary, animated for as short a time as possible. Animated bitmaps increase file sizes. They are better left static in the movie.

- Condense the size of actions on keyframes using as small an amount of space as possible.

- Whenever possible, make the movie dimensions as small as possible. Any unnecessary space should be eliminated.

- Optimize your shapes using the Modify | Optimize | Curves command to smooth out shape. This eliminates unnecessary data used to describe shapes.

16

■ Use device fonts as opposed to embedded fonts. Device fonts don't embed the font information in the SWF file, thus resulting in a smaller movie size.

■ If you embed fonts, try to use as few font families as possible.

■ Try not to use a lot of gradients as they increase file size.

These tips, along with using simple logic will help keep the size of your Flash file smaller.

Test Your Movie Locally

Testing is most crucial to the successful development and delivery of Flash movies because of the broad scope of variables that come into play from the development stage to the end user/audience stage. Often, the end user holds the reigns of control over your movie's playability. Thought must be given to their Internet connection, the browsers being used, the browser versions, and the viewer's computer configuration including processing speed and video display. All these things have a significant impact on the way your movies will play back. You need to be sure that your movie is viewable by the majority of your audience.

To ensure correctness, you need to check and re-check your movie as you work toward its completion. Even after it is up and running, you should still check the movie constantly as problems can always pop up. This will help ensure that problems will be minimal. This section discusses checking the movie locally (testing and previewing it on your computer). If it all looks good on your computer, then it's time to take it to other platforms, browsers, and configurations to rule out one little glitch that could ruin the experience of your movie on thousands of systems.

Throughout this book, you've been testing on the spot using the Control | Play and Control | Test Movie menu options. This is a form of quick local testing. Testing the movie often throughout its development as well as sticking with some good optimizing common sense, puts you in a better position when the movie is ready to be published.

Use the Flash Player

When you test your movie using Test Movie from the main menu, a Flash Player (SWF file) movie is automatically created in the folder where the movie resides. The Flash Player is a plug-in that installs along with your Flash software. You will recognize a Flash Player format file on your computer's desktop by the Flash Player icon (see Figure 16-1), by the Type listing of Flash Player File, or by the .swf extension. When viewing in Test Movie mode, you are seeing the Flash Player file not the FLA version file you use to make your movie.

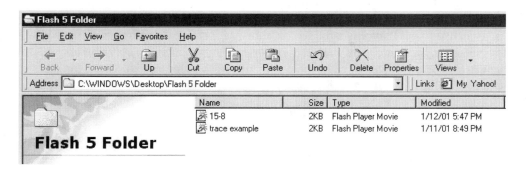

FIGURE 16-1 The Flash Player icon is displayed on your computer when you view files by icon on either the PC or Mac platform

When the Flash Player plug-in is installed, you can view any Flash movie on your system. Likewise, if your audience has the plug-in installed, they too can see your movie on their systems. If you are previewing a file in the Flash Player on a system with Flash 5 installed, you can open and play other SWF files while in the Player window by selecting File | Open from the Player's main menu. By previewing an SWF version of the movie, you will get a good idea of what your audience might be seeing.

It should be noted that the plug-in the viewer uses to see your movie in a browser (or even a self-playing version of your movie) will not have the same extended menu options available as you do if you're previewing the movie from Control | Test Movie. Some additional menu options become available to you in your Flash Player, such as Bandwidth Profiler, Streaming, and Debugging, which are discussed in the next section.

Flash Player Usage   According to the Macromedia site, to date, approximately 92% of Internet users have the Flash Player plug-in loaded on their systems. Because so many Web surfers have the Flash Player installed on their computers, the chance that a large percentage of your audience will be able to view your movie increases greatly. However, these statistics include many users who may have not yet upgraded their Flash Players to version 5. You can save your Flash movies down to earlier versions in the Publish dialog box if you feel this might be an issue.

There are several operating systems and browsers that will install Flash Player for you. These include Macintosh OS 8.1+; Windows 95, 98, and Me; Linux; Netscape Navigator; Netscape Communicator; Internet Explorer 4.5+ for Mac and 5.5+ for Windows; AOL; Prodigy; RealPlayer; QuickTime; @Home; Intel Web Outfitters CD/Web; Web/TV/Liberate; and NeoPlanet.

16

The number of programs that support Flash Player continues to grow because Macromedia's Shockwave format is a recognized and open standard.

Because Flash Player is a plug-in, it ships with all new computers as plug-ins for Netscape Navigator and Internet Explorer. You will need to stay abreast of these trends and changes to chart the percentage of Web surfers who have the ability to see your Flash movie on the Web.

Interpret the Bandwidth Profiler

When you test a movie locally, it plays pretty quickly, regardless of how big it is. When it loads on the Web, that's another story. If the file contains a lot of elements that make it sizable, it could take a while to load. What's worse is when your movie contains heavy animation and isolated frames that contain more and bigger elements than other frames. Because Flash streams, an unbalanced frame load can cause erratic playback on the viewer's end. So utilities such as the Show Streaming feature and the Bandwidth Profiler are important in helping you to measure the efficiency of the playback of the movie in the real world as opposed to playback on your desktop.

To prepare the entire movie for the best-case scenario in playback, you need to find out where problems might be hiding in your movie's frames. The Bandwidth will visually show you which frames are causing the problems such as long download so that you can rework the components of your movie for smoother animations, synchronized sounds, and quick downloads.

Display the Bandwidth Profiler by selecting View | Bandwidth Profiler or CTRL+B/CMD+B while in Player mode (see Figure 16-2). Accessing this tool will help you check frames for download speed and smoothness of streaming with a visual representation.

FIGURE 16-2   Display the Bandwidth Profiler while in Player mode from the View menu

The Bandwidth Profiler displays a graph above the Movie in Player mode with two columns (see Figure 16-3). The column to the left generates important data regarding the file. The following Movie settings are available in this column: dimensions of the movie, frame rate, size of the Player file, duration of the movie in frames and seconds, and preload in frames and seconds.

> NOTE   *You also can use the Bandwidth Profiler to test the efficiency of individual scenes. To do so, while in a particular scene, select Control | Test Scene or CTRL+ALT+ENTER/CMD+OPT+ENTER.*

In the Bandwidth Profiler, the column to the right represents each frame in the movie. Frames are depicted as alternating bars of dark and light gray. The frames can be displayed as two different types of graphs, depending upon your purpose for viewing the information. These two kinds of graphs are the Frame-by-Frame graph and the Streaming graph.

View a Frame-by-Frame Graph   In the Bandwidth Profiler, the column to the right is the actual graph where you can gather information about individual frames. In Figure 16-3, the bars are depicted as a frame-by-frame graph. View the graph in this mode by selecting View | Frame By Frame Graph or CTRL+F/CMD+F from the main menu. When you view the Bandwidth Profiler frame by frame, the graph displays the size of each frame in varying bar heights. Viewing in the Frame By Frame mode makes it particularly easy to spot large frames that might give you trouble.

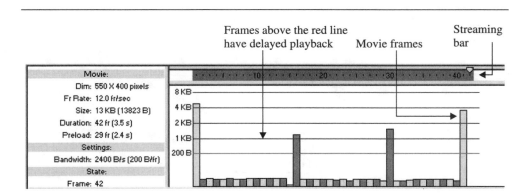

FIGURE 16-3   The Bandwidth Profiler displayed as a frame-by frame graph on a movie gives a visual representation of the movie's playback on different bandwidths

16

Each bar is representative of the size of each frame in bytes and KBs. The corresponding vertical scale gives you a rough indication of what that size is as the height of each frame corresponds directly to this. The red horizontal line at 200 bytes serves as a warning that any bars extending above this red line will take longer to load, therefore, potentially causing erratic behavior at this point in the download. Any frames displayed below the red line will load in real time. The loading preview in Flash is directly attributable to the modem settings you choose in the menu. This is discussed in the next section.

View Bandwidth Profiler as a Streaming Graph   The graph also can be viewed as a streaming graph by selecting View | Streaming Graph or CTRL+G/CMD+G from the menu. A streaming graph depicts how a movie will stream into a browser. In a streaming graph, if frames contain very little information, several bars appear stacked on top of one another in a single time unit. Frames with a lot of data cover several time units (see Figure 16-4). Frames alternate in light and dark gray shading, and are sized according to the time each one takes to download.

NOTE   *A general rule of thumb to keep in mind is, ideally, the amount of time it takes to play the frames in your movie should match the amount of time it takes to download those frames. When the download of frames is longer, it causes pauses and overlaps of frames, and gaps in the playback.*

Show Streaming   Should you decide at any time that you would like to view a download progress bar from Flash Player's Control menu, select View | Show

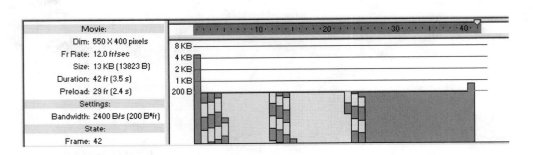

FIGURE 16-4   The Bandwidth Profiler displayed as a streaming graph depicts frames containing a small amount of data stacked on top of one another

Streaming or CTRL+ENTER/CMD+ENTER. While the movie streams, the Timeline at the top of the Profiler displays frames in the process of streaming within a green streaming bar. This indicates where you are in relation to download time as the movie streams, while the actual animation is playing in the test window. It also gives you a real-time simulation of streaming in different settings (from the Debug menu).

Having the ability to see the streaming of a movie is like having an extra pair of eyes to witness the download of the movie on another computer. The streaming feature becomes particularly relevant when viewing a movie with a lot of peaks and valleys represented in the streaming graph. It can be quite surprising to witness frame-loading delays that you might have otherwise not known about if you didn't witnessed it yourself. This convenient feature helps you determine if your movie requires a preloader or some other kind of adjustment, such as repositioning frames with large content to other frames.

Test with Different Baud Rates   The Bandwidth Profiler needs to work in conjunction with one other feature to provide you with a full set of testing tools. In the Debug menu (in the Flash Player window), you can emulate several modem speeds. Depending on what modem speed you've selected in the Debug menu, your Bandwidth Profiler will respond accordingly.

Your audience will consist of viewers with many different bandwidths. There are three modem simulations. When you check any of these settings, the data in the left column of the Bandwidth Profiler changes to reflect the selected setting. The menu lists six speeds to choose from, and they are all customizable. Flash's default will list three common modem speeds, which are 14.4 Kbps (simulated at 1.2 KBps), 28.8 Kbps (simulated at 2.3 KBps), and 56 Kbps (simulated at 4.7 KBps). These are set to simulate real Internet connection rates.

To create a customized setting for a connection speed, choose Customize from the Flash Players' Debug menu and specify the test names and rates in the Custom Modem Settings dialog box (see Figure 16-5).

Your choices in the Custom Modem Settings dialog box let you select from default settings of 14.4 K, 28.6 K, and 56 K speeds. You also can indicate a custom speed you want to simulate in the Bit (bytes) rate box. For example, if you wanted to test a movie at a 36.6 modem setting, you could create and save it in the Custom Modem Settings dialog box. Three additional places to store extra settings include User Setting 4, 5, and 6. Here, you can indicate the custom setting and name it. The default download rate for all these settings is 2.3 KB. The menu text and the baud rate can be customized to simulate various user scenarios that might come into play.

16

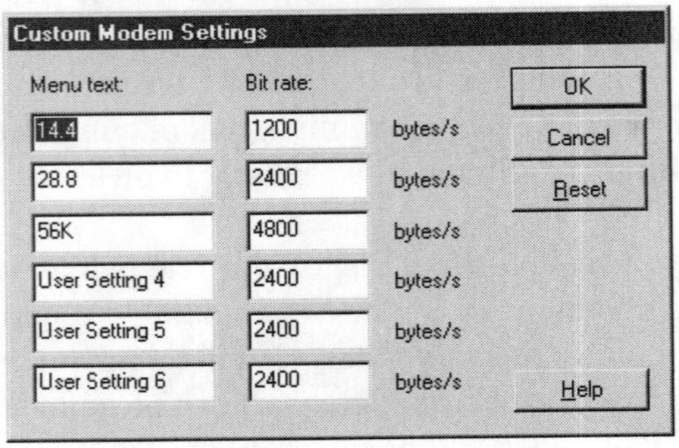

FIGURE 16-5   The Custom Modem Settings dialog box can be accessed from the Debug menu in Player mode

Each time you select a different modem rate while testing the streaming of a movie, depending on how complex the movie is, the streaming will change dramatically from one modem setting to another. In the new millennium, it's highly likely that not many of your audience will be using a 14.4 modem. But when publishing a movie you must weigh all possible scenarios against one another and set priorities accordingly.

Debug a Movie

Whether you're a programmer, Web developer, or designer, a major issue to reckon with in designing movies is to ensure that the movie will play properly and the ActionScript works flawlessly. If you can analyze what happens within your movie as it is playing, you stand a better chance of getting rid of the bugs in your movie before you bring it to the Web or its final destination.

The Debugger is useful from two perspectives. You can track and watch the various parts of your movie while it's playing and actually debug an uploaded movie while it streams from a server.

To debug a Flash Player (SWF) file while it's playing on the Web, check the Debugging Permitted box from the Formats tab in Publish Settings box under Flash editor (see Figure 16-6). When Debugging Permitted is checked, the Password option becomes available underneath the Debugging Permitted box. Use a password if you're debugging from a remote computer. The Flash Publish Settings dialog box is discussed in detail later in this chapter.

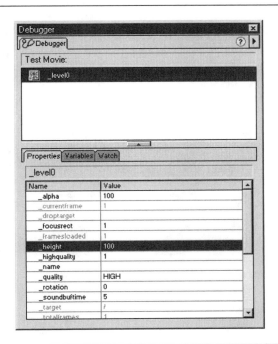

FIGURE 16-6   The Debugger window in Flash

TIP

By setting the password after checking the Debugging Permitted box in the Flash Publish Settings dialog box, you also ensure that you are the only person who can remotely debug your files. The ability to set a password in the Flash Publish Settings dialog box is new into Flash 5.

Flash also offers several other ways to debug a movie while in the Test Movie mode. From the menu in the Player window, you can select List Objects or List Variables.

When you select List Objects, an output window appears listing all objects in the movie with their respective levels and paths indicated. This gives you the opportunity to make sure targets are addressed properly (see Figure 16-7).

The List Variables option provides a list of all variables in the movie. You can check to make sure the values are properly assigned to each variable and that they're working correctly. The List appears in the Output window, as do the Objects.

16

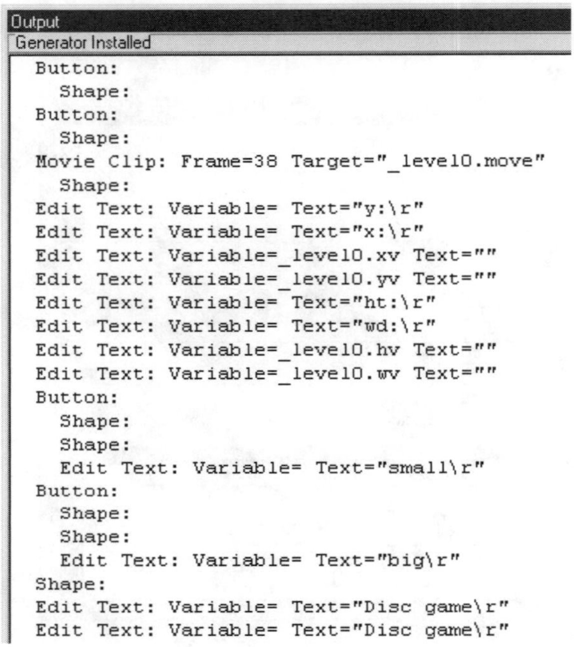

```
Output
Generator Installed
   Button:
      Shape:
   Button:
      Shape:
   Movie Clip: Frame=38 Target="_level0.move"
      Shape:
   Edit Text: Variable= Text="y:\r"
   Edit Text: Variable= Text="x:\r"
   Edit Text: Variable=_level0.xv Text=""
   Edit Text: Variable=_level0.yv Text=""
   Edit Text: Variable= Text="ht:\r"
   Edit Text: Variable= Text="wd:\r"
   Edit Text: Variable=_level0.hv Text=""
   Edit Text: Variable=_level0.wv Text=""
   Button:
      Shape:
      Shape:
      Edit Text: Variable= Text="small\r"
   Button:
      Shape:
      Shape:
      Edit Text: Variable= Text="big\r"
   Shape:
   Edit Text: Variable= Text="Disc game\r"
   Edit Text: Variable= Text="Disc game\r"
```

FIGURE 16-7   An Output window displays with data when you select Debug | List
Objects from the Player window

Another element in Flash that helps to debug a movie is when you place a
Trace action in a movie. Trace actions help test values that might not be easily
tested on the author's end. For example, you might use a Trace action on forms to
make certain the values the user is returning are correct. Here's a quick example
of a Trace action used in a very simple variable example. In Figure 16-8, there are
three text fields. The variables are named according to the names above the text
fields. The text field's salary and wages equal the total text field. However, on this
movie the total text field is just used to pass a value, not display one which makes
it a little hard to test the functionality of this script. The script on the first frame of
the movie is as follows:

```
salary = 200;
wages = 200;
total = salary+wages;
trace (total);
```

Frame Actions
Movie Explorer
Frame Actions
Frame Actions
salary = 200;
wages = 200;
total = salary+wages;
trace (total);
Line 3: total = salary+wages;
Variable: total
Expression
Value: salary+wages
Expression

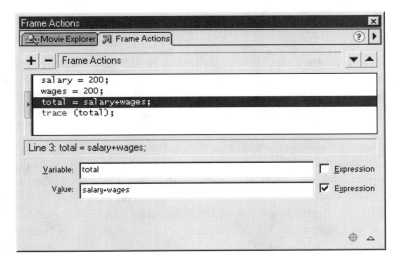

FIGURE 16-8 When a Trace action is placed in a script, it traces the value of a variable in the Output window

When the movie is tested, the Output window traces what this value is and displays it (see Figure 16-9). Generally, you wouldn't be using the Trace action for something this simplistic, but the concept becomes obvious in this simple example; that is to help test and debug elements that you can't see on the local end.

The Trace action should be deleted before the movie is published, as its only purpose is to check values of strings and expressions. Ultimately, Trace actions

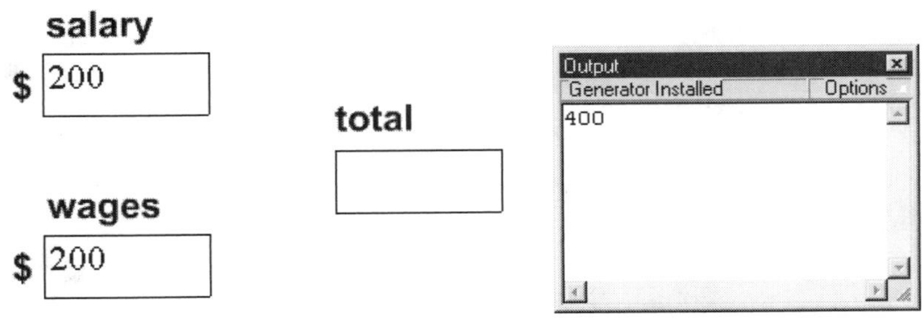

salary
$ 200
total
wages
$ 200
Output
Generator Installed
Options
400

FIGURE 16-9 The Output window with the result of a Trace action displayed

only add to the file size. You also can check the Omit Trace Actions button in the Flash Export dialog box when exporting to SWF format. This removes the Trace action from the SWF file but not from the movie itself.

Test in Different File Formats   It's wonderful to be able to generate alternate file formats in Flash. If you're publishing to the Web, you need to address the other portion of your audience who don't have the Flash Player plug-in or the correct version you're calling for in the Flash Publish Settings dialog box. For this audience, you can alternatively publish your file in several static file formats as well as alternative movie formats. Then, these alternative files can be either embedded in an alternate HTML page or inserted depending upon whether the format requires a plug-in or not. Because of extenuating circumstances in cyberspace, most often you'll be creating more than one version of your Web site so everyone with configurations/browsers new and old will be able to see something.

Just because a percentage of the population might not have the latest plug-ins, you or your clients don't want to lose the business of these techno-dinosaurs. But before you go ahead and publish files in alternative formats, you can preview what they will look like before actually publishing. This is a wonderful feature because it can prevent unexpected outcomes. A beautiful gradient in Flash can look like a mess as an animated or static GIF. Or perhaps a fluid Flash animation might look too jerky as an animated GIF and you might decide a static image gets the message across much better. Opacity and transparency might not translate well in alternative formats. There are too many variables that could go wrong without testing before you establish what the best quality alternative format might be. And remember that you're always balancing quality with file size.

To preview the movie in different formats within a browser, use the File | Publish Preview command. The default settings for the Publish Preview include Default, Flash, and HTML. Default will preview the movie with whatever your current settings are in the Publish Settings dialog box. This box is discussed in detail later in this chapter.

Previewing in Flash displays a Player version of the file, the same as choosing Control | Test Movie. HTML generates an HTML page in the folder where the SWF and FLA files are stored and it embeds the SWF file in the HTML page. This is a convenient feature if ultimately your movie will end up embedded or inserted in an HTML document.

If you select other publishing options in the Publish Settings dialog box such as GIF or JPEG (File | Publish Settings or CTRL+SHIFT+F12/CMD+SHIFT+F12), those settings will also become an option in the Publish Preview pop-up menu (see Figure 16-10). This offers a quick way to test the quality of art on different

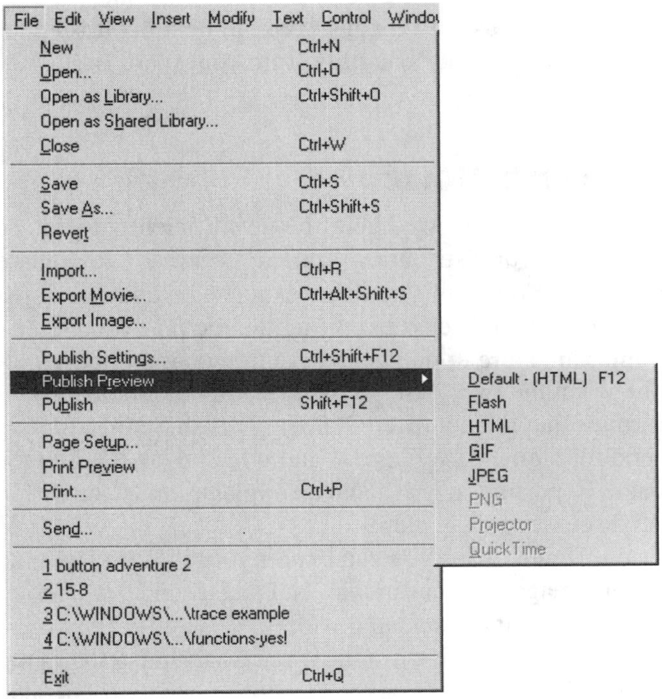

File	Edit	View	Insert	Modify	Text	Control	Windo

```
New                          Ctrl+N
Open...                      Ctrl+O
Open as Library...           Ctrl+Shift+O
Open as Shared Library...
Close                        Ctrl+W

Save                         Ctrl+S
Save As...                   Ctrl+Shift+S
Revert

Import...                    Ctrl+R
Export Movie...              Ctrl+Alt+Shift+S
Export Image...

Publish Settings...          Ctrl+Shift+F12
Publish Preview          ►        Default - (HTML)  F12
Publish                      Shift+F12         Flash
                                               HTML
Page Setup...                                  GIF
Print Preview                                  JPEG
Print...                     Ctrl+P            PNG
                                               Projector
Send...                                        QuickTime

1 button adventure 2
2 15-8
3 C:\WINDOWS\...\trace example
4 C:\WINDOWS\...\functions-yes!

Exit                         Ctrl+Q
```

FIGURE 16-10   When alternative file formats are selected in the Publish Settings dialog box, they appear in the Publish Preview pop-up menu

settings for placement in alternative HTML pages. The Publish Settings are discussed in detail later on in this chapter.

To create this preview, Flash must actually generate the alternative file in the folder where the SWF, FLA, and HTML files reside. Go to this folder if you want to see the file sizes of the new images and how they compare to the SFW version of the movie.

When generating these files, Flash automatically defaults to the proper naming convention by adding an appropriate extension to the current file name. For instance, if you want to generate a JPEG file, Flash automatically adds the .jpg extension or .gif extension for a GIF file, and so on. It also automatically chooses a name for the file format relative to the name of the SWF.

If you want to create your own file names, deselect the Use Default Names option in the Filename area of the Publish Settings dialog box. This feature is

16

solely for the purpose of customizing your names if you want to personalize your files. Remember to always use extensions even on the Macintosh platform. This is proper protocol to ensure all runs smoothly from your platform to other platforms to the server.

Export Your Flash Movie

Once you have tested and previewed your movie sufficiently to determine its suitability and readiness for distribution, you are then ready to prepare the movie for its final destination. You do this by either exporting the movie or publishing the movie. In this section, we'll discuss exporting the movie. Although exporting the movie is similar in nature to publishing the movie, it's important to understand the difference between the two. Also the Export Movie options offer exporting to additional formats that are not offered in the Publish Settings dialog box. Exporting is good for a quick SWF movie and updating an SWF that's embedded in an HTML page. Exporting in Flash and an explanation of the different file formats are also discussed in Chapter 9.

There are two different ways you can export your movie. The first way is to export single-frame images of your movie, and the second way is to export the entire movie and every frame associated with it.

Export a single frame if there's a static piece of art like a logo you might want to use in another movie or a printed piece. To export a single frame in a multi-frame movie, select the frame in the movie you want to export with the playhead. Go to File | Export Image. Give the file a name and choose from one of the available file extensions: .swf, .swt, .spl, .wmf, .eps, .ai, .dxf, .bmp, .jpg, .gif, and .png. The single image will be saved in the folder you select in the Export dialog box.

To export a movie, select File | Export Movie (see Figure 16-11). This setting is useful if you need to export a series of sequential frames to another program. For example, you could save a frame sequence in a PNG format and open each frame individually in FreeHand, Fireworks, or any other program that accommodates sequential files. Or, you could export frames in the AI format and open each file as a frame sequence in Adobe Illustrator. There are many different ways you can export sequential frames into other programs by using the Export Movie command.

The following format extensions are available for saving your movie frames in sequential still frames: .wmf, .eps, .ai, .dxf, .bmp, .jpg, .gif, and .png.

The following format extensions export a movie in a movie format: .swf, .swt, .spl, .avi, .mov, .gif, and for sound, .wav or .aif.

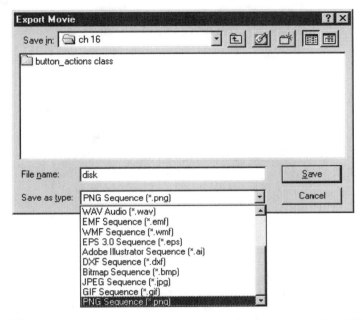

FIGURE 16-11   To export a movie in either a sequential frame format or a movie, use the Export Movie dialog box

As you can see, there are several export formats you can choose from. Most often, you will be exporting your Flash movie from an FLA file type to an SWF file type. During this conversion from FLA to SWF format, Flash will eliminate extra information, sounds, timelines, and bitmaps that are contained in the FLA file to compress the SWF file as small as possible. Sound and bitmap files are also automatically compressed, which also pares the size of the SWF file down tremendously. You might want to take special note of your FLA file size versus the SWF file size. The SWF file is much more compact so it's perfect for use on the Internet where low bandwidths always need to be addressed.

When you export movies to different file formats from the Export Movie/Image dialog boxes, once you select the format, an additional dialog box related to that particular export option will prompt you for special information. For example, if you were to export a movie to a QuickTime format (.mov extenison), you would name the file and select .mov as the Save As Type. Then a QuickTime Settings dialog box would prompt you for such information as Alpha settings, how to read Layers, Compression for Streaming Sound, what kind of movie controller you want, Playback options, and Flatten Movie options (see Figure 16-12).

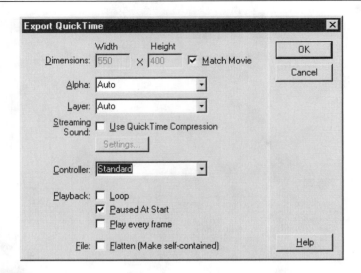

FIGURE 16-12   If you export a movie to a QuickTime format (.mov extension), a dialog box displays where you can customize your settings

Each file type has its own unique settings, which are addressed in the secondary dialog boxes that appear after you export your movie. Dialog boxes also appear when you export an image. Depending on options for that particular file type, the dialog boxes will change here also.

> **NOTE** *If you export a movie or an image from Flash, you must insert or embed your own image/movie into an HTML document. Unlike the Publish command, the Export commands do not automatically generate an HTML file.*

Publish Your Movie

For a multimedia project that's Web-bound, or even to a self-playing projector file, the most commonly used exporting mode is via the Publish Settings dialog box. This offers the most comprehensive set of export options as well as enables you to preview and select all the different settings from the same parent dialog box. You experimented with the Publish Settings dialog box previously in the section on Publish Preview. In this section, all the elements of the Publish Settings dialog box are examined.

As discussed previously, you can export to many different file formats in addition to the Flash SWF format, so the delivery of your animation and interactivity to an audience, who might not have access to Flash plug-ins, becomes an attainable alternative. This is easily accomplished with the Publish Settings and Publish commands, which affords you the ability to publish your Flash movie in up to eight formats simultaneously. This feature also will generate an HTML document so that your published file has the SWF movie already embedded in it.

Interestingly enough, the options for exporting from Flash using the Export Movie command are identical to those in the Publish Settings dialog box. Some of the options for exporting and publishing differ in a sense that some offer more flexibility and customization. For example, when using the Publish Settings dialog box, you are offered the choice to remove gradients from GIF files to keep the file size small. But in the Export GIF dialog box, that choice is not available.

Another difference between publishing and exporting is that Flash will save the Publish Settings with the movie file so if you choose to reuse these settings in subsequent movies or new projects, they are still intact.

To select a movie's publishing format, open the Flash document that you want to publish. Choose Publish Settings from the File menu or CTRL+SHIFT+F12/ OPT+CMD+SHIFT+F12. The dialog box for the Publish Settings will display (see Figure 16-13). Click the Formats tab. There are nine file format publishing options and if you have Generator installed, you are able to choose a tenth option— Generator Template—for server applications.

NOTE *The Macromedia Generator is a powerful workstation and server-side product. By publishing to this format you can create Flash templates that will include Flash graphics in your Web page. These are sophisticated templates that enable you to change content contingent upon user variables. The variables can be graphic variables as well as text. When the user accesses these Flash files in a Generator format, he is ensured a customized Web site viewing to his system's configuration. More information about Generator can be found by visiting the Macromedia Web site, www.macromedia.com.*

When you check a type in the Formats tab, the corresponding tab will appear on the top of the dialog box. You can check as many file formats as you want to generate.

To choose the options for a selected format, select the tab aligned with that format. For example, if you wanted to generate a QuickTime movie, check the QuickTime button, and then click the QuickTime tab to display the QuickTime Settings dialog box (which happens to be the same dialog box as from Export Movie, Figure 16-12). If you want to save these settings with the file you are selecting, click OK. Flash will

16

Format tabs   Publish button

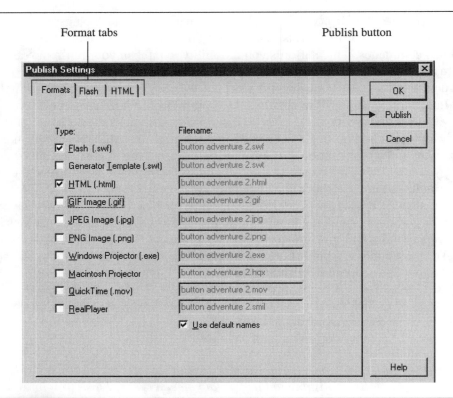

The initial dialog box that displays when you select Publish Settings from the File menu

utilize these settings each time you choose the Publish or Publish Preview command. If you enter test mode (by selecting Control | Test Movie or Control | Test Scene), Flash will use a file's current publish settings. For example, if you selected PNG as your only format type in a movie, if you tested the file, the movie would display in PNG format.

There are ten file format choices in the Publish Settings dialog box, which include SWF, SWT, HTML, GIF, JPEG, PNG, Windows Projector, Macintosh Projector, QuickTime, and Real Player, the settings of which are discussed in the next section.

Publish Settings Dialog Box

The Publish Settings dialog box looks small at first, but its settings are many. Some settings can be quite complex if you don't know what they mean. When you first open the box, there are only three tabs generated from the three default settings, and the first is the Formats tab. This is where you select the type of files you want to export and assign file names. The second tab is the Flash tab. It's assumed that most often you intend to import in a Flash format so Flash is the default publish setting. The third tab is the HTML tab. Although you don't have to publish an HTML document, again it's assumed you probably will. When you select HTML as a type, the Flash format (SWF) always publishes with the HTML page.

Depending on your selection in the Type column of the Formats tab, the tabs on the top of the Publish Settings dialog box will change. Each time you select another type for export, a tab is added to the right of the other tabs. Because the selections are numerous in this dialog box, we will review the different export options and media elements available in the proceeding paragraphs.

The Flash Tab

The first tab we discuss is the Flash tab. When in the Flash tab the first available option is the Load Order (see Figure 16-14).

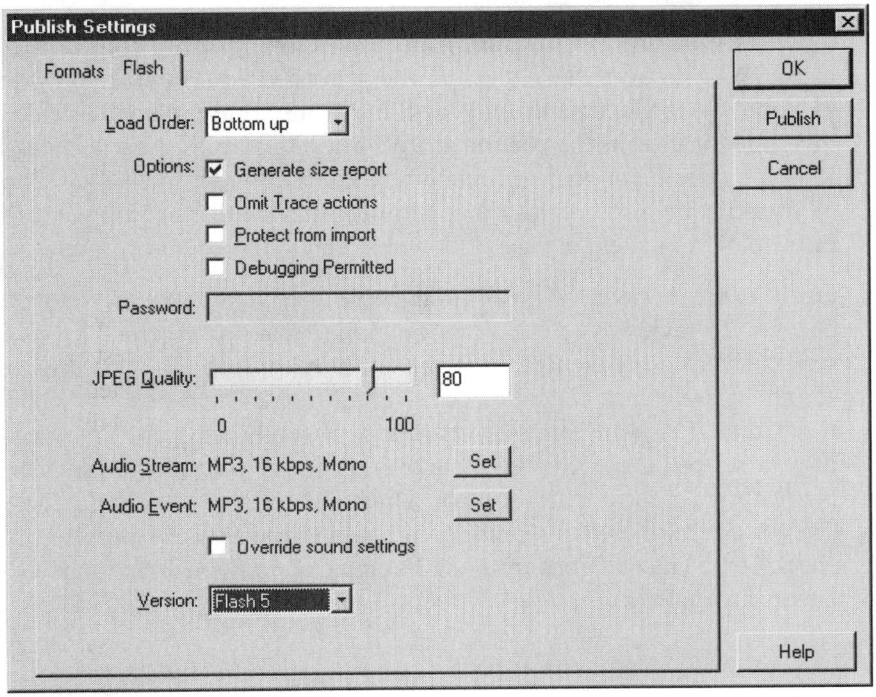

FIGURE 16-14   When the Flash tab is chosen in Publish Settings, the Flash Publish Settings options become available

■ **Load Order**—If you want to select the order in which Flash loads the layers of your movie, you need to address how the first frame of your movie will load. In the Load Order pop-up menu, select from two options. If playback on the Web is slow, Flash will start to display individual layers as they download. The following two selections are available from a pop-up menu:

   ■ **Bottom Up Load Order**—The Bottom Up setting works in the opposite direction.

   ■ **Top Down Load Order**—The Top Down setting downloads and displays the top layer first and then continues down the page to the bottom.

Under Options, the following selections are available:

■ **Generate Size Report**—When you check Generate Size Report, it generates an automatic text file from Flash that supplies you with a detailed report about the size of each frame and the various events that take place in your movie (see Figure 16-15). During the process of exporting your movie as an SWF file from Flash, the text file generated will provide you with extremely valuable data about your file. An ASCII text file will reside in the same location as the generated SWF file. As discussed earlier, this Size Report can help you to determine where the bandwidth-intensive sections of your file are located plus other pertinent information to help you trim the size of your files for ease of downloading to the end user.

■ **Omit Trace Actions**—Trace actions were discussed previously in this chapter. To review, you use a Trace action to make sure certain kinds of scripts are working the right way in your movie. Generally, this involves scripts where values are undetectable in test mode. Trace actions will only work in the Flash-authoring environment. If you broadly use Trace actions in your scripts, they will add to the overall size of your movie file. You can manually trash these actions to consolidate on the size of your published file. As an alternative to searching for them throughout the movie, you can check Omit Trace actions from the Formats tab in Publish Settings box under Flash editor.

```
button adventure 2 Report - Notepad
File  Edit  Search  Help
Movie Report
------------

Frame #      Frame Bytes      Total Bytes      Page
-------      -----------      -----------      ----------------
      1            5252            5252       intro
      2              52            5304       2
      3              53            5357       3
      4              52            5409       4
      5              52            5461       5
      6              53            5514       6
      7              52            5566       7
      8              49            5615       8
      9              53            5668       9
     10              54            5722       10
     11              53            5775       11
     12              53            5828       12
     13              54            5882       13
     14              53            5935       14
     15              18            5953       15
     16            1310            7263       16
     17              49            7312       17
     18              48            7360       18
     19              48            7408       19
     20              49            7457       20
     21              48            7505       21
     22              44            7549       22
     23              48            7597       23
     24              39            7636       24
     25              48            7684       25
     26              48            7732       26
     27              49            7781       27
```

FIGURE 16-15   A Size Report from a published Flash movie

- **Protect From Import**—This option enables you to protect your SWF files from being imported from the Web. When you check this option, you stop hackers and make the movie inaccessible.

- **Debugging Permitted**—Select this option if you want to be able to debug remotely.

16

- **Password Option**—This enables you to set a password so you can debug a file on a remote site from your computer.

TIP *The Publish and Publish Preview commands automatically generate file names in the Publish Settings dialog box. So, if you want to publish several versions of a movie, each containing different settings, you need to ensure that you don't copy over the original, published file. You will need to rename the new file versions, bring the files to a different location or provide a different name in the Formats tab of the Publish Settings dialog box. You must do this to maintain the integrity of your various versions and avoid potential confusion.*

- **JPEG Quality**—This sets the quality of a JPEG image.

- **JPEG Slider**—You can use a slide-rule to adjust the JPEG quality.

- **JPEG Quality Field**—You can enter a value in the Quality field from 0 (low quality) to 100 (high quality).

- **Audio Stream or Audio Event Check Box**—Use either one of these options if your sound is streaming or occurs on an event. You can select from MP3 (Compression), 16 kbps (Bit Rate), or Mono. When you click SET from the Sound Settings dialog box you are offered the following three options:

  - **Compression**—You can set the sound compression parameters for MP3 (the default), ADPCM, Raw Format, or disable sound altogether.

  - **Bit Rate**—Choices are offered for: 8 kbps, 16 kbps, 20 kbps, 24 kbps, 32 kbps, 48 kbps, 56 kpbs, 64 kbps, 80 kbps, 112 kbps, 128 kbps, and 160 kbps.

  - **Quality**—You can choose from Fast, Medium, or Best.

- **Override Sound Settings**—This setting overrules the settings used in the Library Sound Properties dialog box.

- **Version**—You can publish a movie in Player versions 1–5.

It's extremely important that you observe the sampling rates and compression of sounds. This will enable you to maintain a balance between the sound quality and the finished movie's file size. For more on sound settings, refer to Chapter 9.

The HTML Tab

In the beginning, when the Web was new, and even now, embedding your Flash movie in an HTML file is still one of the most common forms of delivering your movie.

To select HTML as a file format to be included with your SWF file, click on HTML for type in the Publish Settings dialog box (see Figure 16-16). Then, click the HTML Formats tab.

Under the Template option you can select from these choices: Accessibility, Ad 3 Banner, Ad 4 Banner, Ad 5 Banner, Ad Any Banner, The Flash Only (Default), Flash With FS Command, Generator Ad Any Banner, Generator Image Output, Generator Only Default, Generator QuickTime, Image Map, Java Player, and QuickTime.

The templates generated by your selection provide a fill-in-the-blanks HTML page with the appropriate script generated for a particular outcome. When you

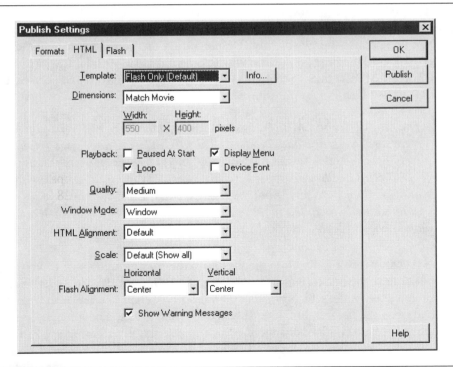

FIGURE 16-16   The HTML Publish Settings

16

select each template, a description of the code that's generated appears to the right of the selection after you click the Info button. For example, if you choose User Choice and press the Info button, the following message displays:

```
Description: Detect if Flash Player 5 is installed.
Use JavaScript and a cookie to allow user to choose
Player or an image. In Publish, select SWF and a
GIF or a JPEG.
```

TIP *The Info button to the right of the Template pop-up menu contains a wealth of information. If your memory fails you and you need to be reminded of the features available, by clicking on the Info button you can get a description of the different formats available to you in this setting.*

The HTML file generated from this selection (User Choice) includes a JavaScript that does exactly what the description says—it detects the player, sends a cookie, and allows the user to select his or her own way of viewing the movie (see Figure 16-17).

When you choose the Flash Only (Default) from the Template pop-up menu, you have selected the most simplistic way to set your HTML code. It will use the OBJECT and EMBED tags so that your Flash movie is displayed and seen by the viewer with the Flash Player plug-in.

NOTE *The OBJECT and EMBED tags in HTML address the two most popular browsers; Netscape and Explorer. The OBJECT tag addresses Explorer technology (ActiveX) and the EMBED tag addresses Netscape issues (SWF plug-in). Both of these tags are necessary in the HTML code to address both browsers. Both the OBJECT and EMBED tags are automatically included in the HTML document when you publish a movie and choose Flash and HTML in the Publish Settings dialog box.*

The HTML default will automatically make the background color of your Web page the same as the background color of your Flash movie. To use a different color, create a template, which you can then modify. When you prepare to publish, be sure to open the default template, save a copy, and give it a new name. In the Flash Only (Default) option, change the line of code and give it a name like Flash Only (*insert your name*) (Background). This will allow Flash to recognize it and add it to the available templates in the Template menu. In the HTML tag, replace

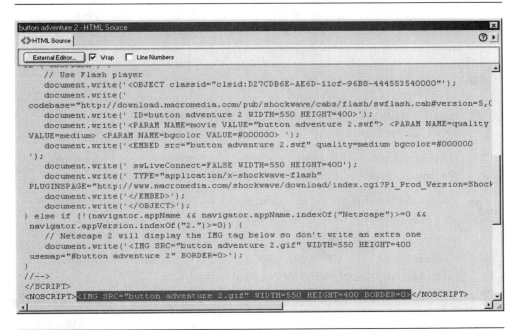

```
button adventure 2 - HTML Source                                          x
<>HTML Source                                                          ⊙ ▶

  External Editor...   �) Wrap   ⬜ Line Numbers
      // Use Flash player                                                  ▲
      document.write('<OBJECT classid="clsid:D27CDB6E-AE6D-11cf-96B8-444553540000"');
      document.write('
 codebase="http://download.macromedia.com/pub/shockwave/cabs/flash/swflash.cab#version=5,0
      document.write(' ID=button adventure 2 WIDTH=550 HEIGHT=400>');
      document.write('<PARAM NAME=movie VALUE="button adventure 2.swf"> <PARAM NAME=quality
 VALUE=medium> <PARAM NAME=bgcolor VALUE=#000000> ');
      document.write('<EMBED src="button adventure 2.swf" quality=medium bgcolor=#000000
 ');
      document.write(' swLiveConnect=FALSE WIDTH=550 HEIGHT=400');
      document.write(' TYPE="application/x-shockwave-flash"
 PLUGINSPAGE="http://www.macromedia.com/shockwave/download/index.cgi?P1_Prod_Version=Shock
      document.write('</EMBED>');
      document.write('</OBJECT>');
 } else if (!(navigator.appName && navigator.appName.indexOf("Netscape")>=0 &&
 navigator.appVersion.indexOf("2.")>=0)) {
      // Netscape 2 will display the IMG tag below so don't write an extra one
      document.write('<IMG SRC="button adventure 2.gif" WIDTH=550 HEIGHT=400
 usemap="#button adventure 2" BORDER=0>');
 }
 //-->
 </SCRIPT>
 <NOSCRIPT><IMG SRC="button adventure 2.gif" WIDTH=550 HEIGHT=400 BORDER=0></NOSCRIPT>   ▼
 ◄                                                                         ►
```

FIGURE 16-17   A movie in which a User Choice template was generated provides a scripting to detect the Flash plug-in and allow the user to select an alternative viewing method

the line code with HTML code for a specific hex color and save the new template in your Flash HTML folder.

The Dimensions option under the HTML heading in Publish Settings will assist you with determining your movie's placement in the browser. The following selections are available in the Dimensions pop-up menu:

- **Match Movie**—This option will allow you to establish the dimensions of your movie.

- **Pixels**—This option allows you to type in values within a range of an integer between 0 and 32000 for Width and Height.

- **Percent**—This option allows you to type in values within a range of 1–100 for width and height. If you input a different width and height from your original Flash movie, you need to tell Flash how you want the new movie scaled. When you decide to resize a movie, keep in mind that it might not

16

fill the rectangle and gaps might occur around the borders of your page. This is a minor design consideration that can be fixed easily, but anticipated nonetheless.

The Playback option offers your viewers several playback choices:

■ **Paused At Start**—This allows your viewer to begin the movie with an event, like a button press.

■ **Display Menu**—Choose this option if you want to develop your own playback options and make them available to your audience.

■ **Loop**—Select this option if you want the movie to repeat itself and start over again when it has reached its last frame.

■ **The Device Font**—This option enables Windows viewers to speed playback on their systems by substituting aliased fonts whenever a Flash movie uses system installed fonts from the viewer's computer.

■ **Quality Setting**—To ensure that your movie plays back at the best quality possible, use this option in the Quality pop-up menu, to select from Low to Best. These choices will control smoothing and antialiasing in the Flash movie. The following settings are available:

   ■ **Low**—When you select Low, Flash will set the antialiasing to "off".

   ■ **Auto Low**—Flash will begin playing back your movie with antialiasing off. If Flash should decide that the viewer's system and Internet connection can control the antialiasing and not disrupt the movie's frame rate, Flash will turn antialiasing on.

   ■ **Auto High**—Flash will turn antialiasing on to start the publishing and turn it off if the playback falls below the frame rate established for the movie's downloading time.

   ■ **Medium**—With this setting, you are at the 50/50 mark, where Flash will handle minor antialiasing but not address smoothing out bitmaps.

   ■ **High**—Flash will apply antialiasing to all graphics except animated bitmaps.

   ■ **Best**—This option allows Flash to maintain antialiasing in the on position throughout the course of publishing the movie.

The overall function of the Quality setting is to balance image quality with playback speed in a published Flash movie.

The following settings are available for Window mode:

■ **Window**—This is the regular default Window mode that plays the movie in a regular browser window.

■ **Opaque Windowless**—If you want to just play the movie in its own Web page window, select Opaque Windowless. This will allow you to block out the background and other elements of the Web page with transparent sections.

■ **Transparent Windowless Effect**—For your Windows Internet Explorer user audience, choose a Transparent Windowless effect while in Window mode from the Publish Settings-HTML menu tab under Window mode. This will allow your Web page elements to show through.

■ **HTML Alignment**—The alignment selected will be added to the HTML template. Choose from the standard HTML settings of Default, Left, Right, Top, and Bottom.

■ **Scale**—This option gives you three choices:

  ■ **Default (Show All)**

  ■ **No Border**—With No Border, you will be able to fill most of the rectangle.

  ■ **Exact Fit**—This will let you change the movie's height and width to the new specifications so it appears to re-proportion the movie.

■ **Horizontal and Vertical pop-up menus**—From Flash Alignment, you can pick the Horizontal and Vertical pop-up menus and choose from Left, Center, or Right alignment.

■ **Show Warning Message**—When you check this box, any problems or conflicts that occur when you publish your file will be brought to your attention. For instance, having QuickTime 4 or over installed on your computer before Flash 5 is installed is crucial. If you select QuickTime as a file format for testing and delivering your movie and you don't have QuickTime 4 or over installed, you will be alerted about this conflict. This option is helpful for spotting potential problems.

16

For more detail about writing, placing, and formatting the HTML code for the Flash aspects of your Web page, if you haven't already done so, you should familiarize yourself with HTML.

The GIF Tab

If your audience doesn't have the Flash plug-in, they won't see your SWF file. For end users who cannot view your Flash elements, the Publish utility will allow you to create a static GIF, JPEG, or PNG pictures of the first frame of your movie or a multiple-image (animated) GIF. Or if you recall, you can generate specific frames using the File | Export Image from the menu.

GIFs are limited to a 256-color palette (indexed color). When you choose a GIF format, you need to define the color characteristics for the file in the lower section of the dialog box. Also important to keep in mind is that animated GIFs are made up of bitmap images so the files they generate might be large, especially if your Flash movie is long. Be sure to monitor the size of the files. The following settings are available in the GIF Settings dialog box (see Figure 16-18):

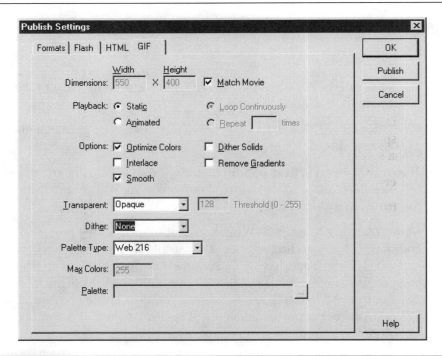

FIGURE 16-18   The GIF Settings dialog box

- **Dimensions**—You select the Width or Height, or match the size of the frame in the movie.

- **Playback**—Playback can be Static or animated. It also can loop continuously.

- **Options**—The five available options include

  - **Optimize Colors**—If you review the dialog box for selecting a GIF file format in the Publish Settings dialog box under Formats, you can optimize colors. This will work toward reducing the colors in the image to make it fit within the 256-color parameters of the GIF format.

  - **Dither Solids**—This option allows you to reduce the number of colors used in your image by replacing solid colors with dithered colors.

  - **Interlace**—When you select Interlace you are specifying that the GIF generate the file so that it can be viewed as the end user downloads. The end user's perception is that of the file downloading more quickly when, in fact, interlacing increases or decreases file size in negligible increments.

  - **Remove Gradients**—If you select this box, you will combine colors and reduce the overall number of colors required to view your image. This option is very much like the Dither Solids box.

  - **Smooth**—When you check Smooth anti-aliases, elements become vector-based prior to the generation of the GIF file.

- **Transparent**—This option allows you to select a color that will be Opaque, Transparent, or an Alpha setting and enables you to set a Threshold for the Alpha setting from 0–255.

- **Dither**—The dither settings include None, Ordered, and Diffusion.

- **Palette Type**—You can select from the following four GIF-appropriate palettes:

  - **Web 216**—The standard Web-safe palette.

  - **Adaptive**—You would use this option if your end user does not have color viewing limitations or if Web-safe color isn't an issue you have to worry about.

  - **Web Snap Adaptive**—This option will yield color results somewhere midway between an 8-bit color palette and your customized or adaptive colors.

16

■ **Custom**—If your viewer's capability is not limited, such as on an intranet, you can use this option, which enables you to load Photoshop Swatch files to help in setting up your image's color palette.

 *Typically, in your image and color designs/selections, you should use the 216 Web-color palette option so that your generated GIF will "default" to these colors.*

The JPEG Tab

A JPEG image renders a continuous tone image. JPEGs are usually used for photographs without a lot of flat color. The following settings are available in the JPEG Settings dialog box (see Figure 16-19):

■ **Dimensions**—You can manually indicate the width and height and Match Movie.

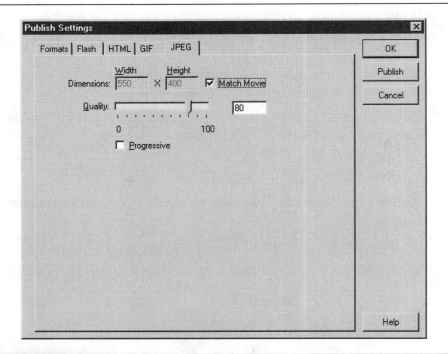

FIGURE 16-19   The JPEG Settings dialog box

- **Quality Settings**—These settings are as follows:

- **JPEG Slider**—This is located in the JPEG Quality area. Use this to adjust the compression of a JPEG bitmap from high, to medium, to low quality.

- **JPEG Quality Field**—This option will allow you to manually enter a specific value in the JPEG Quality field and is to the right of the Slider. When you adjust this setting, you control how Flash will compress your bitmaps as it exports your movie. Using a setting of 0 offers the most compression at the lowest quality. If you use a setting of 100, your bitmaps will be the least compressed at the best quality. JPEG images seem to download quickly because they are read instantaneously even though the entire image is not yet downloaded or visible.

- **Progressive**—This is the JPEG equivalent to interlacing. A low-resolution image appears and as the image progressively loads, it becomes clearer.

The PNG Tab

PNG is the native file format of Fireworks and is quite compatible with FreeHand. Because an 8-bit PNG file is similar to the GIF format, the settings in the PNG dialog box are almost identical to those in the GIF and JPEG dialog boxes (see Figure 16-20). The exception is with the following settings:

- **Bit Depth**—Choose from 8-bit, 24-bit, or 24-bit with Alpha.

- **Options**—Select from the following five options:

  - **Optimize Colors**—This option will work towards reducing the colors in the image to make it fit within the 256-color parameters of the 8-bit PNG format.

  - **Dither Solids**—This option will reduce the number of colors used in your image by replacing solid colors with dithered colors.

  - **Interlace**—This option will let you specify that the PNG generate the file so that it can be viewed as the end user downloads. The end user's perception is that of the file downloading more quickly when, in fact, interlacing increases or decreases file size in negligible increments.

  - **Remove Gradients**—When you check this box you will combine colors and reduce the overall number of colors required to view your image. This option is very much like the Dither Solids box.

16

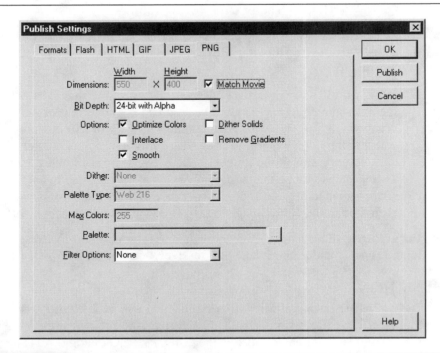

FIGURE 16-20   The PNG Settings dialog box

■ **Smooth**—This allows antialiases, and elements become vector-based prior to the generation of the PNG file.

The PNG format provides most of the capabilities of GIF and JPEG in one format. As mentioned previously, the PNG tab in the Publish Settings window is very similar in content to that of the GIF and JPEG tabs. The big difference is that unlike JPEGs (lossy compression), when a PNG file is compressed, it doesn't lose data (lossless) and will uncompress as the exact same file containing the same data, and so on.

The color capabilities of the PNG format are different from GIFs and JPEGs, also. A PNG file can contain either 8-bit data or 24-bit data. GIFs, as you know, are limited to 256, and JPEG is limited to approximately 24-bit data. PNG can do both or either from a color capacity; however, it does not support animation while a GIF format will. The PNG format is not supported in older browsers, so saving to additional alternative formats might be required to address this issue.

Projector Files

Projector files are primarily used for distributing movies on CD-ROM, DVD, desktop presentation formats, or e-mail. Projector files in Flash Player aren't cross-platform compatible. However, you can create projector files for both Windows and Macintosh platforms separately. Projector file settings generate a tab to a dialog settings box.

- **Windows Projector**—These files are saved with an .exe extension and as such, can only be run in Windows. Concurrently, Macintosh projectors can only be viewed on the Macintosh. You can address both platforms by creating a hybrid CD with both file formats on it.

- **Macintosh Projector**—This format saves with an .hqx extension, which compresses the projector file. This means it needs to be opened with a program like Stuffit or Binhex before the file can be run.

The QuickTime Tab

The QuickTime movie format can be used both on the Web and disk presentations. QuickTime is considered to be one of Apple's miracles—probably one of the longest running and most far-reaching software applications ever developed. QuickTime version 4 and over provides Flash tracks in its architecture to help fully take advantage of sound and media in your Flash movie.

QuickTime supports over 30 file formats, including Flash movies. Flash 5 is fully supported by the capabilities of QuickTime 4. The player comes factory-installed on all Macs and many of the newer Windows computers. Keep in mind, though, that QuickTime is an Apple product so it tends to work better on the Macintosh than on the PC. Audiences using older PCs would, of course, have to have the QuickTime Windows plug-in installed on their systems to view this. Because of this, caution should be used if selecting this as a publishing option for cross-platforms. Test early on in the development of your movie and test frequently if you're going to export to QuickTime.

The following settings are selectable in the QuickTime Settings dialog box:

- **Dimensions**—In this option, you can set the size of the movie in Dimensions by keying in the new Width and Height or Match Movie (matching your original Flash movie).

- **Alpha**—When in the Alpha option, you can control the transparency background of your Flash page on top of QuickTime. You can select from Auto, Alpha Transparent, or Copy.

16

- **Layer**—With the Layer option, you can direct where Flash plays in terms of the stacking order of QuickTime tracks. Select from Auto, Top, or Bottom.

- **Streaming Sound**—Use compression to export streaming sound to a QuickTime sound track.

- **Controller**—In Controller you can select a QuickTime Controller that will control the play of the QuickTime movie. Select from None, Standard, or QuickTime VR.

- **Playback**—The following three Playback options are available:

  - **Loop**—Should you want the movie to repeat itself and start over again when it has reached its last frame, select Loop.

  - **Paused at Start**—This option pauses the movie before it starts playing.

  - **Play Every Frame**—This option will ensure that all the graphical components of the QuickTime file are retained to ensure smoothness.

- **Flatten**—Flatten (Make self-contained) helps to flatten the real movie and store components of the movie outside the QuickTime movie (when working on the Macintosh). Obviously, this would increase the movie's playback while making your movie cross-platform.

The RealPlayer Tab

RealPlayer is another available format within the nine format choices. RealPlayer is a plug-in that enables you to embed player controls into your Web pages much like a QuickTime movie. RealPlayer is a highly visible plug-in with users in the millions. Keep in mind, though, that for viewers to see movies saved in this format as with all plug-ins, your server must recognize this MIME type. Otherwise, the viewer's computer will not recognize this file type.

 The MIME type issue is true for the SWF plug-in also (as well as other plug-ins). The server must recognize the SWF in order for it to work properly. Talk to your Web administrator to find out if these MIME types are included.

If your audience doesn't have RealPlayer 8 or higher installed, your files will not download on their computers. The following options are available in the RealPlayer Settings dialog box (see Figure 16-21):

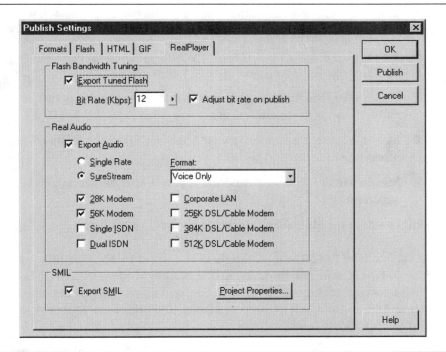

FIGURE 16-21   The RealPlayer options in the Settings dialog box

Flash Bandwidth Tuning. The bandwidth can be tweaked with the following settings:

- **Export Tuned Flash**—When you select this, the following settings become available which enable you to streamline your Flash bandwidth bit rate:

  - **Bit Rate**—Select a higher bit rate for faster Internet connections and a lower bit rate for those slower connections.

  - **Adjust the Bit Rate on Publish**—This will allow you to reset the bit rate to buffer the movie during publishing.

- **Real Audio**—Real Audio is the sister plug-in to RealPlayer. Under Real Audio, you can define the audio speed by selecting from the Single Rate or Sure Stream check box.

16

■ **Format**—Select from one of the four self-explanatory formats that best suits the nature of your Flash movie:

    ■ **Voice Only**—Select this option if your Flash audio only contains voice. Voice requires lower quality than music.

    ■ **Voice With Background Music**—Select this option if your Flash audio contains voice and music.

    ■ **Music**—Select this option if your Flash audio only consists of mono music.

    ■ **Stereo Music**—Select this option if your Flash audio contains stereo music.

Optimal modem speeds can be selected from these check boxes:

■ **28K Modem, 56K Modem, Single ISDN, Dual ISDN, Corporate Lan, 256K DSL/Cable Modem, 384K DSL/Cable Modem, 512K DSL/Cable Modem**—Select any of the modem configurations that you anticipate your Real Audio sound will be streamed from. They represent the range of your target audience's Internet connections.

■ **Export SMIL Box**—This allows you to create a Synchronized Multimedia Integration Language file, which is a markup language that works specifically with multimedia presentation definitions, which is very similar to HTML and XML.

For more information on the applicability of SMIL (a RealPlayer file), go to www.w3org/AudioVideo.

The Generator Tab

This format will only be available if you can access a server with Macromedia Generator capability. Then, the Generator check box in the Publish Settings tab will be available to you. Generator performs complex interactive server tasks. For example, you can create Flash movies with dynamic content and customizable templates that can receive outside data from sources such as Java applets and databases. The scope of Generator reaches far beyond this book, so suffice to say you can customize Generator settings in this tab. For more information on Generator, visit the Macromedia site (www.macromedia.com).

Evaluate Your Movie

Even with all the distribution methods made available to you for delivering your Flash movie to your audience, it is highly unlikely that it will be picture perfect all the time for all audiences. Ultimately, it comes down to the end users' ability to download your movies that direct the sequence of events and the success of delivery. You can try your best, work with bandwidth and data rate of delivery, compress your sound files, and test your movies. With all this, you can determine, using reason and logic, the best-case scenario you can anticipate for the delivery of your information successfully.

Appendix A

Flash 5 Shortcut Keyboard Commands

Keyboard Commands

Command	Menu	Windows	Macintosh
100%	View | Magnification	CTRL+1	CMD+1
Action Panel	Window	CTRL+ALT+A	CMD+OPTION+A
Add Shape Hint	Modify | Transform	CTRL+SHIFT+H	CTRL+SHIFT+H
Align	Window | Panels	CTRL+K	CMD+K
Align Center (Text)	Tex | Align	CTRL+SHIFT+C	CMD+SHIFT+C
Align Left (Text)	Text | Align	CTRL+SHIFT+L	CMD+SHIFT+L
Align Right (Text)	Text | Align	CTRL+SHIFT+R	CMD+SHIFT+R
Antialias	View	CTRL+ALT+SHIFT+A	CMD+OPTION+SHIFT+A
Antialias Text	View	CTRL+ALT+SHIFT+T	CMD+OPTION+SHIFT+T
Bandwidth Profiler	View | Test Movie Mode	CTRL+B	CMD+B
Blank Keyframe	Insert	F7	F7
Bold (Text)	Text | Style	CTRL+SHIFT+B	CMD+SHIFT+B
Break Apart	Modify	CTRL+B	CMD+B
Bring Forward	Modify | Arrange	CTRL+↑	CMD+↑
Bring to Front	Modify | Arrange	CTRL+SHIFT+↑	CMD+SHIFT+↑
Character	Window | Panels	CTRL+T	CMD+T
Character	Text	CTRL+T	CMD+T
Clear Keyframe	Insert	SHIFT+F6	SHIFT+F6
Clear (Stage)	Edit	BACKSPACE	Delete
Close (File)	File	CTRL+W	CMD+W
Convert to Symbol	Insert	F8	F8
Copy (Selection)	Edit	CTRL+C	CMD+C
Copy Frames	Edit	CTRL+ALT+C	CMD+OPTION+C
Cut (Selection)	Edit	CTRL+X	CMD+X
Cut Frames	Edit	CTRL+ALT+X	CMD+OPTION+X
Debug Movie	Control	CTRL+SHIFT+ENTER	CMD+SHIFT+ENTER
Decrease (Tracking)	Text | Tracking	CTRL+ALT+LEFT	CMD+OPTION+Left
Default (Publishing)	File | Publish Preview	F12	F12
Deselect All	Edit	CTRL+SHIFT+A	CMD+SHIFT+A
Duplicate (Selection)	Edit	CTRL+D	CMD+D
Edit Grid	View | Grid	CTRL+ALT+G	CMD+OPTION+G

A

Command	Menu	Windows	Macintosh
Edit Guides	View | Guides	CTRL+ALT+SHIFT+G	CMD+OPTION+SHIFT+G
Edit Symbols	Edit	CTRL+E	CMD+E
Enable Simple Buttons	Control	CTRL+ALT+B	CMD+OPTION+B
Export Movie	File	CTRL+ALT+SHIFT+S	CMD+SHIFT+OPTION+S
Fast (View)	View	CTRL+ALT+SHIFT+F	CMD+OPTION+SHIFT+F
First (Scene)	View | Go To	HOME	HOME
Frame (Add)	Insert	F5	F5
Frame Panel (Show/Hide)	Modify	CTRL+F	CMD+F
Frame-by-Frame (Graph Show)	View (in test movie mode)	CTRL+F	CMD+F
Grid (Show/Hide)	View | Grid	CTRL+'	CMD+'
Group (Selected Items)	Modify	CTRL+G	CMD+G
Guides (Show/Hide)	View | Guide	CTRL+;	CMD+;
Hide Edges	View	CTRL+H	CMD+H
Hide Panels	View	TAB	TAB
Import	File	CTRL+R	CMD+R
Increase (Tracking)	Text | Tracking	CTRL+ALT+→	CMD+OPTION+→
Info	Window | Panels	CTRL+ALT+I	CMD+OPTION+I
Instance Panel (Show/Hide)	Window | Panels	CTRL+I	CMD+I
Instance	Modify	CTRL+I	CMD+I
Italic (Text)	Text | Style	CTRL+SHIFT+I	CMD+OPTION+I
Justify (Text)	Text | Align	CTRL+SHIFT+J	CMD+OPTION+J
Keyframe (Add)	Insert	F6	F6
Last (Scene)	View | Go To	END	END
Library (Show/Hide)	Window	CTRL+L	CMD+L
Lock (Group)	Modify | Arrange	CTRL+ALT+L	CMD+OPTION+L
Lock Guides	View | Guide	CTRL+ALT+;	CMD+OPTION+;
Movie (Properties)	Modify	CTRL+M	CMD+M
Movie Explorer Panel (Show/Hide)	Window	CTRL+ALT+M	CMD+OPTION+M
New	File	CTRL+N	CMD+N

Command	Menu	Windows	Macintosh
New Symbol	Insert	CTRL+F8	CMD+F8
New Window	Window	CTRL+ALT+N	CMD+OPTION+N
Next (Scene)	View | Go To	PAGE DOWN	PAGE DOWN
Open	File	CTRL+O	CMD+O
Open as Library	File	CTRL+SHIFT+O	CMD+OPTION+O
Optimize (Curves)	Modify	CTRL+ALT+SHIFT+C	CMD+SHIFT+OPTION+C
Outlines (View As)	View	CTRL+ALT+SHIFT+O	CMD+SHIFT+OPTION+O
Panels	View	TAB	TAB
Paragraph Panel	Text, Windows | Panels	CTRL+SHIFT+T	CMD+SHIFT+T
Paste (Clipboard Contents)	Edit	CTRL+V	CMD+V
Paste Frames	Edit	CTRL+ALT+V	CMD+OPTION+V
Paste In Place	Edit	CTRL+SHIFT+V	CMD+SHIFT+V
Plain (Text)	Text | Style	CTRL+SHIFT+P	CMD+SHIFT+P
Play (Movie)	Control	ENTER	RETURN
Previous (Scene)	View | Go To	PAGE UP	PAGE UP
Print	File	CTRL+P	CMD+P
Publish	File	SHIFT+F12	SHIFT+F12
Publish Settings	File	CTRL+SHIFT+F12	CMD+SHIFT+F12
Quit	File	CTRL+Q	CMD+Q
Redo	Edit	CTRL+Y	CMD+Y
Remove Frames	Insert	SHIFT+F5	SHIFT+F5
Remove Transform	Modify | Transform	CTRL+SHIFT+Z	CMD+SHIFT+Z
Reset	Text | Tracking	CTRL+ALT+↑	CMD+OPTION+↑
Rewind	Control	CTRL+ALT+R	CMD+OPTION+R
Rulers	View	CTRL+ALT+SHIFT+R	CMD+OPTION+SHIFT+R
Save	File	CTRL+S	CMD+S
Save As	File	CTRL+SHIFT+S	CMD+SHIFT+S
Scale and Rotate	Modify | Transform	CTRL+ALT+S	CMD+OPTION+S
Select All	Edit	CTRL+A	CMD+A
Send Backward	Modify | Arrange	CTRL+↓	CMD+↓
Send to Back	Modify | Arrange	CTRL+SHIFT+↓	CMD+SHIFT+↓
Show All	View | Magnification	CTRL+3	CMD+3
Show Frame	View | Magnification	CTRL+2	CMD+2

Command	Menu	Windows	Macintosh
Show Grid	View | Grid	CTRL+'	CMD+'
Show Guides	View | Guides	CTRL+;	CMD+;
Show Shape Hints	View	CTRL+ALT+H	CMD+OPTION+H
Snap to Grid	View | Grid	CTRL+SHIFT+'	CMD+SHIFT+'
Snap to Guides	View | Guides	CTRL+SHIFT+;	CMD+SHIFT+;
Snap to Objects	View	CTRL+SHIFT+/	CMD+SHIFT+/
Step Backward	Control	,	,
Step Forward	Control	.	.
Streaming (Show/Hide)	View (in Test Movie Mode with Bandwidth Profiler active)	CTRL+ENTER	CMD+ENTER
Streaming Graph	View (in Test Movie Mode)	CTRL+G	CMD+G
Test Movie	Control	CTRL+ENTER	CMD+ENTER
Test Scene	Control	CTRL+ALT+ENTER	CMD+OPTION+ENTER
Timeline	View	CTRL+ALT+T	CMD+OPTION+T
Undo	Edit	CTRL+Z	CMD+Z
Ungroup	Modify	CTRL+SHIFT+G	CMD+SHIFT+G
Unlock All	Modify | Arrange	CTRL+ALT+SHIFT+L	CMD+OPTION+SHIFT+L
Work Area	View	CTRL+SHIFT+W	CMD+SHIFT+W
Zoom In	View	CTRL+=	CMD+=
Zoom Out	View	CTRL+-	CMD+-

Access Tools

Tool	Menu	Windows	Macintosh
Arrow	Toolbox	V	V
Brush	Toolbox	B	B
Dropper	Toolbox	I	I
Eraser	Toolbox	E	E
Hand	Toolbox	H	H
Ink Bottle	Toolbox	S	S
Lasso	Toolbox	L	L
Line	Toolbox	N	N

Tool	Menu	Windows	Macintosh
Magnify	Toolbox	M	M
Oval	Toolbox	O	O
Paint Bucket	Toolbox	K	K
Pen	Toolbox	P	P
Pencil	Toolbox	Y	Y
Rectangle	Toolbox	R	R
Special Arrow	Toolbox	A	A
Text	Toolbox	T	T
Zoom	Toolbox	M, Z	M, Z

Drawing Tools

Tool	Function	Windows	Macintosh
Constrain	Changing shapes, lines, and rotation	SHIFT+drag	SHIFT+drag
Convert	Subsection tool switch corner point to	ALT+drag	OPTION+drag
Arrow tool	Create New Corner Point	ALT+drag a line	OPTION+drag a line
Dropper tool	Set fill and line color	SHIFT-click with Dropper tool	SHIFT-click with Dropper tool
Arrow keys	Move a selected element by one pixel	Arrow keys	Arrow keys
Arrow keys	Move a selected element by 8 pixels	SHIFT+arrow keys	SHIFT+arrow keys
Zoom In and Out	Change between these two while using the Magnifying tool	ALT	OPTION
Drag tool	Drag a copy of selected element	CTRL+drag	OPTION+drag

Appendix B

Flash 5 Resource Guide

As of this writing, the Flash plug-in has been downloaded from the Macromedia site by 325,000,000 visitors. This doesn't include Flash Player distribution with browsers, software applications, and new computers. There's no denying that Flash can be viewed by a tremendous portion of the Web population.

Flash is assuming a more dominant role on the Web than ever before. As a result, more and more designers, programmers, and Web developers are using Flash to build Web sites in addition to numerous other multimedia applications. Because Flash is so popular and so expansive in terms of its scope, there are many resources offered on the Web to help authors find additional information on Flash.

The following is a list of resources to help you keep your skills fine-tuned. Here you will find the information you need to help you gain and keep your momentum working with Flash 5.

Training/Tutorial/Technical Sources

There is no shortage of free Flash 3 and 4 (and for a fee tutorials) on the Web. At the time of this writing, Flash 5 tutorials are scarce because the program is relatively new. More and more Flash 5 tutorials go up on these sites every day, so keep checking back periodically for updated information.

Many tutorials offer sample movies that can be downloaded so you can view the source files or code. Unlike HTML, you can't view the source code of a Flash Player (SWF) file. Unless you're a hacker (in which case you wouldn't be reading this book), you need to obtain the FLA version (original movie) of the file to see how it was made. Being able to view the code in a movie you really like is a great resource in itself.

At the time of this writing, the following sources are recommended for training and tutorials:

www.ehandson.com

This online training company touts instructors who are published and creative professionals in Web design, development, multimedia, video, animation, and graphics. There are several Flash 5 classes available. These classes are offered for a reasonable fee, but they are well worth it. This is one of the better online training centers available.

B

www.flashplanet.com

This is a fascinating and well-made site. With all its resources, tutorials, and links, it can be a handful, but it navigates well and easily, so patience is necessary. The Flash 5 tutorials offer a wide variety of Flash 5 subjects such as the sound basics, start/stop, pan, volume and fading; creating functions; hit test function; and hide, show, and replace the mouse cursor.

www.flashlite.net

This site is excellent for tutorials, source files, and additional resources. It covers a lot of Flash 4 materials so you have to do a little digging to find Flash 5 information.

When entering the site, look under Tutorials. There are two that are noteworthy. One tutors in using the With and Tell Target actions, and the other reviews Effects (faking a draggable mask). You are given choices here. You can either view the tutorial in an HTML file or a PDF file or download the Zip file. The same applies to customizing Flash 5 shortcut keys. You can view it in either HTML or PDF format, but you can't download this tutorial.

www.were-here.com

This site offers a myriad of tutorials for Flash 5 such as creating mouse trails, arrays, multidimensional arrays, drag and drop, dynamic text, and controlling a movie clip with a slider.

www.flashguru.co.uk

This site contains Flash 5 examples with downloadable source files. There are two tutorials worth checking out: one in collision detection, and the other is the random function (deprecated in Flash 5). Check out Resources in this site for the source files that you can download. There also are links to other Flash 5 sites. Look for sound tutorials under More Resources.

www.flashkit.com

The following is a brief list of Flash 5 tutorials available in this site: ActionScripting (call action, setting variable actions, trace action, creating pop-up menus), working with text (you will learn how to create a text mask layer with flashing pictures underneath), and Projector (Flash projector files used in browser-independent scenarios like CDs, emails, and presentations).

Audio

www.flashkit.com

Among other tutorials, open source code and sound files are available through downloading. You can check out tutorials in which you import sound and create movie symbols, buttons, and actions. Tutorial source files are available for download on this site too. Additionally, you can download sound loops for use in Flash projects. This site holds a huge Library of royalty-free music loops.

www.were-here.com

This site offers a huge music loops section, which you can download for the Macintosh in AIF format and WAV format for Windows.

www.webdevelopersjournal.com

Web Developer's Journal. This is a great site, and the resources are endless. You can download multimedia Mac, PC, SWF files, and Web development tools from this site. You can download streaming media servers and MP3 search clients, such as free Napster, CuteMX (a real-time MP3 search engine), Scour Exchange, and iMesh, where you can search for MP3 audio, video, and graphic files. There are looping and sampling software applications such as Fruity Loops, Hammerhead, Tuareg, Acid, and Electrifier Pro. Beatnik and MOD Play software also are available.

www.creativepro.com

You can find some great info here about Flash 5 including optimizing your audio.

www.sitetracks.com

This is a nice-looking site with downloadable audio tracks.

www.panic.com

You can download Audion (a MIDI-like application) from Panic, as well as graphical faces to use in your Flash Web designs. Also, go into Audion 2 from the Panic site where you can learn to handle all your audio playing needs, MP3s, streaming network audio, and encode, mix, edit, and so on.

www.loopz.com

At $1 a loop, there's a nice selection of audio at this site.

Audio Editing Applications

The following are three audio applications you can sample on a free trial basis. Any one of these applications is a fun companion to Flash for those interested in the audio aspects of their movies:

- **Rebirth 2.0** by Propellerheads offers techno musicmaking at its best. Sample this incredible sonic weaponry and download a free trial version at www.propellerheads.com.

- **Groovemaker 2.0**, enables you to create hypnotic, nonstop professional dance tracks in real time. You can mix them, layer in some loops, and create a totally new remix. Download a free trial version from www.groovemaker.com.

- **Acid Pro** by Sonic Foundry is a loop-based music creation tool. Download a free trial version from www.acidplanet.com.

Tips and Techniques

Flash aficionados are abundant. It is through their designs and implied answers to technical questions that we will learn. So, whether it is to review techniques about loops, build ActionScripts, or create special text effects in Flash, the following designer sites should help you obtain most of the answers to your questions.

www.moock.org

This is Colin Moock's site, a well-respected Flash guru. Colin offers answers to technical questions and inspiring examples from the popular to the obscure.

www.canada.cnet.com

This site offers a "help" section with how-tos and tips. You can review the materials online or print out tips and techniques regarding loops, recycling scripts, optimizing variables, preloading audio, and printing Flash files, to name a few.

www.flaxfx.com

You can create text effects for Flash in real time. Be sure to check out the samples at this site.

www.macromedia.com

Of course, Flash's manufacturer, Macromedia, has a great site with lots of pertinent and helpful information. Be sure to look under Macromedia Flash Usability to find usability tips, downloadable source files, and guidelines with extensive hyperlinks to relevant and useful information. Also, Check out the Flash gallery and "site of the day" section. Each day they feature a new site.

Source Code

When you have the ability to download the open source code, you are better able to develop time functions, recordable movements, and a myriad of other Flash components for your movies.

www.flashplanet.com

This is probably the best Flash 5 site around for viewing source files. In addition to great tutorials, if you check out Flash 5 Arena, you will find a plethora of ActionScript source files, such as time functions, buttons that load content into frames, creating recordable movement with playback, how to avoid the pirating of your source files, text substrings, building a progressive percentage preloader, and how to build a virtual shopping cart.

www.were-here.com

This site offers a lot of source code available for downloading from preloaders to shopping carts.

www.sapphire-innovation.com

This site offers a large, royalty-free library of Flash 4 and 5 graphics. There is an archive containing 1,500 symbols in seven libraries.

www.macromedia.com

Check out Macromedia's source code and guidelines.

www.flashpro.nl

With this site, you can download Flash 5 movies to view, along with 100 new effects and source files. If you click on new archives, there's a list of Flash 5 materials.

www.flashguru.co.uk

This site offers Flash 5 samples with downloadable source files. Two tutorials worth checking out are collision detection and random function. Check out the resources in this site and links to other Flash 5 sites and projects.

Noteworthy Flash Movies

These sites are noteworthy because of their technical brilliance and use of design elements. Well-structured Flash sites always provide inspiration when you need to get your creative juices flowing.

www.macromedia.com/showcase-site of the day

genesis by www.digitalorgasm.com

www.flashplanet.com

As mentioned before, this is probably one of the best sites around for Flash 5 materials. Be sure to go into the site and check out Clip Art, which contains galleries of ready-made symbols to add to your Flash libraries. The gamut runs from basic symbols and backdrops to anatomical figures and symbols.

For further inspiration, go into the Directory of Web Sites in this site and take a look at the 40 or so sites listed at the time this book was written. They are all Flash resource sites, most of which contain outstanding Flash materials. Two sites worth a mention are www.thesocalled.com, which contains interesting games in Flash 5, and www.twilomedia.com, which won the Webmaster Award and Golden Web Award and is truly brilliant.

www.were-here.com

This site offers "design" links to many beautiful Flash 4 and 5 sites that offer a plethora of creative ideas.

There's also a "site check" location at this site that enables you to review other Flash 5 sites that people created. By "reviewing" these sites you can get some fresh ideas for your own Flash 5 creations.

www.shop4software.online.com

Be sure to investigate this site so you can purchase Flash Master. This program creates screensavers from Flash files, eliminating the problem of building fully interactive multimedia screensavers. You also can preview sample screensavers made with Flash Master.

altpick.com

Art Mill shows incredible work in these interactive design sites.

www.dvhandbook.com

This is an animation test site for The Idea Exchange. It's an excellent site for inspiration.

www.portfolios.com

You can view many designers' Flash portfolios on this site. Also, be sure to go into Folio Finder so you can review interactive portfolios created in Flash and other interactive software.

www.creativepro.com

This site is for professionals in the field. It holds some interesting links.

Extensions

Flash extensions are fill-in-the-blanks templates that enable you to add interactivity to your movie as well as other miscellaneous things such as Flash clip art and so on. Extensions allow you to create interfaces using pre-built Smart Clips and learn advanced Flash 5 techniques through tutorials. You can incorporate ActionScript code into your projects, add clip art to your pre-existing Libraries and create projects using FLA source files.

www.macromedia.com/downloads

Because of their template-like nature, there's not a lot of room for flexibility with extensions. They are not for everyone, but it's certainly worth the time to explore them, especially for cut-and-dry scripts like counters, tickers, and preloaders.

Here's a quick review of just a few of the Flash 5 extensions that you can download from the Macromedia site.

The Bounce Extension is an ActionScript to help you make movie clips appear to bounce. There are a variety of things you can with this "Bounce" Extension such as drag it, make it collide with other objects, and make it bounce around when hitting the sides of the stage (or work area).

The Text Ticker Extension is a Smart Clip that assists you in creating "stock market" ticker quotes. You also can use it with messages that you might want to convey as a ticker tape alert. You can use the "ticker" with whatever text you are using in your Flash 5 project or link it to an external data file in a Web site to combine with dynamic content.

The FPS Tester Extension is a Smart Clip that is dropped onto any Flash movie to test the frame rate (fps) to determine how the movie plays. This could be extremely helpful in testing your Flash movie to see how smoothly it runs on multi platforms and browsers.

Of course, there are hundreds of other extensions available, with more being added every day. Other sites mentioned in this resource section offer extensions also. However, the extensions on the Macromedia site have been tested, rated, and approved by Macromedia.

Loading Extensions from the Macromedia Site

Before downloading extensions from the Macromedia site, you need to download Macromedia's Extension Manager (if you don't have it already) to ensure the extensions load in the correct folder in Flash so they'll work the right way. The Extension Manager installs extensions and manages them for you, including the ones you might already have.

Download the Extension Manager directly from the Macromedia site. Be sure to select the right version for your computer's operating system (either Windows or Macintosh). Download it to your computer's desktop.

When you use the Macromedia Extension Manager, you can download extensions and then add them to Flash 5. Because developers create new Flash extensions on a continuous basis, check the Macromedia site frequently to help you stay abreast of what's new.

Once you have downloaded Macromedia Extension Manager to your desktop, begin to download the extensions that you like to your computer. There's a quick review of each extension available at the Macromedia Web site.

To use extensions, launch the Macromedia Extension Manager from within Flash 5 by choosing Manage Exchange Items from the Help menu. Be sure to select Flash 5.

The Extensions list themselves in Common Libraries under Window. An Extension displays as its own Library window, and to use most of them you click and drag on the movie clip and display the window panel's clip parameter to view the changeable properties of the extension so you can customize these properties to work with the extension in your Flash file.

Popular extensions do all sorts of things:

- Help you in working with browsers more easily

- Provide tools to help in writing ActionScript code for Flash

- Enable you to add custom styles and formats to your Flash content

- Help you adhere to accessibility guidelines for viewers with disabilities by providing you with Smart Clips and source code to create the required content

- Set up e-commerce solutions such as shopping carts, credit card transactions, and online catalog design

- Educate you by providing educational value in your site or directly through Flash and much more

As you become a more fluent user of Flash 5 and can handle some of the advanced functions and techniques, you might want to experiment with creating your own new extensions.

You can read more about how to do this at the Macromedia Web site. You need to be sure to test your extension completely and copy your files that make up your new extension to the "staging" area so you can package your extension. The correct file format, and so on, is all referenced and explained in the Macromedia site.

Miscellaneous Resources

If you don't own Flash 5, you can download a trial version from the Macromedia Web site. This could be extremely helpful if you bought this book and you don't yet own Flash 5.

Also on the Macromedia site you will find trial versions of Macromedia's Dreamweaver, Fireworks, FreeHand, Director, UltraDev, and other programs. To evaluate these programs you can download them from www.macromedia.com/ downloads. If you use other programs to create your vector, bitmap art, or HTML, Macromedia's products are a wonderful complement to Flash. The interface on all these programs has a familiar look, as does the language.

The Flash 5 Player can be downloaded from this site, too. You might want to direct visitors to your Flash site (who don't have the Flash 5 plug-in) to the Macromedia site to get the proper plug-in.

In the download sections, there is a plug-in for users of CorelDraw that exports their files in SWF format. Macromedia FlashWriter is a plug-in that's available for Adobe Illustrator users. This plug-in expands the export capabilities of Illustrator to the SWF format.

Keep in mind that the Web is an ever-changing form of media and is constantly being updated. Although all the previous Web sites and references were in existence at the time of this writing, some might be changed, gone, or rerouted by the time you arrive.

Index

513

INTERNATIONAL CONTACT INFORMATION

AUSTRALIA
McGraw-Hill Book Company Australia Pty. Ltd.
TEL +61-2-9417-9899
FAX +61-2-9417-5687
http://www.mcgraw-hill.com.au
books-it_sydney@mcgraw-hill.com

CANADA
McGraw-Hill Ryerson Ltd.
TEL +905-430-5000
FAX +905-430-5020
http://www.mcgrawhill.ca

**GREECE, MIDDLE EAST,
NORTHERN AFRICA**
McGraw-Hill Hellas
TEL +30-1-656-0990-3-4
FAX +30-1-654-5525

MEXICO (Also serving Latin America)
McGraw-Hill Interamericana Editores S.A. de C.V.
TEL +525-117-1583
FAX +525-117-1589
http://www.mcgraw-hill.com.mx
fernando_castellanos@mcgraw-hill.com

SINGAPORE (Serving Asia)
McGraw-Hill Book Company
TEL +65-863-1580
FAX +65-862-3354
http://www.mcgraw-hill.com.sg
mghasia@mcgraw-hill.com

SOUTH AFRICA
McGraw-Hill South Africa
TEL +27-11-622-7512
FAX +27-11-622-9045
robyn_swanepoel@mcgraw-hill.com

**UNITED KINGDOM & EUROPE
(Excluding Southern Europe)**
McGraw-Hill Education Europe
TEL +44-1-628-502500
FAX +44-1-628-770224
http://www.mcgraw-hill.co.uk
computing_neurope@mcgraw-hill.com

ALL OTHER INQUIRIES Contact:
Osborne/McGraw-Hill
TEL +1-510-549-6600
FAX +1-510-883-7600
http://www.osborne.com
omg_international@mcgraw-hill.com